Convergence of Cloud with AI for Big Data Analytics

Scrivener Publishing
100 Cummings Center, Suite 541J
Beverly, MA 01915-6106

**Advances in Learning Analytics for Intelligent
Cloud-IoT Systems**

Series Editors: Dr. Souvik Pal (souvikpal22@gmail.com) and Dr. Dac-Nhuong Le (nhuongld@hus.edu.vn)

Publishers at Scrivener
Martin Scrivener (martin@scrivenerpublishing.com)
Phillip Carmical (pcarmical@scrivenerpublishing.com)

Convergence of Cloud with AI for Big Data Analytics

Foundations and Innovation

Edited by

Danda B. Rawat
Lalit K Awasthi
Valentina Emilia Balas
Mohit Kumar
and
Jitendra Kumar Samriya

Scrivener
Publishing

WILEY

Library of Congress Cataloging-in-Publication Data

ISBN 978-1-119-90488-5

Cover image: Pixabay.Com
Cover design by Russell Richardson

Set in size of 11pt and Minion Pro by Manila Typesetting Company, Makati, Philippines

Printed in the USA

10 9 8 7 6 5 4 3 2 1

Contents

Preface

This book was written to discuss the milestones in the development of three recent domains in computer science engineering—Cloud Computing, Artificial Intelligence and Big Data Analytics—and to analyse the convergence of cloud computing with artificial intelligence for big data analytics. Despite the fact that all three domains work separately, they can be linked in interesting ways. However, even though AI and big data can be easily linked, because AI needs a huge amount of data to train the model, they still suffer from a data storage issue. This drawback can be addressed with the help of cloud computing, which makes it possible to provide on-demand services to the client in terms of computer resources, such as storage and computing power, without the need for user management. This book aims to provide the scope of research on the discussed technologies.

Structure of the Book

The 17 chapters of the book cover the intertwining concepts of three key levels that are of interest to the scientific community:

1. Artificial Intelligence
2. Big Data
3. Cloud Computing

A chapter-wise breakdown of the contents of the book follows:

- Chapter 1 discusses the integration of artificial intelligence, big data and cloud computing with the internet of things (IoT).
- Chapter 2 discusses cloud computing and virtualization.
- Chapter 3 presents a time and cost-effective multi-objective scheduling technique for cloud computing environment.

- Chapter 4 discusses cloud-based architecture for effective surveillance and diagnosis of COVID-19.
- Chapter 5 presents smart agriculture applications using cloud and the IoT.
- Chapter 6 presents applications of federated learning in computing technologies.
- Chapter 7 analyzes the application of edge computing in smart healthcare.
- Chapter 8 discusses a smart agriculture application using Fog-IoT.
- Chapter 9 presents a systematic study of the global impact of COVID-19 on the IoT.
- Chapter 10 discusses efficient solar energy management using IoT-enabled Arduino-based MPPT techniques.
- Chapter 11 presents an axiomatic analysis of pre-processing methodologies using machine learning in text mining from the perspective of social media in the IoT.
- Chapter 12 presents an app-based agriculture information system for rural farmers in India.
- Chapter 13 provides a systematic survey on AI-enabled cyber-physical systems in healthcare.
- Chapter 14 discusses an artificial neural network (ANN) aware methanol detection approach with CuO-doped SnO_2 in gas sensor.
- Chapter 15 describes how to detect heart arrhythmias using deep learning algorithms.
- Chapter 16 presents an artificial intelligence approach for signature detection.
- Chapter 17 compares various classification models using machine learning to predict the price range of mobile phones.

Acknowledgment

Writing this book has been a rewarding experience, which was enhanced by the tremendous effort of a team of very dedicated contributors. We would like to thank the authors for their respective chapters and also express our thanks to the list of editors who provided suggestions to improve content delivery. All feedback was considered, and there is no doubt that some of the content was influenced by their suggestions. We especially would like to thank the publisher, who believed in the content and provided a platform to reach the intended audience. Finally, we are thankful to our families for their continued support. Without them, the book would not have been possible.

The Editors
October 2022

Integration of Artificial Intelligence, Big Data, and Cloud Computing with Internet of Things

Jaydip Kumar

Department of Computer Science, Babasaheb Bhimrao Ambedkar University, Lucknow (UP), India

Abstract

The Internet of Things (IoT) provides to the client an effective technique for communicating with the Web world through ubiquitary object enabled networks. The rapid progress in IoT connected devices creates a huge amount of data in a second from personal and industrial devices. This information should be utilized to help business and functional objectives. Thus, there is an urgent requirement for adopting cloud computing, big data, and artificial intelligence techniques to enable storage, analytics, and decision making. In this article, we focused our consideration to integrate Cloud Computing, Big data and Artificial Intelligence technique with the Internet of Things devices. Cloud computing, Big Data, Artificial Intelligence, and IoT are different techniques that are already part of our life. Their adoption and uses are expected to make them more comprehensive and make them essential components of the future Internet. The Internet of Things (IoT) is a system of interconnected gadgets, digital or mechanical machines that are given exceptional identifiers and the capacity to move information over an organization without expecting human-to-human or human-to-pc collaboration.

Keywords: Artificial intelligence, big data, cloud computing, Internet of Things

Email: jaydipkumar2001@gmail.com

Danda B. Rawat, Lalit K Awasthi, Valentina Emilia Balas, Mohit Kumar and Jitendra Kumar Samriya (eds.) *Convergence of Cloud with AI for Big Data Analytics: Foundations and Innovation*, (1–12) © 2023 Scrivener Publishing LLC

1.1   Introduction

With the wide-spread discovery of techniques in the current digital era, increasing physical entities are interconnected to the Internet of Things (IoT) devices. In recent years IoT technologies are applied with different techniques such as Artificial Intelligence, Big Data, and Cloud Computing. Artificial Intelligence (AI) is a technique which has the ability to compute a huge amount of task that is usually done by a human. Artificial Intelligence uses different learning techniques to facilitate automatic rules and regulations for decision making. Artificial intelligence is divided into two different modules such as learning module and predicate module [1]. The learning module is used for effective data collection, training, and data modeling. And the predicate module is used to take action on the current situation. The flow and storage of exponentially increasing data are easily managed by Artificial Intelligence (AI). The integration of cloud computing and IoT are also two different technologies that assume a vital part in our daily life. Cloud computing and the Internet of Things are merged together is expected to break both current and future internet which we called as new paradigm CloudIoT [2]. In the era of the internet which plays a fundamental role in cloud computing, it seems to be represented as a medium or the platform through which many different cloud computing services are accessible or delivered its services. If you are thinking that the internet as a virtual "space" for connecting users from over the globe, it is like a cloud, sharing information by using the internet. Cloud computing is the trending technology in the daily life of everyone which provides on-demand web services such as networking devices, data storage, servers, and applications. It provides higher flexibility and cost efficiency while users try to use cloud computing resources and applications. The different number of connected devices has already exceeded the number of users on the earth. This is due to exponential increase of connected devices rapidly increasing huge amount of data as well. The storage of data locally and temporarily will not be possible to access different devices which are connected to each other. There is a need to be centrally storage space which is provided by cloud storage [3]. And the intense invention in the Internet of Things (IoT) technologies, the Big Data technique has critical data analytics tools which bring the knowledge within the IoT devices to make the better purpose of IoT systems and support critical decision making. Big Data has been divided into five fundamental bases such as volume, variety, velocity, veracity, and value. The volume indicates the size of the data. And the different types of data from different sources are known as variety. The real-time data collection is known as velocity, and veracity is the uncertainty of data and the value which shows the benefits

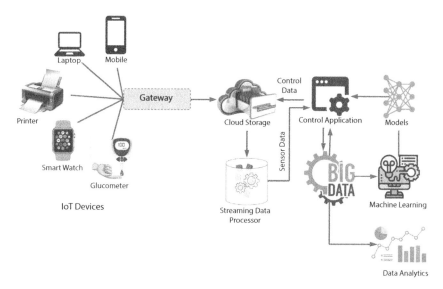

Figure 1.1 Flow diagram of AI, big data, and cloud computing integrated with Internet of Things.

of different industrial and academic fields [4]. The combination of IoT and Big Data has created opportunities to develop complex systems for different industries such as healthcare, smart city, military and agriculture, education, etc. The flow diagram of AI, Big data, and cloud computing integrated with the Internet of Things is given below in Figure 1.1.

1.2   Roll of Artificial Intelligence, Big Data and Cloud Computing in IoT

Internet of Things (IoT) is an interconnection of various devices which are connected to each other through the internet and exchange information. These IoT devices generate a huge amount of information [5]. Artificial Intelligence (AI) uses the decision-making support system to provide data flow and storage in IoT networks. The integration of artificial intelligence (AI) with the Internet of Things (IoT) techniques will generate extraordinary value-creation opportunities. The IoT devices with AI enabled the rise of a "factory of the future" [6]. This increases the efficiency, turnaround, and waiting time and reduces the cost. The IoT with AI is used in different fields such as 3D printing, Robotics, the food industry, manufacturing, logistics, and supply chain management. These fields create lots of information in a regular mode which is centrally stored in cloud computing.

It can be said that the cloud with IoT will be the future of the next generation of the internet. However, the cloud computing services are fully dependent on cloud service providers but IoT technologies are based on diversity [7]. Cloud computing reduces the cost of the use of applications and their services for users. It also simplifies the flow of Internet of Things data capturing and processing and also provides fast and cheapest cost integration, installation, and deployment. And without Big Data analytic applications, the huge amount of data generated by the IoT devices creates an overhead for any business. Due to this any organization must know how to handle this massive amount of data that is collected by the IoT devices. Fetching accurate data is not a problem for any organization; the challenge is to get the necessary skills in the analytical analysis field to deal with big data [8].

1.3   Integration of Artificial Intelligence with the Internet of Things Devices

For addressing any problem AI needs to two-step process which is shown in Figure 1.2. A set of AI models has been created in the first stage. The models are created by the machine learning algorithm with a set of training data. These trained data are processed by the natural language documents or by the encoding of human expertise [14]. The models are invented in different categories like neural networks, decision trees, and inference rules. The models use the inferences from the Internet of Things sensor's input data and guide the operations of the system [9, 18]. There are lots of work have been completed with the integration of Artificial intelligence and Internet of Things. We have mainly surveyed previous works on the personal and industrial applications such as attendance monitoring system, human activity and presence in hospitality, agricultural applications, hospital, human stress monitoring [15, 21]. The short review of IoT applications domains are given below Table 1.1 and the difference between the AI and IoT are given below in Table 1.2.

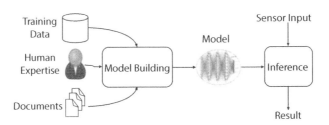

Figure 1.2 Integration architecture of AI in IoT.

Table 1.1 Recent Artificial Intelligence based Internet of Things applications.

Problem	Techniques	Data
Wearable devices	Decision tree, logistic regression	Health data
Human attendance system	Random forest, decision tree etc.	Images
Smart meter operation	Bayesian network, naïve Bayes, decision tree, random forest	Meter reading data
Parking space detection	Clustering algorithms	Camera data
Human stress detection	SVM, logistic regression	Pulse waveform

Table 1.2 Table of differences between the internet of things and artificial intelligence.

Based on	Internet of things	Artificial intelligence
Connection type	A set of interconnecting devices over the network	Interconnection and machine independent is not needed
Capability	Capabilities of the devices are known prior	The capabilities never be predicted of machine
Interaction	Interaction of human between the devices is needed	Interaction of human between the devices is not needed
Future scope	Interaction of human between the devices is needed	Machine can learn and start reacting more than human
Instruction need	Instruction needed to IoT devices	Machines can learn from experiences
Dependency	IoT devices cannot work without artificial intelligence	Artificial intelligence is not dependent on IoT devices
Applications	Smart home, smart city, medical, water monitoring etc.	Fraud prevention, voice assistant, personalized shopping, AI-powered assistants etc.

1.4 Integration of Big Data with the Internet of Things

The generations of the huge amount of data are collected from the Internet of Things devices and its sensors leads to an exponential incremental in data. This data needs to manage, processed, and analyzed by the organization [10] which is shown in Figure 1.3. IoT technology is a major source of Big Data which motivates the organization to deploy Big Data technology and its applications to acquire the needs of IoT technologies. The collected data from the IoT devices is managed, processed, and analyzed by the big data. Big Data provides a framework for data transmission and processing which support IoT data and virtualization. The provided data become deep and more complicated to be stored and analyzed by conventional technology. So the broad consensus is that the big data and Internet of Things techniques are highly interconnected [11]. The architecture of Big Data integrated with the Internet of Things is given below in Figure 1.3 and the comparative study of big data applications is given below [17] in Table 1.3.

1.5 Integration of Cloud Computing with the Internet of Things

The combination of cloud computing and IoT are efficient for every business or user. This enhanced the efficiency of every task and reduced the setup cost for applications, servers, storage spaces, etc. The different cloud provider provides cloud services pay as requirements model, where cloud

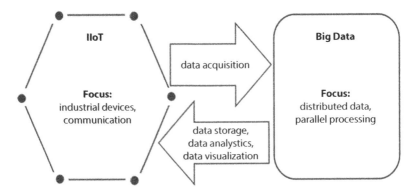

Figure 1.3 Integration architecture of big data with internet of things devices.

Table 1.3 Comparisons of big data applications.

Applications	Sources	Characteristics
Healthcare	Patient and laboratory data, gene expression data, risks and emotions of user's data.	Text, structured, images, videos, hypertext
Government Sectors	Governmental defense data, scientific and technological data, education data, treasury, power and energy records, employment records.	Text, images, videos, audios
Retails and customer products	Sales and purchasing records, marketing, accounting, inventory and feedback data.	Text, audio, videos, hyperlinks, emotional symbols
Agriculture	Weather information, agricultural drones and videos and images, soil's map and fertilities data, global positioning system (GPS) records.	Text, number, images videos
Banking sectors	Transactional information, customer's information, policies, loans, accounts, financial information.	Text, numbers, images
Transportation	Transport information, tracking devices information, GPS information, accidental information, vehicles and products information.	Text, numbers, images, videos, hyperlinks, audios

user can pay for the particular services used [22]. When an organization needs to collect a huge amount of data from the IoT device sensors, each sensor needs a large amount of computation power and storage space. This problem is solved by the combination of Cloud computing and Internet of Things techniques, in which the IoT sensors uses the cloud resources and store the collected information in a centralized manner [12]. The architecture of cloud computing with the Internet of Things is given below in Figure 1.4. Cloud computing and the Internet of Things contain different characteristics which are compulsory for each other which is shown in Table 1.4. Due to these characteristics, the integration of Cloud computing and IoT gives an excellent solution to real-world problems [13].

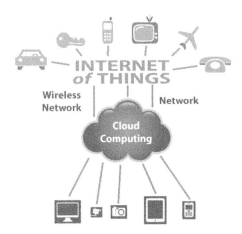

Figure 1.4 Architecture of cloud computing with internet of things.

Table 1.4 Characteristics of the internet of things and cloud computing.

Cloud computing	Internet of things	Characteristics
Give procedure to manage	Producer	Big Data
Provide virtually unlimited	Limited	Storage
Provide virtually unlimited	Limited	Computational services
Centralized services	Widespread	Displacement
Comprehensive	Limited	Reachability
Mode of service providing	Point of convergence	Internet role

The integration of Cloud computing and Internet of Things can be divides in three categories such as cloud platform, infrastructure and IoT middleware. Cloud computing removes the IoT limitations and provided opportunities for the business and it is managed by the cloud infrastructure. The IoT provides interconnection between the IoT devices and Cloud platform for data exchange.

1.6   Security of Internet of Things

The security challenges of IoT technologies are directly related to their applications. The aim of the IoT technique is to provide the combination of both physical and digital world in a single ecosystem which created the new intelligent era of web world [16, 23]. IoT provides huge business and opportunities for organizations such as energy, healthcare, government and other sectors. Due to this enhancement of IoT techniques, it suffers from different security issues which are more challenging to secure its data and applications [19]. The IoT devices faced different security issues such as privacy of data, authorization, verification, access control, data storage management, etc. The few security challenges are given below in Table 1.5. In IoT, the wireless communication channel involves radio communications,

Table 1.5 Internet of Things security requirements.

Security requirements	Description	IoT security properties
Availability	The resources of the IoT devices are readily available.	IoT resources must be attack free from the denial of service (DoS) attacks.
Integrity	It is accuracy, consistency of data and its services, trustworthiness of IoT life cycle.	The security algorithms must be capable of detecting modification and manipulation of data breaches on IoT devices.
Confidentially	The protection from the unauthorized users and access.	
Authentication	It authenticate that the user is genuine user.	The security technique must be capable of verification and authentication of user.
Authorization	Prevented the illegal uses of IoT devices or resources.	Only authorized or legal user can access the network
Access Control	Provided management and prevent unauthorized user and access to IoT resources and data.	Ensured that the IoT devices are verified and authorized to access the IoT data.

transmitters, and receivers for the information exchange between two IoT devices. So this communication channel suffers from different security threats and attacks such as man-in-middle attacks, communication signal loss, hacking of data, Denial of service attacks, protocol tunneling [20].

1.7   Conclusion

The Internet of Things is a wide field and contains incredible and different variety of applications. The main aim of IoT is to provide a facility of exchange information and synergic performance between devices and peoples via global machine-to-machine (M2M) networks. Due to M2M network, exchange of information between the devices creates an exponential amount of data. It is impossible to manage or keep secure these generated personal or organizational data in local devices. The IoT techniques need centrally storage space for personal or industrial data. To avoid these problems, in this paper we have introduced the integration of Cloud Computing, Big Data and Artificial Intelligence techniques with the Internet of Things devices. The integration of cloud computing with IoT techniques stores the information centrally generated by the IoT devices. And the collected data which is centrally stored in cloud computing is managed, processed, and analyzed by the Big Data Techniques. To extract the high volume of IoT data in real-time, processing needs machine learning and AI algorithms.

References

1. Guo, K., Lu, Y., Gao, H., Cao, R., Artificial intelligence-based semantic internet of things in a user-centric smart city. *Sensors*, 18, 5, 1341, 2018.
2. Botta, A., De Donato, W., Persico, V., Pescapé, A., Integration of cloud computing and Internet of Things: A survey. *Future Gener. Comput. Syst.*, 56, 684–700, 2016.
3. Aazam, M., Khan, I., Alsaffar, A.A., Huh, E.N., Cloud of things: Integrating internet of things and cloud computing and the issues involved, in: *Proceedings of 2014 11th International Bhurban Conference on Applied Sciences & Technology (IBCAST)*, Islamabad, Pakistan, 14th-18th January, 2014, IEEE, pp. 414–419, 2014.
4. Ge, M., Bangui, H., Buhnova, B., Big data for internet of things: A survey. *Future Gener. Comput. Syst.*, 87, 601–614, 2018.

5. Mohamed, E., The relation of artificial intelligence with internet of things: A survey. *J. Cybersecur. Inf. Manage.*, 1, 1, 30–24, 2020.

6. Ramadoss, T.S., Alam, H., Seeram, R., Artificial intelligence and Internet of Things enabled circular economy. *Int. J. Eng. Sci.*, 7, 9, 55–63, 2018.

7. Atlam, H.F., Alenezi, A. *et al.*, Integration of cloud computing with internet of things: Challenges and open issues, in: *2017 IEEE International Conference on Internet of Things (iThings) and IEEE Green Computing and Communications (GreenCom) and IEEE Cyber, Physical and Social Computing (CPSCom) and IEEE Smart Data (SmartData)*, IEEE, pp. 670–675, 2017.

8. Alansari, Z., Anuar, N.B. *et al.*, Challenges of internet of things and big data integration, in: *International Conference for Emerging Technologies in Computing*, Springer, Cham, pp. 47–55, 2018.

9. Calo, S.B., Touna, M. *et al.*, Edge computing architecture for applying AI to IoT, in: *2017 IEEE International Conference on Big Data (Big Data)*, IEEE, pp. 3012–3016, 2017.

10. Nasrulla, K. and Anitha K., Perception of relationship between Big Data and Internet of Things, *International Journal of Advanced Research in Computer and Communication Engineering*, 4, 12, 264–267, DOI 10.17148/IJARCCE.2015.41261.

11. Al-Gumaei, K., Schuba, K., Friesen, A. *et al.*, A survey of internet of things and big data integrated solutions for industries 4.0, in: *2018 IEEE 23rd International Conference on Emerging Technologies and Factory Automation (ETFA)*, vol. 1, IEEE, pp. 1417–1424, 2018.

12. Kaur, C., The cloud computing and Internet of Things (IoT). *Int. J. Sci. Res. Sci., Eng. Technol.*, 7, 1, 19–22, 2020.

13. Malik, A. and Om, H., Cloud computing and internet of things integration: Architecture, applications, issues, and challenges, in: *Sustainable Cloud and Energy Services*, pp. 1–24, Springer, Cham, 2018.

14. Sepasgozar, S., Karimi, R. *et al.*, A systematic content review of artificial intelligence and the internet of things applications in smart home. *Appl. Sci.*, 10, 9, 3074, 2020.

15. Yashodha, G., Rani, P.P. *et al.*, Role of artificial intelligence in the Internet of Things–A review, in: *IOP Conference Series: Materials Science and Engineering*, vol. 1055, No. 1, IOP Publishing, p. 012090, 2021.

16. Abiodun, O.I., Abiodun, E.O. *et al.*, A review on the security of the internet of things: Challenges and solutions. *Wireless Pers. Commun.*, 119, 3, 2603–2637, 2021.

17. Bendre, M.R. and Thool, V.R., Analytics, challenges and applications in big data environment: A survey. *J. Manage. Anal.*, 3, 3, 206–239, 2016.

18. Tien, J.M., Internet of things, real-time decision making, and artificial intelligence. *Ann. Data Sci.*, 4, 2, 149–178, 2017.

19. Kouicem, D.E., Bouabdallah, A., Lakhlef, H., Internet of things security: A top-down survey. *Comput. Networks*, 141, 199–221, 2018.

20. Alaba, F.A., Othman, M. *et al.*, Internet of things security: A survey. *J. Netw. Comput. Appl.*, 88, 10–28, 2017.
21. Cui, L., Yang, S., Chen, F. *et al.*, A survey on application of machine learning for Internet of Things. *Int. J. Mach. Learn. Cybern.*, 9, 8, 1399–1417, 2018.
22. Kumar, J., Cloud computing security issues and its challenges: A comprehensive research. *Int. J. Recent Technol. Eng*, 8, 1, 10–14, 2019.
23. Kumar, J. and Saxena, V., Asymmetric encryption scheme to protect cloud data using paillier-cryptosystem. *Int. J. Appl. Evol. Comput. (IJAEC)*, 12, 2, 50–58, 2021.

Cloud Computing and Virtualization

**Sudheer Mangalampalli[1]*, Pokkuluri Kiran Sree[2], Sangram K. Swain[3]
and Ganesh Reddy Karri[1]**

*[1]School of Computer Science & Engineering, VIT-AP University, Amravati,
AP, India*
*[2]Department of Computer Science & Engineering, Shri Vishnu Engineering College
For Women, Bhimavaram, AP, India*
*[3]Department of CSE, Centurion University of Technology and Management,
Odisha, India*

Abstract

Cloud Computing is one of the revolutionized paradigms in the IT industry, which can provide wide variety of services pay-as-you go model to all the customers in different domains like IT industry, Health, education, entertainment etc. These services are provisioned to the user based on the SLA between cloud user and provider virtually. Hypervisors are used to enable the virtualization and to spin up VMs in the cloud paradigm. There are different levels at which virtualization can be implemented, In this book chapter, we are discussing about the overview of cloud computing, different service models, deployment models and different virtualization techniques used for cloud paradigm. For effectiveness of any cloud computing paradigm, a task scheduler is necessary to get seamless services from cloud paradigm. Therefore, in this chapter we have proposed a task scheduling algorithm which uses priorities of tasks and VMs. For this algorithm we have used a nature inspired algorithm chaotic social spider algorithm to model task scheduling algorithm and simulated on CloudSim simulator. Finally, it was compared with existing algorithms PSO and CS and proposed approach is outperformed over existing algorithms with respect to makespan and energy consumption.

Keywords: Cloud computing, Service level agreement (SLA), virtualization, hypervisor, service models, deployment models

---

*Corresponding author: mssudheer2015@gmail.com

Danda B. Rawat, Lalit K Awasthi, Valentina Emilia Balas, Mohit Kumar and Jitendra Kumar Samriya (eds.) Convergence of Cloud with AI for Big Data Analytics: Foundations and Innovation, (13–40)
© 2023 Scrivener Publishing LLC

2.1   Introduction to Cloud Computing

2.1.1   Need of Cloud Computing

Cloud computing is a rapid growing model which is required in many of the fields like healthcare, finance, Education, Government services, Entertainment, Business and not limited to the domains which we have specified here. Initially all the organizations were invested huge amount on their IT infrastructure setup to provide their corresponding services to the customers. They have to invest a lot of up-front investment on the IT infrastructure, which can increase huge burden on the organization and procuring, deploying physical infrastructure is a challenging task, and it takes a huge amount of time for any organization. Physical infrastructure in terms of compute, storage, and network for any organization is limited and it is not scalable. So, the need of cloud computing comes into the point where the resources to the cloud users can be provisioned on demand with the concept named as virtualization. Scalability is also one of the important parameter where in the on premises environment it is not possible to scale up and down the resources on demand, as physical resources are limited. Therefore, with these main limitations like upfront investment and scalability in the existing on premises infrastructures the need for the cloud computing arises in every industry in these days. The below subsection describes about the history of cloud computing.

2.1.2   History of Cloud Computing

Initially in the earlier days in 2010, many of the people thought cloud means huge databases, servers and some may thought this technology actually came from real clouds [2] but it is not true. Cloud Computing is not started in this recent era but it was already existed in the different forms, as we could not confine cloud to a particular architecture either i.e. centralized architecture or distributed architecture. The history [3] of the evolvement of cloud with timelines and is given in the below table in a detailed way in the below table.

From Table 2.1, we can identify cloud computing paradigm was existed years ago and users using the paradigm but no one identifies that this model is cloud computing. When the vendors, which provides infrastructure, and software services on the cloud platforms comes into the picture then everybody is looking at cloud platform as a new model but it is already existed with the base known as virtualization. The above we have given the

Table 2.1 Timeline of cloud computing [3].

Year	Timeline and history of evolvement of cloud
1950	Herb Grosch assumption about operation of Computer terminals using Data Centers.
1960	John McCarthy opinion about computations as public utility
1966	Douglas Parkhill gave his explanation about characteristics of cloud computing
1969	Development of UNIX
1970	Development of Internet
1990	Era of Internet begins
1991	General use of Internet Started
1995	Online Auction website eBay was developed and amazon was also evolved in the same year.
1999	Salesforce developed a cloud platform, which is a Software-as-a-Service.
2006	Amazon started AWS, which is initially started as infrastructure-as-a-Service.
2008	Eucalyptus, Open Nebula were developed which are private cloud platforms.

brief history of cloud computing. The next subsection discusses about the definition of cloud computing.

2.1.3   Definition of Cloud Computing

In this section, we have given the definition for cloud computing which was defined by the NIST. Initially there is no standard definition for cloud computing but after the use of this paradigm by many of the companies NIST [1] in the year 2011 has given a definition for Cloud Computing based on certain characteristics. According to NIST, it was defined as "On demand network access to a shared pool of configurable computational resources which can gives seamless access of services to the users".

2.1.4 Different Architectures of Cloud Computing

In this section, we will discuss about architecture of Cloud Computing. Generally Cloud architecture needs a browser application i.e. to be in any of machine – desktop, laptop, or any device which supports the browser and it should be connected to the Internet and which is again connected again at the backend at the virtual infrastructure which is resided in physical host and which in turn resided in the datacenters. Architecture of Cloud Computing basically divided into two types: i. Generic Architecture and ii. Market oriented Architecture.

2.1.4.1 Generic Architecture of Cloud Computing

This architecture about the generalized version of Cloud Computing and which consists of the components in the below architecture.

The above Figure 2.1 represents Generic architecture of Cloud Computing which consists of three layers [4] i.e. Front end, Network and Infrastructure layers. Front end consists of an application which can be runs from a web browser in any of the device i.e. desktop, laptop, and mobile. Network layer consists of a network which connects both Frontend and backend infrastructure and finally the backend component and finally infrastructure layer consists of virtual machines which are resided in the physical hosts and which in turn resided in datacenters. The above

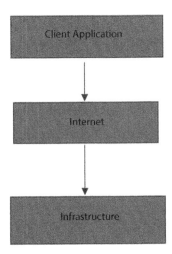

Figure 2.1 Generic architecture of cloud computing [4].

architecture is a generalized architecture which can gives the overview of cloud computing.

2.1.4.2   Market Oriented Architecture of Cloud Computing

This architecture is about the Market Oriented Architecture represented in Figure 2.2, it is a customized architecture for different cloud vendors based on the needs of the customer, and thereby cloud vendor will render the services required for the cloud users. Many of the cloud vendors named as AWS, Azure and Google cloud they are providing the required customized architecture for the users based on the Service Level Agreement made between user and provider. Initially in this architecture, user requests are submitted in the cloud console or interface. On behalf of the user, broker will take these requests and submits them to the task manager where it consists of SLA resource allocator which examines requests made by the user and based on the agreement made by the user and vendor it will allocate resource by dispatching that request through dispatcher to VMs resided in Physical hosts which in turn resided in datacenters. It also consists of Accounting and pricing modules to calculate the price for all the services

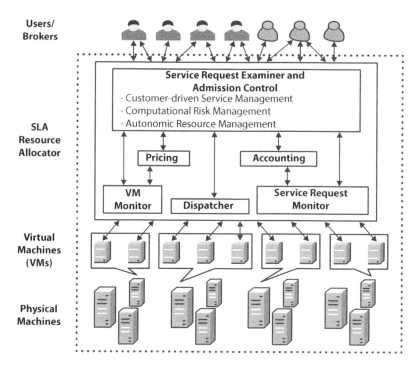

Figure 2.2 Market-oriented architecture of cloud computing [5].

used by the user and automatic pricing will be calculated by the pricing module. It consists of a VM Monitor module which will track the availability of VMs i.e. how many of the VMs are utilized and how many of the VMs are free. These details will be tracked through VM monitor module. For every request given by the user and examined by SLA resource allocator and before assigning it to a virtual machine VM monitor will track the availability of VMs and then based on that it will assign that task to corresponding VM. All these VMs are running in the cloud enabled by a component called hypervisor through which virtual environment will be enabled for the VMs. The below figure represents Market oriented architecture of Cloud Computing. We have presented the architectures of cloud computing in a detailed way. Many of the users chooses different cloud services based on the need of the application and customized version of the cloud platform and services will be provided to the customers so the generic architecture is to assumed as an ideal version and in real time market oriented architecture is to be used by the customers. Now in the below section, we have to discuss about the various applications of cloud computing in different domains.

2.1.5   Applications of Cloud Computing in Different Domains

There are many kinds of applications where cloud computing is used for different purposes. In this sub section some of the applications of cloud computing in different domains are discussed. These are some of the domains mentioned below.

- Healthcare
- Education
- Entertainment
- Government
- Transportation

2.1.5.1   Cloud Computing in Healthcare

In these days, maintaining the patient data manually in the hospitals is a challenging job. Most of the patient health records are in the electronic format and to store these records like test reports, X-rays and scanning reports is easier through cloud storage and to store them in a huge manner it is not that much easier by using standard storage mechanisms. Using Cloud Computing, doctor and patient can easily access the records even if they are sitting remotely. Many of the hospitals and health insurance vendors also maintain their records in cloud for easier processing of insurance for the patients. In this way, Cloud Computing technology is used in health-care domain.

2.1.5.2   Cloud Computing in Education

Pandemic shifted the normal situation into a new normal. To handle this current situation, all the educational institutions are using different tools to teach the students and even for conducting the meetings and other activities. Cloud Computing plays a major role in education domain as many of the organizations uses variety of tools i.e. Microsoft teams from Azure cloud, Google meet from Google cloud and many of the tools are running in the cloud, which can gives greater scalability and flexibility to engage the students in education domain.

2.1.5.3   Cloud Computing in Entertainment Services

This technology gives us a lot of scope to use it in various domains. It can also be used in entertainment where lot of online platforms named as OTT services can be run with the support of cloud computing at the backend. It is difficult to run these services with on premises infrastructure as millions of the people around the world can subscribe these services so there is a chance to get the scalability issue when they run on the on-premises environment. Therefore, these OTT vendors have to use this technology to render their services to the customers with high range scalability by providing seamless services to the users.

2.1.5.4   Cloud Computing in Government Services

Many of the government sector departments also using Cloud Computing technology for running their virtual infrastructure in Cloud. For example, DBS bank runs their total infrastructure on AWS cloud therefore which can reduces their upfront infrastructure cost. It is important for the countries which consist of more dense population and if the people need to use the services in online then there is a definite need to use cloud computing as the technology in many of the Government services.

2.1.6   Service Models in Cloud Computing

In cloud computing, all the components like compute, storage, and network will be rendered as a service to the users. The major services provided by the cloud are mentioned as below.

- Infrastructure-as-a-service
- Platform-as-a-service
- Software-as-a-service

There are many other kind of services like Database-as-a-service, Machine learning-as-a-service and IOT-as-a-service and not limited to these but many more services are available in the various cloud platforms in the below Table 2.2. In this chapter, we briefly discusses about the main services which leverages the services to the users of cloud computing.

Infrastructure-as-a-service: This is the primary layer or service model in cloud computing which can provide virtual infrastructure to the users through which they can get VM instances virtually i.e. compute services through which huge computational tasks or requests can be handled on demand without any upfront investment cost. This layer also provides virtual storage, which can give the advantage of scalability to the corresponding user to store their data in cloud when compared with the on premises environment.

Platform-as-a-service: In cloud computing, there is a chance to develop our own applications on top of the cloud platform which leverages services to the cloud user by enabling the platform to develop their applications on cloud platform with the use of REST API services and different middleware software.

Table 2.2 List of services in major cloud vendors.

Name of the cloud environment	Infrastructure-as-a-service	Platform-as-a-service	Software-as-a-service
Amazon Web Services	EC2, S3, EBS, EFS	Elastic BeanStalk	SNS, Email service
Google Cloud Platform	Compute Engine, Storage and database	Developer tools, APP Engine	Gmail, Google Drive
Microsoft Azure	Azure Virtual machines, Blob Storage, Disks, Files.	Web Apps, Developer Services, Integration services etc.	Microsoft email, one drive

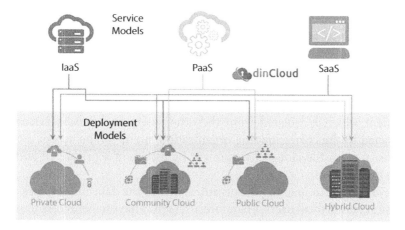

Figure 2.3 Service and deployment models in cloud computing [6].

Software-as-a-service: This layer or service model can be used to run the software on cloud platform rather than in the on premises environment. This service greatly helps the cloud users or customers, which gives seamless access to the software which is running on the cloud.

All the above services are existed in different cloud platforms with different names. The below table represents some of the different services in various cloud platforms.

Figure 2.3 shows various services and deployment models in cloud computing.

In the previous section, we have briefly discussed about various service models in cloud computing, and in the below section, we have briefly given about various deployment models in cloud computing.

2.1.7   Deployment Models in Cloud Computing

This section discusses about various deployment models, which can give overview about how the cloud vendor provides services while deploying the environment and how they can leverage the services to the users in different ways. They are Public, Private, Hybrid, and Community Clouds.

Public Cloud: This is one of the major deployment models in cloud computing through which every user can use the services on a paid basis and the services can be publicly available through online by the cloud vendor. There are many of the cloud vendors, which provide services to the customers seamlessly without any hassle and the vendors are AWS, Google Cloud Platform and Microsoft azure are the major game players in the market.

Private Cloud: This deployment model renders the services to the users by the cloud provider only restricted to that organization. Cloud Provider will renders the services to the users through a virtual private cloud environment which is isolated from the other users and these services are restricted to the corresponding organization and it can be accessed from the users from the cloud environment by means of a private IP address from the user host.

Hybrid Cloud: In many of the organizations all the data and services cannot be accessed to all users. Therefore, users may have to get access to some of the basic services and services which are not accessible to the users can be restricted by private cloud. So, public and private cloud services were combined in this deployment model.

Community Cloud: This deployment model is mainly to be used when resources are collaborated in between organizations in terms of infrastructure virtually. This can be done by the cloud provider itself with corresponding organization or an external third party. This model is especially used for organizations with same type of concerned issues.

This chapter discusses mainly about the role of Virtualization in Cloud Computing, need of virtualization through which cloud vendors provide different services i.e. compute, storage, and network.

2.2   Virtualization

Virtualization is a process of multiplexing of Virtual machines in a single physical host. This process will enable a virtualization layer on top of a physical machine which can be enabled through a hypervisor or otherwise it is called as a Virtual Machine Monitor.

2.2.1   Need of Virtualization in Cloud Computing

Virtualization plays a very important role in Cloud paradigm, as it is difficult to maintain much number of physical hosts in the datacenters to render cloud services to all the users around the world as it is difficult for cloud vendors to maintain physical hosts and it incurs a huge cost for the cloud vendor. It is very difficult for the cloud vendor to spin up and down the servers if they are maintained in a physical host and to handle huge requests on demand by the cloud vendor virtualization is the best process, which separates virtual machine instance from the hardware layer. Therefore, to reduce the costs incurred due to the maintenance of hardware through physical hosts and to increase scalability there is a need to use virtualization in the cloud paradigm.

2.2.2   Architecture of a Virtual Machine

The below figure shows the architecture of a virtual machine which is running on top of a Physical host.

Figure 2.4 shows the architecture of a Virtual machine in which the lower layer shows the actual hardware of a physical host, which consists of the infrastructure. Physical host consists of the next upper layer named as Operating system, which is on top of infrastructure layer. There is a software which can enables virtualization in the physical host named as Hypervisor. It creates a virtual layer on top of physical host, which maps and organizes VMs and maps them onto the physical resources in the host. Each Virtual machine is called as a VM in short form and it consists of a guest OS, library packages and on top of it applications can be run in virtual machines. Each VM can be isolated from another VM and no VM creation; destroying of any VM won't depend on each other. This architecture gives a security perspective and all the resources running in VMs are secured as they are isolated from each other. Therefore, virtualization provides flexibility, security and scalability and due to this reason many of the companies and vendors using virtualization.

The below sub section gives advantages of Virtualization.

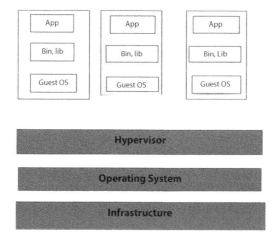

Figure 2.4 Virtual machine architecture.

2.2.3   Advantages of Virtualization

These are some of the advantages of Virtualization technique.

- Efficient use of Hardware Resources.
- Availability
- Speedy recovery
- On demand setup and configuration of a VM
- Easier migration

Explanations of the above advantages are described below.

Efficient use of Hardware Resources: Resources in Physical hosts are always in underutilized mode and it depends on the application which we are using on the hardware resource. To utilize the hardware resources in a proper way, the organization create multiple VM instances on a single host and thereby they can utilize the hardware resources efficiently by using virtualization.

Availability: This is also one of the biggest advantages of virtualization through which servers can be available all the time and round the clock. If the server can be down at any time, we can easily migrate the virtual server from one pool to another. This is not that much easy if any server down occurs in on premises environment. Therefore, availability is one of the greatest advantages we can get by virtualization.

Speedy recovery: It is one of the advantage with virtualization when any VM crashes and if it is down at times then we can easily restore the VM from by using rollback whereas that facility is not available with on premises environment and if any huge load comes onto that VM there is every chance to migrate the VM from that pool to a high end configuration pool.

On demand setup and configuration of a VM: It is very difficult to setup and configure a server in on premises environment. It takes days and months to set up a server in on premises environment. Virtualization made it easier for us to setup and configure a sever within few minutes. Therefore, this reason made virtualization advantageous for a cloud user.

Easier Migration: This is the biggest advantage of virtualization as if the server fails or crashes or down for any reason and if any huge load coming onto server which cannot handled by it through virtualization we can easily spin up a new server in the span of minutes and migrates the overloaded workload onto the VMs easily.

These are some of the advantages of virtualization we have discussed here and to implement this virtualization we have different levels of implementations of virtualization.

2.2.4   Different Implementation Levels of Virtualization

Figure 2.5 represents different levels to implement virtualization. Each of these implementation levels has its own advantages and disadvantages. In this section, we will discuss about only how virtualization can be implemented at these levels.

2.2.4.1   Instruction Set Architecture Level

This is one of the levels of virtualization implementation in which VM will be emulated by performing a binary code translation by using a virtual set Instruction architecture [7] which is to be running in the VM. All the instructions running in the physical host have to be emulated onto the VM by translation of every instruction from the physical host and it also depends on the architecture of the machine currently using at that time for

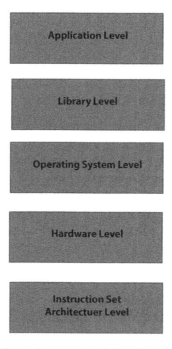

Figure 2.5 Different levels for implementation of virtualization [7].

virtualization. Therefore, this process of virtualization at Instruction Set Architecture Level is relatively slow when compared with the processes of implementing at other levels.

2.2.4.2 Hardware Level

Virtualization at hardware means virtualizing the physical resources such as processor, memory, and I/O devices [7]. This process can be done on top of a bare metal hardware machine with the use of a hypervisor. Most of the organizations use xen hypervisor to enable virtual machine environment.

2.2.4.3 Operating System Level

This is the most frequently used and simple process of implementation of virtualization. On top of an operating system a virtualization layer can be enabled with the help of a hypervisor and it can be viewed as a container [7].

2.2.4.4 Library Level

This virtualization is to be used in most of the cross platform instances where the applications can be run through the support of Libraries such as WINE [7]. In Linux operating system, Microsoft windows applications can be installed and run by using WINE API which can hook the application to the cross platform.

2.2.4.5 Application Level

This is the easiest way for implementation of virtualization as it runs like a process in a machine. Virtualization can be done along with the operating system layer. Best suitable examples of application level virtualization is .NET and JVM running in the physical host [7].

In the above section, we have briefly discussed about the different implementation levels of virtualization and finally in the next section role and importance of server consolidation using virtualization will be discussed.

2.2.5 Server Consolidation Using Virtualization

Server Consolidation using Virtualization is one of the key aspects in datacenters [7] as many of the hardware resources in datacenters are underutilized and most of the physical resources are wasted and which in turn increases energy consumption, increases carbon foot prints and which in turn increases the Power cost and also impacts the environment. For this purpose, most of the datacenters uses a technique called server consolidation to optimize the servers by consolidating the unused servers onto a single physical machine. Server Consolidation provides many advantages and some of the advantages are mentioned below.

- Efficient utilization of Hardware Resources.
- Independent deployment and provisioning of resources in the datacenters [7].
- It can reduces operational costs to the cloud vendor, i.e., minimizing cooling costs, maintenance costs, network hardware requirements.
- It will improve the availability of servers round the clock.
- It will not impact the physical host operating system even if any guest OS can be crashed in the VM as VM templates are readily available as images so that we can quickly set up the servers.

2.2.6   Task Scheduling in Cloud Computing

Task Scheduling is a huge challenge in Cloud Computing as incoming tasks coming onto the cloud interface were varies with respect to size, processing capacity and moreover that they are dynamic in nature i.e. at times tasks were heterogeneous and in order to handle such type of workloads and to map tasks to appropriate VMs an effective task scheduling algorithm is needed. There are several algorithms proposed by many of the earlier authors and all those algorithms were addressing mainly the parameters named as makespan, energy consumption, and operational costs but there is no algorithms mapping tasks onto VMs based on characteristics of tasks. In this section, we have proposed an algorithm, which calculates priorities of tasks and priorities of VMs based on electricity price per unit cost. Priorities of tasks are calculated based on size and processing capacities of tasks. Chaotic social spider algorithm is used as methodology for scheduling tasks. We have used a simulator known as CloudSim for performing the simulation. This proposed approach was compared with existing algorithms which uses nature inspired algorithms like GA, PSO, CS, and CSO. From results, we have identified that our proposed approach shows huge impact over existing approaches in terms of makespan and Energy consumption.

Main Contributions of this proposed algorithm are:

i.   We have used Chaotic Social Spider algorithm [30] used to do scheduling optimization.
ii. Tasks are effectively mapped based on priorities calculated before submitting it to scheduler.
iii. Makespan and Energy consumption are addressed as parameters in this proposed scheduling mechanism.
iv. Simulation results are compared with existing algorithms like PSO and CS algorithms.

The below Table 2.3 represents various existing task scheduling algorithms, which uses nature-inspired algorithms addresses metrics

Table 2.3 Existing scheduling algorithms.

Authors	Used methodology	Simulation environment	Parameters addressed
Mangalampalli *et al.* [8]	Cat Swarm Optimization	CloudSim	Makespan, Total Power cost, migration time, Energy Consumption
Mangalampalli *et al.* [9]	Whale optimization	CloudSim	Makespan, energy consumption and power cost at datacenters
Mangalampalli *et al.* [10]	Hybrid CSPSO	CloudSim	Makespan, migration time and Total Power Cost at datacenters.
Yahia *et al.* [11]	Complement Squirrel Search algorithm	CloudSim	Quality of Service
Prasanna Kumar, K. R. *et al.* [12]	Crow Search algorithm	CloudSim	Makespan

(Continued)

Table 2.3 Existing scheduling algorithms. (*Continued*)

Authors	Used methodology	Simulation environment	Parameters addressed
Bacanin *et al.* [13]	Grey Wolf Optimizer	CloudSim	Quality of service and Robustness
Midya *et al.* [14]	Hybrid Adaptive PSO	Matlab	Response time and energy consumption
Alsaidy *et al.* [15]	Improved PSO	Matlab	Makespan, total execution time, energy consumption
Sharma *et al.* [16]	Enhanced Ant Colony Optimization	CloudSim	Makespan
Arul Xavier *et al.* [17]	Chaotic Spider algorithm	CloudSim	Makespan, load balancing of tasks
Agarwal *et al.* [18]	Cuckoo search Algorithm	CloudSim	Response time, makespan
Abualigah *et al.* [19]	Multiverse GA	Matlab	Total Completion time
Srichandan *et al.* [20]	Hybrid Bacteria foraging algorithm	Customized Cloud environment	SLA violations
Sarah *et al.* [21]	Enhanced Multiverse optimizer	CloudSim	Makespan and Resource utilization
Abualigah *et al.* [22]	Antlion optimization	CloudSim	Makespan and Resource utilization
Basu *et al.* [23]	GA and ACO algorithm	Customized Cloud environment	Makespan

(*Continued*)

Table 2.3 Existing scheduling algorithms. (*Continued*)

Authors	Used methodology	Simulation environment	Parameters addressed
Gamal *et al.* [24]	Hybrid Artificial Bee and ACO	CloudSim	Makespan, response time, execution time
Khorsand *et al.* [25]	Best Worst and Topsis Methodology	CloudSim	Makespan, energy consumption.
Pirozmand *et al.* [26]	Genetic and Energy conscious scheduling	CloudSim	Energy consumption and makespan
Jain *et al.* [27]	Binary Salp Swarm Algorithm	CloudSim	Makespan, resource utilization, throughput.
Fanian *et al.* [28]	Fire fly and Simulated Annealing	CloudSim	makespan
Natesan *et al.* [29]	Grey Wolf optimization	CloudSim	Makespan, Operational costs
Kumar, Mohit, *et al.* [32]	Spider Monkey Optimization	CloudSim	Makespan, Operational costs
Dubey *et al.* [33]	PSO and CS	CloudSim	Energy Consumption
Mohit *et al.* [34]	BPSO	CloudSim	Makespan, Total Execution time.

mentioned in the above Table 2.3. They have not mapped tasks based on [9] priorities of tasks and VMs in the cloud environment. This proposed task scheduling algorithm accurately maps tasks to [9] VMs based on priorities of tasks and VMs so that based on that parameters named as makespan and energy consumption were evaluated. We have used chaotic social spider algorithm used to solve optimization problem and used to model our algorithm, which is based on foraging strategy of spiders [30] and searches for prey based on the vibration on spider web. The below table represents various existing task scheduling algorithms with different objectives.

2.2.7   Proposed System Architecture

In this section, we have carefully designed the system architecture. Initially user requests are submitted at cloud console. On behalf of users broker will submit these requests to the task manager. Here before submitting requests to task manager, we are inducing priority of tasks and priority of VMs in this algorithm. Priorities of tasks calculated based on size of task and processing capacity of tasks. Priorities of VMs calculated based on price per unit of electricity of datacenter's location. This multi criteria help us to map tasks effectively on to appropriate VMs when scheduling tasks in cloud. If all tasks are having the same priority, then scheduler will map all tasks to the VMs where that datacenter is located with low price per unit cost and if resources are exhausted in that pool or if they are overloaded then tasks will be migrated to the next VM in the same pool or different pool in the same datacenter or to the next VMs in the same or different datacenter by using next price per unit cost of electricity. Figure 2.6 gives overview about our proposed system architecture.

2.2.8   Mathematical Modeling of Proposed Task Scheduling Algorithm

This section describes mathematical modeling of proposed system architecture. To formulate accurate mathematical modeling, we have assumed n tasks i.e. $t_n = \{t_1, t_2, \ldots t_n\}$, k VMs i.e. $v_k = v_1, v_2, \ldots, v_k$ and i datacenters i.e. $d_i = \{d_1, d_2, \ldots d_i\}$. Now these n tasks are mapped onto k VMs accurately by calculating priorities of tasks and VMs. The below equation is used to calculate entire load on all VMs. Initially to calculate, priorities of Tasks, we need to calculate overall load on entire VMs and in turn to calculate overall load on physical hosts. The below equation calculates overall load on all VMs.

$$Load^{vm} = \sum_{k=1} Load^k \qquad (2.1)$$

$Load^k$ indicates overall load on k VMs.
The below equation calculates overall load on Physical hosts.

$$Load^{host} = Load^k / \sum_{j=1} Load^j \qquad (2.2)$$

Where $Load^j$ indicates load per physical host.

Priority of task depends on length of task and processing capacity of tasks and the mapping VM of that task. Capacity of a VM can be calculated by using the following equation

$$c^{vm} = p^{no} * p^{mips} \qquad (2.3)$$

Where c^{vm} indicates a capacity of a VM, p^{no} indicates number of processing elements in a VM and p^{mips} indicates number of MIPS cycles it takes to process a request or task.

Now overall capacity of all VMs can be calculated by following equation.

$$Total^{cvm} = \sum_{k=1}^{n} c^{vm} \qquad (2.4)$$

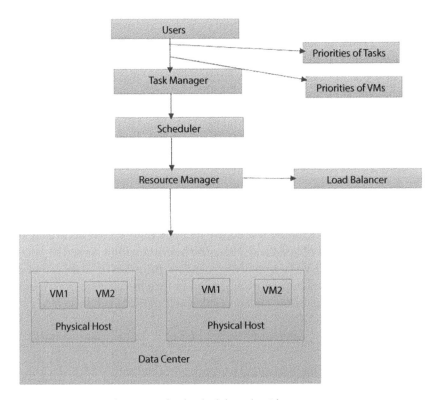

Figure 2.6 System architecture of task scheduling algorithm.

Where $Total^{cvm}$ indicates total capacity of all VMs assumed in mathematical modeling.

Priority of a task depends mainly on length of task and processing capacity of task so that it can be calculated by following equation.

$$t_{len}^n = t^{mips} * t^p \tag{2.5}$$

Now priority of task is calculated as below by following equation.

$$t^{prio} = t_{len}^n / c^{vm} \tag{2.6}$$

Now we have calculated priority of task but we are using a multi criteria decision making system in scheduler which checks for the appropriate VM based on task priority and thereby it needs to map a VM with lower electricity cost VM in the available datacenters.

$$vm^{prio} = \frac{eccost^h}{eccost^{d_i}} \tag{2.7}$$

Where vm^{prio} indicates priority of VM in the available datacenters, $eccost^h$ indicates highest electricity unit cost among all datacenters and $eccost^{d_i}$ indicates electricity unit cost at corresponding datacenter.

We are addressing parameters named as makespan as this is a primary objective of any task-scheduling algorithm and it is calculated by using following equation.

$$m^n = availability_k^{vm} + e^n \tag{2.8}$$

Where m^n is makespan of n tasks and $availability_k^{vm}$ represents availability of k VMs to run n tasks.

After calculation of makespan, energy consumption in cloud paradigm calculated by using following equation.

$$e^c(vm^k) = \int e_{comp}^c(vm^k, t) + e_{idle}^c(vm^k, t)dt \tag{2.9}$$

2.2.9   Multi Objective Optimization

Effective mapping of tasks to VMs by addressing parameters makespan and Energy consumption and inducing priorities into scheduler is a challenging task as cloud paradigm is a dynamic scenario. Therefore, we have decided to use a nature inspired algorithm i.e. chaotic social spider algorithm [30]. We have written fitness function in such a way that it should minimize makespan and energy consumption. The following equation represents fitness function

$$f(x) = min \sum m^n(x), e^c(x) \qquad (2.10)$$

Equation 2.10 is used as fitness function to optimize makespan and energy consumption. To optimize the above said parameters we have used a nature inspired algorithm i.e. Chaotic social spider algorithm and description about algorithm in the below section.

2.2.10   Chaotic Social Spider Algorithm

It is a nature-inspired algorithm [30] proposed by Yu and Li. It is totally based on forging pattern of spiders. This algorithm looks for prey by using a Search Agent based on pattern of spiders by broadcast messages by using search agents. In the initialization phase, spiders were randomly generated in solution space and then when it finds a prey in the web which gives a solution and identifies best solution by using broadcast message and it is calculated as follows.

$$Broad_{msg}(t) = \log\left(\frac{1}{f(x) - C} + 1\right) \qquad (2.11)$$

Where C is the control parameter for identification of feasible solution which is either 0 or 1. After identification of all solutions from all search agents the best solution will be identified and it will compare with current solution and if it is better than current solution it will be identified as the new current solution and checks value of search agent which can be either set to 0 or 1. If a new solution identified and then it sets to 1 or it will be zero. This search agent process will guide all agents to search randomly but not to search the previous location for that searching process given by

$$y^{n+1} = \alpha y^n (1 - y^n) \qquad (2.12)$$

Where y^n is a random number generator for iterations and to avoid previous searching space and to guide search agents in a proper way, an inertia weight added into to the search process. Therefore, selection process is calculated as

$$p(t+1) = p(t) + \left(p(t) - p(t-1)\right) * \beta + \left(p_n - p(t)\right).\alpha \qquad (2.13)$$

$$\beta(t) = \left(\delta_{initial} - \delta_{final}\right) * \left(\frac{it_{mx} - it}{it_{mx}}\right) + \delta_{final} * y^{n+1} \qquad (2.14)$$

Where $\delta_{initial}$ and δ_{final} are initial and final weights which are added in search process. it_{mx} is maximum number of iterations and it is current iteration.

2.2.11 Proposed Task Scheduling Algorithm

Input: set of tasks, VMs and Datacenters.
Output: Mapping of Tasks with VMs by minimization of makespan and energy consumption.

1. Start
2. Initialize search agent population randomly.
3. Calculate priority of task using equation 2.6.
4. Calculate priority of VM using equation 2.7.
5. Calculate fitness function by using equation 2.10.
6. Generate solutions by using equation 2.12.
7. Update search process using equation 2.13.
8. Calculate makespan, energy consumption by using equations 2.8 and 2.9.
9. Randomly pick a VM from all VMs and identify whether calculated solution consists of minimized makespan and energy consumption.
10. If yes keep it as best minimized makespan and energy consumption.
11. Update the solution and identify it as a best VM with optimized makespan and energy consumption.

12. If no identify the next VM rather than already searched VM until best VM found for the addressed parameters.
13. Repeat this process until all iterations are completed. Stop.

2.2.12 Simulation and Results

In this work, simulation was carried out in CloudSim [31]. The entire simulation settings are mentioned in below Table 2.4.

2.2.12.1 Calculation of Makespan

Makespan is evaluated by using CloudSim [31] in which input to tasks are generated randomly which are of from 100 to 1000. Results were compared with existing approaches named as PSO and CS. The below Figure 2.7 represents calculation of makespan.

Table 2.4 Configuration settings for simulation.

Name of the entity	Quantity
Tasks	100, 500, 1000
Task Length	250,000 to 1,00,000
VM Capacity	4096 MB
Number of VMs	100
Number of Hosts	500
Number of Data centers	10

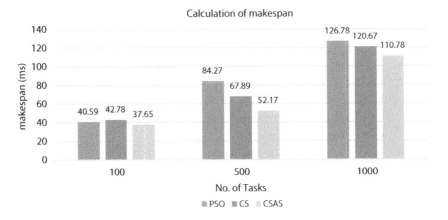

Figure 2.7 Calculation of makespan.

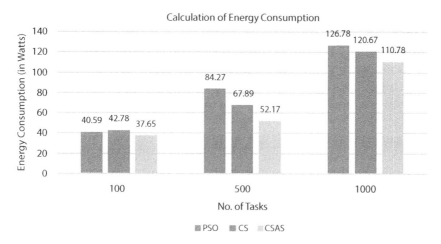

Figure 2.8 Calculation of energy consumption.

In the above Figure 2.7 when input was given as 100, 500 and 1000 tasks. For PSO generated makespan is 1323.6, 1477.5, and 2367.8 ms respectively. For CS generated makespan is 1256.7, 1423.9, and 2158.8ms respectively. For proposed CSAS makespan generated is 1056.2, 1246.9, and 1745.6ms respectively. The proposed approach was evaluated against PSO and CS algorithms and clearly from results; makespan is greatly minimized when compared with other algorithms.

2.2.12.2   Calculation of Energy Consumption

The above Figure 2.8 represents calculation of energy consumption and it was compared with PSO, CS algorithms. In the above Figure 2.8, when input given as 100, 500 and 1000 tasks. For PSO generated energy consumption is 40.59, 84.27, and 126.78 watts respectively. For CS generated energy consumption is 42.78, 67.89, and 120.67 watts respectively. For proposed CSAS generated energy consumption is 37.65, 52.17, and 110.78 watts respectively. The proposed approach was compared with PSO and CS algorithms and it greatly minimizes energy consumption.

2.3   Conclusion

In this chapter, we have clearly discussed about overview of cloud computing paradigm, deployment models, and basic services which give a clear view of basic architectural elements of cloud computing. After that, need of Virtualization and implementation levels of virtualization are discussed. For effectiveness of any cloud computing paradigm appropriate task scheduler is necessary to [9] map tasks to VMs based on priorities of tasks and VMs as this paradigm is dynamic and heterogeneous. We have proposed an algorithm modeled by a nature inspired algorithm i.e. chaotic social spider algorithm. This simulation was done on CloudSim simulator and tasks were generated randomly. It was compared with existing approaches PSO and CS. From results we came to know that our proposed task scheduling algorithm greatly minimizes makespan and energy consumption.

References

1. Mell, P. and Grance, T., Cloud, Hybrid. The NIST definition of cloud computing, *National Institute of Science and Technology*, Special Publication 800, 145, 2011.
2. Walton, Z., Americans think cloud computing comes from actual clouds, WebProNews.com, 29 Aug. 2012, www.webpronews.com/americansthink-cloud-computing-comes-from-actual-clouds2012-08.
3. Bojanova, I., Zhang, J., Voas, J., Cloud computing. *It Prof.*, 15, 2, 12–14, 2013.
4. Sudheer, M.S. *et al.*, An effective analysis on various scheduling algorithms in cloud computing. *2017 International Conference on Inventive Computing and Informatics (ICICI)*, IEEE, 2017.
5. Buyya, R., Yeo, C.S., Venugopal, S., Market-oriented cloud computing: Vision, hype, and reality for delivering IT services as computing utilities, in: *Proceedings of the 10th IEEE International Conference on High Performance Computing and Communications (HPCC)*, Dalian, China, 25–27 September 2008.
6. Stieninger, Mark, and Dietmar Nedbal., Characteristics of cloud computing in the business context: A systematic literature review. *Global Journal of Flexible Systems Management*, 15.1, 59–68, 2014.
7. Hwang, K., Dongarra, J., Fox, G.C., *Distributed and cloud computing: From parallel processing to the internet of things*, Morgan Kaufmann, 2013.
8. Mangalampalli, S., Swain, S.K., Mangalampalli, V.K., Multi objective task scheduling in cloud computing using cat swarm optimization algorithm. *Arab J. Sci. Eng.*, 47, 1821–1830, 2021, https://doi.org/10.1007/s13369-021-06076-7.
9. Mangalampalli, S., Swain, S.K., Mangalampalli, V.K., Prioritized energy efficient task scheduling algorithm in cloud computing using whale optimization algorithm. *Wireless Pers. Commun.*, 85, 1–17, 2021, https://doi.org/10.1007/s11277-021-09018-6.

10. Mangalampalli, S., Mangalampalli, V.K., Swain, S.K., Multi objective task scheduling algorithm in cloud computing using the hybridization of particle swarm optimization and cuckoo search. *J. Comput. Theor. Nanosci.*, 17, 12, 5346–5357, 2020.

11. Yahia, H.S. *et al.*, Comprehensive survey for cloud computing based nature-inspired algorithms optimization scheduling. *Asian J. Res. Comput. Sci.*, 8, 2, 1–16, 2021.

12. Prasanna Kumar, K.R. and Kousalya, K., Amelioration of task scheduling in cloud computing using crow search algorithm. *Neural Comput. Appl.*, 32, 10, 5901–5907, 2020.

13. Bacanin, N. *et al.*, Task scheduling in cloud computing environment by grey wolf optimizer. *2019 27th Telecommunications Forum (TELFOR)*, IEEE, 2019.

14. Midya, S. *et al.*, Multi-objective optimization technique for resource allocation and task scheduling in vehicular cloud architecture: A hybrid adaptive nature inspired approach. *J. Netw. Comput. Appl.*, 103, 58–84, 2018.

15. Alsaidy, S.A., Abbood, A.D., Sahib, M.A., Heuristic initialization of PSO task scheduling algorithm in cloud computing. *J. King Saud Univ.-Comput. Inf. Sci.*, 2020.

16. Sharma, S. and Jain, R., EACO: An enhanced ant colony optimization algorithm for task scheduling in cloud computing. *Int. J. Secur. Its Appl.*, 13, 4, 91–100, 2019.

17. Arul Xavier, V.M. and Annadurai, S., Chaotic social spider algorithm for load balance aware task scheduling in cloud computing. *Cluster Comput.*, 22, 1, 287–297, 2019.

18. Agarwal, M. and Srivastava, G.M.S., A cuckoo search algorithm-based task scheduling in cloud computing, in: *Advances in Computer and Computational Sciences*, pp. 293–299, Springer, Singapore, 2018.

19. Abualigah, L. and Alkhrabsheh, M., Amended hybrid multi-verse optimizer with genetic algorithm for solving task scheduling problem in cloud computing. *J. Supercomput.*, 78, 1, 740–765, 2022.

20. Srichandan, S., Kumar, T.A., Bibhudatta, S., Task scheduling for cloud computing using multi-objective hybrid bacteria foraging algorithm. *Future Comput. Inf. J.*, 3, 2, 210–230, 2018.

21. Shukri, S.E. *et al.*, Enhanced multi-verse optimizer for task scheduling in cloud computing environments. *Expert Syst. Appl.*, 168, 114230, 2021.

22. Abualigah, L. and Diabat, A., A novel hybrid antlion optimization algorithm for multi-objective task scheduling problems in cloud computing environments. *Cluster Comput.*, 24, 1, 205–223, 2021.

23. Basu, S. *et al.*, An intelligent/cognitive model of task scheduling for IoT applications in cloud computing environment. *Future Gener. Comput. Syst.*, 88, 254–261, 2018.

24. Gamal, M. *et al.*, Bio-inspired based task scheduling in cloud computing, in: *Machine Learning Paradigms: Theory and Application*, pp. 289–308, Springer, Cham, 2019.

25. Khorsand, R. and Ramezanpour, M., An energy-efficient task-scheduling algorithm based on a multi-criteria decision-making method in cloud computing. *Int. J. Commun. Syst.*, 33, 9, e4379, 2020.

26. Pirozmand, P. *et al.*, Multi-objective hybrid genetic algorithm for task scheduling problem in cloud computing. *Neural Comput. Appl.*, 33, 19, 13075–13088, 2021.

27. Jain, R. and Sharma, N., A QoS aware binary salp swarm algorithm for effective task scheduling in cloud computing, in: *Progress in Advanced Computing and Intelligent Engineering*, pp. 462–473, Springer, Singapore, 2021.

28. Fanian, F., Bardsiri, V.K., Shokouhifar, M., A new task scheduling algorithm using firefly and simulated annealing algorithms in cloud computing. *Int. J. Adv. Comput. Sci. Appl.*, 9, 2, 195–202, 2018.

29. Natesan, G. and Chokkalingam, A., An improved grey wolf optimization algorithm based task scheduling in cloud computing environment. *Int. Arab J. Inf. Technol.*, 17, 1, 73–81, 2020.

30. James, J.Q. and Li, V., A social spider algorithm for global optimization. *Appl. Soft Comput.*, 30, 614–627, 2015.

31. Calheiros, R.N., Ranjan, R., Beloglazov, A., De Rose, C.A., Buyya, R., CloudSim: A toolkit for modeling and simulation of cloud computing environments and evaluation of resource provisioning algorithms. *Software Pract. Exp.*, 41, 1, 23–50, 2011.

32. Kumar, M. *et al.*, ARPS: An autonomic resource provisioning and scheduling framework for cloud platforms. *IEEE Trans. Sustain. Comput.*, 7, 2, 386–399, 2021.

33. Dubey, K., Sharma, S.C., Kumar, M., A secure IoT applications allocation framework for integrated fog-cloud environment. *J. Grid Comput.*, 20, 1, 1–23, 2022.

34. Kumar, M. *et al.*, Autonomic cloud resource provisioning and scheduling using meta-heuristic algorithm. *Neural Comput. Appl.*, 32, 24, 18285–18303, 2020.

Time and Cost-Effective Multi-Objective Scheduling Technique for Cloud Computing Environment

Aida A. Nasr[1], Kalka Dubey[2]*, Nirmeen El-Bahnasawy[3], Gamal Attiya[3] and Ayman El-Sayed[3]

[1]Information Technology Department, Faculty of Computers and Informatics, Tanta University, Tanta, Egypt
[2]Department of Computer Science and Engineering, RGIPT Jais, Amethi, India
[3]Faculty of Electronic Engineering, Menoufia University, Menouf, Egypt

Abstract

Selection of optimal resources in the cloud is one of the challenging issues that influence the cost and time of this computing paradigm. The main goal of the service provider is to schedule the cloudlets efficiently to avoid the possibility of overutilization and underutilization of resources that directly affects the services of the cloud also the budget of end-users. Several state-of-art techniques have been published to accomplish the requirement of either end-users or service provider's QoS parameters but failed to solve completely. This paper presents a new time and cost-effective Multi-Objective Cloudlet Scheduling Approach (CSA) to overcome the mentioned issue. The main idea of this research work is to convert the large domain scheduling problem in to small size clustering problems while minimizing the makespan and computation cost. The proposed CSA divides the cloudlet list into several clusters and allocate each cluster to the best possible virtual machine without violating resources availability and others constraint. The proposed CSA is implement and validated through cloud simulator i.e. CloudSim and make comparison with existing techniques to test the effectiveness of the developed algorithm. Developed CSA is more efficient than the existing heuristic and meta-heuristic algorithms in terms of time complexity and system performance.

Keywords: Cloud computing, cluster, datacenter broker, load balancing, heuristic

**Corresponding author*: kalka.dubey267@gmail.com

Danda B. Rawat, Lalit K Awasthi, Valentina Emilia Balas, Mohit Kumar and Jitendra Kumar Samriya (eds.) *Convergence of Cloud with AI for Big Data Analytics: Foundations and Innovation*, (41–68) © 2023 Scrivener Publishing LLC

3.1   Introduction

Cloud computing is well known computing paradigm that consists pool of heterogeneous resources and provision to end users over the internet pay per uses basis. Cloud computing offers on-demand resource provisioning, multi-tenant environment for the services, elasticity and scalability at run time, measured the services types of significant characteristics. Cloud computing offers several users beneficiary services through a network where cloud users have the flexibility of accessing the cloud resources, pre-build applications, design own framework, etc. [1]. There are several enterprises that are deploying their services in cost effective manner using cloud platform. Nowadays, cloud computing is becoming an efficient paradigm that provides high-performance computing resources over the Internet to solve large-scale scientific and engineering problems. Several industries and business are shifting their platform from traditional approach to cloud, due to which end users and deployment of web applications are increasing exponentially day by day. On the contrary, expectation of end users (time and cost-effective service) and vendors (maximum profit by utilizing the cloud resources) is raised as cloud-based services become common. However, scheduling of cloudlet over the resources becomes the key challenging issue and it can degrade performance, if it failed to achieve the objectives of either vendors or end users. Cloudlet schedule is characterized by the presence of several cloudlets (i.e. the objects that refer to tasks) that have to be executed on a limited number of virtual machines. Therefore, management of cloud resources is critical especially when many cloudlets are submitted simultaneously to cloud computing [2].

Cloud Computing models utilize the virtualization technology in data center infrastructure for delivering the SaaS, PaaS, and IaaS services to the cloud users [3]. Virtualization allow the decouples of physical machine from the operating system and created an abstraction layer between the host machine and virtual machine to run multiple Operating System (OS) on a single hardware resource [4]. Hypervisor is solely responsible for the creation of abstraction layer which provide the flexibly to run multiple OS concurrently on a single physical machine for efficient utilization of resources. Virtualization technology also supports the live virtual machine migration, dynamic resource allocation, and workload isolation features. Cloud data centers have a large number of computational capabilities with a varying capacity of physical machines which are tightly coupled. There are several expenses like resource management, manpower for maintaining the servers, license for running the software, space, cooling system, power and energy consumption are required to establish a cloud data center [5].

Figure 3.1 shown that the managing and provisioning services of cloud data centers performed in two different levels: task scheduling level and VM application policies level. However, researchers often deal with the above levels separately by developing the task scheduling algorithm for the cost benefits of cloud users and designed VM allocation policies for the benefits for cloud services providers. The major challenge of cloud data center is the efficiently utilizing the infrastructure by cooperative between the user's submitted tasks and generate an optimal allocation sequence of virtual machine to the physical host; therefore, the requirement of an efficient task scheduling algorithm along with an optima VM allocation policy.

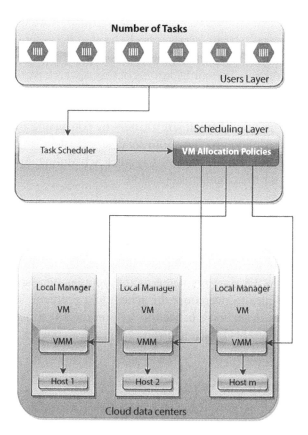

Figure 3.1 Managing and provisioning of task request to the cloud resources.

Many researchers have developed different techniques to solve scheduling problems [3–29]. Some researchers reduce the makespan time of applications, but they ignore other important constraints like requirements of different cloudlets, availability of computing resources, and time complexity of scheduling algorithm. Whenever an algorithm focused at only one parameter, it takes less time to compute the applications. As the number of parameters is increased, the time of algorithms is also increase due to conflicting parameters. Hence, it is tough to find the optimal solution of conflicting parameters in cloud computing. Most of the developed traditional approaches failed to find the solution of contradictory objectives. For example, heuristic algorithms often have low time complexity, but they provide a large schedule length as they provide near-optimal solutions. On the other hand, meta-heuristic algorithms like Genetic Algorithm (*GA*) and Simulated Annealing (*SA*) take more time to schedule a set of cloudlets (i.e. tasks) but they provide a small schedule length. This paper presents a new Cloudlet Scheduling Approach (*CSA*) for the cloud computing environment. The *CSA* enhances the overall performance of cloudlet scheduling by taking into account both the cloudlets requirements and resources available, and improving schedule length, time complexity, and load balancing degree. The contributions of this research work are divided into following two parts:

- Build the several small size clusters by converting the large size scheduling problems into small size clusters.
- Developing a new efficient Cloudlet Scheduling Approach (*CSA*) for the cloudlets allocation.

The remainder part of the research work is organized in six sections. Literature survey is done in Section 3.2. Basic details about cloud computing and cloudlet scheduling problem is covered in the section 3.3. Section 3.4 illustrates the formulation of scheduling problem as an optimization problem. Section 3.5 presents some of the popular heuristic and meta-heuristic techniques to overcome the scheduling problem. The proposed *CSA* is developed in section 3.6. Section 3.7 presents the simulation results while section 8 presents the conclusion of this research work.

3.2   Literature Survey

There have been so many task scheduling algorithms presented in the literature to overcome the scheduling issues in the cloud environments. Several algorithms inspired with the metaheuristic based optimization technique to achieve the desired results in terms of various Quality of Services (QoS) parameters. Guo [6] developed a multi-objective task scheduling algorithm for efficiently and optimally placement of the cloud request to the available number of virtual machines. The developed techniques consider multiple parameters for evaluating the performance. The proposed algorithm is based on the fuzzy self-defense for designing the scheduling scheme. A simulation based experiment performed to validate the effectiveness of the proposed work and compared the results with the existing techniques. Alsaidy *et al.* [7] developed a scheduling algorithm which is inspired from the Partial Swarm Optimization (PSO) to tackle the issue of task scheduling in the cloud environment. The effectiveness of the proposed algorithm was checked by implemented it with the help of CloudSim in cloud environment. The simulation results shown some enhancements in the various parameters compared to the other standard task scheduling algorithms.

NoorianTalouki *et al.* [8] uses optimized cost table to produce the optimal results by placing the higher priority task first and lower priority task on the below order for the execution. The proposed approach follows the HEFT algorithm for reducing the makespan time of dependent tasks. To analyze the performance of proposed technique, a different scientific workflow dataset is used. A significant increment in the performance of the developed technique is notice while comparing other heuristic and metaheuristic based techniques. The performance of the proposed work is checked on the makespan, Schedule Length Ratio (SLR), efficiency, and speed up parameters. Oudaa *et al.* [9] designed a model which is based on the multi-agent system for finding the optimal schedule sequence to allocate the task to the available number of virtual machines. The proposed model uses the Deep Enforcement Learning (DER) for the generation optimal schedule sequence of tasks. A number of experiments performed which shows the effectiveness of the proposed model in the cloud environment. Yang *et al.* [10] focused on the realization of rapid reconfiguration of cloud resources to make the scheduling more flexible and enhancement in the utilization of these resources. A new Software Defined Cloud Manufacturing (SDCM) method for handing the task allocation problem in the cloud environment formalizes the time constraint data traffic problem and divided the tasks into the sub tasks and allocated them to generate an optimal salutation to overcome the data traffic issues. The proposed algorithm combined the two metaheuristic-based approaches for generating the safe schedule sequence. The experiment results demonstrate the usefulness of the algorithm in terms of preventing network congestion and successful to reduce the network latency.

Sanaj *et al.* [11] developed a nature multi objective task scheduling algorithm which use the features of chaotic squirrel search for resolving the task scheduling problem for the independent tasks in the cloud environment. The proposed technique synthesized with the messy local search to enhance the optimal searching ability. To check the performance of the proposed technique, a cloud simulator toolkit is used to implement the proposed technique along with the other standard task scheduling methods. The simulation results proof the effectiveness of the research work. Dubey *et al.* [12] designed a hybrid multi-objective task scheduling framework for the dependent task which combined the features of two metaheuristic-based optimization techniques named as CRO and PSO to overcome the scheduling issue in the cloud. The proposed framework also considers the security aspect during submission of task to the cloud. The proposed framework tested over the CloudSim with the synthetic data set and compared with the other existing technique. The comparison result proves that the proposed framework achieved the desired result.

3.3   Cloud Computing and Cloudlet Scheduling Problem

Cloud computing technology contains four main components namely, *client*, *cloud information system*, *cloud datacenter broker*, and *virtual machines*. Figure 3.2 depicted the major component bs of cloud computing model. Clients are the end users and submitted work in the form of tasks or cloudlet to the cloud datacenter broker for the processing the cloudlet based on the resource requirements. Cloud information system is a repository which stores all the critical information about the cloudlets like cloudlet identification numbers, length, number of resource requirement, and arrival time of cloudlets. This information is used by the datacenter broker for the selection of resources to the cloudlets. Scheduler is responsible for finding the schedule sequence for the submitted cloudlets. Scheduler is the backbone of datacenter broker and determines the order according to which each cloudlet is executed. Virtual machines are the main components in cloud computing environment that responsible for execution of cloudlet and return the results.

In cloud computing environment, several cloudlets arrive to the system at the same time. Each cloudlet needs to be assigned into a suitable VM to be executed in shortest time. However, because the number of available VMs is less than the number of submitted cloudlets, a scheduling algorithm

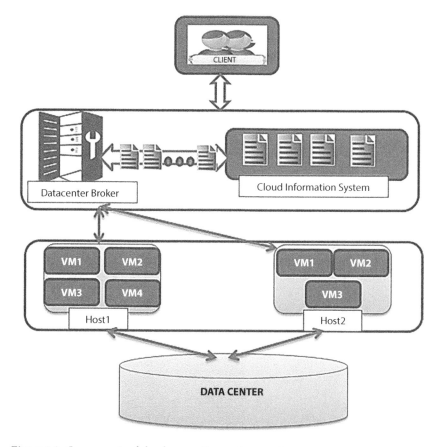

Figure 3.2 Components of cloud computing environment.

is required to schedule the cloudlets onto the available VMs. This problem is called *cloudlets scheduling problem*. Briefly, given a set of n cloudlets to be executed on m of VMs in the cloud computing environment, the cloudlets require certain resources and have computational capacity requirements. On the other hand, VMs are also capacitated. Therefore, need to find the efficient cloudlet execution order so that the cloudlet completion time can be minimized whereas the necessary requirement of cloudlets is met and the virtual machines capacity are not compromised.

3.4   Problem Formulation

The cloudlet-scheduling problem may be formulated as an optimization problem to be solved by optimization approaches. Designing a mathematical model to the cloudlet scheduling problem involves two steps: (i) formulate a cost function to represent the objective of the cloudlets scheduling, (ii) formulate set of constraints in terms of the cloudlets requirements and the availability of the VMs resources.

To formulate the scheduling problem, let n be the number of cloudlets, m is number of VMs, e_{iv} be the execution time of cloudlet i on machine v, and x_{iv} is a binary variable such that x_{iv} is 1 if the cloudlet i is assigned to machine v and 0 otherwise as shown in eq. (3.1).

$$X_{iv} = \begin{cases} 1, & \text{if cloudlet } i \text{ assigned to machine } v \\ 0, & \text{Otherwise} \end{cases} \qquad (3.1)$$

The scheduling problem may be formulated mathematically as:

$$\min Z = \sum_{i=1}^{n} \sum_{v=1}^{m} e_{iv} x_{iv} \qquad (3.2)$$

Subject to

$$\sum_{v=1}^{m} x_{iv} = 1, \qquad \forall \text{ cloudlet} \quad i \qquad (3.3)$$

$$\sum_{i=1}^{n} MI_i \, x_{iv} \le MIPS_v \qquad \forall \, VM \qquad (3.4)$$

$$\sum_{i=1}^{n} mem_i \, x_{iv} \le Mem_v \qquad \forall \, VM \qquad (3.5)$$

In this model, the objective of scheduling is formulated, in eq. (3.2), to minimize the execution time. Indeed, several constraints are modeled to meet the requirements of cloudlets and not violate the availability of virtual resources. The first constrain, eq. (3.3), guarantees that each cloudlet i is assigned to exactly one VMv. The second constraint, eq. (3.4), guarantees that the requirement of *cloudlet$_i$* doesn't exceed the capacity of *VM$_v$.* The third constraint, eq. (3.5), guarantees that total memory requirements should not exceed the maximum available memory.

We can define an optimal solution S_{opt} as a best solution that achieves the lowest makespan. According to reference [3], page (106), the system can achieve the lowest makespan (i.e. optimal solution) if and only if the next conditions are met:

    i.   Each cloudlet is assigned to distinct number *VM*.
    ii.   Each cloudlet starts execution as soon as possible.

By another way, we distributed cloudlets among the *VMs* to balance the workload. Thus, high load balancing is achieved, when optimal solution is founded. We can say that a solution with maximum balancing degree is the near optimal solution.

3.5   Cloudlet Scheduling Techniques

Recently, several cloudlet-scheduling techniques were developed [13]. They may be classified into static scheduling and dynamic scheduling. The distinction indicates the time at which the scheduling decisions are made. In dynamic scheduling, cloudlets are submitted at different time slots, and scheduled during run time (on the fly) based on the current state of VMs. Jing *et al.* [14] is an example of dynamic approaches. In this paper, authors developed a new hybrid meta-heuristic exploiting the features of simulated annealing and particle swarm optimization techniques for maximization of cloud service providers profit and minimizes the execution time. Yuan *et al.* [15] proposed an effectively dynamic task scheduling algorithm for dispatch all arriving tasks to private CDC and public clouds. The disadvantage of scheduling is the overhead incurred to determine the schedule while the program is running. This study concerned with static scheduling. In static scheduling, all cloudlets arrive simultaneously; the number of them is more than the number VMs and information regarding the cloudlets is known prior to execution. In this case, all cloudlets are scheduled first at compile time, before running process. Furthermore, it is easy to implement on the cloud environment while archiving the desired goal of cost saving, makespan time, energy consumption. We can classify a static scheduling into two classes: Heuristic methods and meta-heuristic methods.

3.5.1   Heuristic Methods

Heuristic algorithms use the predictions to achieve near optimal solutions [16–18]. These algorithms have low time complexity. However, they often give high schedule length. Some examples of heuristic algorithms on cloud computing are as follows:

First Come First Serve (FCFS): FCFS is the first technique used in cloud computing model for performing the scheduling of cloudlets on the available number of virtual machine [19]. It is based on the concept of first come first serve similar to the queue in a bank. Cloudlets are schedule to the resources accordance to the order of arrival time. Cloudlets are scheduled to the virtual machine according to the arrival time. FCFS technique is very easy to implement in the cloud environment. However, it does not consider any other criteria associated with the cloudlets while allocating the virtual machine to them. Therefore, the total processing time to execute the cloudlet is very high and resource balancing degree is very low because of less utilization of cloud resources.

Round-Robin (RR): RR technique is very much similar to the FCFS methods for the allotment of virtual machine to the cloudlet [20]. The main difference of this technique, a time slot or time quantum, has been allocated for each cloudlet. After end of time slot of cloudlet, stop the execution of current cloudlet and next cloudlet from the cloudlet provide the resource for the execution. The time slot continuously checks for every cloudlet until the cloudlet finished the execution. Round robin techniques have high resource utilization rate but it finished the execution of cloudlet with very high makespan time.

Min-Min Algorithm: It is the most famous heuristic techniques for scheduling the cloudlet to the virtual machine in the cloud environment [21–23]. It calculates the completion time of each cloudlet against the available number of virtual machine in the cloud datacenters. Then, arrange cloudlets according to the completion time and schedule the cloudlet to the VM which have the minimum completion time. Min-Min technique has very low makespan time due to the better management of cloudlet. However, it has a very low load balancing degree because of allocated smaller task to the high performance virtual machines.

Max-Min Algorithm: it selects the cloudlets with longest completion time to be scheduled on VM that gives it minimum completion time [24, 25]. Therefore, the max-min is more efficient than min-min algorithm, and it considers the system load balancing.

Conductance Algorithm: It is a heuristic technique for solving the scheduling problem in cloud computing environment [26]. This technique represents virtual machine as a pipe and VM can be classified as: thicker VM and thin VM. A thicker pipe has the more water conductance than the thin pipe. Similarly, thicker VM have higher processing power than the thin VM. The developed conductance technique considers four variables: cloudlet length, VM processing power in MIPS, conductance value, and stripe variable for designing the scheduling algorithm for the cloudlet. Cloudlet length measures the size of request task while virtual machine processing power measured in MIPS. Conductance value represents the power capacity of each virtual machine and stripe value find the number of cloudlet which are going to executed on virtual machine according to the conductance value. Furthermore, the proposed technique has a low time complexity but it gives the higher makespan time. Another major drawback of conductance algorithm is that it does not take care of load balancing factor, where it shortlists the number of cloudlet according to the stripe value and the longest cloudlet assign the thicker virtual machine.

3.5.2   Meta-Heuristic Methods

Meta-heuristic techniques are design to solve the cloudlet scheduling problem in cloud environment [27, 28]. These techniques are either single objective or multiple objectives based on the cloudlet requirement set by the cloud user. Heuristic based methods try to find the acceptable solution for the cloudlet scheduling problem with a large search space while meta-heuristic based techniques are population based and begin with initialization of solution which further enhanced after end of iteration by applying various search methods and operation on the exiting solutions. Most famous meta-heuristic based techniques are discussed below.

Genetic Algorithm (*GA*): It is a nature inspired search-based optimization techniques to solve the cloudlet scheduling problems in cloud environment [29–31]. Generally, GA method is used to find either an optimal solution or sub-optimal solution for the specific problem by performing the crossover and mutation function. S. Singh and M. Kalra presented Modified Genetic Algorithm (*MGA*) for cloud computing [32]. The *MGA* algorithm uses *GA* method in which initial solution is initialized with the new version of max-min algorithm. The *MGA* improves performance of scheduling in term of makespan. It has low makespan than the max-min algorithm. However, the time complexity is very high.

Simulated Annealing (**SA**): It has smaller time complexity than *GA* [33, 34]. X. Liu and J. Liu developed new scheduling algorithm based on *SA* for cloud computing. The algorithm uses greedy strategy [35, 36] to guarantee that the initial task scheduling near the optimal solution and improve the efficiency of the search algorithm simulation. *MSA* algorithm is better than the greedy algorithm in terms of makespan and load balancing, but it has high time complexity than the greedy.

Cloudlet scheduling in cloud computing belongs NP Complete problem class and to meta-heuristic based techniques shown a powerful impact for solving the NP complete problems in a reasonable amount of time. Particle swarm optimization [37] is a nature inspired optimization technique and the most useful technique for solving the scheduling problem. Ant Colony Optimization [38] another famous metaheuristic-based technique used by various researcher for cloud scheduling. Furthermore, Chemical Reaction Optimization [39] is new one technique helpful for generating the schedule sequence in cloud domain.

3.6   Cloudlet Scheduling Approach (CSA)

3.6.1   Proposed CSA

The proposed *CSA* is shown in Figure 3.2. The CSA consists of three processes: *Resources Availability and Cloudlet Requirements Process*, *Clustering Process*, and *Resource Selection and Cloudlet Assignment Process*.

- **Process 1:** ***Resources Availability and Cloudlet Requirements,*** Datacenter broker looks for the availability of resources presented in the system and collects information about those resources. This information includes what are the available resources and what are cloudlets requirements. Indeed, the CSA algorithm sorts cloudlet list by descending order to schedule the large cloudlet firstly.
- **Process 2:** ***Clustering,*** the arrived cloudlet list is grouped into several clusters equal to the number of *VMs*. Each cluster has two important values: Cluster Maximum Load (*CML*) and Cluster Total Length (*CTL*). For each *VM*, the algorithm groups some of cloudlets into one cluster according the *CML* value as in equation (3.6).

$$CML\ (C_i) = (MIPS\ (VM_i)\ /\ Total\ MIPS) \times Total\ MI. \qquad (3.6)$$

Where, *Total MIPS* is the summation of *MIPS* for all VMs, and *Total MI* is the summation of *MI* for all cloudlets. CTL (C_i) is the total MI of the cloudlets that belong to cluster C_i. Wherever each cluster takes approximately cloudlets with CTL equals to CML, the schedule length will decrease. Therefore, the algorithm uses ratio value to guarantee that each cluster will take its capacity or approaches it. After 500 experiments, we find that the *Ratio* value at 1.002 is more efficient.

- **Process 3:** *Resource Selection and Cloudlet Assignment,* it is a deciding state in which a specific resource is selected to execute specific cluster. In this process, the *CSA* algorithm assigns the clusters to the available *VMs*. Only one cluster is assigned to specific *VM* and each *VM* executes only one cluster.

3.6.2   Time Complexity

The time complexity of the proposed *CSA* is analyzed according to algorithm shown in Figure 3.2. The time complexity is the summation of time complexity of *Process 1*, *Process 2*, and *Process 3*. In the process 1, the CSA algorithm sorts the arrived cloudlets using quick sort algorithm with time complexity $O(n \log n)$. In the process 2, the algorithm grouped the cloudlets into number of clusters equal to the number of VMs. This process has time complexity $O(n)$. The last process assigns each cluster C_i to specific VM_i with time complexity $O(m)$. So, the overall time complexity of the proposed *CSA* is $O(n \log n + n + m) = O(n (\log n + 1) + m) = O(n \log n + m)$. On the other hand, the time complexity of *SA* [35] is computed by time of greedy algorithm as the initial solution plus the time of *SA* without applying the greedy algorithm. The greedy algorithm has $O(n^2 + nm)$. Because it sorts cloudlets in descending order and then it schedules each one to *VM* which minimize the execution time. The *SA* has $O(itr \times n)$, where *itr* is the number of iterations. The overall running time is $O(itr \times n + n^2 + nm)$. Like *SA*, *MGA* sorts the cloudlets in descending order to select the largest cloudlet. The time complexity of *MGA* [32] is composed from two parts: Max-Min algorithm with time complexity $O(mn^2)$, and the modified genetic algorithm with time complexity $O(G \times P(mn))$. Where, G is the number of generations and P is the number of populations. The overall time complexity of MGA is $O(G \times P(mn)) + n^2m)$.

From the previous analysis, it is noted that the proposed *CSA* has lower time complexity than both *MGA* and *SA* algorithms. The *CSA* collects the advantages of heuristic algorithm and meta-heuristic algorithm, where it gives low makespan and low time complexity.

3.6.3 Case Study

To validate the working sequence of proposed CSA technique, we consider example of ten independent cloudlets as shown in the Table 3.1 allocated to the three virtual machines.

In the first process, the *CSA* collects information about cloudlets requirements and resources availability. It sorts the cloudlets in descending order.

CSA Algorithm

Input: *List of Cloudlets*
Output: *Scheduling Solution*

1. *Collect information about available resources and cloudlets requirements*
2. *Sort cloudlets in descending order of their length*
3. *Create number of Clusters C = Number of VMs*
4. *Calculate CML(Ci) for each cluster*
5. *Set CTL(Ci) = 0;*
6. *Set Ratio = 1.002*
7. *__While__ (Sorted_CloudletList.size() > 0)*
8. *Select cloudlet from sorted cloudletlist*
9. *__For__ i = 0 to C*
10.   *__If__((CTL(C_i) + MI of selected cloudlet)<= (CML(C_i)))*
11.   *Add selected cloudlet to cloudletList of C_i*
12.   *Remove selected cloudlet from Sorted_CloudletList*
13.   *CTL(C_i) += MI of selected cloudlet*
14.   *break*
15.   *__Else if__(CTL(C_i) + MI of selected cloudlet) <= [Ratio×(CML(C_i)])*
16.   *Add selected cloudlet to cloudletList of C_i*
17.   *Remove selected cloudlet from Sorted_CloudletList*
18.   *CTL(C_i) += MI of selected cloudlet*
19.   *break*
20.   *__Else__*
21.   *Ratio=Ratio + 0.0001*
22.   *Continue*
23.   *__End if__*
24.   *__End for__*
25.   *__End while__*
26. *__For__ i = 0 to m*
27.   *select C_i to assign into VM_i*
28. *__End For__*

With the second process, firstly, the *CSA* algorithm creates three empty clusters equal to the number of *VMs*. Secondly; it distributes the cloudlets on the clusters C_0, C_1, and C_2, according to *CML* value for each cluster. According to Eq. (3.6), we can calculate a *CML* value of each cluster as following:

CML (C_0) = *(450/850)*41000 = 21705.9, CML(C_1) = (250/850)*41000 =* 12058.8, and *CML(C_2) = (150/850)*41000 = 7235.3,* where total MI = (1000 + 1500 + 2500 + 3500 + 4000 + 6000 + 6500 + 8000 + 3000 + 5000) = 41000. Finally, the *CSA* algorithm constructs the clusters based on the *CML* value as the follows. C_0 = *{T2, T3, T7, T8, T9}* with *CTL = 22000 ≅ CML (C_0) =* 21705.9, C_1 = *{T1, T4, T6}* with *CTL = 12000 ≅ CML(C_1) = 12058.8,* and C_2 = *{T0, T5}* with *CTL = 7000 ≅ CML(C_2) = 7235.*

By applying process 3 of the *CSA*, C_0 will be allocated into *VM0, C1* will be allocated into VM_1, and *C2* will be allocated into *VM2*. The schedule length is 48.89 sec with running time equals 0.005 sec. By applying conductance, *MGA*, and *MSA* algorithms, the schedule lengths are *65.5 sec, 50 sec, and 50 sec* respectively. In addition, the running times for the algorithms are 0.001 sec for the conductance algorithm, 0.007 sec for *SA*, and *0.015 sec* for the *MGA*.

Table 3.1 Cloudlet length.

Cloudlet	Length MI
T0	1000
T1	1500
T2	2500
T3	3500
T4	4000
T5	6000
T6	6500
T7	8000
T8	3000
T9	5000

3.7   Simulation Results

This section discuss the performance analysis of *CSA*, which is evaluated by considering schedule length, balancing degree, and running time of the *CSA*., In addition, the simulation results are compared with the most recent heuristic technique, conductance algorithm [26], and with the well-known meta-heuristic algorithms, *MGA* [32], and *MSA* [35]. The conductance algorithm is selected because it provides low time complexity. In addition, it finds a good solution than FCFS as the default scheduler of cloud computing model. While, the *MGA* and *MSA* algorithms are selected as the meta-heuristic scheduling algorithms due to (i) firstly, the *MGA* algorithm is the update of the most famous meta-heuristic *GA* technique. Secondly, it gives better solution than Max-min and Min-min algorithms. (ii) The *MSA* algorithm provides low time complexity and better solutions than greedy algorithm.

3.7.1   Simulation Environment

In this study, the well-known *CloudSim* simulator [40] is used to simulate the cloud-computing environment. Indeed, a cloudlet generator is developed to generate random independent set of cloudlets. The generated cloudlets have lengths from 1000 MI to 10,000 MI. In addition, there is a VM generator to generate list of VMs with MIPS in the range of 100 to 1000 MIPS.

3.7.2   Evaluation Metrics

In this study, two evaluation parameters are used to compare the proposed CSA with the other algorithms, namely **schedule length** and **balancing degree**.

1. The schedule length (i.e. makespan) is the maximum execution time for all used virtual machines.
2. The Balancing Degree (BD) is the degree of load balancing between the VMs that achieves after scheduling. By using the optimal solution definition in section (3.4), we can use eq. (3.7) to calculate the balancing degree.

$$BD = SL\ (S_{opt})/SL(S) \qquad (3.7)$$

From Eq. (3.7), we noted that the algorithm with high balancing degree is the near optimal solution.

3.7.2.1   Performance Evaluation with Small Number of Cloudlets

Table 3.2 shows the simulation results of scheduling 10, 20, 40, 60, 80, and 100 cloudlets into three VMs by the proposed *CSA*, *MGA* [32], *MSA* [35], and conductance algorithm [26]. From Table 3.2, we see that the proposed *CSA* provides the best results. It gives low schedule length at low running time. This is because *CSA* algorithm assigns each cluster into the VM that minimizes its execution time. Since *CSA* algorithm gives only one solution using clustering idea, it schedules large number of cloudlets in low running time. Unlike MGA and MSA, they find many solutions. And then they compare the solutions to find the best of them. This operation spends more time.

From the results SL of conductance algorithm, we can see that our algorithm has lower SL than the conductance. This is because the conductance algorithm assigns largest cloudlets in one *VM*. Thus, it doesn't balance between the requirement of computing power and available VMs capacity.

3.7.2.2   Performance Evaluation with Large Number of Cloudlets

Tables 3.3, 3.4, 3.5, and 3.6 show the simulation results of scheduling largest number of cloudlets on different *VMs*. From these tables, we noted that the *CSA* algorithm minimizes the schedule length and running time. The algorithm distributes large number of cloudlets in small number of clusters. After that, it assigns the clusters instead of the cloudlets. This operation takes very small time. Thus, *CSA* algorithm has low running time. The *CSA* provides also the heights *BD* values. This means that it allocates the cloudlets into the available resources with high balancing degree. This balancing increases the system utilization. In addition, the makespan of *CSA* is less than that resulting from the other algorithms. This is because the *CSA* conceders a *VM* capacity. It calculates *CML* and *CTL* values to each cluster. This values balance *VMs* capacity with cluster requirements.

Tables 3.5, 3.6, and 3.7 indicate that the *CSA* is more efficient with large number of cloudlets. It can schedule 2000 cloudlets at only one second. This time is very small compared with the *MGA* and *MSA* algorithms. We see also that the running time with red color of *MGA* algorithm is more than schedule length of it. This means that *MGA* algorithm can't use with large number of cloudlets, because it is not useful. As an example, in Table 3.5, the running time of *MGA* algorithm of 1000 cloudlets at 100 VMs equals 111.

Table 3.2 Scheduling different cloudlets on three VMs.

Cloudlets	VM	CSA			Modified genetic algorithm [22]			Modified simulated annealing [25]			Conductance [16]		
		SL sec	CPU time sec.	BD %	SL sec	CPU time sec.	BD %	SL sec	CPU time sec.	BD %	SL sec	CPU time sec.	BD %
10	3	22.10	0.005	99.5%	23.3	0.008	83%	24.3	0.006	80.6	36.6	0.0001	73%
20	3	33.04	0.005	96%	34.63	0.1	95%	34.999	0.006	94%	48.3	0.0008	74%
40	3	84.8	0.0049	99.8%	86.7	0.156	99%	86.7	0.008	99%	119	0.001	72%
60	3	100.2	0.005	99.8%	100.8	0.179	98%	101.1	0.03	98%	145.6	0.001	71.5%
80	3	207.5	0.005	99.9%	209.5	0.2	97.3%	210	0.04	97.6%	301	0.002	69%
100	3	367.6	0.0061	99.9%	368	0.2	98.6%	368.5	0.041	98%	478	0.002	69%

Table 3.3 Scheduling 100 cloudlets on different numbers of VMs.

VM	CSA			Modified genetic algorithm [22]			Modified simulated annealing [25]			Conductance [16]		
	SL sec	CPU time sec.	BD %	SL sec	CPU time sec.	BD %	SL sec	CPU time sec.	BD %	SL sec	CPU time sec.	BD %
10	115	0.006	99%	115.5	0.285	98.8%	115.5	0.037	98.8%	180.5	0.002	63%
20	57	0.009	96.7%	58.1	0.467	94.6%	58.1	0.041	94.6%	103.6	0.002	57%
40	29	0.037	98%	30.3	0.835	94%	30.3	0.041	94%	51.5	0.0021	51%
60	22	0.04	94%	22.9	1.31	88%	22.9	0.046	88%	39.6	0.0024	54%
80	11	0.045	91%	12	1.87	85%	12	0.053	85%	16	0.0025	61%

Table 3.4 Scheduling 500 cloudlets on different numbers of VMs.

VM	CSA			Modified genetic algorithm [22]			Modified simulated annealing [25]			Conductance [16]		
	SL sec	CPU time sec.	BD %	SL sec	CPU time sec.	BD %	SL sec	CPU time sec.	BD %	SL sec	CPU time sec.	BD %
10	538.2	.011	99.7%	538.5	0.602	99%	538.5	.742	99%	750	0.003	58%
20	385	0.019	99.8 %	385.9	1.5	99%	385.9	0.76	99%	470	0.003	56%
40	143.6	0.088	99%	144.8	4.9	95%	144.8	0.776	95%	250	0.0031	55%
60	111.8	0.089	98%	112.2	10.5	96%	112.2	0.797	96%	220	0.0031	57%
80	61.76	0.32	95%	62.2	18	94%	62.2	0.813	94%	102	0.0033	55%
100	40.8	0.766	96%	41.25	28	93.7%	41.25	0.874	93.7%	90	0.0035	53%

Table 3.5 Scheduling 10C0 cloudlets on different numbers of VMs.

VM	CSA			Modified genetic algorithm			Modified simulated annealing			Conductance		
	SL sec	CPU time sec.	BD %	SL sec	CPU time sec.	BD %	SL sec	CPU time sec.	BD %	SL sec	CPU time sec.	BD %
10	892.8	.024	99.7%	891.43	2.01	99.8%	891.43	2.92	99.8%	985	0.007	59%
20	403.5	0.026	99%	403.5	5.5	99%	403.5	3.5	99%	650	0.0071	55%
40	280	0.119	99%	280.6	19	98%	280.6	3.96	98%	410	0.007	56%
60	163	0.255	98%	164	40.9	96%	164	2.981	96%	258	0.007	55%
80	127.6	0.36	99.2%	128.1	72.5	94.5%	128.1	3.1	94.5%	240	0.0072	54%
100	105	0.8	98.5%	106	111	95.5%	106	3.14	95.5%	198	0.0072	53%

Table 3.6 Scheduling 2000 cloudlets on different numbers of VMs.

VM	CSA			Modified genetic algorithm [22]			Modified simulated annealing [25]			Conductance [16]		
	SL sec	CPU time Sec.	BD %	SL Sec	CPU time sec.	BD %	SL sec	CPU time sec.	BD %	SL sec	CPU time sec.	BD %
10	1235	.026	97%	1230	4.5	99.9%	1230	6.5	99.9%	1401	0.015	60%
20	674.8	.029	99.5%	674	12.5	99.7%	674	6.605	99.7%	851	0.015	57%
40	355	.036	98.2%	355	43	98.2%	355	6.703	98.2%	560	0.015	53%
60	265	0.8	99.4%	265.6	93.4	98.9%	265.6	6.744	98.9%	320	0.015	53%
80	186	1.2	98%	187.5	97	96%	187.5	6.84	96%	242	0.016	50%
100	81	1.9	99%	81.3	125	98%	81.3	7	98%	168.3	0.016	54%

Table 3.7 Scheduling large numbers of cloudlets on different numbers of VMs.

Cloudlets	VM	CSA			Modified genetic algorithm [22]			Modified simulated annealing [25]			Conductance [16]		
		SL sec	CPU time sec.	BD %	SL sec	CPU time sec.	BD %	SL sec	CPU time sec.	BD %	SL sec	CPU time Sec.	BD %
2000	50	323	1	99.8%	323.8	118	99%	323.8	12.5	99%	582	0.027	55.5%
2000	100	169	4.5	98%	170	458	97%	170	13.5	97%	314	0.028	53%
3000	50	433	1.56	99%	431	450	99.6%	431	30	99.6%	790	0.068	53%
3000	100	246	4.8	99%	246.7	1022	98%	246.7	33	99%	446	0.068	54%
4000	50	560	1.7	97%	561	1080	96%	561	37	96	780	0.068	50%
4000	100	281	5	99%	282	1838	97%	282	53.6	97%	455	0.11	56%
5000	100	321	6	99%	322.8	1905	97%	322.8	60	97%	525	0.2	50%
6000	100	456	7.2	99.5%	457	2404	98%	457	81	98%	671	0.4	48%

This value is larger than the schedule length (i.e. 106). Similarly, we see SL of MGA is larger than running time of all red values in Tables 3.6 and 3.7.

From all tables, the proposed *CSA* can achieve lower schedule length than the *MGA*, and *SA*. In addition, it finds a near optimal solution faster than both of them by *99.5%* with *MGA* and *92.9%* with *MSA*.

Although the conductance algorithm gives low time complexity as shown in all of tables, the *CSA* gives very low schedule length compared the conductance algorithm. It gives lower makespan than conductance scheduling algorithm by 41%. The proposed *CSA* not only minimize the schedule length, but also makes the system more balancing than any algorithm. In addition, the *CSA* appears like heuristic algorithm in result stability. It generates only one solution at all run times for specific problem, while the other meta-heuristic algorithms may give more than different solutions at each run for the same problem. In addition, it appears like meta-heuristic in minimizing schedule length.

3.8   Conclusion

In this research work, a new efficient Cloudlet Scheduling Approach has been proposed to solve the cloudlet scheduling problem in cloud computing. The main idea of the proposed approach is to minimize the overall time complexity by converting large size cloudlet scheduling problem into small size cluster scheduling problem and increases the system utilization. The proposed CSA enhances the overall system performance. It increases the balancing degree between the different VMs in the system. The new approach is more efficient than the most recent heuristic and meta-heuristic algorithms. The simulation results depicted that the CSA reduces the makespan than MGA and SA techniques and finds good solutions faster than them by 99.5% with MGA and 92.9% with SA. In addition, the CSA gives lower makespan than heuristic conductance scheduling algorithm by 41%.

References

1. https://www.ibm.com/cloud-computing/learn-more/what-is-cloud-computing/.
2. https://en.wikipedia.org/wiki/Cloud_computing.
3. Dubey, K., Nasr, A.A., Sharma, S.C., El-Bahnasawy, N., Attiya, G., El-Sayed, A., Efficient VM placement policy for data centre in cloud environment, in:

Soft Computing: Theories and Applications, pp. 301–309, Springer, Singapore, 2020.

4. Swathi, T., Srikanth, K., Raghunath Reddy, S., Virtualization in cloud computing. *Int. J. Comput. Sci. Mobile Comput.*, 3, 5, 540–546, 2014.

5. Dubey, K. and Sharma, S.C., An extended intelligent water drop approach for efficient VM allocation in secure cloud computing framework. *J. King Saud Univ.-Comput. Inf. Sci.*, 2020.

6. Guo, X., Multi-objective task scheduling optimization in cloud computing based on fuzzy self-defense algorithm. *Alexandria Eng. J.*, 60, 6, 5603–5609, 2021.

7. Alsaidy, S.A., Abbood, A.D., Sahib, M.A., Heuristic initialization of PSO task scheduling algorithm in cloud computing. *J. King Saud Univ.-Comput. Inf. Sci.*, 2020.

8. NoorianTalouki, R., Shirvani, M.H., Motameni, H., A heuristic-based task scheduling algorithm for scientific workflows in heterogeneous cloud computing platforms. *J. King Saud Univ.-Comput. Inf. Sci.*, 2021.

9. Oudaa, O., Gharsellaoui, H., Ahmed, S.B., An agent-based model for resource provisioning and task scheduling in cloud computing using DRL. *Proc. Comput. Sci.*, 192, 3795–3804, 2021.

10. Yang, C., Liao, F., Lan, S., Wang, L., Shen, W., Huang, G.Q., Flexible resource scheduling for software-defined cloud manufacturing with edge computing. *Engineering*, 2021.

11. Sanaj, M.S. and Joe Prathap, P.M., Nature inspired chaotic squirrel search algorithm (CSSA) for multi objective task scheduling in an IAAS cloud computing atmosphere. *Eng. Sci. Technol., Int. J.*, 23, 4, 891–902, 2020.

12. Dubey, K. and Sharma, S.C., A novel multi-objective CR-PSO task scheduling algorithm with deadline constraint in cloud computing. *Sustain. Comput.: Inform. Syst.*, 32, 100605, 2021.

13. Mathew, T., Sekaran, K., Jose, J., Study and analysis of various task scheduling algorithms in the cloud computing environment. *International Conference on Advances in Computing, Communications, and Informatics (ICACCI)*, pp. 658–664, 2014.

14. Bi, J., Yuan, H., Tan, W., Zhou, M.C., Zhang, J., Li, J., Application- Aware dynamic fine-grained resource provisioning for virtualized cloud data centers. *IEEE Trans. Autom. Sci. Eng. (TASE)*, 14, 2, 1172–1184, 2015.

15. Yuan, H., Bi, J., Tan, W., Zhou, M.C., Li, B.H., Li, J., TTSA: An effective scheduling approach for delay bounded tasks in hybrid clouds. *IEEE Trans. Cybern. (TCYB)*, 47, 11, 3658–3668, 2016.

16. Bi, J., Yuan, H., Tan, W., Li, B.H., TRS: Temporal request scheduling with bounded delay assurance in a green cloud data center. *Inf. Sci. (INS)*, 2016.

17. Kimpan, W. and Kruekaew, B., Heuristic task scheduling with artificial bee colony algorithm for virtual machines. *The 8th International Conference on Soft Computing and Intelligent Systems (SCIS) and 17th International Symposium on Advanced Intelligent Systems (ISIS)*, 2016.

18. Nasr, A., EL-Bahnasawy, N., El-Sayed, A., Performance enhancement of scheduling algorithm in heterogeneous distributed computing systems. *Int. J. Adv. Comput. Sci. Appl.(IJACSA)*, 6, 5, 88–96, 2015.

19. Nasr, A., EL-Bahnasawy, N., El-Sayed, A., A new duplication task scheduling algorithm in heterogeneous distributed computing systems. *Bull. Electr. Eng. Infor. (BEEI)*, 5, 3, 373–382, September 2016.

20. Pavithra, B. and Ranjana, R., A comparative study on performance of energy efficient load balancing techniques in cloud. *International Conference on Wireless Communications, Signal Processing and Networking (WiSPNET)*, pp. 1192–1196, 2016.

21. Chen, H., Wang, F., Helian, N., Akanmu, G., User-priority guided min-min scheduling algorithm for load balancing in cloud computing. *National Conference on Parallel Computing Technologies (PARCOMPTECH)*, pp. 1–8, 2013.

22. Kokilavani, T. and George Amalarethinam, D.I., Load balanced min-min algorithm for static meta-task scheduling in grid computing. *Int. J. Comput. Appl.*, 20, 2, 43–49, 2011.

24. Etminani, K. and Naghibzadeh, M., A min-min max-min selective algorithm for grid task scheduling. *IEEE/IFIP International Conference in Central Asia on Internet*, pp. 1–7, 2007.

25. Devipriya, S. and Ramesh, C., Improved max-min heuristic model for task scheduling in cloud. *International Conference on Green Computing, Communication and Conservation of Energy (ICGCE)*, pp. 883–888, 2013.

26. Chatterjee, T., Ojha, V.K., Adhikari, M., Banerjee, S., Biswas, U., Snáše, V., Design and implementation of an improved datacenter broker policy to improve the QoS of a cloud. *Proceedings of the 5ᵗʰ International Conference on Innovations in Bio-Inspired Computing and Applications IBICA*, Springer International Publishing, pp. 281–290, 2014.

27. Adil, S.H., Raza, K., Ahmed, U., Ali, S.S.A., Hashmani, M., Cloud task scheduling using nature inspired meta-heuristic algorithm. *International Conference on Open Source Systems & Technologies (ICOSST)*, pp. 158–164, 2015.

28. Tawfeek, M.A., El-Sisi, A., Keshk, A.E., Torkey, F.A., Cloud task scheduling based on ant colony optimization. *8ᵗʰ International Conference on Computer Engineering & Systems (ICCES)*, pp. 64–69, 2013.

29. Sindhu, S. and Mukherjee, S., A genetic algorithm based scheduler for cloud environment. *4th International Conference on Computer and Communication Technology (ICCCT)*, September 2013, IEEE, pp. 23–27.

30. Omara, F.A. and Arafa, M.M., Genetic algorithms for task scheduling problem. *J. Parallel Distrib. Comput.*, 70, 1, 13–22, 2010.

31. Kar, I., Parida, R.N.R., Das, H., Energy aware scheduling using genetic algorithm in cloud data centers. *International Conference on Electrical, Electronics, and Optimization Techniques (ICEEOT)*, IEEE, 2016.

32. Singh, S. and Kalra, M., Scheduling of independent tasks in cloud computing using modified genetic algorithm. *International Conference on Computational Intelligence and Communication Networks (CCIN)*, Nov. 2014, IEEE, pp. 565–569.

33. Attiya, G. and Hamam, Y., Task allocation for maximizing reliability of distributed system: A simulated annealing approach. *J. Parallel Distrib. Comput.*, 66, 1259–1266, 2006.

34. Kashani, M. and Jahanshahi, M., Using simulated annealing for task scheduling in distributed systems. *International Conference on Computational Intelligence, Modeling and Simulation*, pp. 265–269, 2009.

35. Liu, X. and Liu, J., A task scheduling on simulated annealing algorithm in cloud computing. *Int. J. Hybrid Inf. Technol. (IJHIT)*, 9, 6, 403–412, 2016.

36. Kahraman, C., Engin, O., Kaya, İ., Öztürk, R.E., Multiprocessor task scheduling in multistage hybrid flow-shops: A parallel greedy algorithm approach. *Appl. Soft Comput.*, 10, 4, 1293–1300, September 2010.

37. Awad, A., EL-Hefnawy, N., Abdel_Kader, H., Enhanced particle swarm optimization for task scheduling in cloud computing environment. *International Conference on Communication, Management and Information Technology (ICCMIT)*, pp. 920–929, 2015.

38. Tumeo, A., Pilato, C., Ferrandi, F., Sciuto, D., Lanzi, P., Ant colony optimization for mapping and scheduling in heterogeneous multiprocessor systems. *International Conference on Embedded Computer Systems, Architectures, Modeling, and Simulation, SAMOS*, pp. 142–149, 2008.

39. Xu, J., Lam, A., Li, V., Chemical reaction optimization for the grid scheduling problem. *IEEE International Conference on Communications*, ICC, pp. 1–5, 2010.

40. Calheiros, R.N., Ranjan, R., Beloglazov, A., De Rose, C.A., Buyya, R., CloudSim: A toolkit for modeling and simulation of cloud computing environments and evaluation of resource provisioning algorithms. *Softw.- Pract. Exp.*, 41, 1, 23–50, 2011.

Cloud-Based Architecture for Effective Surveillance and Diagnosis of COVID-19

**Shweta Singh[1], Aditya Bhardwaj[2]*, Ishan Budhiraja[2]†, Umesh Gupta[2]‡
and Indrajeet Gupta[2]§**

*[1]Department of Computer Science and Engineering, KIET Group of Institutions,
Delhi-NCR, Ghaziabad, India
[2]School of Computer Science Engineering and Technology, Bennett University,
Greater Noida, India*

Abstract

Coronavirus disease 2019 (COVID-19) has spread in multiple countries and caused major worldwide concern. The continual increase in the number of COVID-19 cases is overwhelming the world economy and has become a serious concern to global health. It is supposed to as an absolute to severe acute respiratory syndrome (SARS), formally known as beta-coronavirus, which was termed as COVID-19 through World Health Organization (WHO). Even with its deadly recurrence, several actions have been taken to diagnose and treat the disease as fast as possible. Rigorous quarantine efforts and global containment are being performed. Apart from this, the incidence of pandemics, similar to COVID-19, had been into existence a few decades back. Various techniques and technologies are being introduced previously, by various authors, to tackle the pandemic. Health authorities, worldwide, concluded with surveillance and tracking of individuals, while others opted for application-based techniques to keep track of the infected individuals, etc. The study proposed a cloud-based network to manage pandemic situations like COVID-19. With this proposed scenario and detailed survey, government authorities and researchers (worldwide) can opt for appropriate ways to control its recurrence; and will help to stop further propagation using dynamic surveillance.

*Corresponding author: aditya.cse@nitttrchd.ac.in
†Corresponding author: ishanbudhiraja@gmail.com
‡Corresponding author: umesh.gupta@bennett.edu.in
§Corresponding author: indrajeet.gupta@bennett.edu.in

Danda B. Rawat, Lalit K Awasthi, Valentina Emilia Balas, Mohit Kumar and Jitendra Kumar Samriya (eds.) Convergence of Cloud with AI for Big Data Analytics: Foundations and Innovation, (69–88)
© 2023 Scrivener Publishing LLC

Keywords: Pandemic, COVID-19, cloud-based network, surveillance

4.1   Introduction

A disease is termed as pandemic when it spreads beyond the boundaries of a country and affects people severely to a large extent, hence leading to killings of many. People had been victim to the numerous deadly infectious diseases from past centuries [1]. Few infectious diseases went out of time and did not affect at much higher extent to the countries all around the world. World has been a victim to few infectious diseases from past centuries such as, The Black Death (1330), Spanish flu (1918), HIV/AIDS (1981), The Antonine plague (165 AD), Ebola (21st Century), Tuberculosis, Asian flu (1957), Smallpox (1633), Camp fever, plague of Athens (430 BC), COVID-19 (2019), etc. [1, 2]. Every pandemic leaves the country with numerous political, economic, and social disruptions.

Hence, it becomes equally impossible and more complex to manage the circumstances during any pandemic, as almost every sector of growth is affected at a wider extent. Several precautionary and preventive measures have been followed by countries to manage and stop further propagation of a pandemic. To some extent, the techniques fulfill the criteria, but lacks in providing more reliable and effective techniques to manage the circumstances during a pandemic. Every country is working beyond limits to safeguard the world from the deadly propagation of the disease. With every new era, new technology-based solutions are being provided.

Various authors have proposed technology-based solutions to manage the propagation of disease and safeguard the people. Few authors proposed an android application-based surveillance and detection of infected individuals in an area. Few previous solutions are based on Artificial Intelligence (AI) [3] based architectures that can detect and diagnose using Drone technology [4]. Others provided the review of various blockchain-based technologies [5] that can be utilized to detect the infected person more effectively. But technologies proposed so far lacks in one or the other way. Hence, in this study we explored how cloud-based technology could be used to provide solution of pandemic situation like COVID-19 [6, 7]. In this paper, a framework of cloud-based technology has been implemented that will help various government authorities to diagnose and track the individuals in more efficient manner. An individual will be able to coordinate for the resources via web service utilizing through cloud-based architecture.

The main contributions of this chapter are as follows:

- Proposed cloud-based network to provide solution of pandemic situation like COVID-19.
- Explored factor to perform data analysis of the proposed approach.
- Conducted reliability and validity test for factors analysis in proposed solution.

Furthermore, the chapter is structured in following sections, as: Section 4.2 describes different technologies that has been implemented worldwide to manage circumstances during any pandemic. Section 4.3 describes the proposed Cloud-based network to manage the circumstances for future pandemics similar to COVID-19. Section 4.4 describes survey findings by drawing attention to different factors and outcomes of implementing proposed cloud-based technology in various diagnosis & treatment activities; Section 4.5 includes conclusion and future scope that will help in developing such technology for better sustenance.

4.2   Related Work

From lockdown practices to the technology-based surveillance of the people, various methodologies have been implemented by the countries all around the world. In [8], authors have provided the framework to assist the people online through IoT and blockchain-based architecture [9, 10]. The author has proposed a four-layer architecture to detect the infected people using smartphones. To detect the symptoms based on readings received via sensors, IoT-enabled technology is utilized, and to secure the transfer of information, blockchain-based technology is facilitated.

In [11], author proposed a systemic review of the mobile applications that have been utilized for information gathering and detection of the disease during pandemic in past two years. Thereafter, an analysis of the mobile applications has been done based on certain set of features and quality factors, such as functionality, reliability of the information provided by the application, etc. In [12], authors have discussed about various AI based techniques [13] that can help combat with the deadly propagation of the disease. The authors have provided the detailed description on importance of AI in combating with the pandemic through drone-based technology in various ways related to the prevention, testing, treatment, etc. In [14], authors have proposed an AI-based model to diagnose the disease using radiology images [15]. The authors have proposed COVID-19 Detection Neural Network (COVNet) model to detect and diagnose the community that has acquired the infection from somewhere. Based on the CT-Scan and X-Ray images received, a model will predict about the status of the health of an individual.

In [16], authors proposed a Neural Network (NN) [17] model that will detect the infected people based on an abnormality in the respiratory patterns of an individual. The model proposed by the authors relies on the set of 05 factors, namely, Susceptible, Exposed, Infectious, and Recovered or Removed (SEIR). A classifier model has been utilized to classify the patterns for the estimation of the infection to an individual. In [18], author has provided the detailed explanation and description of various AI-based models that have been proposed by various researchers all around the world. Based on the parameters, such as accuracy, sensitivity, and specificity of every proposed algorithm, the author has concluded the existing models need to be modified for more accurate results, so that difficulties related to transparency and interpretability can be rectified.

In [19] and [20], authors have proposed a model to detect the level of infection in an individual using smartphone. An individual need to record an audio of the cough and using an additional apparatus, body temperature will be measured and saved. And based on the measurement of both cough and temperature of an individual, a decision will be taken whether a person is infected or not. In [21], authors have provided the detailed description of various blockchain-based technologies to detect and deal with the pandemic. Authors have concluded that technologies such as cloud computing [22, 23], AI, big data along with blockchain technology can effectively work in a scenario to handle the spread of any deadly infection in near future.

In [24], authors have proposed a surveillance model based on IoT and Edge technologies [25]. The model works on real-time values received via set of sensors through an IoT-enabled gadget. The authors have proposed a five-stage architecture that will work through a dedicated android application and based on the current health state of an individual, a suspect can be grabbed to safeguard others in his surroundings. The author has implemented an alarm monitoring system for other people who stay nearby an infected person.

Hence, it can be summarized that when it comes to manage the data and resources at a larger extent, cloud-computing is the widely used technology. Cloud-based technology is utilized around the world due to its set of salient features, such as improved agility, performance, increased productivity, security [26], etc.

4.2.1   Proposed Cloud-Based Network for Management of COVID-19

This section represents the proposed cloud-based network to effectively detect and diagnose during pandemic like COVID-19. Figure 4.1 describes the proposed scenario where cloud-based technology is utilized as the basis of more effective and reliable surveillance for the disease.

As shown in Figure 4.1 for the proposed cloud-based network, state of a country is being partitioned into separate regions that will stay connected via web service. For each state there will be a centralized data storage center for resources and equipment that may be required in future. One centralized committee of doctors and security authorities will also be made, so that they can manage the data at a centralized region. Every region will be equipped with group of users, that may have few infected people, a regional repository of data storage, resources, and equipment required, along with the dedicated team of doctors and security authorities at regional level. Every regional committee is hereby responsible to update the centralized committee for the status of the regional health. Following steps are to be followed to implement a more reliable and efficient cloud-based surveillance architecture:

1) The architecture is based on cloud-enabled technology, which is operated and managed through any web service.
2) Through this architecture better diagnosis and surveillance methods can be attained.
3) States of the country is to be partitioned into various regions, and for each region, separate data storage & resource centers are to be maintained, for both medical & security authorities.

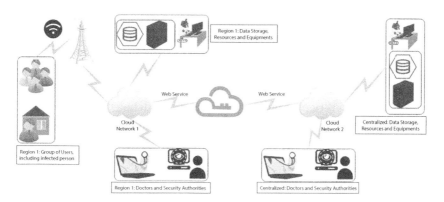

Figure 4.1 Proposed cloud-based network for management of COVID-19.

4) Individuals at each region will be allowed to find relevant information about COVID-19 as and when required through a particular web service.

5) Weekly survey pings will be sent to every individual in particular regional area, so that health–related updates are reached at time to the responsible authorities.

6) Similarly, centralized data & resource centers will be maintained along with the centralized control of medical and security authorities.

7) With this, centralized diagnosis & surveillance centers will be maintained, so that all regional committees can send updates for better management of recurrence of this pandemic.

8) Every individual is required to operate a kind of web service, and for that, their location and Bluetooth should always remain active.

9) The services of Identity (ID) tracing will help authorities to trace an infected person and will help other individuals to avoid visiting to those infected zones.

10) Along with this, special authority should be given to every medical store in various regions, so that they can send update on time-to-time, to the responsible authorities is any individual buy's medications required in their zone.

11) Though this cloud-based technology, further propagation of COVID-19 can be backed up to some level, as it is secure, efficient, faster, and requirement of time. Figure 4.2 shows working steps for the proposed cloud-based network for management of COVID-19.

Figures 4.1 and 4.2 conclude the overall architecture that is to be followed in proposing scenario to tackle with the propagation of pandemic similar to COVID-19 through cloud-based technology. Figure 4.2 states the overall blueprint of all the features of the proposed scenario. From the Figure 4.2, the summary of the proposed scenario can be concluded in just 05 steps. Whereas Figure 4.1 describes a detailed architecture for cloud-based technology (how cloud-based technology is to be utilized to gain maximum to prevent further propagation). From Figure 4.2, it can be concluded that regional and centralized distribution of resources and equipment will help the individuals to meet their needs during an adverse situation. Hence, maintaining data storage and other relevant information

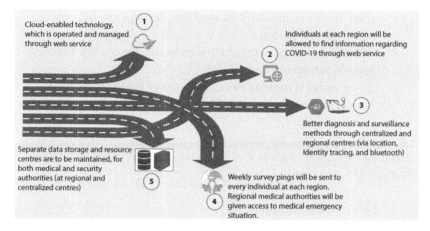

Figure 4.2 Working steps for the proposed cloud-based network.

at sub-regional and centralized region will help the government authorities to better coordinate in the extreme conditions.

4.3   Research Methodology

The existing treatment programs and diagnosis phenomenon of the "Novel Coronavirus" has not been defined clearly [27]. Hence, it becomes necessary to introduce improved technology-based practices that will help in better surveillance and diagnosis during future pandemic. There are less efficient and effective solutions provided by various authors to manage suspicious patients and lacks in appropriate treatment methods. To better interact and to overcome the treatment difficulties, a cloud-based assistance is required that provides a frontline to interact the medical experts. With this, suspicious patients will be monitored in a timely manner and misdiagnosis can be avoided this way.

The present area of study relies on the following specific objectives:

a. To validate the above proposed cloud-based architecture to manage the circumstances in future pandemics, a survey has been performed.

b. To generate the factors which contributes for surveillance and diagnosis practices for future pandemics.

c. To consider the list of generated factors for data analysis and find the most impacting factor out of them and justify their inter-connectivity to stop its propagation in a more sophisticated manner.

d. The survey has been conducted based on the circumstances seen so far during COVID-19.

e. Since world is moving towards an era of Smart Things [28], hence Internet-based solutions will be best suited for the coming century.

From above literature study and data analysis, a set of following impacting factors are conceived:

1) Ease of using technology
2) Smart gadgets
3) Ease of using Internet
4) Applications as travel guides
5) Reliability on applications
6) Efficiency of applications
7) Awareness about COVID-19
8) Awareness about protective & preventive measures
9) COVID-19 declared as pandemic
10) Initiative by government
11) Satisfaction from government
12) Guidelines issued by government
13) Role of technology in managing COVID-19

4.3.1   Sample Size and Target

The investigation is performed on suspects in North-East Delhi region. The target sample size at initial was set to 430 out of which approximately 398 respondents validated with appropriate responses. To achieve subjectivity of this study, an analysis is to be performed, that explains the impact of COVID-19 on majority, and how technology can help in avoiding misdiagnosis procedures. Since their survey is being done during COVID-19, hence, the questionnaire was prepared related to the pandemics similar to COVID-19. We have restricted our study to certain parameters in due consideration of technological issues due to time and resource constraints. A convenient sampling method was utilized so that people were surveyed as per convenience.

The research more relies on evaluating the impact of eight different factors found that can play a vital role to overcome the pandemic in a country. Total count of thirteen factors was taken at initial for the data analysis, but further analysis methods reduced them to eight factors. Data collected through questionnaire is primary in nature, which will further act as basis of report formulation. Though, authors agree to certain constraints that may restrict the study as more descriptive in nature to a certain point than being exploratory.

Pilot Testing

To attain the lucidity in questionnaire and the reliability of variables, several pretesting methods [29] need to be performed. These pre-testing surveys are performed so that questions that are hard to understand or confusing can be easily rectified, and questionnaire is to be non-confusing. Under study, a count of 70 pre-test surveys was preferred from a non-probability sample respondent.

4.3.1.1 Sampling Procedures

Research relies on a survey technique to gather information via questionnaires distributed to various suspects in North-East Delhi region. These suspects were mixed who were aged between 12 years and above. An appropriate sampling technique was utilized while investigation. These 440 participants were distributed properly prepared questionnaire that contained COVID-19 and questions related to the technology-based solutions. The questionnaire method was containing 65 items. Our survey technique bifurcated questionnaire items to 13 different factor loads relevant to manage the propagation of COVID-19.

4.3.1.2 Response Rate

A count of 440 questionnaires was circulated out of which 396 satisfactory responses are received. Though a satisfactory response rate of 90% is attained, rest mentioned issues such as lack of interest, busy schedules, or other personal reasons. While the data analysis was going on, no invalid responses were considered.

4.3.1.3 Instrument and Measures

While designing the questionnaire, various factors like smart gadgets, reliability on applications, advantage of technology in managing COVID-19, etc., (total count of 13 factor dimensions) were taken into consideration. The overall process has resulted in mainly 65 items in questionnaire consisting of both generalized and proposed scenario related questions.

Data Analysis

Exploratory Factor Analysis (EFA) [30, 31] was performed to cut-off the count of proposed items to some level. It is a two-way approach mainly. In the initial stage, to satisfy the level of reliability and validity of the conception, an individual measurement model must be examined. Furthermore, with second stage, the procedure of factor analysis is performed, and respondents answered to items according to their own excuses.

4.3.2   Reliability and Validity Test

An IBM SPSS Statistics software (22.0) [32, 33] is used to perform reliability test on 65 items in questionnaire. Table 4.1 depicts the alpha coefficients calculated for each factor involved. To improve the scales, those adapted from previous studies, Cronbach's alpha coefficient [34] and EFA were applied. On considering the multi-dimensionality intended for the factors, coefficient alpha was evaluated regarding every factor. Reliability test [35] for analysis about cloud-based network in managing pandemic similar to COVID-19 was done on set of 13 factors, separately. Survey findings stated that minimum 5 items should be included for which separate alpha coefficients are to be assigned.

As recommended by testing research theory (Nunnally & Bernstein, 1994) [36], a cut-off level is to be fixed at 0.7. Thus, eliminating the factors, those are unsatisfactory in level of reliability. Optimized item-to-total correlation [37] is facilitated that helps to choose which item is to be removed. Multiple recompiling for alpha values is performed further, which helped to cut-off the list of items to some extent. Further, on investigating optimized item-to-total correlations at times, all irrelevant items are deleted. This multiple elimination practice helps in improving corresponding alpha values. After recurrence to a lot of times, count of 40 items for 8 constructs (to which, 65 items for 13 constructs were initially proposed) are found most relevant.

4.3.3   Exploratory Factor Analysis

Unlikely to factor analysis, an appropriate methodology is utilized to determine the dimensionality of 65 items scale. EFA is used basically to cut-off the count of items in questionnaire, and to evaluate validity for the construct. The very famous, Kaiser-Meyer-Olkin (KMO) and Bartlett's Test [38, 39] are opted by most researchers to validate the robustness for each factor analysis and sampling adequacy procedures [40]. Table 4.2 depicts KMO calculate of sample adequacy as (0.855) which is approximately 1.

Table 4.1 Reliability test for factors in relevance to Cloud-based solution to manage future pandemics similar to COVID-19.

S. no.	Factors considered	Cronbach's Alpha	
1	Ease of using technology	0.612	Calculated Alpha coefficients for factors namely 2, 3, 4, 5, 7, 11, 12, 13 has met the considerable range of reliability that lies in between 0.713 and 0.876. Though, factors like 1, 6, 8, 9 and 10 didn't met the minimum reliability with loads as 0.612, 0.667 , 0.634, 0.539 and 0.685. Thus, these indicate inadequate level of reliability in relation to role of cloud-based network in managing pandemic. To achieve constancy, unsatisfactory factors were removed, and was restricted to further load the factors with minimum of 0.7.
2	Smart gadgets	0.785	
3	Ease of using Internet	0.876	
4	Applications as travel guides	0.830	
5	Reliability on applications	0.713	
6	Efficiency of applications	0.667	
7	Awareness about COVID-19	0.773	
8	Awareness about protective & preventive measures	0.634	
9	COVID-19 declared as pandemic	0.539	
10	Initiative by government	0.685	
11	Satisfaction from government	0.747	
12	Guidelines issued by government	0.834	
13	Role of technology in managing COVID-19	0.801	

Table 4.2 KMO and Bartlett's test.

Test		Adequacy
Kaiser-Meyer-Olkin measure of sampling adequacy		0.855
Bartlett's Test of Sphericity	Chi-Square	10752.627
	Significant Value	0.000

Moreover, while applying Bartlett's Test of Sphericity, a considerable value (p = 0.000) is received i.e., approximately 0.05 (such that p-value <0.5). Hence, it can be stated that sample and factors extracted are now more optimized and satisfactory.

4.4   Survey Findings

Tables 4.1 and 4.2 depicts the optimized count of total factors (8 factors) after applying reliability tests on set of factors. Figures 4.3 and 4.4 conclude the results drawn after a survey is done on factors related to the circumstance of the COVID-19 epidemic and awareness in public regarding technological solutions. The factors that are most relevant to findings related to advantages of technology for better diagnosis and surveillance are, smart gadgets, ease of using Internet, applications as travel guides, reliability on applications, awareness about COVID-19, satisfaction from government, guidelines issued by government, and Role of technology in managing COVID-19.

Figure 4.3 describes the factors that most essential this survey, after analysis is performed. It is found that factor named Ease of using Internet

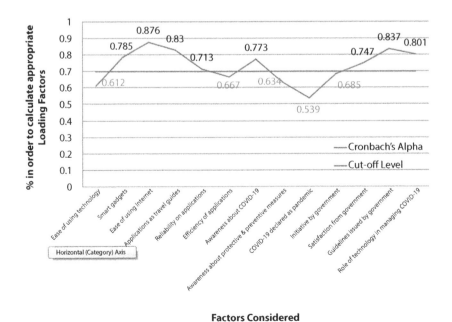

Factors Considered

Figure 4.3 An open-source factor analysis for analyzed 13 factors using Cronbach's alpha.

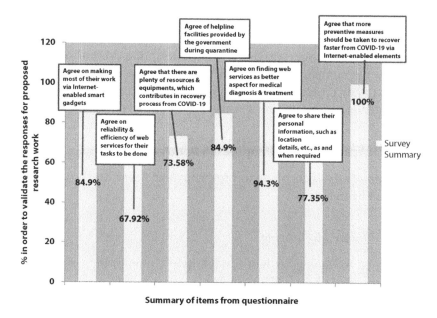

Figure 4.4 Survey summary to validate the proposed scenario of cloud-enabled network.

has received greatest loading factor. This means that people make maximum work out of Internet-based services. Second most appropriate factor found is Applications as travel guides that contribute much for security authorities, as users of such applications agree to its prescribed terms & conditions of usage. That is, they are ready to share their location related information, as and when required by the government. This feature will help authorities to trace the infected person, and to update the people nearby to him.

Figure 4.4 concludes the summary report as per the items distributed to various respondents. It can be stated clearly from the Figure 4.4, that respondents have validated the proposed cloud-based scenario. According to the above figure, 84.9% of total respondents agree to make their most of the work done via Internet and with the ease of using smart gadgets. Similarly, 94.3% of the total respondents find web and related services as appropriate ways to find information and being updated. Also, 100% stated that more preventive measures should be introduced that can be utilized via Internet-enabled elements. Hence, it can be concluded from survey findings that majority of respondents agree that cloud-based technology should be encouraged for better diagnosis and surveillance related activities, by the government, for the sake of every individual.

It is found from both the surveys and factor analysis method, most appropriate factor to be considered is role of technology in managing COVID-19. Technology is playing a vital role in almost every aspect worldwide, as it has numbers of advantages over traditional methods of finding solutions to any problem. Further, this the study carried out in this paper can be extended with container-based virtualization [41, 42].

4.4.1   Outcomes of the Proposed Scenario

The key points that contribute to providing better services through technology can be stated as:

4.4.1.1   Online Monitoring

Cloud-based technology is best in identifying, monitoring, and guiding better diagnosis and surveillance online.

4.4.1.2   Location Tracking

Can be best fitted to trace the infected individuals and provide appropriate treatment procedures.

4.4.1.3   Alarm Linkage

Alarms or pings can be sent to individuals as in case there is some probability of being infected in some circumstances.

4.4.1.4   Command and Control

The command to offload data at cloud data center can be easily executed. Further, the working method would also provide controlling run time data through the cloud manage servers.

4.4.1.5   Plan Management

The preset criteria of managing and timely treatment can be provided for suspected, confirmed, and suspicious cases found. This will help in attaining measures for better surveillance-related activities.

4.4.1.6   Security Privacy

In the healthcare sector, data protection and security are the primary factors for patient perspective. Nowadays, services of cloud computing are provided across the entire computing spectrum through secure data centers.

4.4.1.7   Remote Maintenance

Through remote locations, easy graded diagnosis and treatment facilities can be utilized through web service.

4.4.1.8   Online Upgrade

Automatic medical and other information will be updated to individuals via web service and other aspects, so that necessary precautions are taken in time.

4.4.1.9   Command Management

Through cloud-based network, information can be collected, and better results can be attained.

4.4.1.10   Statistical Decision

On collecting data through different practices, statistical reports can be made, and different problem identifiers, experiences, and solutions can be proposed through various experts and managers.

Factors with minimum loading factor are, such as Ease of using technology, Efficiency of applications, Awareness about protective & preventive measures, COVID-19 declared as pandemic, Initiative by government. The factors with minimum value for Cronbach's Alpha, also contributes to managing and controlling misdiagnosis & surveillance in some way or the other.

4.4.2   Experimental Setup

This section represents the experimental setup that has been made for the proposed scenario. An individual is allowed to operate while roaming into various regions. The regions are connected through the cloud-based architecture. The individual will be allowed to gain information through web

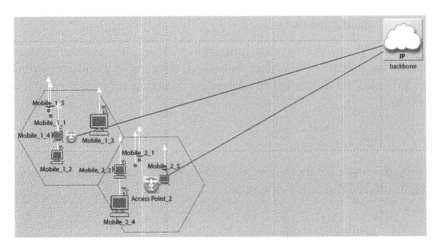

Figure 4.5 Experimental setup for the proposed cloud-based network.

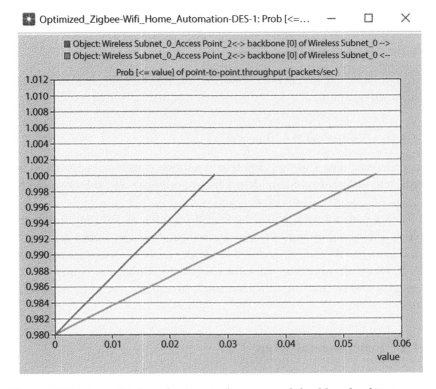

Figure 4.6 Point-to-point throughput received via proposed cloud-based architecture.

service-based architecture. Figure 4.5 represents the experimental setup for the proposed scenario.

For the experimental setup of the current scenario, two regions are taken into existence. Each region will have a group of people communication while roaming. An individual can be traced or provided with diagnosis more effectively.

To validate the performance metrics for the proposed cloud-based architecture, the simulation represents the outcome as increased throughput. Figure 4.6 represents the simulation analysis based on the performance metrics in terms of throughput.

4.5   Conclusion and Future Scope

Researchers round the world are keenly finding technological solutions to combat with the deadly pandemic. Solutions such as IoT and AI-based have been provided by various authors in different perspectives. But an area of improvement in the strategy is required for effective surveillance and diagnosis of the people all around the world. In the paper, a cloud-based architecture is proposed that contributes to providing better aspects to manage COVID-19 and finds measures to stop further propagation of this pandemic. A user is supposed to operate the services via web service. States of a country are divided into various regions and, every region is then managed through a centralized location for a particular state. Furthermore, a survey is performed on various factors that contribute to validate the proposed cloud-based scenario for effective surveillance and diagnosis methods. In this paper, a primary questionnaire was made, to which Cronbach's Alpha factor is applied that support the substantial factors from proposed set of factors. From the overall study, it can be stated that introducing Internet-based services is given as main concern, so that they can be updated from remote locations, as and when required. The purpose behind such research is to provide intelligent diagnosis, treatment to the majority, and overcome the fear of being infected in between the people. With this technology, authorities can easily trace at remote locations and can stop further propagation by applying certain monitoring procedure.

References

1. Huremović, D., Brief history of pandemics (pandemics throughout history), in: *Psychiatry of Pandemics*, pp. 7–35, Springer, Cham, 2019.

2. Murti, B., *History of epidemiology*, FK University, Surakarta, March 1 2010.

3. Jiang, F., Jiang, Y., Zhi, H., Dong, Y., Li, H., Ma, S., Wang, Y., Dong, Q., Shen, H., Wang, Y., Artificial intelligence in healthcare: Past, present and future. *Stroke Vasc. Neurol.*, 2, 4, 2017.

4. Scott, J.E. and Scott, C.H., Models for drone delivery of medications and other healthcare items, in: *Unmanned Aerial Vehicles: Breakthroughs in Research and Practice*, pp. 376–392, 2019.

5. Srivastava, G., Parizi, R. M., Dehghantanha, A., The future of blockchain technology in healthcare Internet of Things security. Blockchain cybersecurity, trust and privacy, pp. 161–184, 2020.

6. Abdali-Mohammadi, F., Meqdad, M.N., Kadry, S., Development of an IoT-based and cloud-based disease prediction and diagnosis system for healthcare using machine learning algorithms. *IAES Int. J. Artif. Intell.*, 9, 4, 766, 2020.

7. Singh, S. and Tripathi, A.K., Analyzing for performance factors in cloud computing. *International Conference on Sustainable Computing Techniques in Engineering, Science and Management (SCESM 2016), International Journal of Control Theory and Applications (IJCTA), Scopus Indexed*, vol. 9. No. 21, 2016.

8. Alam, T. and Benaida, M., Internet of Things and blockchain-based framework for coronavirus (COVID-19) disease. *Int. J. Online Biomed. Eng. (iJOE)*, 1–9, 2022, Available at SSRN: https://ssrn.com/abstract=3660503

9. Kashani, M.H. *et al.*, A systematic review of IoT in healthcare: Applications, techniques, and trends. *J. Netw. Comput. Appl.*, 192, 103164, 2021.

10. Singh, S., Chaudhary, H., Tripathi, A.K., IoT-enabled intelligent public transportation system. *Des. Eng.*, 3459–3474, 2021.

11. Davalbhakta, S. *et al.*, A systematic review of smartphone applications available for corona virus disease 2019 (COVID19) and the assessment of their quality using the mobile application rating scale (MARS). *J. Med. Syst.*, 44, 9, 1–15, 2020.

12. Preethika, T., Vaishnavi, P., Agnishwar, J., Padmanathan, K., Umashankar, S., Annapoorani, S., Subash, M., Aruloli, K., Artificial intelligence and drones to combat COVID - 19. *Preprints*, 2020, 2020060027. (doi: 10.20944/preprints202006.0027.v1).

13. Islam, M.N., Inan, T.T., Rafi, S., Akter, S.S., Sarker,I. H., Islam, A. K.M., A survey on the use of AI and ML for fighting the COVID-19 pandemic, arXiv pp. 1–10, 2020.

14. Wang, S., Kang, B., Ma, J., Zeng, X., Xiao, M., Guo, J., ... Xu, B., A deep learning algorithm using CT images to screen for corona virus disease (COVID-19). *Eur. Radiol.*, 31, 8, 6096–6104, 2021.

15. Singh, S., Karimi, S., Ho-Shon, K., Hamey, L., Show, tell and summarise: Learning to generate and summarise radiology findings from medical images. *Neural. Comput. Appl.*, 33, 13, 7441–7465, 2021.

16. Wang, Y., Hu, M., Li, Q., Zhang, X. P., Zhai, G., Yao, N., Abnormal respiratory patterns classifier may contribute to large-scale screening of people infected with COVID-19 in an accurate and unobtrusive manner. pp. 1–6, 2020. arXiv preprint arXiv:2002.05534

17. Egmont-Petersen, M., de Ridder, D., Handels, H., Image processing with neural networks—A review. *Pattern Recognit.*, 35, 10, 2279–2301, 2002.

18. Kumar, A., Gupta, P.K., Srivastava, A., A review of modern technologies for tackling COVID-19 pandemic. *Diabetes Metab. Syndr.: Clin. Res. Rev.*, 14, 4, 569–573, 2020.

19. Maddah, E. and Beigzadeh, B., Use of a smartphone thermometer to monitor thermal conductivity changes in diabetic foot ulcers: A pilot study. *J. Wound Care*, 29, 1, 61–66, 2020.

20. Alqudaihi, K.S. *et al.*, Cough sound detection and diagnosis using artificial intelligence techniques: Challenges and opportunities. *IEEE Access*, 9, 102327–102344, 2021.

21. Sharma, A., Bahl, S., Bagha, A.K. *et al.*, Blockchain technology and its applications to combat COVID-19 pandemic. *Res. Biomed. Eng.*, 38, 173–180, 2022. https://doi.org/10.1007/s42600-020-00106-3

22. Ernest, and Rivera, L., The pandemic accelerated cloud: Application, impact and challenges of cloud computing in COVID-19 pandemic, in: *Impact and Challenges of Cloud Computing in COVID-19 Pandemic*, December 13, 2021.

23. Tripathi, A.K. and Singh, S., A comparative analysis on internet protocols in cloud-mobile environment. *International Conference on Sustainable Computing Techniques in Engineering, Science and Management (SCESM 2016), International Journal of Control Theory and Applications (IJCTA), Scopus Indexed*, vol. 9. no. 17, 2016.

24. Ashraf, M.U. *et al.*, Detection and tracking contagion using IoT-edge technologies: Confronting COVID-19 pandemic. *2020 International Conference on Electrical, Communication, and Computer Engineering (ICECCE)*, IEEE, 2020.

25. Hayyolalam, V., Aloqaily, M., Özkasap, Ö., Guizani, M., Edge intelligence for empowering IoT-based healthcare systems. *IEEE Wirel. Commun.*, 28, 3, 6–14, 2021.

26. Tripathi, A.K. and Singh, S., Ensuring reliability in cloud computing and comparison on IPv6 encouraged with protocols. *Proceedings of International Conference on Science, Technology, Humanities and Business Management*, Bangkok, 2016.

27. Mbunge, E. *et al.*, A critical review of emerging technologies for tackling COVID-19 pandemic. *Hum. Behav. Emerging Technol.*, 3, 1, 25–39, 2021.

28. Ghazal, T.M. *et al.*, IoT for smart cities: Machine learning approaches in smart healthcare—A review. *Future Internet*, 13, 8, 218, 2021.

29. Green, R., Pilot testing: Why and how we trial, in: *The Routledge Handbook of Second Language Acquisition and Language Testing*, pp. 115–124, Routledge, USA, 2020.

30. Summers, A., A practical example of exploratory factor analysis and critical realism. *Nurse Res.*, 29, 1, 1–2, 2021.

31. Bhardwaj, A. and Rama Krishna, C., Efficient multistage bandwidth allocation technique for virtual machine migration in cloud computing. *J. Intell. Fuzzy Syst.*, 35, 5, 5365–5378, 2018.

32. Tripathi, A.K., Singh, S., Pandey, N., Impact of technology on human behavior during COVID-19, in: *Recent Trends in Communication and Electronics*, pp. 355–360, CRC Press, London, 2021.

33. Kirkpatrick, L.A., *A simple guide to IBM SPSS Statistics-Version 23.0*, Cengage Learning, US, 2015.

34. Bhardwaj, A. and Krishna, C.R., Virtualization in cloud computing: Moving from hypervisor to containerization—A survey. *Arab. J. Sci. Eng.*, 46, 9, 8585–8601, 2021.

35. Leech, N.L., Barrett, K.C., Morgan, G.A., *IBM SPSS for intermediate statistics: Use and interpretation*, Routledge, New York, 2014.

36. Sijtsma, K. and Pfadt, J.M., Part II: On the use, the misuse, and the very limited usefulness of cronbach's alpha: Discussing lower bounds and correlated errors. *Psychometrika*, 86, 4, 843–860, 2021.

37. Adriani, M. *et al.*, Determining the validity, reliability, and utility of the forgotten joint score: A systematic review. *J. Arthroplasty*, 35, 4, 1137–1144, 2020.

38. Kline, R.B., Book review: Psychometric theory. *J. Psychoeduc. Assess.*, 17, 3, 275–280, 1999.

39. Lorenzo-Seva, U. and Ferrando, P.J., Not positive definite correlation matrices in exploratory item factor analysis: Causes, consequences and a proposed solution. *Struct. Equ. Model.: A Multidiscip. J.*, 28, 1, 138–147, 2021.

40. Shrestha, N., Factor analysis as a tool for survey analysis. *Am. J. Appl. Math. Stat.*, 9, 1, 4–11, 2021.

41. Singh, S. *et al.*, Social issues under digital India, a campaign towards digitalization. *International Conference on "E-governance in Digital India: Prospects and Opportunities for Entrepreneurship & Innovation", International Journal of Science Technology and Management (IJSTM)*, vol. 6, pp. 1–8, 2020.

42. Bhardwaj, A. and Krishna, C.R., A container-based technique to improve virtual machine migration in cloud computing. *IETE J. Res.*, 68, 1, 401–416, 2022. doi: 10.1080/03772063.2019.1605848

Smart Agriculture Applications Using Cloud and IoT

Keshav Kaushik

School of Computer Science, University of Petroleum and Energy Studies, Dehradun, India

Abstract

The Internet of Things (IoT) is a game-changing technology that symbolizes the future of computers and telecommunications. Agriculture is the lifeblood of the majority of people on the planet. As a result, sophisticated IT solutions are required to integrate conventional agricultural processes. Modern technology may help manage costs, servicing, and performance monitoring. In today's agriculture, satellite and aerial photography are critical. Agriculture's most essential need is irrigation. The appropriate use of water resources is critical, and there is a pressing need to conserve water. Farmers in poor nations, resulting in inefficient use of environmental assets, mostly use traditional agricultural cultivation methods. This chapter highlights the applications of smart agriculture using the concept of IoT and cloud infrastructure. The chapter also discusses the open research challenges in the domain of smart agriculture. Moreover, the cyberattacks on the IoT applications in smart agriculture is also the part of this chapter.

Keywords: Cloud, smart agriculture, Internet of Things (IoT), IoT applications, quantum drones, cybersecurity, smart irrigation, security challenges

5.1 Role of IoT and Cloud in Smart Agriculture

The Internet of Things (IoT) is a game-changing innovation that facilitates future of communication and information technology. Agriculture is the

---

Email: officialkeshavkaushik@gmail.com

Danda B. Rawat, Lalit K Awasthi, Valentina Emilia Balas, Mohit Kumar and Jitendra Kumar Samriya (eds.) Convergence of Cloud with AI for Big Data Analytics: Foundations and Innovation, (89–106)

lifeblood of the majority of people on the planet. As a result, smart IT techniques are required to integrate traditional agricultural methods. Modern technology may help manage costs, maintenance, and performance monitoring. In today's agriculture, satellite and aerial photography are critical. Smart Agriculture is a rising, cost-effective approach for agricultural and food production that is both efficient and reliable. It's a technique for incorporating connected gadgets and cutting-edge innovation into agriculture. The IoT has brought great advantages to agriculture, including efficient water usage, input augmentation, and many more. The immense gains that have lately changed farming were what made all the difference. IoT-based Smart Farming improves the overall agricultural system by monitoring the field in real-time.

Because of sensors and connectedness, the IoT in Farming has not only reduced farmers' time but also reduced resource waste such as electricity and water. It keeps track of a number of factors, including moisture, temperature, and soil, and displays them in a crystal-clear real-time display. In order to meet increased demand and decrease production losses, IoT applications in agriculture are directed at conventional agricultural tasks. In agriculture, drones, UAVs, sensor systems, and computer imaging are used in conjunction with ever-improving machine learning and data mining techniques to observe crops, measure and map fields, and transmit data to farmers for cost-effective farm management. In aggrotech, the IoT is a system that combines sensitive physical equipment with analytical software. The majority of the time, an analytical dashboard is a piece of software that processes data collected by equipment. As a result, a solid technical grasp of robotics and computer-based intelligence is required for operating, maintaining, and comprehending the thoughts of these priceless machines. Because IoTs need actual equipment, each farm will require its own collection of sensors and bots to capture data specific to that farm. As a result, each farm will have its own dashboard to see the data. It is not feasible to connect and scale IoT for several fields in a single platform, unlike SaaS aggrotech like CropIn, which allows you to integrate and manage global operations via a single platform.

Sensors have been downsized as a result of recent advances in developing technologies, and attempts to utilize them in a variety of disciplines have been effective. Furthermore, the adoption of IoT and Cloud Computing in any area is resulting in the notion of "Smart," which includes Smart Health Systems [1], Pervasive Computation, Smart Mobility, Embedded Systems, Security Systems, and Smart meters [2], among others. Agriculture is one of the fields of research where this acceptance has occurred, culminating in Smart Agriculture. Agriculture is a critical source of revenue and lifestyle for the world's most populated countries, including India, China, and

Table 5.1 Comparative study of smart agriculture and IoT and cloud related papers.

Author	Year	A	B	C	D	E	F	Major findings
Mekala *et al.* [3]	2017	✓	✓	✓	✗	✗	✗	The authors looked at several common uses of farming IoT Sensor Surveillance Communication networks with the use of Cloud technology as the backbone in this article. This study is being used to better expose the various techniques and to develop long-term smart agriculture. A wireless network is used to handle a simple IoT agricultural concept.
Namani *et al.* [4]	2020	✓	✓	✓	✓	✗	✗	This paper gives a basic description of a Smart Drone for agricultural production, in which real-time information from the drones, combined with IoT and Cloud Technology, aids in the construction of a feasible Smart Farming system.
Lakhwani *et al.* [5]	2018	✓	✓	✓	✗	✓	✓	Developments of IoT in agricultural production were researched and evaluated in this study, which also included a concise introduction to IoT technology, agricultural production IoT, a list of certain promising application subject areas where IoT can be used in the farming sector, advantages of IoT in agricultural production, and a review of some publications.

(Continued)

Table 5.1 Comparative study of smart agriculture and IoT and cloud related papers. (*Continued*)

Author	Year	A	B	C	D	E	F	Major findings
Mekala *et al.* [6]	2019	✓	✓	✓	✓	✓	✓	The temperature quotient is calculated in this study based on the quantity of water vapor and density in the air, which is used to assess plant development. The level of comfort is calculated by subtracting the relative humidity from the conventional constant optimum temperature. As a result, real-time data tests using the CLAY-MIST assessment index reveal an accurate judgment and a full report given to farmers. As compared to current thermal comfort methodologies, the findings are 94 percent accurate and take less time to execute.
Ramachandran *et al.* [7]	2018	✓	✓	✗	✗	✓	✓	This study describes an automatic watering system that uses IoT, cloud computing, and optimization techniques to minimize water use in farming. Low-cost sensors are used in the automated irrigation system to detect factors of relevance such as humidity, pH level, soil conditions, and temperature variations. For tracking storage, the information is kept in the Thingspeak cloud service. The data from the agriculture ground is sent to the cloud using a GSM mobile networks and Wi-Fi connections.

(*Continued*)

Table 5.1 Comparative study of smart agriculture and IoT and cloud related papers. (*Continued*)

Author	Year	A	B	C	D	E	F	Major findings
Kalyani *et al.* [8]	2021	✓	✓	✗	✗	✓	✗	The main goal of this study is to gather all important research and development of new computer concepts and smart agriculture, as well as to offer a new architectural model based on the interaction of cloud, Fog and Edge architecture. It also investigates and analyzes agricultural application fields, research methods, and the utilization of various combinations. In addition, it examines the components utilized in architectural models and quickly examines the networking systems used to communicate from one layer to the next. Lastly, the paper briefly mentions the limitations of smart agriculture as well as future studies possibilities.
Suma V. [9]	2021	✓	✓	✗	✗	✗	✗	Multiple linear regression analysis, IoT devices with cloud administration, and protection devices for multi-culture in the agricultural sector are all covered in this study, which takes into account farmers' previous experiences. It also emphasizes the difficulties and issues that might be anticipated when incorporating contemporary technologies into traditional agricultural practices. Depending on qualitative and numerical methodologies, the existing agricultural system may be revolutionized more effectively.

A: Blockchain B: 5G C: IoT D: Artificial Intelligence E: Smart contracts F: Security.

many others. Incorporating IoT and Cloud Computing into the agricultural industry would result in improved crop production by regulating costs, tracking progress, and maintaining equipment, all of which would assist farmers and the country as a whole. The comparative study of latest papers related to Smart Agriculture and IoT is shown above in Table 5.1.

The growing need for food, in terms of quantity and quality, has hastened the need for agricultural industrialization and aggressive techniques of production. A rising IoT market is proposing various unique ideas at the vanguard of the new farming era. Connecting with IoT allows research institutions and scientific associations to expand their reach and speed, bringing technologies and goods to a variety of farm sectors. The IoT is a developing framework that aims to synchronize various smart devices in order to modernize multiple domains. Several IoT-based frameworks have been proposed to record and handle agricultural areas with optimum human interaction in an automated way. Farmers [10] may use IoT apps to stay up to date on the recent developments and advances in their area. Furthermore, the availability of cloud-based smart apps and models aids farmers in maintaining control over their crops. Such technologies, for instance, have the capacity to gather data, analyses it, and predict the optimal response in various scenarios in order to tackle the anticipated issue. Problems like this arise as a consequence of unfavorable weather and a variety of crop diseases.

The IoT is transforming agriculture by giving farmers with a varied collection of tools to handle a variety of difficulties they experience on the farm. IoT-enabled technology allows farmers to communicate to their farm from practically anywhere and at any time. Sensors and actuators monitor the agricultural procedure, in which, wireless sensor networks are utilized to regulate the farmland. To access the farm remotely and gather information in the form of films and photographs, wireless sensors and cameras were utilized. Farmers can also utilize IoT to monitor the present state of their agricultural land from anywhere in the world using a smart phone. IoT-enabled solutions have the ability to reduce crop production costs while also increasing agricultural production.

5.2   Applications of IoT and Cloud in Smart Agriculture

IoT Modern electronic agriculture is made possible by smart technology. To handle today's issues, innovation has become a requirement, and various industries are automating their processes using the latest advancements.

Smart agriculture [11], which is built on IoT technology, is designed to help producers and farmers minimize waste and increase output by regulating fertilizer use to increase process efficiency. Farmers can better regulate their animals, develop crops, decrease expenses, and conserve resources using IoT-based Smart Agriculture. Farmers have benefited from the use of IoT in a variety of ways, including monitoring water quantities in tanks. This is all done in real time, which improves the effectiveness of the entire irrigation operation. The monitoring of seed growth is another thing which has been made feasible by the introduction of IoT technology. Producers can now monitor resource use and the time it takes for a seed to completely mature into a plant.

The adoption of IoT in farming was akin to the Green Revolution's second wave. Farmers have reaped two main advantages from the IoT. With the support of reliable data collected via IoT, they can now do the same number of jobs in less time while simultaneously increasing agricultural yields. Sensors monitor every aspect of crop production, including moisture in the soil, temperature, sunlight, climate, and irrigation management automation. This technique enables farmers to keep an eye on their fields from anywhere. When compared to traditional farming, IoT-based farming is significantly more efficient. Smart farming based on IoT not only aids in the modernization of traditional farming techniques, but also targets alternative agricultural methods such as sustainable agriculture, family farming, and boosts extremely transparent farming. Smart farming based on the IoT is also good for the environment. It may assist farmers in making better use of water and optimizing inputs and treatments. Now, we will look (Figure 5.1) at the applications of IoT and cloud in the smart agriculture that are transforming the agricultural industry.

- IoT powered drones: In recent years, technology has advanced dramatically and at a faster pace. Agricultural drones are an excellent illustration of this trend. Drones are being used in agriculture to enhance a variety of agricultural processes. Drones are used in agriculture for crop health evaluations, cultivation practices, pest management, drainage, sowing, and field analysis, both on the ground and in the air. These drones acquire spectral bands, thermal, and visual pictures during their flight. Crop health surveillance, integrated GIS mapping, improved efficiency, ease of use, and enhanced agricultural yields are just a few of the benefits of drones. Numerous benefits have been predicted for real-time applications as a result of recent breakthroughs in

Figure 5.1 IoT and cloud applications in smart agriculture.

quantum drones, the Internet of Quantum Drones [12], and Drone-to-Satellite connection. We can give the agriculture industry a high-tech makeover if we integrate surveillance drones with effective planning and strategy based on real-time data collecting.

- *Observing Livestock:* Large farm operators use wireless IoT apps to keep track of their cattle's whereabouts, health, and well-being. This knowledge [13] aids them in identifying ill animals and separating them from the flock, as well as caring for them and preventing the sickness from spreading to other livestock. It may also help owners save money on labor since IoT-based sensors can assist them find their animals.

- *Intelligent Greenhouses:* Greenhouse farming aims to increase vegetable, agricultural, and fruit yields, among other things. In greenhouses, climate effects are managed via human interaction or a proportional control system. On the other side, manual participation leads in reduced productivity, power dissipation, and labor expenses. Therefore, the concept of greenhouses has been made obsolete. Consequently, smart gardens are the better alternative. A smart greenhouse might be developed with the help of IoT. Autonomous greenhouses, on the other hand, monitor and control the atmosphere without requiring human intervention.

- *Irrigation Monitoring:* Computer imaging mostly entails deploying sensor cameras strategically positioned across the farm to create pictures that are then processed digitally. Irrigation throughout time assists in the mapping of irrigated fields. This allows determining whether to produce or not harvest during the pre-harvest season.
- *Weather Monitoring:* Crop productivity is influenced by the weather. Varied crops need different climatic conditions to develop, and even a rudimentary understanding of climate has a significant impact on crop amount and quality. Farmers may use IoT technologies to get real-time weather updates. Sensors installed in agricultural fields gather information from the environment, which farmers use to select a crop that can thrive in certain climatic circumstances.
- *Accurate Farming:* Precision farming, often known as smart farming, refers to any method of raising animals and cultivating crops that renders the entire process more precise and regulated. Sensors, robots, automation trucks, control mechanisms, automated equipment, variable rate innovation, and other advancements are all important components of this farming approach.
- *Remote Sensing:* Sensors installed along fields, such as meteorological stations, are used in IoT-based remote sensing to collect data, which is then sent on to analysis instruments for study. Farmers may keep an eye on their crops using analytical interfaces, and take action based on the information gleaned.

5.3   Security Challenges in Smart Agriculture

The IoT is a collection of physical items that can recognize themselves to other gadgets and utilize integrated technology to communicate with intrinsic or extrinsic states. Many computing devices with monitoring and communication capabilities are now linked due to advances in technology. Such devices [14] collect information from the environment, process it, and then either retain or transfer the information to another device with comparable characteristics. A few examples [15] of IoT applications are smart homes, intelligent buildings, smart grids, and smart cars. For remote access, collection, distribution, and processing, these applications need distributed information delivery architectures. As a consequence, communication among smart things opens up new possibilities for applications aimed at improving human health. Enormous communication inside these cyber-physical systems, on the other hand, raises a slew of security issues. Such security [16] flaws have the potential to disrupt whole applications/ systems, perhaps resulting in death. As a result, modern IoT applications must have high levels of trust and security. To that aim, it's critical to comprehend the major security issues that smart IoT applications face, such as those in the e-health, agricultural, and energy industries. As a result, in order to improve the security of smart IoT applications, this article describes and addresses the key security issues and needs.

Attacks on the IoT system may be interpreted or characterized from a variety of perspectives, depending on whether they are aggressive or passive. These may also be used to determine if the assault is coming from the inside of the network or from outside. In any instance, information security and anonymity must be protected. In IoT case studies, the customer has access to the data and the authorized machine, information confidentiality is a critical concern. It involves addressing two key features: first, a means for validating and verifying identities, and second, an admission limitation and penalty process. The verification of a legal IoT device is the confirmation of the identification of the IoT based networks for internet or fog-based services. To utilize the cloud services safely, IoT apps must verify their identity. User confidentiality is another difficult issue with real-time apps. With IoT applications where devices are interconnected, privacy is another major challenge. The IoT related common cyberattacks in smart agriculture are given below in Figure 5.2.

- *Routing Protocols attacks:* Such type of attack targets the various routing protocols used in the IoT communication and is responsible for packet loss, downgrading network bandwidth, poor throughput, and data loss.
- *Internal/External attacks:* Internal attacks are those attacks that are done by the insider of the organization or in which some internal person of the organization is involved. The extremal attacks are those in which some external factor is involved like attack from outside the organization e.g. phishing, etc.

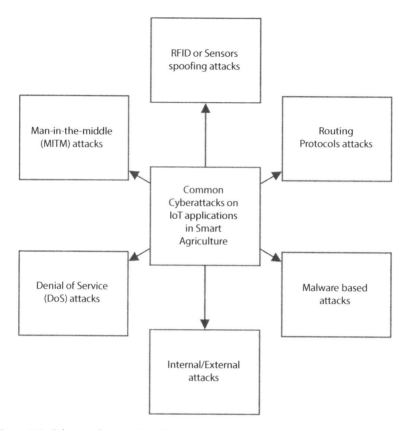

Figure 5.2 Cyberattacks on IoT applications in smart agriculture.

- *Malware based attacks:* In this type of attacks, some malware is involved like rootkit, Trojan, virus, worm, etc. This attack may lead to the data theft, unnecessary utilization of resources, privacy breach, and data tampering.
- *Denial of Service (DoS) attacks:* This attack comes into picture when some non-legitimate user(s) is trying to restrict the legitimate user(s) from using the services. This attack may also lead to network flooding, unavailability of the resources and system crash.
- *RFID or Sensors Spoofing Attacks:* In this attack, RFID/ sensors are faked out to fool the target. This type attack may lead to modification of data and manipulation of it.
- *Man in the Middle (MITM) attacks:* MITM attacks are due to network eavesdropping, when an intruder wiretaps the

network to sniff it. This attack may leads to breach of confidentiality and privacy, and data leakage.

Agricultural knowledge and digitization are addressed by smart agriculture. With the advancement of agriculture spurred on by current digital technology, however, data security risks must be addressed. Three distinct smart sustainable agriculture modes are discussed in this research [17]. Sustainable farming is still in its infancy, with few security mechanisms. Future solutions will rely on data accessibility and accuracy to aid farmers, and security will be critical to constructing reliable and productive systems. Because smart agriculture carries a wide variety of resources and huge amount of data, security must handle challenges such as interoperability, less number of resources, and enormous data. The aim of this study [18] is to assess the existing level of smart agricultural security, especially in open-field farming, by explaining its design, outlining security difficulties, and providing important obstacles and future perspectives. In the agricultural industry, new information technologies and applications will be increasingly employed to maintain and enhance operations, efficiency, and productivity. The widespread use of information, meanwhile, brings with it significant security dangers and weaknesses, and the industry is now being attacked like never before. Using an analytical technique, some comments on the security difficulties that Smart Farming technologies confront are presented in this study [19].

5.4   Open Research Challenges for IoT and Cloud in Smart Agriculture

Smart Agriculture is a promising field that is evolving day by day due to the support of advanced technologies like IoT, Cloud Computing, Artificial Intelligence, Cybersecurity, Blockchain etc. Due to its wide nature, it provides a vast array of research scope and opportunities. This section highlights the open research challenges for IoT and cloud computing in Smart Agriculture. IoT is a developing paradigm that aims to link various smart hardware elements for various domain upgrading. Several IoT-based definitions have been developed to autonomously manage and monitor agricultural areas with minimum human interaction. The primary components, new technology, security problems, obstacles, and emerging developments in the agricultural area are all discussed in depth in this article [20]. The open research challenges for IoT and cloud in smart agriculture is shown below in Figure 5.3.

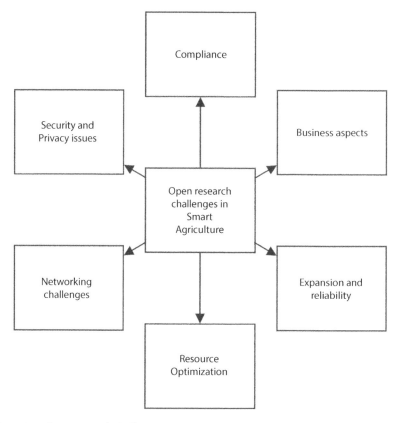

Figure 5.3 Open research challenges in smart agriculture.

- *Compliance:* The legislative and legal mechanisms regulating the administration and custody of agricultural data between farm employees and data businesses must be sorted out. In accordance with the service offering, technical problems, profitability, information security, and security, regulations differ per nation. Various regulations in different parts of the globe might influence how IoT is used in certain applications like surveillance and food production.
- *Business aspects:* Because the agriculture industry has a low market share, it is necessary to balance the deployment of IoT-enabling technology with the anticipated advantages. Installation and operational expenses are two types of costs connected with IoT adoption in agriculture. The installation fee includes the cost of IoT devices necessary to create a

smart agricultural setting. A lack of information of IoT and its uses, particularly among rural farmers regions, is a major impediment to IoT adoption in agribusiness.

- *Expansion and reliability:* Huge count of IoT devices and detectors are used in smart agriculture, requiring the employment of a smart IoT management system to identify and regulate each node. IoT devices are designed to be put in the open air. This exposing the devices to harsh external conditions, which might lead to sensor degradation and communication issues over time.

- *Resource optimization:* To increase profitability, farmers need a resource optimization procedure to determine the ideal count of access points, IoT devices, conveyed data, and cloud storage. This is complicated by the fact that different farms have different dimensions and need different kinds of sensors to identify agricultural factors for specific crops or animals.

- *Network challenges:* The connectivity between numerous sensor units in smart agriculture poses a challenging task. Sensors [21] do enormous calculations that need a lot of energy, yet sensor batteries are limited. As a consequence, efficient energy storage is required by networks. These issues don't simply exist at the device implementation level; they also emerge at the network level.

- *Security and privacy issues:* Physical tampering [22], such as burglary or assaults by rats and cattle, as well as differences in physical location or link, are all possibilities in the smart agricultural area. At various tiers of IoT, the authors [23] tackled various security breach situations such as security breaches, SQL Injection attacks, and so on. The perception layer is primarily focused on physical devices such as sensors and actuators. Accidental or intentional human action, viruses, or hackers may lead to physical equipment to fail.

Information became fragmented since the number of research and initiatives regarding IoT-based sustainable farming grew rapidly, and he related communications systems were not previously studied and addressed in prior reviews. To achieve the wonderful ahead expansion in smart agriculture, more emerging communications systems should be utilized in agricultural production, according to the report [24].

5.5   Conclusion

IoT allows for the collection of massive amounts of data through sensors, allowing for improved management of internal operations and, as a consequence, fewer production hazards. The Internet of Things allows for effective monitoring of the agricultural environment. By providing remote monitoring, the Internet of Things allows farmers to watch their farms from numerous places. Decisions may be taken instantly and from any location. In this chapter, the applications of smart agriculture using Cloud and IoT are discussed. Moreover, the cyberattacks on IoT applications in the field of smart agriculture is also highlighted in this chapter. Smart agriculture relies largely on the IoT, which reduces the need for local farmers to do physical work and so boosts productivity in every manner possible. The book chapter highlighted the role of IoT and cloud in smart agriculture. The chapter also enlightened the readers about the research scope of IoT and cloud in Smart Agriculture. The chapter is also helpful for the IoT enthusiasts, cloud security experts, Ph.D. scholars, researchers and students.

References

1. Singh, K., Kaushik, K., Ahatsham, Shahare, V., Role and impact of wearables in IoT healthcare. *Adv. Intell. Syst. Comput.*, 1090, 735–742, 2020.
2. Jain, S., Kaushik, K., Sharma, D.K., Krishnamurthi, R., Kumar, A., Sustainable infrastructure theories and models, in: *Digit. Cities Roadmap*, pp. 97–126, Apr. 2021.
3. Mekala, M.S. and Viswanathan, P., A survey: Smart agriculture IoT with cloud computing. *2017 Int. Conf. Microelectron. Devices, Circuits Syst. ICMDCS 2017*, Dec. 2017, vol. 2017-January, pp. 1–7.
4. Namani, S. and Gonen, B., Smart agriculture based on IoT and cloud computing. *Proc. - 3rd Int. Conf. Inf. Comput. Technol. ICICT 2020*, Mar. 2020, pp. 553–556.
5. Lakhwani, K. *et al.*, Development of IoT for smart agriculture a review. *Adv. Intell. Syst. Comput.*, 841, 425–432, 2019.
6. Mekala, M.S. and Viswanathan, P., CLAY-MIST: IoT-cloud enabled CMM index for smart agriculture monitoring system. *Measurement*, 134, 236–244, Feb. 2019.
7. Ramachandran, V., Ramalakshmi, R., Srinivasan, S., An automated irrigation system for smart agriculture using the Internet of Things. *2018 15th Int. Conf. Control. Autom. Robot. Vision, ICARCV 2018*, Dec. 2018, pp. 210–215.

8. Kalyani, Y. and Collier, R., A systematic survey on the role of cloud, fog, and edge computing combination in smart agriculture. *Sensors*, 21, 17, 59225922, Sep. 2021.

9. Suma, V., Internet of Things (IoT) based smart agriculture in India: An overview. *J. ISMAC*, 03, 01, 1–15, 2021, https://doi.org/10.36548/jismac.2021.1.001

10. Tawalbeh, M., Quwaider, M., Tawalbeh, L.A., IoT cloud enabeled model for safe and smart agriculture environment. *2021 12th Int. Conf. Inf. Commun. Syst. ICICS 2021*, pp. 279–284, May 2021.

11. Gaur, C., IoT in smart agriculture solutions and applications | Use case, Oct. 20, 2021, https://www.xenonstack.com/use-cases/iot-smart-farming (accessed Dec. 01, 2021).

12. Kumar, A., Bhatia, S., Kaushik, K., Gandhi, S. M., Devi, S. G., Diego, Di. A., & Mashat, A., Survey of promising technologies for quantum drones and networks. *IEEE Access*, 9, 125868–125911, 2021, https://doi.org/10.1109/ACCESS.2021.3109816

13. Pathak, R., 7 Applications of IoT in agriculture | Analytics steps, Dec. 23, 2020, https://www.analyticssteps.com/blogs/5-applications-iot-agriculture (accessed Dec. 01, 2021).

14. Kaushik, K. and Singh, K., Security and trust in IoT communications: Role and impact, in: *Advances in Intelligent Systems and Computing*, vol. 989, pp. 791–798, 2020.

15. Tariq, N., Khan, F.A., Asim, M., Security challenges and requirements for smart Internet of Things applications: A comprehensive analysis. *Proc. Comput. Sci.*, 191, 425–430, Jan. 2021.

16. Kaushik, K. and Dahiya, S., Security and privacy in IoT based e-business and retail. *Proc. 2018 Int. Conf. Syst. Model. Adv. Res. Trends, SMART 2018*, pp. 78–81, Nov. 2018

17. Yang, X. *et al.*, A survey on smart agriculture: Development modes, technologies, and security and privacy challenges. *IEEE/CAA J. Autom. Sin.*, 8, 2, 273–302, Feb. 2021.

18. Rettore de Araujo Zanella, A., da Silva, E., Pessoa Albini, L.C., Security challenges to smart agriculture: Current state, key issues, and future directions. *Array*, 8, 100048, Dec. 2020.

19. Barreto, L. and Amaral, A., Smart farming: Cyber security challenges. *9th Int. Conf. Intell. Syst. 2018 Theory, Res. Innov. Appl. IS 2018 - Proc.*, Jul. 2018, pp. 870–876.

20. Sinha, B.B. and Dhanalakshmi, R., Recent advancements and challenges of Internet of Things in smart agriculture: A survey. *Future Gener. Comput. Syst.*, 126, 169–184, Jan. 2022.

21. Saha, H.N., Roy, R., Chakraborty, M., Sarkar, C., IoT-Enabled agricultural system application, challenges and security issues, in: *Agric. Informatics*, pp. 223–247, Mar. 2021.

22. Haseeb, K., Din, I.U., Almogren, A., Islam, N., An energy efficient and secure IoT-based WSN framework: An application to smart agriculture. *Sensors*, 20, 7, 20812081, Apr. 2020.
23. Demestichas, K., Peppes, N., Alexakis, T., Survey on security threats in agricultural IoT and smart farming. *Sensors*, 20, 22, 64586458, Nov. 2020.
24. Tao, W., Zhao, L., Wang, G., Liang, R., Review of the internet of things communication technologies in smart agriculture and challenges. *Comput. Electron. Agric.*, 189, 106352, Oct. 2021.

6

Applications of Federated Learning in Computing Technologies

Sambit Kumar Mishra*, Kotipalli Sindhu, Mogaparthi Surya Teja,
Vutukuri Akhil, Ravella Hari Krishna, Pakalapati Praveen
and Tapas Kumar Mishra

SRM University, AP, India

Abstract

Federated learning is a technique that trains the knowledge across different decentralized devices holding samples of information without exchanging them. The concept is additionally called collaborative learning. In federated learning, the clients are allowed separately to teach the deep neural network models with the local data combined at the deep neural network model at the central server. All the local datasets are uploaded to a minimum of one server, so it assumes that local data samples are identically distributed. It doesn't transmit the information to the server. Because of its security and privacy concerns, it's widely utilized in many applications like IoT, cloud computing; Edge computing, Vehicular edge computing, and many more. The details of implementation for the privacy of information in federated learning for shielding the privacy of local uploaded data are described. Since there will be trillions of edge devices, the system efficiency and privacy should be taken with no consideration in evaluating federated learning algorithms in computing technologies. This will incorporate the effectiveness, privacy, and usage of federated learning in several computing technologies. Here, different applications of federated learning, its privacy concerns, and its definition in various fields of computing like IoT, Edge, and Cloud Computing are presented.

Keywords: Federated learning, computing technology, cloud computing, edge computing, IoT, neural network

Corresponding author: skmishra.nitrkl@gmai.com

Danda B. Rawat, Lalit K Awasthi, Valentina Emilia Balas, Mohit Kumar and Jitendra Kumar Samriya (eds.)
Convergence of Cloud with AI for Big Data Analytics: Foundations and Innovation, (107–120) © 2023
Scrivener Publishing LLC

6.1   Introduction

Google first presents the idea of federated learning in 2016, which is helpful in many applications to require care of privacy policy. Federated learning is used to collaboratively train the global machine learning model, with distributed datasets, protecting user's data privacy. In this article, we are going to work on different applications of federated learning in computing technology. Here, we divided the Applications of federated learning into different sections.

Section 6.1: Federated Learning in Cloud Computing
This section works on federated learning in cloud computing, its applications in different fields like cloud mobile edge-computing and cloud edge-computing [1, 2].

Section 6.2: Federated Learning in Edge Computing
This section deals with Edge computing, federated learning in edge computing, and applications in various fields like vehicular edge processing and intelligent recommendation [1].

Section 6.3: Federated Learning in Internet of Things (IoT)
This section is on IoT, federated learning in IoT, and its applications in different fields like Correspondence productive Federated Learning for wireless edge devices and blockchain and federated learning for privacy-protected data sharing [3, 4].

Section 6.4: Federated Learning in Medical Fields
This section presents on its different medical fields like Medical Healthcare and Data privacy in healthcare [5, 20].

Section 6.5: Federated Learning in Blockchain
This section deals on Blockchain and its applications in different fields like Blockchain-based federated learning [6, 7].

6.1.1   Federated Learning in Cloud Computing

The consistent development of intelligent gadgets requiring preparation has prompted moving AI calculation from server to edge nodes, leading to the edge processing worldview. Federated learning is a favorable circulated machine learning arrangement that utilizes nearby local computing with the local data to train the Artificial Intelligence (AI) model [8].

Attributable to the restricted limit of edge computing nodes, the presence of famous applications in the edge nodes brings about critical upgrades in client's fulfillment and administration achievement. Consolidating local data processing and Federated learning can prepare an impressive AI model for guaranteeing local information protection while utilizing versatile customers' assets. However, the heterogeneity of local information in the gadgets, that is, Non-free and indistinguishable circulation (Non-IID) and lopsidedness of regional information size may prevent the utilization of federated learning in mobile edge computing (MEC) systems. In specific circumstances, federated learning acquired consideration for performing, taking in methods from information dispersed across different clients, keeping the data untouched.

As of late, the consistently expanding scattering in our day-by-day life of Smart gadgets like wearable gadgets, cell phones, smart cards, sensors, etc., has set off the expansion of various conveyed network gadgets creating gigantic amounts of heterogeneous information to be handled and deciphered. Inferable from such excellent proportions of data with sensational advancement designs and the typical private nature of these data, sending all the data to a far cloud gets impossible, unnecessary, and stacked with assurance concerns [9, 21]. Thus, these parts have added to the ascent of the new adaptable, mobile edge processing (MEC) perspective, which handles the progress in the limit and computation breaking point of current devices for pushing, getting ready, and taking care of strategies locally on the simple contraptions. The MEC approach includes the participation of edge nodes with the far-off cloud to give rise to a processing framework ready to help huge scope tasks preparing and dealing with the climate. Inside this specific situation, the proficient and powerful treatment of enormous information brings out data and natural highlights covered up in the datasets, valuable for some application zones.

Applications of federated learning in cloud computing are explained as follows.

6.1.1.1   Cloud-Mobile Edge Computing

Machine Learning (ML) procedures comprise a vast part of considerable information control. A multi-hidden up multi-layered convolutional neural organization is received to serve information validation in a hearty portable group detecting issue, targeting improving detecting unwavering quality, and decreasing the general dormancy [11].

Here, we have a scenario shown in Figure 6.1, where the cloud is in a remote area where the network cannot be reached [10]. Here, we have a set

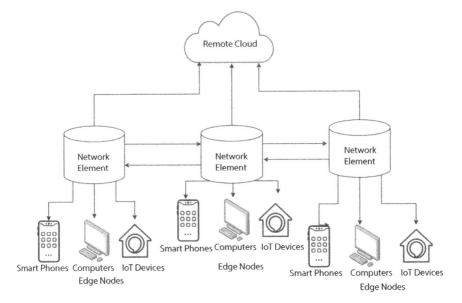

Figure 6.1 Cloud–MEC network architecture [2].

of network elements representing NE and we have a set of edge nodes representing ED. Here once the requested trained model is completed in the ED it passes the model to the network element [11]. If the training model is not present in on edge node it passes the model to the nearest node to perform the task in this way it automatically this task is performed several times and the trained model is sent to NE's.

The AI calculations utilized in federated learning are not restricted to edge network calculations yet incorporate different measures, like random forests. Federated learning comprises a variable function and so many edge nodes [12]. The edge nodes are responsible for gathering inclinations moved by each edge node, reviving the parameters of the structure as demonstrated by the smoothing out computation and keeping up the global parameters. The available nodes master nodes gain from the delicate information autonomously and locally. After every cycle, nodes transfer inclinations to the parameter worker, and the worker sums up and refreshes the global parameters [12]. At that point, edge nodes compute the refreshed global parameters outside of the parameter server, overwriting their old local parameters and continuing to the following cycle. During the entire learning measure, nodes just communicate with the parameter server. Learning nodes can't acquire any data about the excess nodes, except for the global parameters that are kept up, which ensures the classification of the private information. The Federated Learning for Edge Network

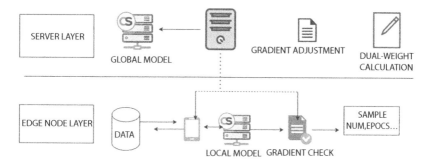

Figure 6.2 Privacy-protected federated learning framework for edge network computing [1].

Computing, which depends on the customary federated learning structure, is shown in Figure 6.2. This method has two layers: parameter server layer and edge node layer. The self-versatile limit slope pressure module is at the edge node layer, and the non-concurrent federated learning module traverses the two layers.

6.1.1.2   Cloud Edge Computing

Edge node application administrations diminish the amounts of information that should be transferred, the ensuing traffic, and the distance that data should travel. It calculates the lower latency and decreases transmission costs. Calculation offloading for constant applications, like facial acknowledgment calculations, showed extensive upgrades accordingly, as shown in early exploration. Further examination showed that utilizing these machines made cloudlets close to portable clients, which offer administrations usually found in the cloud, given upgrades in execution time when a portion of the errands is offloaded to the edge node. Then again, emptying each task may bring about a stop because of move times among gadgets and nodes, so relying upon the responsibility can characterize an ideal setup [13].

Another utilization of this engineering is cloud gaming, where a few parts of a game could run in the cloud, while the delivered video is moved to lightweight customers running on gadgets like cell phones, VR glasses, and so forth. This kind of streaming is otherwise called pixel streaming. Other remarkable applications incorporate associated vehicles, self-driving vehicles, smart city areas, automated industry, and home robotization frameworks. The pervasiveness of IoT gadgets and the expanding refinement of cyber-attacks suggest a need to improve existing cyber-attack discovery instruments. As of late, DL has been generally fruitful in cyber-attack recognition [13]. Combined with FL, cyber-attack recognition models can be adapted cooperatively while keeping up client security. Given the calculation and capacity limit limitations of edge workers, some computationally concentrated undertakings of end gadgets must be offloaded to the distant cloud worker for calculation. Moreover, usually mentioned records or then again administrations should be put on edge workers for quicker recovery, i.e., clients don't need to speak with the far-off cloud when they need to get to these records again benefits. Accordingly, an ideal reserving and offloading calculation plan can be cooperatively educated and advanced with FL.

6.1.2 Federated Learning in Edge Computing

Federated learning is a technique that is similar to machine learning technique. And one more advantage of federated learning is security or privacy, and this is the main reason why federated learning. These types of federated learning techniques train an algorithm throughout the different decentralized aspect devices containing the local information (data) without exchanging the local information (data) to others [14, 15]. Edge Computing is open IT architecture, dispensed those functions mobile computing and technologies that are Internet of Things (IoT), processing power decentralized. In the Edge computing, the devices process the data by itself or by local computers or by any servers. Like capturing traffic signals and calculating the Reduced Latency, Speeds Processing, Optimizing Bandwidth, etc. [14]. These types of analyses are done by devices itself without transmitting the data to datacenters. But in cloud computing captured traffic signals images need to be transmitted into the datacenter and it may lead to data privacy policies.

Federated Learning is a model that is similar to machine learning, here the model, using the locally stored data, may be discovered through some of dispensed nodes. It gives better data privacy or security because these locally stored data or trained information (data) is not sending it to the central (principal) server. The actual technology together with self-driving cars is VR and AR. These are the new architectures for data processing [16]. For this case cloud computing is unsuitable due to the variances in latency and bandwidth [17]. The new model of computation termed edge computing is suitable, because of low latency and high bandwidth. In remote control locations, cloud computing is not better than edge computing, because processing data needs to be done by time to time.

Applications of federated learning in edge computing explained as follows.

6.1.2.1   Vehicular Edge Computing

Federated learning is a well-known machine learning algorithm; wherein customers are enabling to teach the models (local Deep Neural Networks (DNN)) with the usage of district information and at the central server combine together to form a global (DNN) version [14]. The point of the Vehicular Edge Computing (VEC) is at the brink of vehicular organizations misusing the correspondence and calculation assets. In vehicular edge computing federated learning has the capability to satisfy the growing needs of AI packages in Intelligent Connected Vehicles (ICV). Image category is the one of the most important AI programs in VEC. We encouraged a selective aggregation version wherein "fine", Local DNN fashions are decided on after which dispatched to the central servers by comparing the nearby photo excellence and the computation functionality. For the execution of version choice, the imperative server always aware about the photo pleasant and computation functionality within side the vehicular customers, whose privacy is exactly maintained below federated learning agenda. To triumph over the evidence, we have a 2-Dimensional settlement principle as an allotted framework to recognize the interplay among central (principal) server and vehicular customers [14]. The expressed hassle is then converted right hooked on a dutiful hassle thru sequentially enjoyable and simplifying the constraints, and eventually solved through the usage of a grasping algorithm. Here we're the usage of datasets that is MNIST & Belgium TSC choosy version combination is used to outclass the unique federated Averaging (Fed-Avg) method in phrases of efficiency and exactness. As compared to the baseline model, our approach has higher utility at the central servers.

6.1.2.2   Intelligent Recommendation

Intelligence advice is a beneficial feature in cell phone or computer programs that expect consumer selections so that customers can without difficulty get entry to and use it. Contrasted and well-known AI draw near, edge federated learning can proficiently prepare adaptable models for suggestion under-takings, because aspect nodes are located in a perfect region and feature comparable obligations for performance and price causes. The prediction of emojis and the evaluation effect shows that the model on every node has an excellent typical overall performance because of the truth that models are adjusted to one of a type of language and traditional pattern in a particular region [16].

Display that the browser alternative proposal version skilled with federated learning can assist customers quickly discovers the internet site they want through coming into fewer characters. The paintings may be progressed in aspect federated learning structures to offer exclusive customers with rather customized fashions with the aid of exploring personal similarities without violating personal privacy and security [16].

6.1.3   Federated Learning in IoT (Internet of Things)

The core plan behind federates learning is decentralized learning, where the user information is rarely sent to the central server. Data is usually created by nervy devices like smart phones or IoT sensors. Federated learning is a solution that permits device machine learning while not transferring the user's non-public information to a central cloud. For the Internet of things (IoT), together with cloud, fog, dew, edge computing is essential, which provides aggregation and processing from detector networks and individual devices associated with the physical world. It is a network of well-connected devices providing wealthy information [3, 18]. However, it may also be a security nightmare. Federated learning will facilitate come through personalization as well as enhance the performance of devices in IoT applications. Federated learning trains a framework in IoT, big information, and multimedia system communications. Federated learning may be a possible resolution to unravel the issues of knowledge islands, break information barriers, and shield information security and privacy, particularly within the context of the IoT and massive information [19]. Distributed IoT and enormous information users got to collaboratively train a classification or regression model to implement excellent information prediction results while not compromising privacy. Not like privacy-preserving outsourced coaching, instead of submitting information to the centralized cloud server, users train information domestically in the American state. The federate center is barely answerable for aggregating the gradient info (or model parameters) uploaded by users and distributing the worldwide coaching model.

Applications of Federated Learning in IoT are explained as follows.

6.1.3.1   *Federated Learning for Wireless Edge Intelligence*

The quickly increasing range of IoT devices is generating vast quantities of knowledge; however public concern over information privacy suggests that user's square measure apprehensive to sending information to a central server. They simply modified the behaviors of edge infrastructure that software-defined networks provide to collate IoT information, wherever federate learning may be performed, while not uploading information to the server. Fed-Avg is an Associate in nursing federated learning algorithmic rule that has been the topic of abundant study. Regardless, it suffers from an extensive range of spherical to confluence with non-independent identically distributed (non-IID) consumer information sets and high communication prices. They proposed adapting Fed-Avg to reduce the number of rounds to convergence and novel compression strategies to provide communication-efficient Fed-Avg (CE-Fed-Avg). They tend to perform intensive experiments with the consumer information, and variable numbers of purchasers, consumer participation rates, and compression rates. The CE-Fed-Avg will converge to target accuracy in up to 6xless rounds than equally compressed Fed-Avg, whereas uploading up to 3xless information, is additionally strong, aggressive compression. Experiments on Associate in Nursing edge-computing like testbed exploitation Raspberry Pi purchasers show that CE-Fed-Avg is ready to succeed in a target accuracy in up to one 7xless real-time than Fed-Avg [3, 22, 23].

6.1.3.2 Federated Learning for Privacy Protected Information

The speedy increase within the volume of knowledge generated from connected devices in the industrial net of things paradigms parades new potentialities for enhancing the standard of service for the rising applications through information sharing. However, security and privacy considerations square measure major obstacles for information suppliers to share their information in wireless networks. The outpouring of personal information will result in severe problems on the far side loss for the suppliers. We tend to initial style a blockchain scepters secure information sharing design for distributed multiple parties during this article. Then, we tend to formulate the information sharing drawback into a machine-learning (ML) drawback by incorporating privacy-preserved federate learning [19]. Privacy is well-maintained by sharing the information model rather than revealing the particular data. Finally, we tend to integrate federate learning within the agreement method of permission blockchain, so the computing work for the agreement may also be used for federate coaching. Numerical results derived from real-world information sets show that the projected data sharing theme achieves sensible accuracy, high potency, and increased security.

6.1.4   Federated Learning in Medical Computing Field

Federated learning is an AI strategy that prepares a calculation across various workers, and it keeps the information tests without trading information. This methodology makes the stands instead of unified, and AI and the informational indexes are in one worker. Machine learning models are helpful without sharing data [4]. This helps us with critical issues such as data privacy, data security, and data access rights and to data. Different industries across the world use this application. A few investigations say that the capability of profound learning in distinguishing complex examples prompting indicative identification of sufficiently large datasets. For training is a significant challenge in medicine and rarely found in individual institutions. Furthermore, the multi-institutional joint efforts dependent on halfway shared patient information face under the security and different difficulties. For information private multi-institutional joint effort model learning all accessible and information without dividing information among the organizations by appropriating the information proprietors and conglomerating their outcomes, clinical reception of united learning is relied upon to prompt models prepared on a dataset of uncommon size and thus it has a synergist sway towards the customized medication.

AI has arisen as a promising methodology for building precise measurable models from the clinical information gathered in tremendous volumes by the cutting-edge medical services frameworks. Existing clinical information isn't completely abused by ML since its information and protection concerns limit admittance to this information. Notwithstanding, without admittance to adequate information, ML will be kept from arriving at its maximum capacity and eventually making progress from examination to clinical practice. To properly consider key components adding to the issue, investigating how unified learning may give us an answer for the fate of computerized wellbeing features and difficulties in contemplations this should be tended, for instance, preparing an AI-based tumor finder requires an enormous data set incorporating the full range of potential life structures, pathologies, and information types. Information like this is difficult to acquire because wellbeing information is exceptionally delicate, and its utilization is firmly controlled. Regardless of whether information anonymization could sidestep these constraints, it is currently surely known that eliminating metadata, for example, patient name or the date of birth, is frequently insufficient to save privacy. It is, for instance, conceivable to recreate a patient's face from the processed tomography and attractive reverberation imaging information. Another motivation behind why information sharing isn't deliberate in medical care is that gathering, curating, and keeping a great informational index takes impressive time, exertion, and cost. Thus, such datasets may have critical business esteem, making them more out-landish they will be openly shared. All things considered; information authorities frequently hold fine-grained command over to information they have accumulated.

Applications of federated learning in medical computing field are explained as follows.

6.1.4.1   Federated Learning in Medical Healthcare

Federated learning holds extraordinary guarantees on medical services information examination. For instance, assembling model for foreseeing emergency clinic readmission hazard with the patient Electronic Health Records and buyer patient-based applications and screening atrial fibrilla-tion with electrocardiograms caught by brilliant, the touchy patient infor-mation can remain either in nearby organizations or with singular buyers without going out during the federated learning measure which adequately ensures the patient protection. This paper aims to survey the arrangement of federated learning, examine the overall performances and difficulties, and imagine its applications in medical services [19]. EHRs have arisen as a critical wellspring of genuine medical services information utilized for a blend of significant biomedical examination and machine learning research.

6.1.4.2   Data Privacy in Healthcare

Nowadays, artificial intelligence is facing many challenges. Among the many challenges, two of the major challenges are data in the form of isolated forms in most industries [5]. The other is to increase the strength of data and privacy and security. To solve this problem, we propose a solution to secure federated learning. In 2016 Google intro-duced the first federated learning. We introduced a better secured fed-erated framework that includes both vertical and horizontal learning and federated transfer learning [5]. The applications of the federated learning frameworks provide a comprehensive survey in this subject in addition to this, and we also propose to build a data network among the different organizations to get an effective solution based on a federated mechanism that allows sharing the knowledge without compromising user privacy.

6.1.5 Federated Learning in Blockchain

It is an open-source technology where a blockchain could be a growing list of records (blocks), which are unit-connected mistreatment cryptography [7]. Every block has a scientific discipline hash of the last block, a time-stamp, and dealing knowledge (delineated as a Merkle tree). By design, a blockchain is a proof against modification of its knowledge. This is often as a result of once recorded, the information in any given block cannot be altered retroactively while no alteration of all subsequent blocks. For each round of federated learning, the user's update will be added to the buffer with other information on the update process [21]. A committee consisting of several members responsible for verifying the update will conduct the consensus. If more than half of the members confirm an update meets all the criteria, it will be added to the blockchain.

Committee consensus:

We should have to verify these before adding the block to the blockchain.

1. If the update of local parameters is qualified for aggregation.
2. If the generated hash of the block is valid and satisfies the difficulty criteria.
3. If the previous hash stored in the block matches the hash of the latest block in the blockchain [7].

Committee consensus allowed the overall validation of a local model update before being further aggregated into a global model. End-point data corruption with varying degrees of noise and occlusion added was employed to evaluate the adaptability and robustness of the scheme.

Applications of federated learning in Blockchain are as follows.

6.1.5.1 Blockchain-Based Federated Learning Against End-Point Adversarial Data

Researcher considered scenarios, where an adversarial user in the scheme trains the local model with corrupted training data purposely. A scheme consists of three users who train their local convolution neural networks to classify the binary images of handwritten digits from the MNIST dataset. We divided the training set, with a total of 60000 images, randomly into three datasets, as the local dataset of the user.

Salt and pepper noise: Adding random noise to the local data.
Occlusion: Using a randomly positioned circle with various diameters.

6.2 Advantages of Federated Learning

Data privacy and data secrecy: The data is divided into small parts, so it is difficult for others to hack it. The parameters are encoded before sharing between local data rounds for computation. It is more personalized. It has more data protection. It keeps private data local. Information sharing is through model parameters sharing. Parameter aggregation is at the central server for global model generation. It is used in developing self-driving cars, health department, IoT, Cloud computing, Edge computing, and many more [7].

6.3 Conclusion

In this chapter, we have focused on various applications of federated learning in computing technologies. In each section, we have explained multiple applications of federated learning in various fields. Using this theoretical bound, we will implement models related to federated learning to maintain privacy and secrecy. Future work can investigate how to make the most efficient use of federated learning.

References

1. Lu, X., Liao, Y., Lio, P., Hui, P., Privacy-preserving asynchronous federated learning mechanism for edge network computing. *IEEE Access*, 8, 48970–48981, 2020.
2. Fantacci, R. and Picano, B., Federated learning framework for mobile edge computing networks. *CAAI Trans. Intell. Technol.*, 5, 1, 15–21, 2020.
3. Nguyen, T.D., Marchal, S., Miettinen, M., Fereidooni, H., Asokan, N., Sadeghi, A.D., IoT: A federated self-learning anomaly detection system for IoT, in: *39th IEEE International Conference on Distributed Computing Systems (ICDCS)*, 2019.
4. Rieke, N., Hancox, J., Li, W., Milletari, F., Roth, H.R., Albarqouni, S., Cardoso, M.J., The future of digital health with federated learning. *NPJ Digital Med.*, 3, 1, 1–7, 2020.
5. Choudhury, O., Gkoulalas-Divanis, A., Salonidis, T., Sylla, I., Park, Y., Hsu, G., Das, A., *Differential privacy-enabled federated learning for sensitive health data*, arXiv preprint arXiv:1910.02578, 2019.
6. Kim, H., Park, J., Bennis, M., Kim, S.L., Block-chained on-device federated learning. *IEEE Commun. Lett.*, 24, 6, 1279–1283, 2019.
7. Sun, Y., Esaki, H., Ochiai, H., Blockchain-based federated learning against end-point adversarial data corruption, in: *19th IEEE International Conference on Machine Learning and Applications (ICMLA)*, pp. 729–734, 2020.

8. He, K., Zhang, X., Ren, S., Sun, J., Delving deep into rectifiers: Surpassing human-level performance on ImageNet classification. *Presented at the IEEE Int. Conf. Comput. Vis. (ICCV)*, Dec. 2015.

9. Mishra, S.K., Sahoo, B., Parida, P.P., Load balancing in cloud computing: A big picture. *J. King Saud Univ.-Comput. Inf. Sci.*, 32, 2, 149–158, 2020.

10. Mishra, S.K., Puthal, D., Sahoo, B., Jena, S.K., Obaidat, M.S., An adaptive task allocation technique for green cloud computing. *J. Supercomput.*, 74, 1, 370–385, 2018.

11. Wu, Q., He, K., Chen, X., Personalized federated learning for intelligent IoT applications: A cloud-edge based framework. *IEEE Open J. Comput. Soc.*, 1, 34–44, 2020.

12. Gour, L. and Waoo, A., Implementing fault resilient strategies in cloud computing via federated learning approach. *J. Innov. Appl. Res.*, 4, 1, 2021.

13. Liu, L., Zhang, J., Song, S.H., Letaief, K.B., Client-edge-cloud hierarchical federated learning, in: *IEEE International Conference on Communications (ICC)*, 2020.

14. Ye, D., Yu, R., Pan, M., Han, Z., Federated learning in vehicular edge computing: A selective model aggregation approach. *IEEE Access*, 8, 23920–23935, 2020.

15. Mishra, S.K., Puthal, D., Sahoo, B., Sharma, S., Xue, Z., Zomaya, A.Y., Energy-efficient deployment of edge data centers for mobile clouds in sustainable IoT. *IEEE Access*, 6, 56587–56597, 2018.

16. Vyas, J., Das, D., Das, S.K., Vehicular edge computing based driver recommendation system using federated learning, in: *2020 IEEE 17th International Conference on Mobile Ad Hoc and Sensor Systems (MASS)*, pp. 675–683, 2020.

17. Mishra, S.K., Khan, M.A., Sahoo, S., Sahoo, B., Allocation of energy-efficient task in cloud using DVFS. *Int. J. Comput. Sci. Eng.*, 18, 2, 154–163, 2019.

18. Mishra, S.K., Sahoo, S., Sahoo, B., Jena, S.K., Energy-efficient service allocation techniques in cloud: A survey. *IETE Tech. Rev.*, 37, 4, 339–352, 2020.

19. Qiu, T., Wang, X., Chen, C., Atiquzzaman, M., Liu, L., TMED: A spider web-like transmission mechanism for emergency data in vehicular ad hoc networks. *IEEE Trans. Veh. Technol.*, 67, 9, 8682–8694, Sep. 2018.

20. Xu, J., Glicksber, B.S., Su, C., Walker, P., Bian, J., Wang, F., Federated learning for healthcare informatics. *J. Healthc. Inform. Res.*, 5, 1, 1–19, 2021.

21. Pokhrel, S.R. and Jinho, C., Federated learning with block chain for autonomous vehicles: Analysis and design challenges. *IEEE Trans. Commun.*, 68, 8, 4734–4746, 2020.

22. Mishra, S.K., Puthal, D., Rodrigues, J.J., Sahoo, B., Dutkiewicz, E., Sustainable service allocation using a metaheuristic technique in a fog server for industrial applications. *IEEE Trans. Industr. Inform.*, 14, 10, 4497–4506, 2018.

23. Mishra, S.K., Puthal, D., Sahoo, B., Jayaraman, P.P., Jun, S., Zomaya, A.Y., Ranjan, R., Energy-efficient VM-placement in cloud data center. *Sustain. Comput.: Inform. Syst.*, 20, 48–55, 2018.

7

Analyzing the Application of Edge Computing in Smart Healthcare

Parul Verma* and Umesh Kumar

Amity Institute of Information Technology, Amity University, Uttar Pradesh, Lucknow, India

Abstract

The evolution of IoT devices is not only to facilitate the human lives, but at the same time its potential is exploited by various industries that include agriculture industry, healthcare industry, manufacturing industry, and everything in between. It provides wide range of applications to these industries and makes them to work more smartly, accurately and efficiently. IoT Architecture consists of various connected devices; they may be sensors, smart phones, or wearables that produce data which is transmitted to the cloud through IoT gateway. After processing and analyzing the data, the resultant data is forwarded back to the device for execution of further tasks. The volume of the collected raw data is huge that consequences various challenges like low latency, high bandwidth, data analysis and many more. Integrating edge computing into existing IoT architecture is a possible solution to overcome these challenges. Edge computing supports data processing near to the devices that generates it. In this chapter we are going to present an analytical view of application of edge computing for Smart Healthcare and discuss various edge architectures that are available and are being exploited by the smart healthcare applications along with the prospective uses cases in healthcare sector.

Keywords: IoT, edge computing, smart healthcare, real time analytics

---

Corresponding author: pverma1@lko.amity.edu

Danda B. Rawat, Lalit K Awasthi, Valentina Emilia Balas, Mohit Kumar and Jitendra Kumar Samriya (eds.) Convergence of Cloud with AI for Big Data Analytics: Foundations and Innovation, (121–156) © 2023 Scrivener Publishing LLC

7.1   Internet of Things (IoT)

In last years, the scope of the internet is expanded, and it is not limited between two or more computers but something more than that. Now internet allows connecting wide range of devices or things which are around us like bulb, refrigerator, washers, and dryers, AC, wearables, and so on. Interconnection of such devices to the internet is coined a term as IoT (Internet of Things). IoT devices are capable in sending data, receiving data and computing the data without human intervention. Such devices are considered as smart devices and allow us to live smart life. Such smart devices change our way of living and transform it into smart living. For example: Handling your home appliances with smart phone from remote location. Gubbi *et al.* [1] presented an implement of IoT setup that is cloud based and elaborated the technologies and applications to be used in near future.

In addition to our smart home appliances, IoT (Figure 7.1) is an essential technology in other industries like smart healthcare, smart farming, smart manufacturing, smart transportation and many more. In manufacturing industry, it allows companies to automate processes that reduce the overall cost, reduce wastage of materials, and improve quality of product. In healthcare sector it helps in early detection of diseases and remote monitoring of patient. If we talk about smart transportation it helps to predict traffic congestion.

7.1.1   IoT Communication Models

The standard guidelines in the form of architectural document were released by Internet Architecture Board (IAB) in the year 2015. The guidelines outlined four communication models for IoT devices. Rose *et al.* [2]

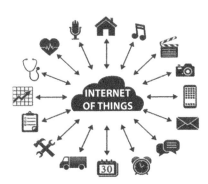

Figure 7.1 Internet of Things.

briefly discuss the various technical communications models described by IAB and highlight the flexibility of connecting IoT devices. The discussion below explains key characteristics of each model.

Device-to-Device (D-to-D) Communication: In this type of communication two or more devices connect and communicate without intervention of any other device. Such devices connect and communicate with each other using different types of protocols like Bluetooth, Z-wave, and Zigbee. This communication model (Figure 7.2) is commonly used in to control home appliances (like smart light bulb, smart door lock, smart switch etc.) where small packet of information needs to be communicated with low data rate. The limitation of this model is interoperability. It means devices belong to Z-wave protocols are not compatible with devices belongs to Zigbee protocols.

Device-to-Cloud (D-to-C) Communication: In Figure 7.3, this type of model IoT devices directly communicates to cloud service provider. This model support data storage and computation in cloud due to the limited data storage and computation power of IoT devices. It uses existing communication structure like wired Ethernet or WiFi connection to connect devices with cloud server. The performance of this model basically depends on bandwidth and available network resources.

Device-to-Gateway (D-to-G) Communication: In Figure 7.4, device-to-gateway communication model IoT devices are connected to cloud service provider through gateway. Application layer gateway will act as an intermediary between devices and cloud service provider. This model improves the security and brings some level of computation at application layer that improves the performance of IoT devices. For instance, Smartphone act as a gateway that runs some application to communicate with IoT devices and the cloud.

Figure 7.2 D-to-D communication model.

Figure 7.3 D-to-C communication model.

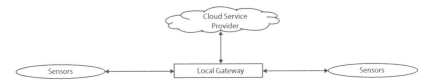

Figure 7.4 D-to-G communication model.

7.1.2   IoT Architecture

IoT architecture (Figure 7.5) is basically classified into three layers. The upcoming and latest technologies are upgrading these layers day by day. Sethi and Sarangi [3] had elaborated IoT architecture in their work. They also explained about protocols, and various applications of IoT in versatile domain.

IoT Devices

IoT devices collect data through various sensors that are connected to each other. The data collected by these sensors is transferred further to IoT gateway. These devices are called as data generator devices and they generate different types of data like environmental data, health data, and motion data to name a few.

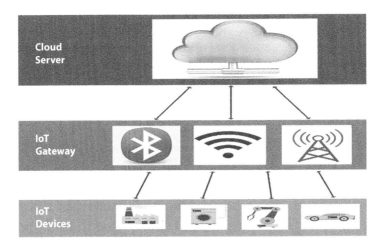

Figure 7.5 Layered architecture of IoT.

IoT Gateway

The role of IoT gateway is to perform data processing on the collected data from variety of sensors. The initial processing of data will convert it into meaningful data which is further transmitted to the cloud server. There are many data transfer technologies that might be used like- ZigBee, Bluetooth, Wireless Area Network, Wi-Fi etc.

Cloud Server

Cloud servers are used to store huge volume of data generated by sensors and passed to them through IoT gateway. Data is processed and analyzed and drawn results, by application of various machine learning algorithms. The results are transmitted to the end user in the form of some alert message, text message of may be through email. For example: Any fluctuations in health related data of the patients will send alarm to the concerned healthcare center.

7.1.3   Protocols for IoT

The protocols can be defined as collection of norms that mention common set of standards for data exchange among various devices. In a previous section, the role of different layers in IoT architecture were described, now in this section the focus is to explain the different protocols (Figure 7.6) responsible for seamless communication among the layers. Shadi *et al.* [4] describes various protocols used in different layers for communication of data.

7.1.3.1   *Physical/Data Link Layer Protocols*

The section will elaborate various physical and MAC layer protocols. The role of these protocols is to connect various IoT devices; it may be two

Application Layer		MQTT, CoAP, AMQP, XMPP .....
Transport Layer		TCP, UDP
Network Layer	Encapsulation	6LowPAN, 6Lo, 6TiSCH ....
	Routing	RPL, CORPL, CARP ....
Physical/Data Link Layer		BLE, ZigBee, Z-Wave, WiFi, LoRaWAN, 802.11 AH ....

Figure 7.6 IoT protocol stack.

sensors or sensors and gateway. There are many protocols functioning at this layer, but some most commonly used protocols are discussed below:

Bluetooth: It is used for short range communications and works at 2.4 GHz in ISM band. It works on the concept of master and slave. In two connected Bluetooth device one may by master and other one will be slave [5]. Two new protocols are introduced under IoT protocols Bluetooth Low Energy (BLE) or Bluetooth Smart for the low power consumption devices. As compared to classical protocol it uses less power and less latency as well. These protocols use adverting and data frames, when nodes are communicating then only, they are awake.

ZigBee: This IoT protocol is meant to be used in applications with less frequent data exchange. The connectivity range between nodes is 100 meters and data transmission rate is 250 Kbps. The protocol is normally used with the applications related to building and home automation, industrial control system etc. It is latest version 3.0 is based on IEEE 802.15.4 standard. It is the unification of the various ZigBee wireless standards into a single standard. Another variant ZigBee smart energy is developed for variety of IoT applications, and it supports different types of topologies as well like peer-to-peer, cluster-tree, or star. This protocol is easier to install and maintain. Zigbee Alliance [6] established in 2002 is responsible for maintaining and publishing the Zigbee standards.

Z-Wave: This wireless protocol uses low energy radio waves and it is basically meant to be used with home appliances. Z-wave [7] allows the user to control the home appliances remotely like light control, door lock, thermostats etc. via the internet from a smart phone or tablet. In different countries it operates at different frequencies and covers physical range 100 meters. It supports data rates up to 100kbit/s. Like Bluetooth it also follows master/slave architecture where master sends the command to slaves and controls the whole network. It is MAC protocol and uses CSMA/CA for collision detection to avoid the possibility of data loss. [RFC 5826] elaborates the basic requirements for the data routing over lossy and low power networks specifically for home appliances.

LoRaWAN: This Long Range Wide Area Network protocol covers long range and consumes less power. It is basically used for the intercommunication between smart devices that consume low power and meant to be used in smart cities. The LoRaWAN [8] uses varied frequency in variety of networks and the data transmission rate is varied between 0.3

Kbps-50 Kbps. [RFC 8376] describes an overview of the LoRaWAN protocol and architecture.

WiFi: The IEEE 802.11 standard (also called WiFi). The commonly used protocol for intercommunication among devices to transfers the high-speed data i.e. up to 1 Gbps. The frequencies are 2.4GHz and 5GHz bands. The range it covers is 50 m. It works in integration of IP (Internet Protocol) IEEE 802.11, but it is not appropriate for IoT applications due to power consumption and frame overhead issue. To overcome this problem IEEE 802.11ah was developed. The elementary 802.11ah MAC layer had features like efficient bidirectional packet exchange, increase sleep time, short MAC frame.

7.1.3.2 Network Layer Protocols

The basic functions performed by network layer are Routing and Encapsulation. Packet formation is facilitated by protocols at encapsulation layer whereas for selecting the optimal path for packet transfer is facilitated by protocols at routing layer. Some important protocols are discussed below.

Routing Protocol for Low-Power and Lossy Networks (RPL): The protocol works on distance vector algorithm. Each node maintains a record of routing table. The algorithm works on the principal of periodic updating of routing table by fetching information from neighbor node. RPL [9] organize a topology as a Direct Acyclic Graph (DAG) that is partitioned into one or more Destination Oriented DAGs (DODAG). DODAG has only one route from each leaf node to the root. To establish communication between leaf node and any other node, it sends Destination Advertisement Object (DAO) to its parent node and then further DAO it is transmitted to root node. Finally, root node will take decision to send the communication request to the respective node at it has complete knowledge of entire DODAG. [RFC 6550] specifies the IPv6 routing protocol for low-power and lossy networks that supports point to point, multipoint to point and point to multipoint traffic. An extension of RPL is Cognitive RPL (CORPL) that is designed for cognitive network.

Channel-Aware Routing Protocol (CARP): It is a lightweight distributed routing protocol used for IoT. It is a protocol design for underwater wireless sensors. It provides significant performance in term of latency and power consumption. CARP avoids loops and forward the packets in a hop-by-hop manner. The drawback of the protocol is to not support reusability of data collected earlier. E-CARP is an enhancement of CARP that overcomes the problem of reusability of data and reduce the communication overhead.

IPv6 over Low power Wireless Personal Area Network (6LoWPAN): Due to quite long addresses in IPv6 they are not fit for data frames for IoT data link as the frames are smaller in size. 6LoWPAN [10] allows encapsulating IPv6 datagram in MAC layer frames for use in IoT applications. The important features of this protocols that makes it suitable for IoTs are: supports different network topologies, low bandwidth, low power consumption, long sleep time, mobility, scalability, reliability, and size cannot exceed 128 byte length. 6LoWPAN uses four headers: 00, 01, 10, and 11 which means No 6LoWPAN headers, dispatch headers, mesh headers, and fragmentation headers respectively. 00 is used to discard that frames that does not follow 6LoWPAN specification, 01 used for multicasting and compression, 10 is used for broadcasting and 11is used to break long headers. [RFC 8138] specifies IPv6 over 6LoWPAN routing header that supports low power and lossy network.

IPv6 over Time-Slotted Channel Hopping (6TiSCH): These are the protocols to make specifications for passing long headers through TSCH [11] mode of IEEE 802.15.4e data links.It specifies ways to pass long IPv6 headers through TSCH [11] mode of IEEE 802.15.4e data links. The working is based on channel distribution matrix that consist available frequencies in column and their time slots in row. The complete matrix is classified into various sections that consist of information related to time and frequencies which are visible to all nodes in a network. [RFC 8180] mentions minimal mode of operation for an IPv6 over the TSCH mode of IEEE 802.15.4e network.

7.1.3.3   Transport Layer Protocols

Transport layer focuses on end-to-end communication and ensure complete delivery of packets. It also ensures that packets are arriving in order at destination, congestion avoidance, and flow control in network. Transmission Control Protocol (TCP) and User Datagram Protocol (UDP) are two most common protocols working in this layer.

Transmission Control Protocol (TCP): It is a connection-oriented protocol that provides reliable data transmission. It means there is a guarantee that data will reach to destination without losing the integrity of data. TCP [12] protocol establish the virtual path before sending the data to destination, once connection is established then sends the data and finally terminate the connection after successful delivery of data. The packet overhead is very large and consumes more power from the devices, so it is not suitable for the low power devices. [RFC 9006] provide guidance on how to implement and use TCP in constrained node network and explains various techniques to simplify a TCP stack.

User Datagram Protocol (UDP): It is a connectionless and non-reliable protocol as there is a chance of packet loss before reaching to destination but provide fast data transmission in comparison to TCP protocol. Here each packet is independent and select their own path to reach to the destination, there is no predefined path like TCP that is why there is a chance that some packets may struck somewhere in a network and considers as lost packet. After reaching to destination all packets will rearrange because there is possibility that packets will reach in different order as they selected different paths. It is a light weighted protocol that is the reason it is suitable for wireless sensor network communications. UDP protocol is useful for real time application like watching live on your mobile.

7.1.3.4   Application Layer Protocols

This layer protocols helps to provide services offered by any application to the users in a seamless manner. There are many protocols working in this layer, but some common protocols are discussed below.

Message Queue Telemetry Transport (MQTT): The MQTT was initially presented by IBM in the year 1999 and later on in the year 2013 OASIS finally standardized it. It is transport meant for the purpose of messaging and works on the principal of publish/subscribe. It is heterogeneous in nature and its basic role is to monitor heterogeneous devices in the network [13]. It is made up of three basic components- subscriber, publisher, and broker. Publishers are generally light weighted sensors that generate data and transmit data to the subscribers with the help of broker. Initially data is sent from publisher to broker, then the data is classified in topics at broker and finally broker informs to subscribers for any new arrival of data and reverts them their topic of interest.

Advanced Message Queuing Protocol (AMQP): It works at application layer and its major role is to transmit data seamlessly and in a secure manner.

Its basic role is to transmit data between cloud and other connected devices with the help of TCP protocol. AMQP [14] architecture is very much similar to MQTT instead of broker is sub divided into two parts. Broker has three core components: Exchange, Binding, and Message Queue. The role of exchange is to receive message and put them in queue. The message queue stores the message until consumed by client app. The binding component is meant for connecting, exchanging, and messaging queue data. Initially exchange will receive the publisher message, then distributes to message queue according to predefined role and conditions there it is classified as topics and finally subscribed by subscriber whenever data is available in message queue.

Constrained Application Protocol (CoAP): It works on the principle of client-server model and its basic role is to make HTTP protocol adaptable to the low power devices and gadgets. CoAP [15] architecture is classified into messaging and request/response layer. UDP (User Datagram Protocol) is used to connect two ends. The messaging technique of CoAP is classified as confirmable, non-confirmable, piggyback and separate that represents reliable transmission, non-reliable transmission, response is send with acknowledgement and response and acknowledgement sends separately respectively. [RFC 7252] defines specification of CoAP usage in the constrained network and it is designed to be get easily integrated with HTTP protocol.

Extensible Messaging and Presence Protocol (XMPP): There are two architecture supported by XMPP – publish/subscribe and request/response and any one of them can be selected by developer. The base of XMPP [16] protocol is XML language and is basically used as communications protocol. Lot of power consumption is involved with XML messages due to headers and tags involved in it and hence considered appropriate for IoT applications. However, later the architecture is enhanced so that XML communication may support IoT applications. Various mode of communications is allowed by this protocol like voice/video calls, chat (multi party), routing of XML data to name a few. The protocol does not support end to end encryption and QoS.

7.1.4   IoT Applications

IoT applications make our life smart and safe. There are many sectors where we found it is playing an important role like smart house, smart healthcare, smart farming, smart manufacturing, smart transportation and many more. Zeinab and Elmustafa [17] reviewed various application of IoT and suggested future avenues for many related technologies. Some applications are discussed below.

Smart Home: The concept of smart home refers to a technology where home appliances and devices can be controlled remotely from anywhere with the help of smart phone, laptop or tablet. The wide range of devices and home appliances are interconnected through the internet that makes the user to control it remotely like room temperature, light, door lock, washers and dryers, refrigerator and many more. Electricity prediction and home security are the most useful applications in smart home as it helps to forecast home energy consumption and allows monitoring home remotely. Matta and Pant [18] addresses the current trends, major research challenges, and application domains in the field of Internet-of-Things (IoT).

Smart Healthcare: Healthcare is one of the applications of IoT that makes many researchers, industries and the public sector to work on it. IoT technology makes doctors to monitor the patient remotely and allows patient to visit virtually. In this way it improves the quality of care and reduces the cost of care in comparison of traditional method of healthcare. It also helps hospital to track patient, staff, and various equipment. As many healthcare devices IoT it helps in early detection of diseases. Dang *et al.* [19] in the year 2015 gave an analytic review on the prominent usage of IoT devices in the healthcare industry.

Smart Farming: Smart farming is a concept of farming integrating it with technologies like IoT, Artificial Intelligence, Drones, Sensors, Robotics. IoT may help in resolving many critical issues of traditional farming and improves productivity at a lower cost. Smart farming includes various activities like remote monitoring of crop, automation of irrigation, weather forecasting, analyzing ideal time of plantation and harvesting, detection of pests, observing soil conditions and many more [20]. Smart farming relates to improvement in both quality and quantity with low risk. Gill *et al.* [21] suggested an automatic information system for smart farming based on cloud server. The system provides updated and required information the end-users automatically.

Smart Manufacturing: Industry 4.0 or in other word smart industry represents revolution in manufacturing industry. It is a fourth generation of industry where entire manufacturing process is automated that increases the overall profit of company. It changes how products are invented, manufactured and shipped. Each machines and various industrial equipment are embedded with sensors that generate data which is helpful to analyze the errors in productions process and takes correct action. Vuksanović *et al.* [22] discussed the role of IoT devices and its usage in the future scenario of the factories.

Smart Transportation: The idea of smart transportation deals with predicting the traffic congestion in advance that helps the user to avoid unnecessary traffic jam by knowing the alternative route. As in many countries' government is supporting to design electric vehicles to reduce the fuel cost and impact of global warming. In some countries there is a progressive research in the direction of designing self-driving car. In such types of research IoT will perform an important task like detecting pedestrians, traffic signs, obstacles etc. Ferdowsi *et al.* [23] discuss deep learning in intelligent transportation systems for traffic flow prediction, self-driving car and traffic signal.

7.1.5 IoT Challenges

Internet of things applications outlined above is rapidly increasing over last few years but still there are some challenges while implementing IoT. Omid Helmi *et al.* [24] analyzed and elaborated different types of challenges that are there in IoT environment. Following are the area of concern-

Security and Privacy: IoT devices do share lot of personalized data of the end user, this leads to the various security and privacy concerns for that data. In a study it has been observed that almost 70 percent of IoT devices are vulnerable in nature due to non-availability of standard encryption and authentication techniques. The manufactures and policy makers should frame some standards to deal with this scenario. Alansari *et al.* [25] elaborated about vulnerabilities of IoT systems and discussed about various model that may be used to protect data and systems.

Interoperability: IoT includes millions of interconnected devices over the internet. These devices are smart devices and able to process the information. But each device has different information, processing, and communication capabilities as the manufacturing companies around the globe produce various product categories. Interoperability among heterogeneous devices connected in any application is one of the critical issues with IoT devices. There are numerous interoperability challenges that can be dazed by the proposed CoRE framework by Mazayev *et al.* [26].

Data Analytics: The voluminous amount of data generated by heterogeneous IoT devices cannot be analyzed in a proper manner due to poor quality of data. It is a tough task to segregate useful and useless data among such huge volume of data. There are numerous challenges regarding data management that are pointed by Cooper and James [27].

Volume of Data: Some IoT applications include frequent communication between devices and continuous collection of data that will increase the volume of raw data. The processing, storing and management of huge amount of data is another challenging task with IoT technology. Constante *et al.* [28] in his work analyzed the impact of large volume of data and the processing challenges. They also draw attention towards research works tools used for such data analysis.

Power Supply: The smart IoT devices are not connected with continuous power supply hence they need self-reliant energy source. The power consumption depends mainly on data processing, transmission, and sensing as well. The power supply requirement for the wireless technologies is towards higher side be it Bluetooth or Wi-Fi. This generates a demand of less power consuming wireless technologies. Perković *et al.* [29] developed power estimation analysis system. The core work of their system it the sum up the various possibilities for its future use.

7.2   Edge Computing

Centralization and Decentralization is the core of computing. In a history in each decade a wave shifts from centralization to decentralization. Starting from mainframes and then shifting to personal computers and then again moving on to the cloud. In the last two decades we were storing each and everything on cloud even our personal data. Cloud has it pros and cons like any other technology; privacy of data and cost management are the two major drawbacks of cloud [30].

The latest wave of decentralization is in the name of Edge computing. It lies between the date generation sources like sensors and other IoT devices and cloud server. Weisong *et al.* [31] addressed the various issues related to the edge computing, current status and future avenues. Edge resolves the latency issue of cloud and bandwidth issue by transferring only relevant data to the cloud after performing real-time processing.

7.2.1 Cloud vs. Fog vs. Edge

In this section, Table 7.1 compare cloud computing, fog computing and edge computing.

Table 7.1 Cloud vs. fog vs. edge.

	Cloud computing	Fog computing	Edge computing
Architecture	Centralized	Distributed	Distributed
Processing of data	Central cloud server which is very far from source of data.	LAN hardware or IoT gateway	Sensors connected devices
Processing Power	Advanced processing technology	Low processing	Low processing
Storage	High	Medium	Low
Purpose	Data analytics for long term processing	Quick analysis for real time response	Real Time Analytics
Advantages	Scalable, Big data processing, Unlimited storage	Low latency, Data security, Low bandwidth, Reduce network traffic	Low latency, Data security, Low bandwidth, Reduce network traffic, low power consumption
Disadvantages	High latency, Slow response time, High power consumption	Limited processing and storage	Limited processing and storage

7.2.2   Existing Edge Computing Reference Architecture

The new paradigm of computing in network environment is edge computing, where resources and services are now shifting from cloud to the edge. Edge is now gaining momentum and various researchers provided different architecture, capabilities, terms and features for Edge architecture. The following section elaborates various reference architectures (RA) with respect to edge computing.

7.2.2.1   FAR-EDGE Reference Architecture

FAR-EDGE RA [32] is an effort of leading experts in manufacturing, industrial automation and future internet (FI) technologies. According to this RA there are two viewpoint of a factory automation- functional viewpoint and structural viewpoint. Functional viewpoint focuses the functionality of the industries and divided it into three domains- Automation, Analytics and Simulation whereas structural viewpoint represents the detailed structure of factory automations that covers the various steps from collecting the data to utilizing the processed data. Figure 7.7 represents four tiers under structural viewpoint – Field Tier, Edge Tier, Ledger Tier and Cloud Tier.

7.2.2.2   Intel-SAP Joint Reference Architecture (RA)

Intel and SAP [33] developed reference architecture for edge computing environment that delivers solutions for cloud and sensors integration. The

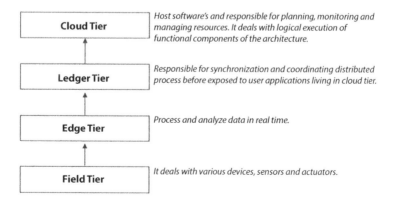

Figure 7.7 FAR-EDGE reference architecture.

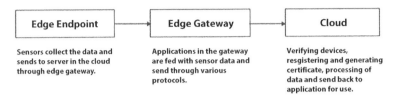

Figure 7.8 Intel-SAP joint reference architecture.

RA facilitates the enterprises to understand the secure management of smart network of IoT devices. The network of IoT devices collects, manages and analyze the data and combine it with business intelligence. Figure 7.8 represents the various blocks of Intel-SAP joint RA.

7.2.3   Integrated Architecture for IoT and Edge

The integrated architecture of IoT and edge (Figure 7.9) helps in eradication of various challenges in the existing architecture. It handles voluminous data, issue of latency, privacy and many more. The edge facilitates processing of collected data near to the source like gateway, router, laptop etc. The core of edge computing is to reduce overhead on cloud. Wei Yu *et al.* [34] briefed the integration of IoT with edge and elaborated its challenges and benefits.

Sensors and Actuators: In IoT environment data is generated through sensors and they are capable to sense the surrounding environment such as temperature sensors, humidity sensors, motion sensors, smoke sensor, gas sensor etc. The role of actuators is to convert energy into motion.

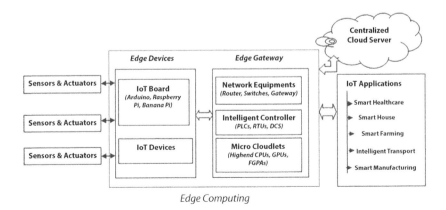

Figure 7.9 Integrated architecture for IoT and edge.

Sensors are capable data collection only, so the data collected with these sensors pass to IoT board that is capable in data processing and data communication.

Edge Computing: The latency in case of edge computing is reduced in various real time applications by performing data processing just near to the source of data generating devices. Edge computing improves the performances of IoT devices, reduces bandwidth utilization and provided better security and privacy. It helps to offload the various important tasks which are earlier performed by the centralized server called cloud server. It includes two major components one is called edge devices and the other one is edge gateway.

Edge Devices: Edge devices perform real time data processing based on the trained model. These devices are either IoT devices which is a primary source of raw data or IoT board that is directly connected to the sensors which collects the real-world data. There are some single board computing devices are also available that are so powerful and smart enough to replace the desktop in near future. These devices are even capable to execute machine learning algorithms and very small in size and low in cost. Some of the popular single board computers and their specifications are – Raspberry Pi 4 model, Latte Panda Alpha, Udoo Bolt and Jetson Nano (NVIDIA).

Edge Gateway: Edge gateway performs pre – processing of data, allows data storage and various intelligent algorithms are installed. The devices that can be used as edge gateway are network devices (like routers, switches, and gateway), intelligent controllers (like PLCs, RTUs, and DCS) and micro cloudlets. Micro cloudlets are also called as micro data centers with high end processing speed, large amount data storage capacity and high bandwidth wireless LAN. The Edge gateway provides communication standards for various interfaces like wire, radio-based and technologies like – Bluetooth, 3G mobile radio, ZigBee, Z-Wave, LTE. Preprocessing of data and preliminary learning of data at edge gateway will help to offload the work of centralized cloud server that results the performance of the time sensitive applications will improve and provides the benefits to the end user.

Centralized Cloud Server: Cloud server is accountable for further processing of data received from edge computing layer, enhance the analysis of data by introducing advanced machine learning techniques and store the data as a historical data for future research. It mainly handles large set of data by using big data processing tools and technologies. Some of the best big data tools are Hadoop, HPCC, Storm, Qubole and many more. These tools are cost effective and incorporate time management in various data analytics tasks. It also includes some advance learning techniques called deep learning. Deep Learning (DL) creates multi-layered structure of neural networks. In comparison to ML algorithms Deep learning algorithms are step ahead. Popular DL algorithms are ANN (Artificial Neural Network), CNN (Convolutional Neural Network), RNN (Recurrent Neural Network), RBM (Restricted Boltzmann Machines), DBN(Deep Belief Network), LSTM (Long Short Term Memory Networks) to name a few. Training and testing of models are performed at cloud server and finally the trained model is deployed over edge devices to take early decision.

IoT Application: IoT applications are various apps that are delivering the services to end user and act as a user interface with the help of API (Application Programming Interface). These apps help the user to access the real time data and make them to take early decision. There are various sectors where sectors where IoT plays an important role.

7.2.4   Benefits of Edge Computing Based IoT Architecture

Introducing edge computing in IoT architecture brings various benefits in IoT implementation that includes less response time, low bandwidth and efficient communication. This section will elaborate various benefits of integrated architecture of IoT and Edge.

Network Performance: The network performance of Edge Computing environment can by evaluated on latency, network bandwidth and network traffic. Edge computing improves the performance of applications by reducing latency. Latency is basically dependent on delays (transmission, propagation, computing, and queuing). Krittin *et al.* [35] studied the effect of communication and computational latency in edge environment. The major contribution of edge is to pre-process data that results into its size reduction before transmitting it to cloud. SpanEdge reduces latency and bandwidth consumption as proposed by Sajjad *et al.* in [36].

Efficient Data Management: Processing data at edge computing will provide efficient data management. It is like preprocessing of raw data before sending to cloud server for further processing and analysis. The preprocessing involves cleaning, integration and transformation of data. Huge amount of data is collected by IoT devices, but some small percentage of total data is important that needs to be sent to cloud server. Edge computing will allow finding out important data and aggregating it that results reduced data size which will improve the analysis and helps various applications to perform their task efficiently. The advancements in edge computing with respect to its impact on IoT applications are analyzed by Hassan *et al.* in [37].

Data Analytics and AI: Edge computing will allow some extend of data analytic and artificial intelligence to those IoT services which need fast response. Artificial Intelligence (AI) is achieved by introducing machine learning models at edge itself. It will improve the learning performance as well as reduce network traffic. For example, self-driving vehicles fast response is necessary to avoid any hazardous consequences. Wazir *et al.* [38] highlighted the significant role of edge computing in versatile real time applications where sending responses in real time is the fundamental requirement of applications like healthcare applications.

Security and Privacy: Edge computing offers many operations closer to the devices that collect data. By applying various advanced tools and techniques edge will provide security of data. The distributed nature of edge computing will have limited impact if there is any attack on the network. Security services at the edge can be used to ensure that the devices which are more vulnerable will isolate easily and protect from any attack. In addition to security aspects of IoT, additional areas like confidentiality, access control, data integrity and authenticity is also in consideration to improve security and privacy. Edge and IoT integration was presented by Lin *et al.* in [39]. They also conducted a summary of IoT with respect to system architecture.

Low Power Consumption: Edge computing also contributes in reduction of power consumption by reducing data transmission load on network. Processing data near to the devices that produce it leads to reduction of power consumption. Improvement in latency may also improve battery life of IoT devices as communication channels are opened for short span of time. Impact of energy consumption in various IoT devices is analyzed by Mocnej *et al.* [40]. They also elaborated the utilization of edge computing in the IoT.

7.3 Edge Computing and Real Time Analytics in Healthcare

The concept of application of ML in integrated environment of Edge Computing and IoT is rising day by day. The combination of these technologies is now in application phase and is being deployed by many industries in various use cases. Smart devices may use ML and DL techniques at edge and reducing the burden on cloud as the processing will be performed at the local or device level.

Traditionally the data collected by IoT devices are processed by the cloud sever. The huge volume of such data overburdened cloud servers; the edge here plays a crucial role in diminishing the load of cloud server by application of ML/DL algorithms and classifying which data to be processed at edge and the other needs to be processed at cloud server by more powerful algorithms. There are many applications which need real time analytics to be performed on some crucial data especially healthcare and some financial applications; the application of ML/DL techniques at edge is an added performance benefit for such applications. Edge ML also deals with the security aspects of an application where personalized information is being stored at Cloud which is global in nature.

Healthcare sector is more and more focusing on providing better support to patients. The role of Deep Learning is becoming a promising and transformative in healthcare. Basically Deep learning models consists of multiple layers, the input data passes through multiple layers and each layer performs a kind of matrix multiplications on data. After passing through multiple layers the last layer will ultimately produces a feature set or final output. There are variety of deep learning models used in a specific scenario like – DNN (Deep Neural Network), CNN (Convolutional Neural Network) and RNN (Recurrent Neural Network). Integration of deep learning with edge computing improves real time processing which is a crucial aspect in case of healthcare systems. To address the issue of latency and quick performance in real time applications, variety of integration model of edge with deep learning are proposed.

The general architecture of an Edge Computing Environment includes a sensor/smart device and edge/fog/cloud computing node. The edge layer is being used to bridge the gap between the cloud server and the IoT devices. IoT layer consists of variety of healthcare sensors each having unique identification. The data collected from these sensors is further transferred to the edge layer using WiFi, Bluetooth, or ZigBee.

The variety of devices is being used by researchers in various healthcare models categorized as smart device, medical instruments or IoT based sensor kits. The edge devices are growing day by day starting from Nokia mobile or PDA in their initial days. The latest smart phones are now being used in variety of healthcare applications. Smart phones sensors though are easy to use but have limitation of embedding variety of sensors in it. Using dedicated medical sensors helps in collecting and handling large volume of health data that may lead to more accurate diagnosis [41].

Author Liu *et al.* [42] proposed RMCS (Remote Medical Care System) model for miners to assess their physical and mental health by making use of biosensors. They applied emotion shift theory knowledge and made use of EHR (Electronic Health Record) to draw inferences. The brain wave sensors are fixed in miner's helmet which collects data about physical and mental status of minors and issue early warning signals. The overall system uses ZigBee network. The information collected through sensors will be transmitted to minor's mobile phone and from there the information will be transmitted to backend system where the physical and mental status of miners is evaluated using EHR ontology model. In case of emergency miner's family and paramedic facilities are automatically informed.

Dubey *et al.* [43] developed a fog computing architecture (Figure 7.10) that emphasized on data reduction, low power consumption and highly efficient. Their proposed architecture is service oriented, and its main asset is low power embedded computer. The model performs data mining techniques and analytics on the data collected by number of wearable devices. The data read is in time series pattern and further analyzed by embedded computer. The analytics helps in identifying the unusual data in the series of data which are further transmitted to cloud for analysis.

The Intel's Edison processor used by them is low power device that is supported by rechargeable battery. They used the DTW (Dynamic Time wrapping) algorithm for pattern mining in data. The role of DTW is to find similarity between two data series. Further they used CLIP (Clinical Speech Processing Chain) that is a series of operation to filter speech data. To compress data they used GNU zip for compression and decompression algorithm. Fog processor reduces data transmission and storage at cloud by processing it at local level for data for healthcare.

Figure 7.10 Fog computing architecture.

Speech Monitoring for Patients of Parkinson's Disease: They collected speech data from smart watches and sent it to fog gateway. The Intel Edison processor at fog computer processes the speech data by DTW and CLIP. The features and patterns extracted at fog are further sent to the cloud. The data compression performed by DTW, CLIP and GNU. Among all CLIP achieved 99 percent of data reduction.

The authors proposed a cascading architecture as mentioned in Figure 7.10 based on fog computing which has three sub-systems as – BSN (Body Sensor Network) is used for data acquisition, the second sub-system is a fog gateway which will process the acquired data and for further back-end analysis cloud server is used. The role of fog gateway is to filter out the relevant information that needs to be transferred to the cloud server for further processing.

Gaura *et al.* [44] in their proposed work moved analytics at IoT nodes that leads to less transmission of data hence reducing network loads. This edge mining techniques takes place at the edge of IoT device. L-SLIP (Linear Spanish Inquisition Protocol), Class Act and BN (Bare Necessities) these three algorithms developed by authors are used to reduce sensing messages and eventually reducing less energy and less storage as well. Various sensors transmit redundant data, edge mining focus on saving packets rather than bits and hence improve performance.

The authors proposed the processing of data collected by various sensors at the edge nodes that are near to the sensors only and they convert raw signals into some meaningful information. The real work of edge nodes is to estimate the states and convert it into some meaningful information that is required for the application. The raw data from the sensors may give raw information like someone entered the room; however the state information like how many people are there in the room may be inferred from filtering information collected from the sensors. Further to state estimation, event detector will decide about the significant change in state.

The purpose of L-SIP algorithms is to acquire data from sensing applications and re-construct the signal if it's loses energy. The purpose of Class Act algorithm is to recognize human posture and store the various timestamps in the change in posture. The BN algorithm provides the time spent in different positions. The overall performance is recorded as L-SIP reduces the packet transmission rate by 95%, BN reduces 99.8%, and Class Act reduces packet transmission by 99.6%. The results justified the importance of edge mining in various IoT based applications.

Bhargava *et al.* [45] proposed a WNS based system for the localization of elderly suffering from Alzheimer disease. The author proposed a system that will perform analysis of data collected at the local level close to the data source for better response and detailed analysis is performed at cloud level based on historical data. The fog based wireless sensor network system was proposed by authors for outdoor localization of elderly people. The analysis was performed on data collected through wearable devices obtained from the Kasteren dataset. The proposed system is a combination of two nodes – wearable device and cloud gateway. They used genetic algorithm for the activity recognition using IEM (Iterative Edge Mining) that facilitates localization. The mining algorithms on edge are based on SIP (Spanish Inquisition Protocol) that converts raw data into application specific states. The data is further transmitted to a cloud only if it is not predicted by past estimation or approximation model. The general SIP models are as follows -

L-SIP works on sensing applications where reconstruction of original signal is required.

Class Act approach is used to detect human postures; it stores and transmits timings of change in human postures but not the original signal. It is based on decision trees; it takes signals from body worn accelerometer sensors and then performs posture estimation. It is well suited for embedding in wireless sensors, it is simple and closely knitted with the application and hence capable of making strong assumptions about the output.

BN does not keep a record of timing it is appropriate to get summarized information of time duration of different states. States are being represented in the form of distributed and non-overlapping bins. Change in distribution of these bins represents occurrence of any event. Class Act and BN are destructive approaches hence preferably used in the applications where reconstruction of signals is not required. The results confirm that our system can achieve a high positional accuracy despite a short initial training period and low frequency of data computations on the resource constrained sensor devices.

Althbeyan *et al.* [46] proposed system that collects patient data like temperature, glucose level and other activities and transmits that data to the cloudlets. The abnormal values are further transmitted to the MEC (Mobile Edge Computing) servers and removed immediately from the memory in order to maintain privacy. The decision support system attached with MEC system has to analyze only abnormal value instead of bulk of values. This reduction technique to reduce computing complexity is called inexact computing used along with morphological filtering to reduce data processing.

The model proposed consists of four major components- cloudlets, MEC system, DSS (Decision Support System), DCS (Data Collection System). Their proposed model observed reduction in power consumption and per user delay.

Bhunia et al. [47] applied fuzzy techniques for selection of data to be transmitted for analysis of data collected through IoT sensors. Authors used this technique for the identification of heart condition of the patients. They prepared knowledge base and rules for the detection of some early signs of any serious heart trouble in real time. The data collected from the various sensors is aggregated and send to fuzzifier. The role of fuzzifier is to classify the parameters using some predefined functions. Finally, fuzzy inference system processes fuzzy sets that are based on the input from rule engine.

They programmed fuzzy system on the Arduino board which they used as an aggregator in the healthcare application. The selection of data to be transmitted is done by fuzzy rules. Required data to generate alert is only transmitted. They compared normal data collection technique with their proposed technique, and they observed considerable reduction in energy consumption. By adopting this approach, they can reduce energy consumption by sending only required data over costly communication channel.

Borthakur et al. [48] proposed usage of machine learning approach on the edge computing device which requires considerable fewer amounts of resources. They collected speech data of patients suffering from Parkinson's disease through smart watches used by patients. They employed Intel Edison and Raspberry Pi as a Fog computer architecture. In general machine learning model are implemented at cloud to process physiological data for the traditional telecare model. K-means clustering algorithms are used for the analysis of data. Clustering of unlabeled data is performed at fog layer. This clustering can be helpful for the real time sub-grouping of Parkinson's disease data. They collected 164 speech samples and selected features as average fundamental frequency and intensity. The feature extraction is done using Praat an acoustic software for analysis. K-means algorithm used for clustering is implemented in Python. Their proposed architecture is useful in handling speech processing and disorders in real time. Fog computing architecture reduces the dependency on cloud server. Their work utilized low resource machine learning approach on fog device and the results show that proposed architecture is promising for low-resource machine learning.

Hosseini et al. [49] developed a system for the monitoring and regulation of epilepsy. An automated edge computing framework (Figure 7.11)

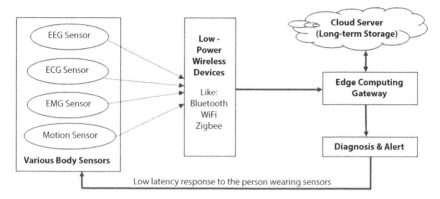

Figure 7.11 Automated edge computing framework.

proposed by them to process volume of data generated which is a part of decision support system. The estimation model for the estimation of epileptogenic network using EEG and rs-fMRI is also developed. An unsupervised technique based on Deep CNN to differentiate between interictal epileptic discharge (IED) periods and nonIED periods using electrographic signals from electrocorticography (ECoG).

Their proposed framework is divided into three layers- Sensing layer, Edge computing gateway and cloud computing layer. Sensing layer consists of various biosensors to collect physiological data like heart rate, motion etc. The sensors are wearables and implantable also and the data collected is transferred to the Edge Gateway through Bluetooth, ZigBee and Wi-Fi as well. The Edge gateway does not work just like simple Access Point or Base Station it performs initial diagnosis and finally data is being transferred to cloud layer for long term storage.

The volume of data that is collected by the Biosensors is pre-processed at the edge layer before it is transferred to the cloud environment for further processing. Pre-processing of data at edge layer will provide real-time services to the patients. The EEG and rs-FMRI data collected is processed at local level. The data pre-processing is performed by Butterworth band pass filter which cuts frequencies and removed unwanted frequencies. Further for the identification of abnormalities at functional level re-clustering is applied. Wavelet transformations are applied to capture rhythmic nature of an epileptic seizure and for high level feature extraction. An edge computing gateway operates constantly even in the situation when connectivity between cloud and monitoring system is lost. Edge gateway supports cloud-based system by supplementing them in terms of real-time computing, low latency, heterogeneity, and scalability.

Sood *et al.* [50] proposed fog computing based system for the continuous monitoring and analysis of hypertensive patients. The data is collected through IoT sensors at fog layer for the identification of various stages of hypertension in the patients. After identification of stages, further analysis of risk level is done by application of Artificial Neural Network (ANN).

The fog-based system collects health related temporal data in a specified time window. This helps in risk assessment of hypertensive patients. The granulation of temporal data collected is associated with attribute of data values that is collected in a window time. The real time processing of data collected is performed for diagnosis. The diagnosis will produce an alert message on the end users phones to take preventive measures on time. The results show promising efficiency in bandwidth, minimum delay good response time, and higher accuracy.

Shammin *et al.* [51] proposed an edge computing-based system to control spread of COVID-19 epidemics. The biggest challenge of real-time monitoring of epidemic is to collect and process pathological, radiographic, and other types of information. They used Deep Neural Network for the processing and analysis of data collected during epidemic. Their three-layered framework - in which bottom layer consists of end users, stakeholders, hospitals and the decision makers. At this layer general health data is being collected like Blood pressure, temperature, and cough quality through app by patients. AI based module will investigate these preliminary symptoms and will categorize further action as per the rules. Middle layer is the combination of edge server, cache, and nodes. The topmost layer is cloud that consists of cloud servers and global storage.

Deep learning model works on cloud that contains servers with high computational power. The global storage area at cloud stores hospital and physiological test signals. These signals are in form of variety of images (X-Ray, CT-scan, protease sequences), and other physiological features like body temperature, blood pressure so on. The signals are collected from the connected network of hospitals. Three Deep Learning models are adopted ResNet50, deep tree, and Inception v3. Various streams are used for different types of image signals. Final step is decision fusion that is performed by each stream that helps in decision making even if any of the modality is missing.

The middle layer during the off-peak times downloads the DL model and shifts it to edge. The edge server is located nearby to the specified hospital. The collected data samples are transferred to edge through wireless technologies. The role of edge server is to secure the data using blockchain and further forward it to DL model. The explainable AI at edge is used for the understanding of output of each layer of DL model in the healthcare applications. The test data from hospitals and other symptoms are analyzed at edge using latest high power edge computers.

Ejaz *et al.* [52] developed an integrated system of edge computing and blockchain for the smart healthcare system. The objective of their system is to avoid long operating times, network issues, security and cost in highly dynamic network conditions. They assessed their system on the basis of following key terms like latency, power consumption, network utilization and computational load and compared the performance with the systems where blockchain is not used. Their model monitored various health parameters of the elderly person like blood pressure, heart rate, oxygen or blood sugar level. In case the parameters value goes beyond the range the alert message is issued for the healthcare centers.

Figure 7.12 represents a proposed framework consists of 3 layers – local tier, access tier and core tier. The local tier consists of variety of sensors that may collect data from various resources and then pass it on further to the edge or cloud servers for further processing.

At local tier, the edge nodes that are resource constrained do pass the data to the higher computational capacity node. The local nodes of edge are in the vicinity of the elderly or disabled person. The permissioned

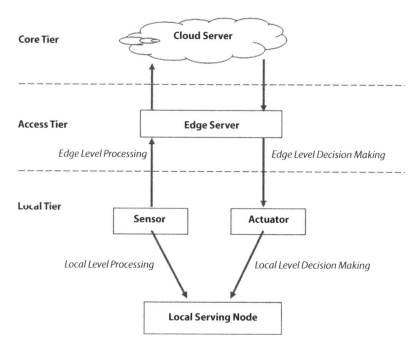

Figure 7.12 Integrated edge computing and blockchain architecture.

blockchain will run at the local edge nodes for the transfer of trusted information among different entities of the system like end users, healthcare workers, emergency units etc.

The access tier is much richer as compared to local tier and includes edge server, MEC servers and their role is to provide computational capabilities to the monitoring services. The basic role of this tier is to perform data analytics, decision making, security and privacy services, and allocation of resources. At this layer only blockchain provides an auction/renting of various resources for processing and storage capacity and/or for healthcare services as well.

Core tier is the richest in term of resources it provides huge number of resources. The major role of this tier to provide service logic that is used to manage overall working of healthcare systems and provide required resources.

The integration of edge and blockchain results into secure, trusted and delay-critical healthcare services for remote monitoring cases such as monitoring of elderly and disabled people. Their proposed Health-BlockEdge framework brings resources near to the end users and performs real time data analytics and decision-making functions to improve system-level resource efficiency.

7.4   Edge Computing Use Cases in Healthcare

The current scenario of pandemic has raised the demand of digital healthcare system. The fast-spreading disease like COVID-19, need real time responses from the healthcare industry, and put a pressure on healthcare providers to work in tight margins. Digital health is necessary now to meet the requirements of better resource management and collaboration across the healthcare industry. The key driver for the digital health in the coming future will be edge computing. Edge computing is all set to revolutionize the healthcare services. Following are few of the use cases.

Ambulance Service

The emergency services in healthcare system require prompt ambulance services to transport the patients to the healthcare centers. The unstructured way of ambulance management is one of the key reasons for so many causalities in recent time of pandemic. In emergency real time alerts and reachability of the services is required.

The promising performance of edge computing (along with 5G) with low latency, and high data processing capabilities may enable accurate and fast diagnosis and treatment by healthcare centers. It can provide more coarse information at the healthcare centers about the status and location of incoming patients and centers may take appropriate measures and be prepared to handle any adverse situation.

It can be achieved by the following:

- The data is transmitted to the hospital collected through body cams (enabled through 5G). This information will give live updates about the patient situation and healthcare staff will plan for potential treatment before patient reaches there.
- Real time analysis of patient data regarding blood pressure, heart rate at the edge and response by the healthcare personnel.
- To display patient's information like treatment history and other details can displayed on augmented reality glasses at edge to empower healthcare personnel.
- Diagnostics by remote ultrasounds using Haptic-enabled tools. Haptic also known as 3D touch is a technology where electronic and mechanical movements can be experienced through an interface.

Companies like Vodafone and BT are exploring the potential of this use case and trying to develop point of care to deliver services by exploiting the potential of 5G and MEC (multi-access edge computing). STL partners are also looking forward and trying to quantify its potential in the industry.

Patient Monitoring

Variety of monitoring devices is being used by healthcare sector like glucose monitors, various sensors, and health tools as well. These monitoring devices are either not connected or they store data at cloud. The security concern for such data is very high and limits its adoption.

The solution can be on-premise edge where data will be stored locally to maintain privacy. It will also facilitate processing of hospital data from various sources and extracting meaningful information. Edge is capable of sending notifications to doctors about unusual symptoms of patient behavior through analytics. Implementing edge at local level will observe significant resource efficiency, increase in productivity and will definitely decrease cost per patient.

Few implementations in this context are as follows:

Google Deep Mind/Google Health used for the early prediction of kidney injury so that early action can be taken to regulate it.

CareAI – This is a platform used majorly for the monitoring of critical patients, even when they come out of the critical situation. It helps in improving the quality of healthcare services an also improves their operational efficiency.

AWS Outposts – AWS is all set to target healthcare industry integrating it with its own on-premise edge technology. They are more concerned about the security and privacy of personalized healthcare data. AWS is set to provide power of core cloud to the healthcare industry.

Remote Care

The lifestyle and pressure of various factors on people lives is directly reflecting in their health and this needs prompt and reachable healthcare services. In the present scenario the healthcare staffs are overburdened. Treatment of chronic diseases such as diabetes, cardiac disease needs regular monitoring. Another scenario where rural peoples are not able to access the healthcare services due to reach ability issues or expensiveness.

Remote monitoring of patients (elderly and living in rural areas) may improve healthcare scenario. Wearable, sensors, IoT devices may provide real time updates of patient's health status and can alert healthcare workers to take action.

Processing health data at cloud is not safe as there are lot of critical information of patient's health is there. Data at edge is safe as it is processed at local level between patient and healthcare provider only. The low latency is required to process data in a real-time scenario can be will supported by edge. Processing data at edge reduces cost by processing data close to the source itself.

Examples:
Intel and Flex created an innovative Healthcare Application Platform. It enables healthcare solutions to deliver their services in a secure manner across the connected and always expanding healthcare edge and cloud. The Intel and Flex IoT engine enhance robustness and ease of use for various healthcare solutions.

Dibatacare monitors blood sugar level through mobile apps and devices; it sends the data to the healthcare centers, clinicians. Personalized treatment is provided to patients as per the requirements and periodic visits are adjusted to the nearest clinic in case of any emergencies.

TELUS Home Health Monitoring is used for remote monitoring of patients. It helps in reducing the pressure on healthcare systems. It regularly monitors basic health factors and reports any deviation from the standard values to the healthcare centers/providers.

7.5   Future of Healthcare and Edge Computing

Integration of 5G and edge computing has the potential to bring revolution in the healthcare industry. Edge computing creates a safe environment for the healthcare devices and also trying to remove dependency on cloud environment. Latest technologies like Internet of Things, Augmented Reality, and Virtual Reality are playing crucial role in virtual healthcare systems. Removing dependency on cloud resolves various issues of downtime, network congestion and latency as well. In healthcare solutions small delay leads to the critical situations.

Edge computing is contribution these days in recording patients vital through wearables and other connected devices. CPE (Customer Premises Equipment) and VCPE (Virtual Customer Premises Equipment), gateway and switches send the collected vitals to the edge servers. The data at edge syncs with the cloud in specific time interval. Sometimes edge computational device is also implemented at edge for real time data processing, analysis and drawing conclusions.

The latest reports of GM insights the IoT healthcare market is going to grow by 15% by 2024. The demand for remote monitoring applications in healthcare sector is getting hike. The Business Insider reports that 5.6 billion IoT devices are in use by the organizations and government for collecting data and for processing it in 2020 and will keep on growing in the coming years as well. These reports visualize the future of real time processing in healthcare systems using edge computing in the upcoming years.

7.6   Conclusion

This chapter provides a detailed overview of integration of edge computing technology with the traditional IoT architecture which helps to discover the solution of various challenges we are facing with existing model. In edge computing based IoT architecture, processing of data, analysis of data and some extend of data storage is occurred at edge of network. That results low latency, improved data security, low bandwidth, reduce network traffic, more efficient data management, scalability, and long battery life for

IoT devices. This concept will also improve the QoS (Quality of Service) of such application that needs real time data for processing and analyzing. To summarize our work, we have investigated various researchers work in healthcare sector and found that most of the researchers observed promising results by the application of edge/fog computing layer in the framework of modern healthcare systems.

References

1. Gubbi, J., Buyya, R., Marusic, S., Palaniswami, M., Internet of Things (IoT): A vision, architectural elements, and future directions. *Future Gener. Comput. Syst.*, 29, 7, 1645–1660, 2013.

2. Rose, K., Eldridge, S., Chapin, L., The Internet of Things: An overview, in: *Proc. Internet Society (ISOC)*, pp. 1–53, 2015.

3. Sethi, P. and Sarangi, S.R., Internet of Things: Architectures, protocols, and applications. *J. Electr. Comput. Eng.*, Hindawi, 2017, 1–25, 2017, https://doi.org/10.1155/2017/9324035.

4. Al-Sarawi, S., Anbar, M., Alieyan, K., Alzubaidi, M., Internet of Things (IoT) communication protocols: Review. *8th International Conference on Information Technology (ICIT)*, IEEE, 2017.

5. Nieminen, J. *et al.*, IPv6 over BLUETOOTH(R) Low Energy, IETF RFC 7668, October 2015, https://tools.ietf.org/html/rfc7668.

6. Zigbee Alliance, Connectivity Standards Alliance, 2021, https://zigbeealliance.org/solution/zigbee/.

7. Brandt, A. *et al.*, Home automation routing requirements in low-power and lossy networks, IETF RFC 5826, April 2010, https://tools.ietf.org/html/rfc5826.

8. Farrell, S. (Ed.), Low-Power Wide Area Network (LPWAN) Overview, IETF RFC 8376, May 2018, https://tools.ietf.org/html/rfc8376.

9. Winter, T. (Ed.), *et al.*, RPL: IPv6 Routing protocol for low-power and lossy networks, IETF RFC 6550, March 2012, https://tools.ietf.org/html/rfc6550.

10. Thubert, P. (Ed.), *et al.*, IPv6 over Low-Power Wireless Personal Area Network (6LoWPAN) routing header, IETF RFC 81338, April 2017, https://datatracker.ietf.org/doc/html/rfc8138.

11. Vilajosana, X. (Ed.), *et al.*, Minimal IPv6 over the TSCH mode of IEEE 802.15.4e (6TiSCH) configuration, IETF RFC 8180, May 2017, https://datatracker.ietf.org/doc/html/rfc8180.

12. Gomez, C. *et al.*, TCP usage guidance in the Internet of Things (IoT), IETF RFC 9006, March 2021, https://datatracker.ietf.org/doc/html/rfc9006.

13. *MQTT version 3.1.1*, A. Banks and R. Gupta (Eds.), OASIS Standard, 29 October 2014, http://docs.oasis-open.org/mqtt/mqtt/v3.1.1/os/

mqtt-v3.1.1-os.html. Latest version: http://docs.oasis-open.org/mqtt/mqtt/v3.1.1/mqtt-v3.1.1.html.

14. OASIS Advanced Message Queuing Protocol (AMQP) Version 1.0 Part 0: Overview, OASIS Standard, 29 October 2012, http://docs.oasis-open.org/amqp/core/v1.0/os/amqp-core-overview-v1.0-os.html.

15. Shelby, Z. *et al.*, The Constrained Application Protocol (CoAP), IETF RFC 7252, June 2014, https://datatracker.ietf.org/doc/html/rfc7252.

16. Saint-Andre, P., Extensible Messaging and Presence Protocol (XMPP): Core, IETF RFC 6120, March 2011, https://tools.ietf.org/html/rfc6120.

17. Mohammed, Z.K.A. and Ahmed, E.S.A., Internet of Things applications, challenges and related future technologies. *World Sci. News*, 67, 2, 126–148, 2017.

18. Matta, P. and Pant, B., Internet-Of-Things: Genesis, challenges and applications. *J. Eng. Sci. Technol.*, 14, 3, 1717–1750, 2019.

19. Minh Dang, L., Jalil Piran, Md., Han, D., Min, K., Moon, H., A survey on Internet of Things and cloud computing for healthcare. *Electronics*, 8, 768, 2019.

20. Verma, P. and Kumar, U., Smart farming: Using IoT and machine learning techniques, in: *Internet of Things and machine learning in agriculture*, J.M. Chatterjee, A. Kumar, P.S. Rathore, V. Jain (Eds.), pp. 3–20, De Gruyter, Berlin, Boston, 2021, https://doi.org/10.1515/9783110691276-001.

21. Gill, S.S., Chana, I., Buyya, R., IoT based agriculture as a cloud and big data service. *J. Organ. End User Comput.*, 29, 4, 1–23, 2017, https://doi.org/10.4018/ JOEUC.2017100101.

22. Vuksanović, D., Ugarak, J., Korčok, D., Industry 4.0: The future concepts and new visions of factory of the future development. *SINTEZA, International Scientific Conference on ICT and E-Business Related Research*, 2016.

23. Ferdowsi, A., Challita, U., Saad, W., Deep learning for reliable mobile edge analytics in intelligent transportation systems. *IEEE Veh. Technol. Mag.*, 14, 1556–6072, March 2019.

24. Helmi, O., Ehsankanani, Sokeh, M.A., Sepidnam, G., The challenges facing with the Internet of Things. *Int. J. Sci. Study*, 5, 4, 527–533, July 2017.

25. Alansari, Z., Anuar, N.B., Kamsin, A., Belgaum, M.R., Alshaer, J., Soomro, S., Miraz, M.H., Internet of Things: Infrastructure, architecture, security and privacy, in: *2018 International Conference on Computing, Electronics Communications Engineering (ICCECE)*, Aug 2018, pp. 150–155.

26. Mazayev, A., Martins, J.A., Correia, N., Interoperability in IoT through the semantic profiling of objects. *IEEE Access*, 6, 19379–19385, 2018.

27. Cooper, J. and James, A., Challenges for database management in the internet of things. *IETE Tech. Rev.*, 26, 5, 320–329, 2009.

28. Constante, F., Silva, F., Herrera, B., Big data analytics in IoT: Challenges, open research issues and tools, in: *Trends and Advances in Information Systems and Technologies*, pp. 775–788, March 2018.

29. Perković, T., Damjanović, S., Šolić, P., Patrono, L., Rodrigues, J., Meeting challenges in IoT: Sensing, energy efficiency, and the implementation. *Fourth International Congress on Information and Communication Technology*, January 2020, pp. 419–430.

30. Kumar, U., Verma, P., Qamar Abbas, S., Bringing edge computing into IoT architecture to improve IoT network performance. *2021 International Conference on Computer Communication and Informatics (ICCCI)*, pp. 1–5, 2021.

31. Shi, W., Pallis, G., Xu, Z., Edge computing. *Proc. IEEE*, 107, 8, 1474–1481, August 2019, Digital Object Identifier 10.1109/JPROC.2019.2928287.

32. P. FAR-EDGE, FAR-EDGE Project H2020, 2017, Available online: http://faredge. eu/{#}/.

33. INTEL-SAP, *IoT joint reference architecture from Intel and SAP, Technical report*, INTEL-SAP, 2018, Available online: https://www.intel.com/content/dam/www/public/us/en/documents/reference-architectures/sapiot-reference-architecture.pdf.

34. Yu, W., Liang, F., He, X., Hatcher, W.G., Lu, C., Lin, J., Yang, X., A survey on the edge computing for the Internet of Things. *IEEE*, 6, 6900–6919, 2018, Digital Object Identifier 10.1109/ACCESS.2017.2778504.

35. Intharawijitr, K., Iida, K., Koga, H., Yamaoka, K., Practical enhancement and evaluation of a low-latency network model using mobile edge computing. *41st Annual Computer Software and Applications Conference (COMPSAC)*, IEEE, 2017.

36. Sajjad, H.P., Danniswara, K., Al-Shishtawy, A., Vlassov, V., SpanEdge: Towards unifying stream processing over central and near the-edge data centers, in: *Proc. IEEE/ACM Symp. Edge Comput. (SEC)*, Oct. 2016, pp. 168–178.

37. Hassan, N., Gilani, S., Ahmed, E., Yaqoob, I., Imran, M., The role of edge computing in Internet of Things. *IEEE Commun. Mag.*, 56, 99, May 2018.

38. Khan, W.Z., Ahmed, E., Hakak, S., Yaqoob, I., Ahmed, A., Edge computing: A survey. Article *Future Gener. Comput. Syst.*, 97, 219–235, February 2019.

39. Lin, J., Yu, W., Zhang, N., Yang, X., Zhang, H., Zhao, W., A survey on Internet of Things: Architecture, enabling technologies, security and privacy, and applications. *IEEE Internet Things J.*, 4, 5, 1125–1142, Oct. 2017.

40. Mocnej, J., Miškuf, M., Papcun, P., Zolotová, I., Impact of edge computing paradigm on energy consumption in IoT. *IFAC PapersOnLine*, 51, 6, 162–167, 2018, 10.1016/j.ifacol.2018.07.147.

41. Hartmann, M., Hashmi, U.S., Imran, A., Edge computing in smart healthcare systems: Review, challenges and research directions. Special Issue Article *Emerging Telecommun. Technol.*, © 2019 John Wiley & Sons, Ltd., 1–25, 2019.

42. Liu, L., Yang, Y., Zhao, W., Du, Z., Semi-automatic remote medicine monitoring system of miners. *UbiComp/ISWC'15 Adjunct: Adjunct Proceedings of the 2015 ACM International Joint Conference on Pervasive and Ubiquitous Computing and Proceedings of the 2015 ACM International*

Symposium on Wearable Computers, September 2015, pp. 93–96, https://doi.org/10.1145/2800835.2800879.

43. Dubey, H., Yang, J., Constant, N., Amiri, A.M., Yang, Q., Makodiya, K., Fog data: Enhancing telehealth big data through fog computing. *Proceedings of the ASE Big Data & Social Informatics 2015ASE BD & SI '15*, ACM, New York, NY, USA, pp. 14:1–14:6, 2015.

44. Gaura, E.I., Brusey, J., Allen, M., Wilkins, R., Goldsmith, D., Rednic, R., Edge mining the Internet of Things. *IEEE Sens. J.*, 13, 10, 3816–3825, 2013.

45. Bhargava, K. and Ivanov, S., A fog computing approach for localization in WSN. *2017 IEEE 28th Annual International Symposium on Personal, Indoor, and Mobile Radio Communications (PIMRC)*.

46. Althebyan, Q., Yaseen, Q., Jararweh, Y., Al-Ayyoub, M., Cloud support for large scale e-healthcare systems. *Ann. Telecommun.*, 71, 9, 503–515, 2016.

47. Bhunia, S.S., Dhar, S.K., Mukherjee, N., iHealth: A fuzzy approach for provisioning intelligent healthcare system in smartcity. *2014 IEEE 10th International Conference on Wireless and Mobile Computing, Networking and Communications (WiMob)*, pp. 187–193, 2014.

48. Borthakur, D., Dubey, H., Constant, N., Mahler, L., Mankodiya, K., Smart fog: Fog computing framework for unsupervised clustering analytics in wearable Internet of Things. *2017 IEEE Global Conference on Signal and Information Processing (GlobalSIP)*, pp. 472–476, 2017.

49. Hosseini, M., Tran, T.X., Pompili, D., Elisevich, K., Soltanian-Zadeh, H., Deep learning with edge computing for localization of epileptogenicity using multimodal rs-fMRI and EEG big data. *2017 IEEE International Conference on Autonomic Computing (ICAC)*, pp. 83–92, 2017.

50. Sood, S.K. and Mahajan, I., IoT-fog-based healthcare framework to identify and control hypertension attack. *IEEE Internet Things J.*, 6, 2, 1920–1927, 2019.

51. Hossain, M.S., Muhammad, G., Guizani, N., Explainable AI and mass surveillance system-based healthcare framework to combat COVID-19 like pandemics. *IEEE Network*, 34, 4, 126–132, July/August 2020.

52. Ejaz, M., Kumar, T., Kovacevic, I., Ylianttila, M., Harjula, E., Health-blockedge: Blockchain-edge framework for reliable low-latency digital healthcare applications. *Sensors*, 21, 2502, 2021, https://doi.org/10.3390/s21072502.

8

Fog-IoT Assistance-Based Smart Agriculture Application

Pawan Whig[1]*, Arun Velu[2] and Rahul Reddy Nadikattu[3]

[1]*Vivekananda Institute of Professional Studies, New Delhi, India*
[2]*Department of CSE, Equifax, Atlanta, United States*
[3]*University of the Cumberlands, Williamsburg, KY, United States*

Abstract

Increased agricultural activity is supposed to be of crucial importance as intelligent agriculture or precision agriculture. Increased agricultural activity is supposed to be of crucial importance as intelligent agriculture or precision agriculture. The bandwidth and the information repository are too much for an old cloud-based system that largely employs IoT devices. Reduced latency, better battery life for IoT systems, a lot more efficient cash knowledge acquisition, accessibility to intellectual capital, and AI, ML IoT-EDGE style platform are suggested or may be used. When opposed to using the cloud to process and store information, the edge for the IoT provides prospective edges for various IoT installations, as well as the elimination of interval in combination with geometrical communication potency. Several IoT procedures, for example, will also have a high level of technology at the sting, resulting in minimal latency and quick processing. The current cloud-based systems, which are built on traditional cloud concepts, cannot handle the large quantities and different data produced by linked IoT devices. To facilitate real-time decision-making based on the data collected, it is critical to move data processing closer to the roots of their production. This will be solved by using fog-based models, which will be addressed in this chapter.

Keywords: IoT, cloud computing, artificial intelligence, machine learning, latency, communication, edge computing, networking

*Corresponding author: pawanwhig@gmail.com

Danda B. Rawat, Lalit K Awasthi, Valentina Emilia Balas, Mohit Kumar and Jitendra Kumar Samriya (eds.) *Convergence of Cloud with AI for Big Data Analytics: Foundations and Innovation*, (157–176) © 2023 Scrivener Publishing LLC

8.1   Introduction

Fog computing is a decentralized computing architecture in which data, computers, stores, and applications are located everywhere inside the data foundation and fog [1]. Fog computing (FG), like edge computing, conveys the benefits of the control of the fog closer to where data is created and used. Fog and edge computing are frequently used in the place of each other since they both include delivery intelligence and meting out earlier to anywhere data is generated. It is frequently done to increase efficiency, but it may also be performed for safety or a specific condition [2].

Fog computing brings the cloud's power closer to the point where data is created and consumed. In other words, more individuals may be online [3]. It suggests the identical interacting and cloud facilities as before, nonetheless by increased safety and obedience.

Basic Characteristics

IDC estimates that by 2025, 45 percent of all data will be produced at the network edge, with 10 percent of that data coming from edge devices such as phones, smart watches, connected automobiles, and other connected gadgets [4]. Fog computing is the solitary skill that will opinion the exam of the period, and it will level outperform AI, IoT Apps, and 5G in the succeeding ten years.

The situation delivers highly virtualized storing, calculating, and interacting facilities to cloud end devices from traditional data centers. Fog computing has little dormancy, site consciousness, edge location, change of site, actual data connectivity, and capability for connected mist interaction [5].

Instead of batch processing, fog applications rely on real-time interactions and often connect to mobile devices [6]. Fog nodes have also been used in diverse contexts with different form factors. The basics of fog computing are shown in Figure 8.1.

Although a lot has been published and investigated on fog-computing, how various fog actors will align in the future is not simple to say. Based on the nature of major services and applications, it is nonetheless clear to conclude: subscriber models will have an extensive role in fog computing (smart grid, clever cities, linked cars, etc.) [7].

Suppliers of worldwide services are expected to collaborate. New holders, including transport providers, vehicle manufacturers, government authorities, etc., will enter the fog domain. Some recognized fog players

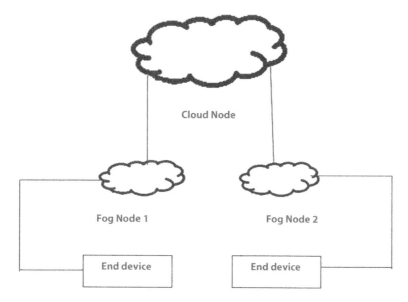

Figure 8.1 Basics of fog computing.

are cloud-based providers like Apache CloudStack7, OpenStack6, and OpenNebula8 [8].

8.1.1 Difference Between Fog and Edge Computing

The cloud enables users to access computer, networking, and storage choices quickly and conveniently [9]. It might lead to reduced productivity or latency for devices that are not linked to the internet.

Leading-edge calculation aims to reduce processing time and distance by bringing data sources and equipment closer together. In principle, this enhances both applications' and smartphones' efficiency and performance [10].

Fog computing (FC), to use a Cisco tenure, also brings the computer to the net's control. It mentions the requirements aimed at this procedure's optimal performance. Figure 8.2 depicts a pyramidal model of fog, cloud, and edge computing.

Process delay is eliminated or considerably reduced by locating storage and computing systems as close to the programs, parts, and systems that make them as feasible. That's also especially crucial for IoT devices, which

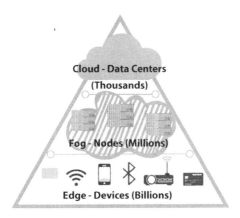

Figure 8.2 Fog, cloud, and edge comparison.

create large volumes of data. Because they are nearer to the source of data, these gadgets have a significantly lower delay in fog computing [11, 12].

The difference between cloud, fog, and edge computing is shown in Table 8.1.

To distinguish between edge devices and fog nodes, fog is the model that enables consistent, well-structured, scaled execution inside the editing environment. Information is compiled, analyzed, and saved close together and in edge computing, it's a kind of cloud computing. Edge processing, and also the network and application connections required for data transit, are all part of sensor networks [13].

That's because, with both fog and portable edge calculation, the goal is to decrease inactivity and boost efficiency while processing data in diverse locations. Cutting edges are most common when sensors are linked to equipment and data is collected—there is a bodily link between the information basis and the dispensation place. Fog computation reduces the remoteness between the dispensation site and the information basis by performing edge computing on or within the LAN processors connected to an IoT or fog node [14]. This causes a physically longer processing distance between the sensors and no additional delay [15].

Merits of Fog Computing

Some merits/advantages of fog computing is described below.

Latency

System breakdowns, line shutdowns, and other significant challenges can be avoided by keeping analysis closer to the data source, especially in

Table 8.1 Difference between cloud fog and edge computing.

	Cloud computing	Fog computing	Edge computing
Architecture	• Central processing based model • Fulfils the need for large amounts of data to be accessed more quickly, this demand is ever-growing due to cloud agility • Accessed through internet	• Coined by CISCO • Extending cloud to the edge of the network • Decentralized computing • Any device with computing, storage and network connectivity can be a fog node, can be put on railway track or oil rig • Fog computing shoves intelligence down to the local area network level of network architecture, processing data in a fog node or IoT gateway	• Fog computing usually work with cloud or fog • Edge is limited to smaller number of peripheral layers • Edge computing pushes the intelligence, processing power and communication of an edge gateway or appliance directly into devices like programmable automation controllers (PACs)

(*Continued*)

Table 8.1 Difference between cloud fog and edge computing. (*Continued*)

	Cloud computing	Fog computing	Edge computing
Pros	• Easy to scale • Low cost storage • Based on Internet driven global network on robust TCP/IP protocol	• Real time data analysis • Take quick actions • Sensitive data remains inside the network • Cost saving on storage and network • More scalable than edge computing • Operations can be managed by IT/OT team	• Edge computing simplifies internal communication by means of physically wiring physical assets to intelligent PAC to collect, analysis and process data • PACs then use edge computing capabilities to determine what data should be stored locally or sent to the cloud for further analysis
Cons	• Latency/Response time • Bandwidth cost • Security • Power consumption • No offline-mode • Sending raw data over internet to the cloud could have privacy, security and legal issues	• Fog computing relies on many links to move data from physical asset chain to digital layer and this is a potential point of failure	• Less scalable than fog computing • Interconnected through proprietary networks with custom security and little interoperability. • No cloud-aware • Cannot do resource pooling • Operations cannot be extended to IT/OT team

Table 8.1 Difference between cloud fog and edge computing. (*Continued*)

	Cloud computing	Fog computing	Edge computing
Misc.		• Less sensitive and non-real-time data is sent to the cloud for further processing • Fog node can be deployed in private, community, public or hybrid mode	• PACs (programmable automation controllers) then use edge computing capabilities to determine what data should be stored locally or sent to the cloud for further analysis • Intelligence is literally pushed to the network edge, where our physical assets are first connected together and where IoT data originates • The current edge computing domain is a sub-set of fog computing domain

vertical systems that count every second. Faster warnings imply less danger to users and less time lost, allowing for real-time data processing.

8.1.1.1   Bandwidth

Maintain adequate bandwidth in the network. Many information analysis responsibilities, smooth the most serious ones, organize not necessitate the use of fog-based storing and handing out. Connected devices continually create

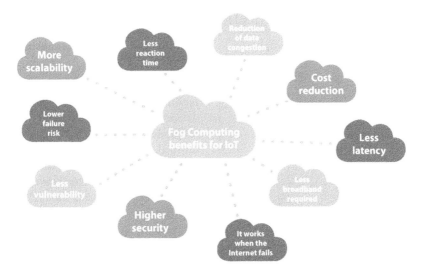

Figure 8.3 Merits of fog computing.

more data for analysis. To free up bandwidth for other important tasks, the majority of this massive amount of data is delivered via fog computers [16].

Costs of operation are lowered. Operational costs are lowered as a result of local processing and network bandwidth retention. Increase the level of safety. It is critical to protect IoT data throughout transmission and storage [17]. Users may monitor, protect, and enable fog nodes throughout the whole IT system using the same controls, policies, and processes. The merits of fog computing is shown in Figure 8.3.

8.1.1.2 Confidence

Conditions may be harsh since IoT devices are typically employed in extreme environmental and emergencies. Fog computing can increase reliability and minimize the data transfer burden in certain situations. Deepen your understanding without jeopardizing your privacy [18]. In its place of risking a data opening by uploading searching data to the fog for study, This may study it in the vicinity on the plans that gather, examine, and supply the statistics. In terms of statistics safety and secrecy, fog computation is a better option for highly sensitive data.

8.1.1.3 Agility

Improve the business's agility. Companies can only respond quickly to customer demand if they recognize the resources consumers require, where these resources are needed, and where assistance is required. Developers may easily construct and deploy fog apps using fog computing [19]. Fog computation skill also permits operators to provide additional specialized facilities and explanations to their clients depending on existing capabilities and infrastructure, as well as identify data and data tools in which they are best handled.

Fog computing issues are caused by a high dependence on information transit. Although the deployment of the 5G system has addressed this subject, there are still limitations in terms of availability, speeds, and high-frequency congestion. Near fog nodes, extra caution is required for speed and safety [20].

Disadvantages of Fog Computing

Because fog computing is related to a physical location, some of cloud computing's advantages are harmed.

Security

In the right circumstances, fog computing may be exposed to security threats such as IP spoofing or middle man attacks (MitM).

Costs

Fog computing is a system that makes use of edge and cloud resources, hence the hardware is costly.

Ambiguous

While there is a significant misunderstanding in the idea of fog computing across various organizations, even though fog computing has been around for a while there are suppliers that describe it differently.

8.1.2   Relation of Fog with IoT

IoT and end-users are becoming more powerful. The cloud now handles a large amount of data in real-time. IoT devices using fog computing [21] are shown in Figure 8.4. Furthermore, fog computing provides several benefits to the IoT app development process:

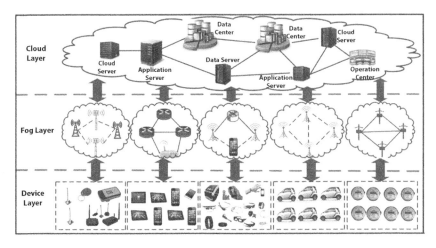

Figure 8.4 Fog computing with IoT.

Agility for Business

With the right tools, you can design and deploy fog apps. In the hands of the user, the device can function similarly to these programs.

Safety

Fog computing performances are a substitution for strategies that limit their resources and keep their security software and credentials up to date. It uses fog nodes in various parts of the IT infrastructure, all of which follow the same policies, processes, and controls. Data processing is a complex distributed system that uses a large number of nodes to assess the security condition of almost connected devices.

Delay

Have you noticed how quickly Alexa asks? This is because fog computing has low latency. Also because fog is closer to all users (and gadgets), it responds quickly. This device is ideal for any operation that requires a quick response.

Bandwidth

Fog control allows speedy and effective information dispensation founded on available applications, computer capitals, and schmoozing. Instead of being sent through a single path, information is blended at numerous points. This decreases the quantity of information that must be moved to the fog, preserving net capacity which helps in lowering costs.

Services

Even if the network connection to the cloud is limited, fog computing can operate independently and deliver uninterrupted services. Furthermore, due to a large number of connected channels, connection loss is almost impossible.

User Experience

Stronger protocols, such as Zigbee, Z-Wave, or Bluetooth, are used by edge nodes. Edge computing offers immediate connectivity between mobile and home consumers, independently of the network, improving user experience.

8.1.3   Fog Computing in Agriculture

The agriculture industry has gained and been changed as a result of fog computing. The SWAMP project, which stands for Smart Water Management Platform, is an excellent example in this regard [22]. Water, which accounts for 70% of freshwater use, is a critical component of the agricultural industry, making it the most significant consumer. Leaks in distribution and irrigation systems in-field application methods frequently result in resource waste.

Surface irrigation waste has high-water content since it only watered areas where plants are not favorable. Local irrigation here provides for more effective and efficient use of water, which eliminates the need for irrigation or irrigation. The fundamental issue is that farmers provide enough water to avoid under-irrigation. It not only reduces output but also increases the waste of a critical resource [23]. As a result, farmers required a technique to deal with these events and provide an effective response. And it is at this point that the SWAMP project identifies and addresses IoT, data analysis, stand-alone devices, and so on.

SWAMP develops a smart water system idea for agriculture with the help of fog computing, ensuring that water wastes are reduced to a minimum [24]. Fog computing also allows the system to collect and analyze sensor data from the field to improve water distribution. An example of fog computing in agriculture is shown in Figure 8.5.

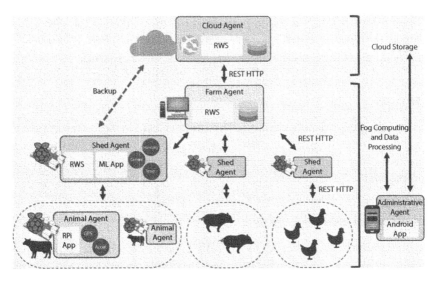

Figure 8.5 Fog computing in agriculture.

The SWAMP project has published an essay about the concept of a smart agricultural environment, in which data is collected and stored in real-time for analysis. The technique [25] discusses two different approaches to using fog to filter data. The experiment filters the methodologies and employs a real-time data package that includes temperature and moisture readings. Another use of fog computing in agriculture is Agrifog, or smart agriculture or precision agriculture, which has enabled IoT-based agricultural systems [26]. iFogSim was used to construct the program.

Through data processing, it aims to reduce latency in real-time decision-making. IoT-Fog is a low-cost, comparative study of data gathered from the cloud and fog-based technologies. As a platform, fog computing has transformed the agriculture and agricultural sectors, allowing farmers to reduce waste and interpret and analyze processed data to find methods to profit from it. Fog computing in healthcare.

New technologies are frequently employed in the medical field to improve services and solutions. In addition, similar to earlier technological breakthroughs [27], fog computing was leveraged to its advantage. One of the most important uses of fog computing in healthcare is eHealth an example shown in Figure 8.6. eHealth is an online and print platform that gracefully guides health workers across the healthcare continuum, which is characterized by frequent and exciting changes as a result of escalating technical and other structural changes [28].

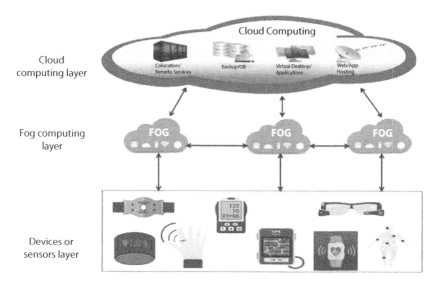

Figure 8.6 Example of fog computing in healthcare.

They employ a network mix that connects medical devices to cloud platforms. The application organizes, transmits, stores, and records data relevant to the treatment, payment, and recording processes. Because professionals have access to electro-medical records (EMR), which comprise documents such as X-rays, ultrasounds, CT scans, and MRIs, fog computing makes diagnosis and evaluation procedures easier. It also keeps data safe on a private cloud [29].

Instead of keeping a physical duplicate, the application may preserve confidential data on many networks and monitor it via fog computing. The recorded information enables a physician to quickly access and diagnose the patient's condition, as well as get the patient's medical records. Fog computing also allows eHealth to provide quick responses to critical medical requirements [30]. Similarly, wall, a separate health solution, creates a smart home environment with a fog computer by creating a customized sensor-based context-conscious application.

8.1.4   Fog Computing in Smart Cities

Intelligent cities are urban areas that gather data from residents who are able or unable to live there utilizing technological gadgets. The data then adds to the town's overall quality of life. People opt to stay and make such smart cities their home since they have more job opportunities and better

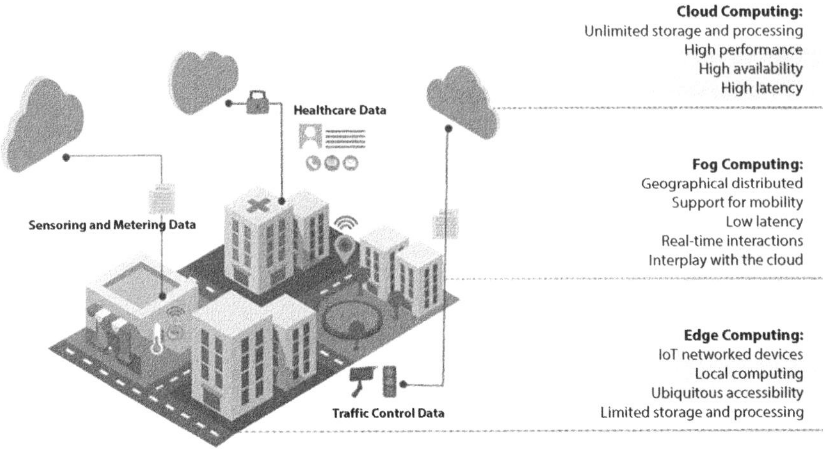

Figure 8.7 Example of fog computing in smart cities.

living circumstances. Fog computing develops cost-effective, real-time, and latency-sensitive surveillance technologies to protect residents' and visitors' privacy as shown in Figure 8.7 [31]. Fog computing has already worked wonders in several locations, reducing traffic congestion. People are tracked down, and GPS technology predicts traffic and suggests other routes and arrival times.

Another fascinating use of fog computing is driverless vehicles, which require the processing of large amounts of data. Fog computing is critical for linking low-level sensors and enabling high bandwidth real-time processing.

Intelligent waste management solutions must be addressed in smart cities that are safe and considerate of their residents' demands. Sensor data and improvised garbage control strategies can be used by the local council here. Waste management solutions that are intelligent are employed. Smart cities are advancing at a faster rate every day, thanks to the availability of new technological solutions. The amount of data that can be captured and analyzed is unlimited with a fog computing platform.

8.1.5 Fog Computing in Education

The education business has evolved as a result of technological advancements, particularly in light of COVID-19 [32]. The whole industry was heavily reliant on electronic gadgets, and many professionals who wished to further their careers used online programs to do it. The fog computing

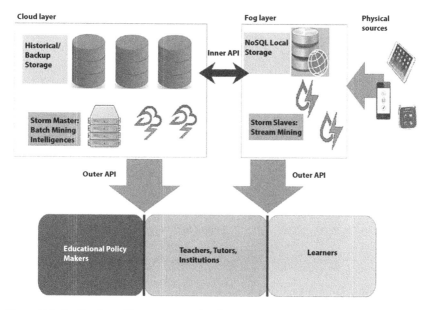

Figure 8.8 Application of fog computing in education.

Platform facilitates communication while also ensuring network data storage and administration. It improves scalability, flexibility, and redundancy for education systems to safeguard privacy and safety as shown in Figure 8.8.

Computers and Entertainment for Fog

In recent decades, the entertainment business has gone a long way. Both customers and producers have reported high demand. Consider sports, where all live broadcasts of events covering wide fields, such as ESPN, NBA TV, NBC Sports Network, and others, are expected to provide high-quality and accurate coverage of every game minute [34].

8.1.6   Case Study

With 10% of all data created and processed outside of the cloud or centralized data centers, edge computing is steadily gaining traction in several industries [33]. However, considering that the ratio will reach 75% by 2025, we may expect rapid growth in the use of edge computing. Figure 8.9 depicts the smart agriculture model. For good reason, edge computing in agriculture has already become a major IoT trend. In terms of speed and efficiency, edge computing is gaining ground on cloud infrastructure [35, 36].

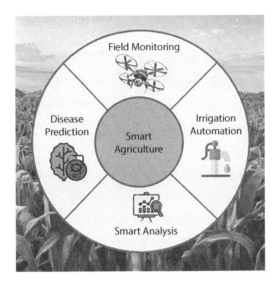

Figure 8.9 Model of smart agriculture.

While the benefits of IoT applications in agriculture cannot be overstated, smart farming technologies, particularly those that rely on the cloud, might present some challenges. There are a few major roadblocks to IoT cloud computing. Agriculture is both clever and intelligent [37].

Case1
Security issue: When data is sent from a field device to the cloud, the chances of a data breach are relatively significant. Furthermore, every device or sensor in the IoT network might be a potential vulnerability point [38].

Possible answer: Continuous computing reduces the risk of data infringement or theft when data is being captured – on the device itself.

Case 2
Speed Concern: Data gathering, transmission, and analysis are all time-consuming tasks. As a result, some businesses may face the dilemma of deciding between the depth and speed with which to absorb information-derived insight. This is especially true in the case of distant agricultural tools in the field [39, 40].

Simple solution: Edge computing solves this problem by improving network and data processing efficiency. The acquired data and input may be processed in each network device, resulting in faster processing rates and more insight [41].

Case 3

Cost difficulty: The expenses of cloud computing are generally based on the volume of data generated by the objects and transferred across the network. Given the number of devices used by a single smart farming system and the amount of data it produces, cloud computing costs might quickly rise. Using cutting-edge computers in agriculture eliminates the need to overcrowd or shift your warehouse with unneeded and worthless data. Solution: As a result, both storage and bandwidth expenses in your cloud may be decreased [42, 43].

There are many instances of intelligent farming, from monitoring climate change and the monitoring of crop/cattle conditions to automatic greenhouse processing and even end-to-end agricultural management solutions that are IoT-enabled. The application of edge calculations for smart agriculture is a key opportunity within the so-called "precision agriculture." Farmers that use this technique rely on data to better manage their businesses, improve their operational efficiency, and lower their operating costs [44].

Conclusion and Future Scope

This chapter discusses how fog computing is linked to IoT and how it benefits many industries, notably the agricultural sector. The Internet of Things (IoT) is changing the world by offering a range of approaches and technologies, such as cloud, fog, and edge computing. The cloud has existed in our universe for a long time, and the fog and the edge are fresh modernizations. Both of these are comparable, with the exception that the edge is quicker and has a larger latent value than just the fog and cloud. Computing has been used in the cattle industry and others. Agriculture has not been updated and continues to use antiquated practices. If done properly, edge computing has the potential to transform things and give the agriculture industry a huge boost. For researchers in the same subject, this chapter is quite beneficial. With the progress of technology, we will soon see a new revolution in agriculture called agriculture 4.

References

1. Schaffers, H., Komninos, N., Pallot, M., Trousse, B., Nilsson, M., Oliveira, A., Smart cities and the future internet: Towards cooperation frameworks for

open innovation. *The Future Internet Lect. Notes Comput. Sci.*, vol. 6656, pp. 431–446, 2011.

2. Cuff, D., Hansen, M., Kang, J., Urban sensing: Out of the woods. *Commun. ACM*, 51, 3, 24–33, Mar. 2008.

3. Dohler, M., Vilajosana, I., Vilajosana, X., Llosa, J., Smart cities: An action plan. *Proc. Barcelona Smart Cities Congress*, Dec. 2011, pp. 1–6.

4. Vilajosana, Llosa, J., Martinez, B., Domingo-Prieto, M., Angles, A., Vilajosana, X., Bootstrapping smart cities through a self-sustainable model based on big data flows. *IEEE Commun. Mag.*, 51, 6, 128–134, Jun. 2013.

5. Hernández-Muñoz, J.M., Vercher, J.B., Muñoz, L., Galache, J.A., Presser, M., Hernández Gómez, L.A. *et al.*, Smart cities at the forefront of the future internet. *The Future Internet Lect. Notes Comput. Sci.*, vol. 6656, pp. 447–462, 2011.

6. Mulligan, C.E.A. and Olsson, M., Architectural implications of smart city business models: An evolutionary perspective. *IEEE Commun. Mag.*, 51, 6, 80–85, Jun. 2013.

7. Walravens, N. and Ballon, P., Platform business models for smart cities: From control and value to governance and public value. *IEEE Commun. Mag.*, 51, 6, 72–79, Jun. 2013.

8. Lynch, J.P. and Kenneth, J.L., A summary review of wireless sensors and sensor networks for structural health monitoring. *Shock Vib. Dig.*, 38, 2, 91–130, 2006.

9. Nuortio, T., Kytöjoki, J., Niska, H., Bräysy, O., Improved route planning and scheduling of waste collection and transport. *Expert Syst. Appl.*, 30, 2, 223–232, Feb. 2006.

10. Al-Ali, A.R., Zualkernan, I., Aloul, F., A mobile GPRS-sensors array for air pollution monitoring. *IEEE Sens. J.*, 10, 10, 1666–1671, Oct. 2010.

11. Maisonneuve, N., Stevens, M., Niessen, M.E., Hanappe, P., Steels, L., Citizen noise pollution monitoring. *Proc. 10th Annu. Int. Conf. Digital Gov. Res.: Soc. Netw.: Making Connec. Between Citizens Data Gov.*, pp. 96–103, 2009.

12. Li, X., Shu, W., Li, M., Huang, H.-Y., Luo, P.-E., Wu, M.-Y., Performance evaluation of vehicle-based mobile sensor networks for traffic monitoring. *IEEE Trans. Veh. Technol.*, 58, 4, 1647–1653, May 2009.

13. Lee, S., Yoon, D., Ghosh, A., Intelligent parking lot application using wireless sensor networks. *Proc. Int. Symp. Collab. Technol. Syst.*, 19–23 pp. 48–57, May 2008.

14. Kastner, W., Neugschwandtner, G., Soucek, S., Newmann, H.M., Communication systems for building automation and control. *Proc. IEEE*, 93, 6, 1178–1203, Jun. 2005.

15. Fielding, R.T., *Architectural styles and the design of network-based software architectures*, pp. 76–85, Ph.D. Thesis, University of California, Irvine, 2000.

16. Efficient XML Interchange (EXI) format 1.0, in: *World Wide Web Consortium*, Feb. 2014.

17. Castellani, A.P., Bui, N., Casari, P., Rossi, M., Shelby, Z., Zorzi, M., Architecture and protocols for the Internet of Things: A case study. *Proc. 8th IEEE Int. Conf. Pervasive Comput. Commun. Workshops (PERCOM Workshops)*, pp. 678–683, 2010.
18. Castellani, A.P., Dissegna, M., Bui, N., Zorzi, M., WebIoT: A web application framework for the Internet of Things. *Proc. IEEE Wireless Commun. Netw. Conf. Workshops*, 2012.
19. Li, Y. *et al.*, IoT-CANE: A unified knowledge management system for data-centric internet of things application systems. *J. Parallel Distrib. Comput.*, 131, 161–172, 2019.
20. Atzori, L., Iera, A., Morabito, G., The internet of things: A survey. *Comput. Netw.*, 54, 15, 2787–2805, 2010.
21. Bellavista, P., Cardone, G., Corradi, A., Foschini, L., Convergence of MANET and WSN in IoT urban scenarios. *IEEE Sens. J.*, 13, 10, 3558–3567, Oct. 2013.
22. Laya, A., Bratu, V.I., Markendahl, J., Who is investing in machine-to-machine communications? *Proc. 24th Eur. Reg. ITS Conf.*, Oct. 2013, pp. 20–23.
23. Whig, P. and Ahmad, S.N., A novel pseudo NMOS Integrated ISFET device for water quality monitoring. *Act. Passive Compon.* Hindawi, 1, 1, 1–9, 2013, article i.d 258970.
24. Bhatia, V. and Whig, P., Modeling and simulation of electrical load control system using RF technology. *Int. J. Multidiscip. Sci. Eng.*, 4, 2, 44–47, 2013.
25. Whig, P. and Ahmad, S.N., Development of economical ASIC for PCS for water quality monitoring. *J. Circuits Syst. Comput.*, 23, 6, 1–13, 2014.
26. Whig, P. and Ahmad, S.N., CMOS integrated VDBA-ISFET device for water quality monitoring. *Int. J. Intell. Eng. Syst.*, accepted Publ., 7, 1, 5–14, 2014.
27. Whig, P. and Bhatia, V., Performance analysis of multi-functional bot system design using microcontroller. *Int. J. Intell. Syst. Appl.*, 02, 69–75, 2014.
28. Whig, P. and Ahmad, S.N., Development of low power dynamic threshold PCS system. *J. Electr. Electron. Syst.*, 3, 3, 1–6, 2014.
29. Whig, P. and Ahmad, S.N., Novel FGMOS based PCS device for low power applications. *Photonic Sens. (Springer)*, 5, 2, 1–5, 2015.
30. Whig, P. and Ahmad, S.N., Impact of parameters on the characteristic of novel PCS. *Can. J. Basic Appl. Sci.*, 3, 2, 45–52, 2015.
31. Ruchin, Mahto, C., Whig, P., Design and simulation of dynamic UART Using Scan Path Technique (USPT). *Int. J. Electr. Electron. Comput. Sci. Eng.*, 1, 6–11, 2015.
32. Sharma, A., Kumar, A., Whig, P., On the performance of CDTA based novel analog inverse low pass filter using 0.35μm CMOS parameter. *Int. J. Sci. Technol. Manage.*, 4, 1, 594–601, 2015.
33. Whig, P. and Ahmad, S.N., Simulation and performance analysis of low power quasi floating gate PCS model. *Int. J. Intell. Eng. Syst.*, 9, 2, 8–13, 2016.
34. Whig, P. and Ahmad, S.N., Ultraviolet Photo Catalytic Oxidation (UVPCO) sensor for air and surface sanitizers using CS amplifier. *Glob. J. Res. Eng.*, 16, 6, 1–13, F 2016.

35. Whig, P. and Rupani, A., Novel economical social distancing smart device for COVID19. *Int. J. Electr. Eng. Technol.*, 2, 2, 1–10, 2020.

36. Velu, A., The spread of big data science throughout the globe. *Int. J. Sustain. Dev. Comput. Sci.*, 1, 1, 11–20, 2019.

37. Velu, A., A stable pre-processing method for the handwritten recognition system. *Int. J. Mach. Learn. Sustain. Dev.*, 1, 1, 21–30, 2019.

38. Whig, P., Exploration of viral diseases mortality risk using machine learning. *Int. J. Mach. Learn. Sustain. Dev.*, 1, 1, 11–20, 2021.

39. Whig, P., A novel multi-center and threshold ternary pattern. *Int. J. Mach. Learn. Sustain. Dev.*, 1, 2, 1–10, 2019.

40. Velu, A. and Whig, P., Protect personal privacy and wasting time using NLP: A comparative approach using AI. *Vivekananda J. Res.*, 10, 42–52, 2021.

41. Velu, A., Influence of business intelligence and analytics on business value. *Int. Eng. J. Res. Dev.*, 6, 1, 9–19, 2021.

42. Khera, Y., Whig, P., Velu, A., Efficient effective and secured electronic billing system using AI. *Vivekananda J. Res.*, 10, 53–60, 2021.

43. Velu, A. and Whig, P., Impact of COVID vaccination on the globe using data analytics. *Int. J. Sustain. Dev. Comput. Sci.*, 3, 2, 1–10, 2021.

44. Khera, Y., Whig, P., Velu, A., Framework of Perceptive Artificial Intelligence using Natural Language Processing (P.A.I.N). *Artificial & Computational Intelligence*, Published Online: July 2021.

9

Internet of Things in the Global Impacts of COVID-19: A Systematic Study

Shalini Sharma Goel[1], Anubhav Goel[2]*, Mohit Kumar[3] and Sachin Sharma[4]

[1]*Computer Science and Engineering Department, MIET Meerut, Meerut, India*
[2]*Polymer and Process Engineering Department, IIT Roorkee, Roorkee, India*
[3]*Information & Technology Department, NIT Jalandhar, Jalandhar, India*
[4]*School of Electrical and Electronic Engineering, Technological University Dublin, Dublin, Ireland*

Abstract

COVID-19 is highly contagious in nature. It marked a grievous impact on the world's social and economic status and disrupted the other related domains as well. Global mental health is debatable in present scenario. Travel and Tourism industry is one of the hardly hit sectors which clearly and badly influenced the aviation industry. In this article, we highlight some of the major global sectors which are highly affected by the pandemic, including social and financial turmoil caused by COVID-19, healthcare front, environment, education, and travel. A reasonable weightage is given to situation in India while discussing about the different impacts. Since the outbreak, researchers have been working feverishly to leverage a broad range of technologies to tackle the global threat. The Internet of Things (IoT) is one of the forerunners in this field. The Internet of Things (IoT) has gained popularity as a new research field in a variety of academic and industry fields in recent years, particularly in healthcare. This article investigates and highlights the overall applications of the well-proven IoT tools and technologies in all the COVID-19 impacted domains by providing a perspective roadmap to combat this global threat. Various myths or misconceptions regarding COVID-19 have also been discussed and explained logically.

Keywords: COVID-19, global impacts, Internet of Things (IoT), smart wearables, robots, drones

**Corresponding author*: agoel@pe.iitr.ac.in

Danda B. Rawat, Lalit K Awasthi, Valentina Emilia Balas, Mohit Kumar and Jitendra Kumar Samriya (eds.) Convergence of Cloud with AI for Big Data Analytics: Foundations and Innovation, (177–204)
© 2023 Scrivener Publishing LLC

9.1   Introduction

The Human coronaviruses are not unfamiliar and were first discovered in 1960's [1], they mainly target epithelial cells of the respiratory tract in humans, causing mild to severe respiratory illness [2]. Depending upon the coronavirus species, they can transmit from one host to another either by fomite, aerosol or fecal oral route [3, 4]. An infected carrier can shed viruses to the surrounding environment. The recent outbreak of coronavirus, commonly called COronaVIrus Disease-2019 (COVID-19) is a new strain of Betacoronavirus (β-CoV lineage B) producing symptoms that are potentially severe [3]. The name of virus causing COVID-19 is severe acute respiratory syndrome Coronavirus 2 (SARS-CoV-2) or new Coronavirus which is a positive sense single stranded RNA virus (+ssRNA) which belongs to coronavirus family as its seventh member. The scientific name given to this group of related viruses is orthocoronavirinae or coronavirinae of family coronaviridae [5]. The initial cases of SARS-CoV-2 traces back to a wet market named Huanan Seafood Market, Wuhan, China, in December 2019 [6]. World Health Organization (WHO) initially named it as 2019-nCoV and declares it as a public health emergency of global disquietude on January 30, 2020 and subsequently as a pandemic on March 11, 2020 [7]. SARS-CoV-2, as renamed by international committee on taxonomy of viruses (ICTV) on February 11, 2020 [8] is the successor of SARS-CoV-1 [6] and is widely believed to have zoonotic origin especially similar to bat coronaviruses [8].

A person infected with COVID-19 may be symptomatic, asymptomatic, presymptomatic [9]. The most common symptoms are cough, sore throat, fatigue, fever, and loss of smell while some acute symptoms are sputum production, headache, hemoptysis, diarrhea, dyspnea, and lymphopenia [6, 10, 11]. It is usually transmitted when a person somehow comes in close contact with the contaminated surface or inhales contaminated respiratory droplets and afterward touches their eyes, nose and mouth without washing or sanitizing their hands [11, 12]. The transmission basically occurs via contaminated respiratory droplets within a range of 1.8 m (6 ft.) [12]. Different research studies are still being conducted at a high pace for the amount of time the virus remains tenable or grounded on different surfaces. It is suggested that it can survive for 3 days on stainless steel and plastic (polypropylene i.e. PP), approximately 4 hours on copper, one day on cardboard, and 3 hours on aerosols [13]. When a person is exposed to the virus, the symptoms generally appear after an incubation period of 2 to 14 days with an average of approximately 5.2 days [9, 11]. During this incubation period, the organism or virus multiplies itself to reach a maximum threshold to produce symptoms in the host person [11].

The WHO published various testing protocols for the COVID-19 disease. The ideal method being widely used is real time reverse transcription polymerase chain reaction (rRT-PCR) [14]. Chest radiographs and Computed Tomography (CT) scans, serological testing, and viral sequencing may also be found supportive in diagnosing COVID-19 in suspected individuals [9]. By far, there is no pharmaceutical intervention (PI) i.e. specific antiviral drug or vaccine against COVID-19 infection. What people should do is to take protective and preventive measures known as Non Pharmaceutical Intervention (NPI) [9]. Currently, the strategy to fight COVID-19 is to trace, quarantine, test, isolate, and treat. Every person should maintain good personal hygiene i.e. washing or cleaning hands with soap and water or alcohol based sanitizer, avoid touching eyes, nose, mouth with unwashed hands, shun travelling, wear a mask, self-isolate as much as possible and most importantly follow social distancing [15]. A physical distance of 1m (3 ft.) is recommended by WHO [11], whereas the US CDC (United States-Center for disease control and prevention) advised maintaining a social distance of 2m (6 ft.) [12]. It is also mentioned to disinfect and clean the often touched surfaces in public places or homes on a day-to-day basis.

COVID-19 leaves a disastrous global impact. All the public and the private sectors around the world are dreadfully destabilized with the onset of its outbreak. The impacts of COVID-19 on the economy, education, human health, and different sectors are appalling as illustrated in Figure 9.1. It is noteworthy that articles studying the impacts of COVID-19 are limited to one concern or another. A study summarizing the various impacts as a whole is missing. This study concentrates on this requirement and covers the global impacts of the COVID-19 in all domains of life and economy. In each of the global impacts that we have specified to discuss, there is a special emphasis given to India.

Since the outbreak, researchers have been working furiously to harness a wide variety of technologies to combat the global challenge, and the Internet of Things (IoT) is one of the frontrunners in this field. IoT is a recent advancement in information technology that refers to the integration of real-world physical objects with internet-enabled technologies to make them smart [16]. Several technologies are grouped under a single platform in order to communicate and share data over a network protocol with no human interaction. In the case of COVID-19, IoT connected/enabled devices or applications are being used to limit

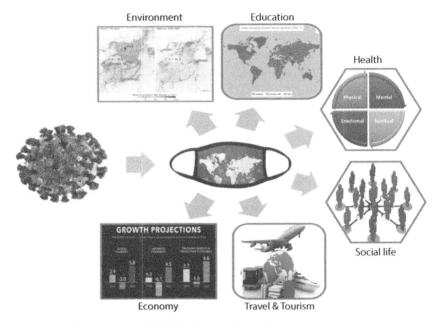

Figure 9.1 Global impacts of COVID-19 on different domains.

the spread of the virus. Ndiaye *et al.* [17] reviewed the in-depth contributions of IoT in virus mitigation and the effects of a pandemic on the transformation of IoT architecture. The challenges associated with the deployment of sensor hardware in the wake of current pandemic are also highlighted in their study [18] emphasized on the role of IoT in healthcare and suggested an IoT architecture based on actuator activation and further reading data from the sensor, to shrink the outspread of COVID-19. Singh *et al.* [19] also discussed the importance of IoT in healthcare and highlighted 12 major IoT applications which can be used to combat COVID-19 pandemic. IoT is playing an eminent role in all fields affected by the current pandemic by its broad spectrum of technological advancements. In this article, we investigate and highlight the overall applications of the well-proven IoT tools and technologies in all the COVID-19 impacted domains by providing a perspective roadmap to fight against it.

This article also discusses several myths going round, related to the COVID-19 and the facts are explained logically and scientifically [20].

9.2   COVID-19 – Misconceptions

a) *Antibiotics can cure COVID-19*: SARS-CoV-2 belongs to the broad family of viruses known as coronaviridae. Antibiotics work against bacterial infection, not viruses. Some people infected with COVID-19 can also develop bacterial co-infection, so in that case, antibiotics may be prescribed. Currently, there is no specific medicine or vaccine to cure COVID-19.

b) *Alcohol kills SARS-CoV-2*: Alcohol poses significant health risks and can be dangerous to the health of an individual. Alcohol does not prevent an individual from COVID-19.

c) *Hydroxychloroquine can cure COVID-19*: Presently no proof is available to support that Hydroxychloroquine or any other drug already available in the medicinal world can cure or prevent from COVID-19. Instead, its misuse can cause severe illness and also lead to death.

d) *Disinfectants protect against COVID-19*: Chlorine (Bleach) or any other disinfectants should not be used or sprayed onto the body. They can cause irritation and also damage the skin and eyes. Disinfectants can be poisonous if ingested. Also, drinking chlorine, menthol, and ethanol can be extremely dangerous to health. They are used to clean a virus on the surface, not in the body. It can harm the internal organs in the body and can cause disability and death.

e) *5G mobile network can spread COVID-19*: Virus cannot travel on a cellular network. COVID-19 spreads through contaminated respiratory droplets or surfaces and then by touching your eyes, nose, and mouth without washing your hands. Countries without the 5G network are also shaking with the COVID-19 outbreak.

f) *Higher temperature can kill the COVID-19*: The virus causing COVID-19 is also outspreading in the countries having very hot and humid weather. At present, no studies support this statement. The normal body temperature is itself 36.5°C and 37°C disregarding the external temperature.

g) *COVID-19 can spread through houseflies and mosquitoes*: COVID-19 is a respiratory virus and no evidence suggests that it can spread through houseflies and mosquito bites.

h) *Hand dryers and UV lamps can disinfect hands and body from COVID-19*: To protect against the new COVID-19, frequently washing the hands with soap and water or alcohol based sanitizer is important. UV rays can harm the skin and eyes and should be avoided.

i) *Pneumonia vaccines can kill COVID-19*: Pneumococcal vaccine and *Haemophilus influenza* type B (Hib) vaccine cannot protect against COVID-19. Many potential vaccines are under human trials around the world for this new coronavirus.

j) *Cleansing nose with isotonic solution can protect against COVID-19*: No documentation supports that continuously rinsing the nose with saline solution can protect against the new coronavirus.

k) *Young population is not susceptible to COVID-19*: This new coronavirus is infecting people of all ages. Many studies support that a person of any age can be affected by COVID-19.

l) *Steam bath can safeguard from COVID-19*: The normal body temperature is itself 36.5°C and 37°C regardless of the external temperature. Taking a hot bath cannot protect against COVID-19.

m) *Eating pepper and garlic defends against COVID-19*: Garlic possesses antimicrobial properties that boost the immunity of an individual. But adding pepper and garlic to the diet does not guarantee the prevention of the new coronavirus.

n) *Recovery from COVID-19 is not possible*: Most of the people who are getting infected with COVID-19 are recovering from it. The number of patients getting recovered from COVID-19 is more than the number of active cases [21].

o) *Continuous use of the medical mask can cause CO_2 intoxication and O_2 deficiency*: Prolonged use of masks though uncomfortable but it can neither cause CO_2 intoxication nor O_2 deficiency if worn properly. Although damp and disposable mask should not be reused.

9.3   Global Impacts of COVID-19 and Significant Contributions of IoT in Respective Domains to Counter the Pandemic

Beyond the fast and vast outbreak of the disease, the consequences of the new COVID-19 pandemic are catastrophic. Around the globe, the repercussions of this new coronavirus cannot be reverted. The prevailing COVID-19 has pernicious effects on mortality and morbidity, effectuating massive public health emergencies. In this part of the article, major disruptions caused by the outbreak of COVID-19 in several fields and the considerable contributions of IoT in each of them are illustrated explicitly.

9.3.1   Impact on Healthcare and Major Contributions of IoT

The pandemic marks a dreadful impact and gives rise to unprecedented challenges for the global mental and physical health of common people and health workers who are on the front line in combat with this disease. Typical reasons of mental stress in general population involves fear of getting infected or dying, worried of being placed in quarantine with other infected, avoiding healthcare for some previous illness due to the fear of catching the virus, nervous for losing the job and distressed about financial condition in case of contamination. The suspected case of COVID-19 placed in quarantine may experience boredom, anxiety, loneliness, and symptoms which they are showing further cause emotional pain or fear of contracting the virus. There has also been a magnified concern for the people suffering from Obsessive-Compulsive Disorder (OCD) as the self-hygiene guidelines are triggering the related compulsions in OCD patients even more [22].

Psychological tension is there among frontline workers, owing to using strict biosecurity measures, elongated and tiresome working hours, insufficient self-care, and fear of getting infected due to long term exposure to patients. In order to support the emotional and psychosocial well-being of different classes of people's, an interim is published by WHO during the COVID-19 outbreak [23].

Along with the medical experts and doctors from the respiratory department, the surgical medical staff (surgeon and anesthesiologists) also plays a vital role in resisting COVID-19 by treating the patients with other critical health issues. A survey was conducted on 120 people from surgical staff divided into two groups in one of the China's hospital at two different time periods i.e. (outbreak period: January 28, 2020 to February 29, 2020) and (Non-epidemic outbreak period: March 2, 2020 to March 21, 2020). Anxiety Scale, Dream anxiety score, Depression Score, and SF-36 scale were four different scales taken to validate the survey. The amount of all criteria on staff during the outbreak period was found to be higher than that of the other group's surgical staff during the non-outbreak period [24]. To cope up with the mental issues of both patients and healthcare workers, it is appreciable to deploy Mental Health Professionals (MHPs) in all COVID-19 hospitals. As mental and physical well-being goes hand in hand, the MHPs have a prominent role to play in this course of pandemic. The Consultation-Liaison (CL) Psychiatrists should identify and analyze the mental health issues of healthcare workers, of people currently in quarantine or diagnosed with COVID-19 infection and their families while also addressing the pre-existing mental illness among all [25]. Harvard Medical School initiated a digital platform to foster the importance of global mental health named 'EMPOWER' in the recent years. It was designed to ratchet up psychological therapies based on evidences, through which providers i.e. any non-specialist therapists can learn and master psychosocial treatments [26].

Many patients with several health issues other than the recent outbreak are also suffering, as either they are not seeking timely treatment or they have not been given required medical attention. Ekiz and Pazarlı [27] showed that obesity related conditions if found in an infected individual, worsens the effects of COVID-19. The influence of COVID-19 on patients, who underwent bariatric surgery (gastric bypass, gastric sleeve, and other weight loss surgeries), has been found substantial [28]. The psychosocial care of those patients is essential. Ozoner *et al.* [29] studies the effect of the outbreak on neurosurgery practice and suggests the postponement of surgeries that do not require immediate intervention. Patients suffering from musculoskeletal tumors are also facing a delay or postponement of promptly required surgery [30]. Diagnosis, treatment, and impact of COVID-19 in patients who have cancer, including solid tumors and hematological malignancies, have been elaborated in one more recent report [31]. The effects of COVID-19 on Liver Transplant (LT) have been reported in one of the research [32]. Due to the lack of ICU beds and the COVID-19 infection concerns in both patients and healthcare workers, there are reports of an extreme cutback in the number of LTs performed in Italy. A study on dentistry has also been conducted and it is found out that due to direct exposure to blood and saliva, dental practitioners are also at a high risk of contracting the disease [33]. Proper protective measures should be taken while examining and treating dental patients. The implications and impact of the outbreak on cardiovascular disease has also been reported in a study [34].

Apart from all these health concerns during the pandemic, drug shortage has also been noticed due to lockdown policies worldwide which superinduces the problems in health facilities. WHO organized a fundraising event named 'Telethon' for 40 countries to raise $8 billion to aid the swift development of COVID-19 vaccines. Likewise, the Coalition for Epidemic Preparedness Innovatives (CEPI) organized a similar fundraising campaign for $2 billion for the same cause. In India, one of the National Health Mission (NHM) reports indicated that there is a sudden fall of 69% for measles, mumps, and rubella vaccination in small children in response to the outbreak. A sharp 50% reduction in clinical attendance for severe cardiac events, 21% drop in institutional deliveries and a steep 32% decline in patients with pulmonary illness conditions was noticed in March 2020 as compared to March 2019 [35].

In the subject of COVID-19, IoT linked/enabled devices and applications can be used to reduce the risk of spreading the virus too quickly to others by detecting it early, tracking infecting patients and following a set of guidelines even after patient's recovery. COVID-19 is being combated with industrial IoT-based solutions in three phases: early detection, quarantine, and recovery [36]. Early detection and diagnosis will result in fewer infections and, therefore, better healthcare for infected patients. By quarantining the COVID-19 infected or suspected people and by implementation of needful restrictions the number of positive cases can be reduced. Following up on COVID-19 patients after they've recovered can aid in the monitoring of reoccurring symptoms and the possibility of a relapse. The various IoT devices and applications which can majorly be utilized to fight against this virus are wearables, smartphone applications, drones, IoT buttons, and robots.

In the first phase i.e. early detection, by collecting data through sensors and then analyzing the data for patients, healthcare professionals, and authorities to identify and monitor this infectious disease, IoT devices make the detection process quicker and more effective. The appropriate wearable devices which may be used in the first phase are smart thermometers in any form i.e. touch, patch, and radiometric to constantly measure body temperature. There are many smart thermometers available in the market which can report body temperature on a smartphone at any time for example Kinsa's, Tempdrop, Ran's Night, iFever, and iSense [37].

Smart helmets attached with a thermal camera detecting if there is a high temperature of the person wearing the helmet and sending the image taken by optical camera and location of the person using Google location history to the assigned mobile device or a health officer. For example, the KC N901 is a smart helmet made in China that detects high body temperatures with a 96% accuracy [36]. IoT base smart glasses embedded with optical and thermal cameras to monitor crowd. Up to 200 individuals can be monitored using smart glasses with infrared sensors. Using unmanned aerial vehicles (UAV) and, in particular, another approach to speed up the process of identifying sick persons and zones during this pandemic is to use IoT-based drones, which can eliminate human interaction and reach difficult locations. Pandemic drone application which is a thermal imaging drone combined with virtual reality for remotely detecting and monitoring any case of infection by capturing temperature, heart rate and any sneezing or coughing. IoT linked robots can fasten the process of early diagnosis by collecting throat swab samples. Intelligent care robot developed by Vayyar Imaging and Meditemi detects COVID-19 symptoms in 10 seconds with a distance of 1 meter [38]. IoT buttons, a programmable device which performs repetitive tasks such as alerting authorities. Wanda QuickTouch is an IoT button developed by Visionstate [39] has been deployed in hospitals as a cleaning alert system. Developing application for smartphones using Internet of Medical Things (IoMT) by which people can update their health status to the cloudIoT and receive online health advice. The smartphone applications being widely used in the first phase of COVID-19 are nCapp, MobileDetect, and Stop Corona.

In the quarantine phase, IoT devices could help in reducing serious challenges by monitoring patients carefully. IoT wearable bands connected through Bluetooth to patient's smartphone can be monitored by healthcare authorities using a web interface every 2 minutes. For example, IPT Q-Band, a wrist band is used in Hong Kong [40] to track new arrivals and ankle monitors or bracelets are being used in United States. Drones that can be used in quarantine phase are Disinfectant Drone and Medical/Delivery Drone. Robots play a vital role in keeping the staff away from isolated patients. Telerobots, remotely operated by humans can perform remote diagnosis, surgeries, and treatments. Collaborative robots or cobots though not as effective as telerobots in this pandemic but can be used during quarantine phase. Asimov Robotics in India and eXtreme Disinfectant Robot (XDBOT) are examples of this category of robot [41]. Autonomous robots are also highly being used these days. Disinfectant robot developed by Xenex and UVD robots created by Danish company falls under this category of robots. Social robots can communicate with isolated patients to save them from potential mental stress. One such example is Paro social robot. If the health condition of a patient deteriorates, by pressing the Sefucy IoT button, the family members and healthcare providers can be alerted. The smartphone applications used during quarantine phase are social monitoring, Selfie App, Civitas and The StayHomeSafe.

In the recovery phase of COVID-19, patients need to be extra cautious, the wearable IoT devices can be used. EasyBand [42] is to ensure that people are implementing social distancing. It works in a certain radius and if people come in close proximity to each other, the LED lights glow and band starts beeping to remind them of social distancing. One more example is Proximity Trace and Instant Trace. In the after recovery phase, many drones such as Surveillance drones can be used to monitor crowd. MicroMultiCopter and Cyient [43] are examples of this class of drones. Announcement drones and multipurpose drones are also being used these days. Robots may also be used in the third phase for example, Spot, a four-legged robot, reminds crowds in public places to implement social distancing. The smartphone applications which can be used in recovery phase are Aarogya Setu, TraceTogether, Hamagen, Coalition, BeAware Bahrain, eRouska, and social media application – Whatsapp. In the future, having IoT enabled smart cities and IoT-based smart home technologies can help prevent any pandemic to a certain level. There are some concerns regarding IoT-based and enabled devices and applications also. One such issue is privacy, where patients are asked to share their data. Before sharing private information, establishing a safe communication network and encryption techniques would be a possible area of research.

9.3.2   Social Impacts of COVID-19 and Role of IoT

Stay at home in order to maintain physical distancing, by all the governments worldwide to prevent the social gathering of people has had a rational effect on every individual. All the large gatherings like marriages, scientific and business meetings and conferences, schools, colleges, multinational companies, religious ceremonies, political rallies, and all such sort of events where people come in contact with each other have been either postponed or cancelled globally. Notable sports events, 32nd Summer Olympics 2020 and Paralympics 2020 to be held in Tokyo starting July 24, 2020 and the 11th World Games to be organized in Birmingham, Alabama, initially planned for July 2021 had also been postponed. It does have a significant detrimental effect on many individuals. Lockdowns imposed by all governments provoked hoarding of essential commodities everywhere, which in turn proved to be calamitous for population belonging to low socio-economic stratum (SES) [44]. The lack of necessities and awareness has seen a significant increase in depression, anxiety, alcohol dependence, chronic stress, and augmented physical (domestic violence), emotional and sexual abuse [44, 45]. The pandemic has gravely inflamed the cases of racism and xenophobia worldwide. It was initially against the Chinese and other East Asian people and then moved further to the people of Italy. Muslims in India also faced discrimination for an event organized in Delhi, India.

In India, the National Commission for Women (NCW) reported a sudden shoot up of 45% in domestic violence cases during the first lockdown period. The pandemic has indirectly intensified preexisting inequalities and sexual discrimination [46]. NCW re-launched a WhatsApp number to allow women to contact them immediately in case of domestic torment. Social distancing measures like self-isolation and quarantine taken to cope up the outbreak has accidentally resulted in loss of jobs for millions of people. This situation has intensified the mental stress, especially for the class with low income, which witnessed a spike in suicidal tendencies or cases all over the world. In the health and social sectors, women accounts for up to 70% of the total workforce. That is the reason behind a large number of COVID-19 cases in female health workers than their male counterparts in some countries [47].

Using proper sanitization techniques and maintain social distancing is the key to fight COVID-19. IoT tools and applications are proving to be valuable in these times. Wearables, smartphones applications, drones, IoT buttons and robots etc. are being widely used to ensure proper sanitization, physical distancing, surveillance, medical delivery, observe patients, recording symptoms and social monitoring etc. Drones are used everywhere for disinfecting and sanitization purposes on a large scale. Social robots can communicate with isolated patients to save them from potential mental stress. One such example is Paro social robot. The role of telehealth and digital tools is very productive to deliver social and mental care in today's crisis.

9.3.3 Financial and Economic Impact and How IoT Can Help to Shape Businesses

In the hour of COVID-19 pandemic, where more than one third of the global population had been placed under lockdown, the world has marked the largest global recession in history. The pandemic has ignited the economic turbulence and had a ruinous impact upon international stock market, crude oil, and gold market in March 2020. Due to the travel restrictions and the reduction in factory activity, the global oil demand got knocked off. To balance the loss in demand of oil, a meeting of the Organization of Petroleum Exporting Countries (OPEC) was conducted in Vienna on March 5, 2020, to discuss over proposed oil-production cuts [48]. The failure of OPEC deal sparked price war among Saudi Arabia and Russia. In order to retaliate, Saudi Arabia instead increased the production of crude oil by 25% compared to February i.e. 9.7 to 12.3 million barrels per day (bbl/d) and sold it for massive discounts of $6 to $8 to US, Asia and Europe [45]. Brent Crude witnessed the largest drop of 30% since 1991 [49] and West Texas Intermediate reported the lowest drop since February 2016. Ultimately in April 2020, the leaders agreed to the biggest oil production cuts of 10 million bbl/d or 10% of global population for the month of May and June. Whiting Petroleum and Diamond Offshore oil companies were bankrupted during the COVID-19 pandemic [50].

Since the 2008 financial downturn, the international stock market divulged their biggest single week falloff on February 28, 2020 [51]. The failure of OPEC deal led both Saudi Arabia and Russia to augment oil production, which in succession led the oil prices to fall by 25% [48, 49]. The gold prices surged to a 7 year high. By March 2020, the stock markets worldwide recorded a decline by over 30% due to the ongoing COVID-19 pandemic and the cost conflict between Russia and Saudi Arabia. The COVID-19 outbreak interacted negatively with the international stock market returns [52]. The NPI policies adopted by various governments worldwide to combat COVID-19 had a significant effect on the global stock market.

There have been many reports of supply shortages of Fast Moving Consumer Goods (FMCG) items due to panic buying around the globe. Due to huge requirement of personal protection equipment's, the prices are reaching sky-high along with a delay of four to six months in supply of medical items. The pandemic marks a disruptive impact on the manufacturing industry as well. Due to the advised self-isolation globally, work from home in the manufacturing industry is not a practicable option. Since the 2008 financial crisis, the chemical industry had witnessed the slowest growth in the current prevailing outbreak, as its global production grows by 1.2% in 2020, which is much slower than 2019 [53]. The automotive industry also suffered a significant loss during this time. The arts and entertainment sector has observed a considerable impact of the outbreak due to social restrictions. COVID-19 resulted in reduced revenues from zoos, museums, performing arts etc., as all of them involve a large gathering of people. Also, it delayed or stopped the production and release of various television programs. The global box office slumped by billions of dollars as movie theatres have been closed, film releases have been delayed indefinitely, film festivals and award functions have been either shelved or cancelled. The pandemic has also adversely affected the global food industry as the social distancing measures do not allow people to dine in the restaurants and hotels. There are many reports of employees being fired from their jobs during the pandemic when all the restaurants and hotels were shut down by the government. Rate of agricultural commodities also drops by 20% due to universal crash in needs from hotels and restaurants, which at once and harshly affects small scale farmers [45].

In India, an estimated 14 crore people lost their jobs during the lockdown period and the unemployment rate rose from 6.7% to 26% within a month [55]. Major public and private sector units such as Larsen & Toubro, Bharat Heavy Electricals Limited (BHEL), Aditya Birla Group, UltraTech Cement, TATA motors and many more have provisionally halted or reduced operations. In India, Stock markets reported their worst falloff in history in March. NSE NIFTY fell by 1150 points (12.98%) and SENSEX fell by 4000 points (13.15%) [56]. International monetary fund (IMF) forecasted a global recession due to COVID-19 and projected that in 2020, the global economy is projected to shrink by (-)3% and speaking of India, its Gross Domestic Product (GDP) growth rate reached 1.9% as compared to 4.2% in 2019 (Figure 9.2) [54]. Overall, India's exports in April 2020 exhibits a negative growth of (-) 36.65%, while imports indicate a negative growth of (-) 47.36% in April 2020 when compared to April 2019 [57]. Up to 53% of businesses in India have specified a certain amount of impact due to shut down. Also, India witnessed the biggest exodus of migrant daily wages workers as they lost their jobs due to the lockdown. Many economic relief measures are taken by the Indian government to pull back the diminishing economy.

Apart from all the measures taken by governments all over the world, COVID-19 has forced businesses to rely on high-tech developments such as the Internet of Things (IoT) for their everyday operations. The use of IoT

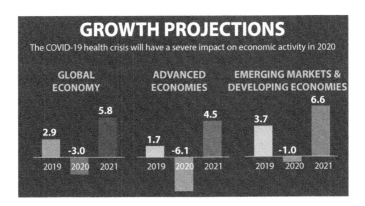

Figure 9.2 Global impact of COVID-19 on economic activity [54].

application development services assists businesses in adapting to the new reality and addressing the challenges posed by the coronavirus. According to a survey, the value of the global IoT market will rise to $243 billion by 2021 as a result of the pandemic. By 2025, the number of connected devices is expected to reach 75.44 billion [16]. The world of interconnected devices enables businesses to make the most of data exchange. The pandemic has given IoT more opportunities to be deeply embedded in digital infrastructure. Many applications areas in which IoT proves to be beneficial are covered in [16]. Here are some ways that eco-friendly businesses can benefit from these apps.

> **Build up new business opportunities**: Businesses may analyze consumer preferences and upgrade or add new products and services using IoT-powered data.
>
> **Reduced expenses**: By troubleshooting issues before they have an effect on business activities, IoT devices may dramatically reduce maintenance costs.
>
> **Improved flexibility**: IoT technologies allow businesses to conduct business in the digital world with remote employees in a seamless manner.
>
> **Increased productivity**: Analyzing data via IoT will reveal which tasks help to streamline operations and which hinder them.

People are unable to stroll back to their workplaces, so with the help of IoT applications and tools like remote computer access, cloud platform, and smartphones, companies are demonstrating efficient performance and are getting back on track. IoT sensors and devices provide remote monitoring solutions and getting the work done from distributed locations. Industrial IoT sensors detect possible shortcomings and provide real-time data. The trend in contactless payment has seen an upward surge during the pandemic and is likely to continue in the future. IoT innovative technologies combined with data analytics provide valuable insights for smart retail, smart farming, and energy markets. The energy sector's increasing acceptance of process changes and technical advances has made the energy sector to generate noteworthy revenues.

9.3.4   Impact on Education and Part Played by IoT

To contain the spread of COVID-19, nearly all governments around the globe have temporarily closed all educational institutions from pre-primary to tertiary level. According to the UNESCO monitoring report, by mid-April, 194 countries had implemented nationwide school closures, which directly affected 1.725 billion students worldwide and that makes up to about 99% of the world's total student population [58]. As of June 23, 2020, 118 countries implemented nationwide closure of schools and colleges in response to the pandemic, affecting 1.09 billion learners of the total 1.725 billion learners which make 62.2% of the total enrolled learners as shown in Figure 9.3. Some countries have imposed localized closures affecting 0.531 billion learners and only 0.104 billion learners are physically able to attend the schools, colleges, and universities as some countries have obviated the closure restrictions [58]. The psychological impact of these closures can be troublesome, giving rise to anxiety, uncertainty, stress, and loneliness to both student's and teacher's fraternity [59]. Also, the lockdown of educational institutions has overarching social and economic effects on students, teachers, as well as their families. To minimize the obstruction in imparting education, UNESCO and many other government organizations have urged the use of digital learning. E-learning portals and access to other virtual options are being explored to fill the gap of learning process to ensure that the impact on education due to this pandemic is the least. The impact is far more severe on underprivileged children and their families who are unable to explore online learning.

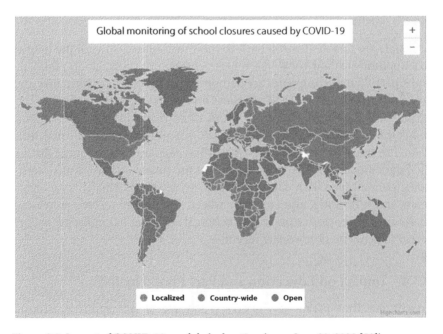

Figure 9.3 Impact of COVID-19 on global education (as on June 23, 2020 [58]).

As it has triggered interrupted learning, lack of nourishment and food insecurity, a gap in childcare, high economic costs, rise in dropout rates [60].

In India, the union government declared a nationwide closure of educational institutions on March 16, 2020 which put all ongoing primary and board examinations on hold till further notification along with the competitive exams which are to be held in the near future. As of April 26, 2021 there is still a country-wide closure of schools, colleges, and universities. The total number of affected learners in India, according to UNESCO are 0.320 billion out of which 0.158 billion are female and 0.162 are male and majority of them are either in primary or secondary level [58]. Various e-learning portals and applications have been launched by educational bodies and government of India such as DIKSHA portal, e-Pathshala, Swayam, STEM based games, etc. In India, most of the teaching community is undergoing stress as they have not been properly trained to use digital platforms and web resources for teaching effectively. Some are facing internet connectivity issues or poor internet if they are residing in far flung areas. Many teachers of schools, colleges, and universities are also perturbed about their salaries and jobs. This pandemic for sure leaves a deep scar on education system globally. Post pandemic, various workshops concerning the use of online teaching and learning, needs to be conducted by all educational institutions. Also stress management courses for all students and teachers should be made imperative [61].

Initially due to COVID-19, all the educational institutes were physically closed which created a great disruption in imparting education as discussed above. But later with the help of digital tools, online collaboration and continuity of educational activities was achieved. IoT may play a crucial role in imparting education, which cannot be overlooked, especially now that we are facing a global pandemic. We should well be prepared for future advancements in the education sector. The key goal of implementing IoT in education is to create an atmosphere that promotes information acquisition in a modern, normal, and productive manner that meets the needs and expectations of students. There are several benefits of using IoT in education: creating interactive smart labs and classrooms, implementing customized digital models of education which can maintain the active participation of students in the learning process, also encouraging their creativity and making the real time assessment of their cognitive activities. An IoT based distance learning framework integrating both teaching and examination activities is proposed for higher education [62].

A collection of IoT sensors provides each student's input data. Real-time streaming data is retrieved and stored by the system. Data is transmitted from a sensor to a receiver, using wired or wireless technology (Zigbee,

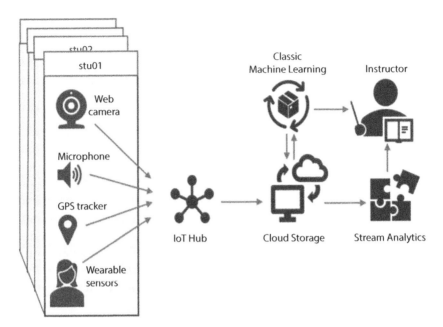

Figure 9.4 IoT framework for managing the educational process in distance learning [62].

Bluetooth, etc.). IoT hub links students' computers to task-specific software on Cloud for data storage and processing as shown in Figure 9.4. Stream Analytics and Machine Learning (ML) algorithms are used to process the collected data. Findings are sent to the lecturer's dashboard and accordingly they can adjust their approach between teaching and examination. Recently, machine learning algorithms and IoT devices have become a backbone of learning activities. This is marked with a exponential rise in publications concerning the IoT in education, currently, making it a hot research area [63, 64]. The COVID-19 situation provides yet another impetus for researchers to look into the use of this emerging technology in online teaching and learning.

9.3.5 Impact on Climate and Environment and Indoor Air Quality Monitoring Using IoT

Due to the travel restrictions imposed by the government worldwide in the wake of COVID-19, the positive effect on the environment and climate can easily be noticed. There was a considerable drop in air pollution because of the reduced economic activity like road and air traffic, coal consumption, and oil refining. The pollutants contributing majorly to air pollution and arousing strong public health concerns includes carbon monoxide (CO), ozone (O_3), sulphur dioxide (SO_2), nitrogen dioxide (NO_2), and particulate matter. There are majorly two harmful particulate matter, a coarse fraction containing the larger particles of size ranges from 2.5 to 10 μm (PM_{10} to $PM_{2.5}$) and a fine fraction carrying small particles of size ranges from 0.1 to 2.5 μm ($PM_{2.5}$ to $PM_{0.1}$) [65]. In the initial days of lockdown in China, 25% reduction in greenhouse gas emissions which are often measured in carbon dioxide (CO_2) equivalent and a whopping 50% curtailment in nitrogen oxide ($NO_X = NO + NO_2$) emissions were recorded [66]. NASA (National Aeronautics and Space Administration) and ESA (European Space Agency) detected a significant drop in NO_2 gases in China in the initial lockdown period as depicted in Figure 9.5 [67].

Similar drops in NO_2 emissions are also recorded in Spain, France, Italy, and USA [68]. A similar study was conducted in four air quality stations in Sao Paulo, Brazil during the lockdown period to analyze air pollutants concentration variation. It was found that there is up to 64.8% decrease in CO concentrations (parts per million, ppm), up to 77.3% reduction in NO

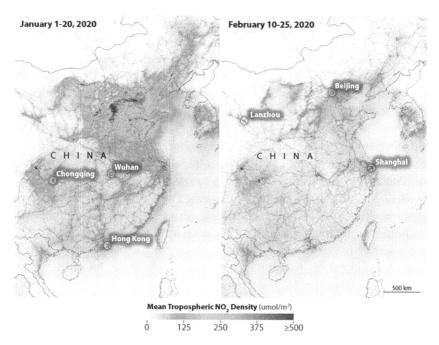

Figure 9.5 NO_2 emissions before and after lockdown in Eastern China [67].

concentrations ($\mu g/m^3$), up to 54.3% drop in NO_2 concentrations ($\mu g/m^3$) and approximately 30% increase in O_3 concentration ($\mu g/m^3$) [69].

In India, similar studies have been conducted and significant results are obtained. India also observed a large restriction in human and economic activity since the mid of March 2020. A study that involves 22 cities of different regions of India is analyzed for six criteria pollutants from March 16 to April 14 from 2017 to 2020. It was observed that there is a decrease of 43% in $PM_{2.5}$, 31% decrease in PM_{10}, 10% reduction in CO, 18% decline in NO_2, a considerable 17% increase in O_3, and negligible changes in SO_2 during the lockdown period as compared to previous year values. Reduction of 29%, 32%, 44%, 33% and 15% in east, west, north, south, and central India, respectively, in Air Quality Index (AQI) is also mentioned in the analysis [70]. A remarkable improvement in water quality and wildlife can be seen around the globe. Various reports of clear water and animals roaming freely are doing rounds these days. This is the only territory where the current pandemic marks a positive impact.

On the contrary, before the surge of COVID-19, monitoring the indoor air quality was never a priority in public places like hospitals, shopping malls, banks, educational institutions, and restaurants. Indoor air, unlike outdoor air, is constantly filtered, trapped, and accumulates contaminants that may aid virus transmission. Now that, some people are still working from home while some started going to jobs and the public places are being reopened such utmost protection from the virus is the only need of hour. So, there is an emergent situation to monitor indoor air quality of confined spaces where people come in close proximity of each other and the ventilation system sucks the outdoor air and recycles it constantly. It causes the air to get trapped and build up pollutants which may facilitate rapid virus transmission. This is where IoT comes into effect, as using the gas and particle sensors, air quality can be monitored and whenever the sensor readings exceed the pre-defined thresholds, alarms are generated. A study was conducted by Mumtaz et al. [71] to monitor indoor air quality and predicting solutions, efficiently based on IoT sensors and Machine learning capabilities. An IoT node consisting of several pollutants along with humidity and temperature, communication module for data transmission and a server for data management were the major components of that study. A similar study was conducted by [72], where the author describes an IoT-based platform for indoor air monitoring that records air quality information and transfers it to a web server for interpretation and classification. Various studies to monitor and maintain indoor air quality have been conducted by many researchers using IoT technologies.

9.3.6   Impact on Travel and Tourism and Aviation Industry and How IoT is Shaping its Future

The tourism and travel industry is going through a lot of tussles to survive in the difficult time of COVID-19. Due to the stern government guidelines to implement social distancing and restricting non-essential travel to contain the spread of the virus, the tourism sector along with the travel industry becomes one of the sorely hit by the current outbreak. According to World Travel and Tourism board, around 50 million jobs may be at compromised in the global travel and tourism [45]. A 22% decline of 67 million international arrivals has been reported by United Nations World Tourism Organization (UNWTO) in the first quarter of 2020, which makes US$80 billion in receipts (exports from tourism). There is an estimation of a 60–80% decline in international arrival of tourists that translates to 850 million to 1.1 billion, steering to a possible loss of US$910 billion to US$1.2 trillion that comes from export revenues in tourism sector [73]. Foreign arrivals in India fell by 66.4% on year on year basis in March 2020 [74].

Due to this significant drop in tourism and a plunge in demand of travelers, the aviation industry is also facing a massive reduction in revenues. It leads to the firing of employees and declaring bankruptcy by airlines; 80% of flight movements were obstructed globally by April, 2020. Due to the huge cancellation of passenger flights, the International Air Transport Association (IATA) projected a total revenue loss of US$419 billion and a net loss of US$84.3 billion by June 2020 with a total number of flights cancelled from January to July is 7.5 million. It calculates to a 54% reduction in demands [75].

Although IoT technology can benefit a variety of industries as it is already discussed above, the travel and tourism industry is especially well-positioned to benefit because it can allow more automation, personalization, and a better customer experience. In travel industry IoT technology facilitating a higher level of personalization inside in flights and hotels. This is mainly accomplished via a centralized systems like internet enabled lighting, heating, air conditioning, television etc. that allows customers to monitor more equipment or services. At airports, IoT enabled sensors can be used to quickly locate the luggage of passengers by sending an alert to their smartphones when their luggage is nearby. To create a more seamless the check-in process in hotels, an electronic key cards can be sent to guests phone then by enabling them as preferred, automatic check-in could be possible without making them wait at reception. Contactless systems have been implemented at airports and travel hubs to improve passenger safety and control.

9.4   Conclusions

Along with an immense medical emergency, COVID-19 irrupted with a global development crisis with far reaching impacts. In this article, global impacts of COVID-19 are discussed and the role of Industrial IoT based solutions available to fight this disease, are elaborated. Different impacts and the part played by IoT in each of them to reshape the life are summarized here, which can help readers to relate with the ongoing pandemic. While discussing each global impact of COVID-19, a concise exploration of Indian scenario is also covered. It is said that partial knowledge is a dangerous thing, in reference to COVID-19, people are falling for many misconceptions. Brief and useful information is also provided for the same to ensure unharmed safety of people.

References

1. Kahn, J.S. and McIntosh, K., History and recent advances in coronavirus discovery. *Pediatr. Infect. Dis. J.*, 24, 11 Suppl., 223–227, 2005.
2. King Andrew, C.E.B., Lefkowitz, E., Adams Michael, J. (Eds.), *Virus taxonomy - 1st edition, Ninth report of the International Committee on Taxonomy of Viruses*, Ist editio, pp. 806–28, Elsevier, Oxford, 2011.
3. Hui, D.S. *et al.*, The continuing 2019-nCoV epidemic threat of novel coronaviruses to global health — The latest 2019 novel coronavirus outbreak in Wuhan, China. *Int. J. Inf. Dis.*, 91, 264–266, Feb. 01, 2020.
4. Han, Q., Lin, Q., Jin, S., You, L., Coronavirus 2019-nCoV: A brief perspective from the front line. *J. Infect.*, 80, 4, 373–377, 2020.
5. Wu, C. *et al.*, Analysis of therapeutic targets for SARS-CoV-2 and discovery of potential drugs by computational methods. *Acta Pharm. Sin. B*, 10, 5, 766–788, May 2020.
6. Zhu, N. *et al.*, A novel coronavirus from patients with pneumonia in China, 2019. *N. Engl. J. Med.*, 382, 8, 727–733, Feb. 2020.
7. WHO Director-General's opening remarks at the media briefing on COVID-19, WHO, Switzerland, 11 March 2020, https://www.who.int/dg/speeches/detail/who-director-general-s-opening-remarks-at-the-media-briefing-on-covid-19—11-march-2020 (accessed Jun. 21, 2020).
8. Gorbalenya, A.E. *et al.*, The species severe acute respiratory syndrome-related coronavirus: Classifying 2019-nCoV and naming it SARS-CoV-2. *Nat. Microbiol.*, 5, 4. Nature Research, 536–544, Apr. 01, 2020.
9. Acter, T., Uddin, N., Das, J., Akhter, A., Choudhury, T.R., Kim, S., Evolution of severe acute respiratory syndrome coronavirus 2 (SARS-CoV-2) as

coronavirus disease 2019 (COVID-19) pandemic: A global health emergency. *Sci. Total Environ.*, 730, 1–19, 2020.

10. Huang, C. *et al.*, Clinical features of patients infected with 2019 novel coronavirus in Wuhan, China. *Lancet*, 395, 497–506, 2020.

11. Q&A on coronaviruses (COVID-19), World Health Organization, Switzerland, Accessed: Jun. 21, 2020. [Online]. Available: https://www.who.int/emergencies/diseases/novel-coronavirus-2019/question-and-answers-hub/q-a-detail/q-a-coronaviruses.

12. How coronavirus(COVID-19) spreads, Centre for Disease Control and Prevention (CDC), USA, Accessed: Jun. 21, 2020. [Online]. Available: https://www.cdc.gov/coronavirus/2019-ncov/prevent-getting-sick/how-covid-spreads.html.

13. Van Doremalen, N. *et al.*, Aerosol and surface stability of SARS-CoV-2 as compared with SARS-CoV-1. *N. Engl. J. Med.*, 382, 16, 1564–1567, Apr. 16, 2020, Massachussetts Medical Society.

14. Corman, V.M. *et al.*, Detection of 2019 novel coronavirus (2019-nCoV) by real-time RT-PCR. *Eurosurveillance*, 25, 3, 1–8, 2020.

15. Advice for the public, World Health Organization, Switzerland, https://www.who.int/emergencies/diseases/novel-coronavirus-2019/advice-for-public (accessed Jul. 04, 2020).

16. Goel, S.S., Goel, A., Kumar, M., Moltó, G., A review of Internet of Things: Qualifying technologies and boundless horizon. *J. Reliab. Intell. Environ.*, 7, 1, 23–33, 2021.

17. Ndiaye, M., Oyewobi, S.S., Abu-Mahfouz, A.M., Hancke, G.P., Kurien, A.M., Djouani, K., IoT in the wake of COVID-19: A survey on contributions, challenges and evolution. *IEEE Access*, 8, 186821–186839, 2020.

18. Kumar, K., Kumar, N., Shah, R., Role of IoT to avoid spreading of COVID-19. *Int. J. Intell. Networks*, 1, 32–35, July 2020.

19. Pratap, R., Javaid, M., Haleem, A., Suman, R., Internet of Things (IoT) applications to fight against COVID-19 pandemic. *Diabetes Metab. Syndr.: Clin. Res. Rev.,* 14, 521–524, January, 2020.

20. Advice for public: Myth busters, World Health Organization (WHO), Switzerland, Accessed: Jun. 22, 2020. [Online]. Available: https://www.who.int/emergencies/diseases/novel-coronavirus-2019/advice-for-public/myth busters.

21. COVID-19 map, Johns Hopkins Coronavirus Resource Center, USA, Accessed: Nov. 19, 2020. [Online]. Available: https://coronavirus.jhu.edu/map.html.

22. Banerjee, D.D., The other side of COVID-19: Impact on obsessive compulsive disorder (OCD) and hoarding. *Psychiatry Res.*, 288, 112966, 2020.

23. Mental health and psychosocial considerations during COVID-19 outbreak, World Health Organization, Switzerland, 2020.

24. Xu, J., Xu, Q. h, Wang, C. m, Wang, J., Psychological status of surgical staff during the COVID-19 outbreak. *Psychiatry Res.*, 288, March, 112955, 2020.

25. Grover, S., Dua, D., Sahoo, S., Mehra, A., Nehra, R., Chakrabarti, S., Why all covid-19 hospitals should have mental health professionals: The importance of mental health in a worldwide crisis! *Asian J. Psychiatr.*, 51, April, 102147, 2020.

26. Patel, V., Empowering global mental health in the time of COVID19. *Asian J. Psychiatr.*, 51, 102160, 2020.

27. Ekiz, T. and Pazarlı, A.C., Relationship between COVID-19 and obesity. *Diabetes Metab. Syndr. Clin. Res. Rev.*, 14, 5, 761–763, 2020.

28. Sockalingam, S., Leung, S.E., Cassin, S.E., The impact of coronavirus disease 2019 on bariatric surgery: Redefining psychosocial care. *Obesity*, 28, 6, 1010–1012, 2020.

29. Ozoner, B., Gungor, A., Hasanov, T., Toktas, Z.O., Kilic, T., Practice during coronavirus disease 2019 (COVID-19) pandemic. *World Neurosurg.*, 140, 198–207, June, 2020.

30. Thaler, M., Khosravi, I., Leithner, A., Papagelopoulos, P.J., Ruggieri, P., Impact of the COVID-19 pandemic on patients suffering from musculoskeletal tumours. *Int. Orthop.*, 44, 1503–1509, 2020.

31. Raymond, E., Thieblemont, C., Alran, S., Faivre, S., Impact of the covid-19 outbreak on the management of patients with cancer. *Targeting Oncol.*, 15, 3, 249–259, 2020.

32. Umberto, M. *et al.*, The impact of the COVID-19 outbreak on liver transplantation programs in Northern Italy. *Am. J. Transplant.*, 20, March, 1–9, 2020.

33. Passarelli, P.C., Rella, E., Manicone, P.F., Garcia-Godoy, F., D'Addona, A., The impact of the COVID-19 infection in dentistry. *Exp. Biol. Med.*, 245, 11, 1–5, 2020.

34. Gupta, M.D., Girish, M.P., Yadav, G., Shankar, A., Yadav, R., Coronavirus disease 2019 and the cardiovascular system: Impacts and implications. *Indian Heart J.*, 72, 1, 1–6, 2020.

35. Cash, R. and Patel, V., Has COVID-19 subverted global health? *Lancet*, 395, 10238, 1687–1688, 2020.

36. Nasajpour, M., Pouriyeh, S., Parizi, R.M., Dorodchi, M., Valero, M., Arabnia, H.R., Internet of Things for current COVID-19 and future pandemics: An exploratory study. *J. Healthc. Inform. Res.*, 4, 4, 325–364, 2020.

37. Tamura, T., Huang, M., Togawa, T., Current developments in wearable thermometers. *Adv. Biomed. Eng.*, 7, April, 88–99, 2018.

38. Vayyar Imaging LTD, World's most advanced 4D imaging sensor, https://vayyar.com/ (accessed Apr. 26, 2021).

39. Visionstate ships first IoT buttons for rapid response to cleaning alerts TSX venture exchange:VIS. https://www.globenewswire.com/news-release/2020/03/23/2004645/0/en/Visionstate-Ships-First-IoT-Buttons-for-Rapid-Response-to-Cleaning-Alerts.html (accessed Apr. 26, 2021).

40. Hong Kong uses tracking wristbands for coronavirus quarantine, Quartz, New York, 2020. https://qz.com/1822215/hong-kong-

uses-tracking-wristbands-for-coronavirus-quarantine/ (accessed Apr. 26, 2021).

41. Cobots v Covid: How universal robots and others are helping in the fight against coronavirus, https://roboticsandautomationnews.com/2020/06/19/cobots-v-covid-how-universal-robots-is-helping-in-the-fight-against-coronavirus/33285/ (accessed Apr. 26, 2021).

42. Tripathy, A.K., Mohapatra, A.G., Mohanty, S.P., Kougianos, E., Joshi, A.M., Das, G., EasyBand: A wearable for safety-aware mobility during pandemic outbreak. *IEEE Consum. Electron. Mag.*, 9, 5, 57–61, 2020.

43. Cyient provides drone-based surveillance technology to support Telangana State Police in implementing COVID-19 lockdown. https://www.cyient.com/prlisting/corporate/cyient-provides-drone-based-surveillance-technology-to-support-telangana-state-police-in-implementing-covid-19-lockdown (accessed Apr. 26, 2021).

44. Gopalan, H.S. and Misra, A., COVID-19 pandemic and challenges for socio-economic issues, healthcare and National Health Programs in India. *Diabetes Metab. Syndr. Clin. Res. Rev.*, 14, 5, 757–759, 2020.

45. Nicola, M. *et al.*, The socio-economic implications of the coronavirus pandemic (COVID-19): A review. *Int. J. Surg.*, 78, March, 185–193, 2020.

46. Nigam, S., COVID-19, lockdown and violence against women in homes. *SSRN Electron. J.*, Apr. 2020.

47. United Nations, The impact of COVID-19 on women, pp. 1–10, 2020, Accessed: Jun. 21, 2020. [Online]. Available: https://www.un.org/development/desa/dpad/.

48. OPEC's pact with Russia falls apart, sending oil into tailspin, Reuters, Canada, Accessed: Jun. 21, 2020. [Online]. Available: https://www.reuters.com/article/us-opec-meeting/opecs-pact-with-russia-falls-apart-sending-oil-into-tailspin-idUSKBN20T0Y2.

49. Oil prices, stocks plunge after saudi arabia stuns world with massive discounts, NPR, USA, Accessed: Jun. 21, 2020. [Online]. Available: https://www.npr.org/2020/03/08/813439501/saudi-arabia-stuns-world-with-massive-discount-in-oil-sold-to-asia-europe-and-u-.

50. Shale pioneer chesapeake considers bankruptcy filing after oil rout, Reuters, Canada, Accessed: Jun. 21, 2020. [Online]. Available: https://in.reuters.com/article/chesapeake-enrgy-bankruptcy/shale-pioneer-chesapeake-considers-bankruptcy-filing-after-oil-rout-idINKBN22O0C4.

51. Global downturn looms as countries struggle to contain coronavirus outbreak, Reuters, Canada, Accessed: Jun. 21, 2020. [Online]. Available: https://www.reuters.com/article/us-china-health/coronavirus-spreads-in-three-continents-markets-brace-for-global-recession-idUSKCN20M069.

52. Al-Awadhi, A.M., Alsaifi, K., Al-Awadhi, A., Alhammadi, S., Death and contagious infectious diseases: Impact of the COVID-19 virus on stock market returns. *J. Behav. Exp. Finance*, Canada, 27, 100326, Sep. 2020.

53. Chemical industry - BASF online report 2019. Accessed: Jun. 21, 2020. [Online]. Available: https://report.basf.com/2019/en/managements-report/forecast/economic-environment/chemical-industry.html.

54. World economic outlook, April 2020: The great lockdown; IMF Report on growth projections. https://www.imf.org/en/Publications/WEO/Issues/2020/04/14/weo-april-2020#Introduction (accessed Jul. 03, 2020).

55. Vyas, M., Unemployment rate over 23%, Centre for Monitoring Indian Economy (CMIE), Mumbai, Accessed: Jun. 21, 2020. [Online]. Available: https://www.cmie.com/kommon/bin/sr.php?kall=warticle&dt=2020-04-07 08:26:04&msec=770.

56. Prabhakara, B.N., Impact of COVID-19 on the Indian economy-A study. *International Journal of Emerging Technologies and Innovative Research*, 7, 1664–1672, 2020. [Online]. Available: www.jetir.org.

57. India's foreign trade: April 2020 pib.gov.in 'Ministry of Commerce and Industry. 10, April, 1253–1267, 2010.AU: Please provide journal title.

58. COVID-19 Educational disruption and response, UNESCO, London, Accessed: Jun. 23, 2020. [Online]. Available: https://en.unesco.org/covid19/educationresponse/consequences.

59. de O. Araújo, F.J., de Lima, L.S.A., Cidade, P.I.M., Nobre, C.B., Neto, M.L.R., Impact of SARS-COV-2 and its reverberation in global higher education and mental health. *Psychiatry Res.*, 288, March, 112977, 2020.

60. Adverse consequences of school closures, UNESCO, London, Accessed: Jun. 23, 2020, [Online]. Available: https://en.unesco.org/covid19/educationresponse.

61. Gautam, R. and Sharma, M., 2019-nCoV pandemic: A disruptive and stressful atmosphere for Indian academic fraternity. *Brain. Behav. Immun.*, 88, 1–2, 2020.

62. Ilieva, G. and Yankova, T., IoT in distance learning during the COVID-19 pandemic. *TEM J.*, 9, 4, 1669–1674, 2020.

63. Pruet, P., Things "(IoET) in rural underprivileged areas. *2015 12th Int. Conf. Electr. Eng. Comput. Telecommun. Inf. Technol.*, 2015.

64. Teräs, M., Suoranta, J., Teräs, H., Curcher, M., Post-COVID-19 education and education technology 'solutionism': A seller's market. *Postdigit. Sci. Educ.*, 2, 3, 863–878, 2020, doi: 10.1007/s42438-020-00164-x.

65. WHO, Ambient air pollution: Health impacts. Accessed: Jun. 26, 2020. [Online]. Available: https://www.who.int/airpollution/ambient/health-impacts/en/.

66. Zhang, R., Zhang, Y., Lin, H., Feng, X., Fu, T.M., Wang, Y., NOx emission reduction and recovery during COVID-19 in East China. *Atmosphere (Basel)*, 11, 4, 1–15, 2020.

67. Airborne nitrogen dioxide plummets over China. earthobservatory.nasa. gov." Accessed: Jun. 26, 2020. [Online]. Available: https://earthobservatory. nasa.gov/images/146362/airborne-nitrogen-dioxide-plummets-over-china.

68. Muhammad, S., Long, X., Salman, M., COVID-19 pandemic and environmental pollution: A blessing in disguise? *Sci. Total Environ.*, 728, 138820, 2020.

69. Nakada, L.Y.K. and Urban, R.C., COVID-19 pandemic: Impacts on the air quality during the partial lockdown in São Paulo state, Brazil. *Sci. Total Environ.*, 730, 139087, 2020.

70. Sharma, S., Zhang, M., Anshika, Gao, J., Zhang, H., Kota, S.H., Effect of restricted emissions during COVID-19 on air quality in India. *Sci. Total Environ.*, 728, 138878, 2020.

71. Mumtaz, R. *et al.*, Internet of Things (Iot) based indoor air quality sensing and predictive analytic—A COVID-19 perspective. *Electron.*, 10, 2, 1–26, 2021.

72. Jo, J., Jo, B., Kim, J., Kim, S., Han, W., Development of an IoT-based indoor air quality monitoring platform. *J. Sensors*, 2020, 13–15, 2020.

73. International tourist numbers could fall 60-80% in 2020, UNWTO reports, UNWTO, 2020, Spain, Accessed: Jun. 27, 2020. [Online]. Available: https://www.unwto.org/news/covid-19-international-tourist-numbers-could-fall-60-80-in-2020.

74. News for airlines, airports and the aviation industry, Centre For Aviation (CAPA), Australia, 2020. https://centreforaviation.com/news/visitor-arrivals-to-india-down-226-in-1q2020-arrivals-down-664-in-mar-2020-993794 (accessed Jun. 27, 2020).

75. Industry statistics - fact sheet, International Air Transport Association (IATA), Canada, 2020. www.iata.org.

10

An Efficient Solar Energy Management Using IoT-Enabled Arduino-Based MPPT Techniques

Rita Banik[1]* and Ankur Biswas[2]

[1]Department of EEE, ICFAI University Tripura, Agartala, Tripura, India
[2]Department of CSE, Tripura Institute of Technology, Narsingarh, Tripura, India

Abstract

The amount of irradiance falling on a photovoltaic (PV) system has a significant impact on its performance. To achieve a constant peak power generation in a PV, maximum power point tracking (MPPT) approach is utilized, which employs a control system to enable PV system to run at their highest power output. The study proposes a method to design solar Maximum Power Point (MPP) Tracker based on an improved, fast, and reliable algorithm. The algorithm is inspired by existing Perturb and Observe (P&O) approach for monitoring solar photovoltaic (SPV) maximum power point. The tracker has been created with a low-cost Arduino UNO development kit, powered by an ATmega328P microcontroller that runs at a 16MHz frequency. The model is fast, accurate and utilizes very low power due to its high frequency operations. The circuit was simulated using Proteus and a hardware prototype to realize the operation has also been established. MPPT was responded in a quick and accurate manner to the changes in solar radiation. The algorithm can significantly minimize the power loss as it removes the oscillation around the MPP. The efficiency offered by the tracker is 99.21% under a Standard Test Condition (1000 W/m^2 irradiance at 25°C).

Keywords: MPP tracker, perturb and observe, Arduino, microcontroller, SPV

*Corresponding author: rita.nit@gmail.com

Danda B. Rawat, Lalit K Awasthi, Valentina Emilia Balas, Mohit Kumar and Jitendra Kumar Samriya (eds.) Convergence of Cloud with AI for Big Data Analytics: Foundations and Innovation, (205–228)
© 2023 Scrivener Publishing LLC

List of Symbols

MPP	Maximum Power Point
PV	Photovoltaic
MPPT	Maximum Power Point Tracking
P&O	Perturb and Observe
Inc. Cond.	Incremental Conductance method
PSO	Particle Swarm Optimization
PCE	Power Conversion Efficiency
ΔP	Change in output power
ΔV	Change in output voltage
I_L	Photo generated current
I	Output current
I_D	Diode current
I_{SH}	Shunt resistor current in amperes
I_{ref}	Photo current at standard reference condition
α_T	Relative temperature coefficient of the short-circuit current
G	Irradiation on the Solar PV module
G_{ref}	Reference irradiation (1000 W/m²)
T_{ref}	25°C
I_{sc}	Short Circuit Current
V_{oc}	Open Circuit Voltage

10.1 Introduction

Energy sources like coal, oil, and natural gas, are the significant source of energy for the world. But, the combustion of these sources is the primary reason of global warming. Therefore, renewable sources are growing more prevalent amongst two categories of energy viz., conventional and non-conventional, presently. The rising degree of pollutants and dwindling use of traditional energy sources necessitate the utilization of clean and sustainable renewable energy. It is now known that non-renewable resources, such as coal, oil, and others, are nearly on the brink of ending and stocks are expected to be depleted during the next 50 to 120 years. These preceding challenges highlight the need of investigating renewable energy sources that are cleaner, economical, and sustained. Hence, the transition towards solar, wind and hydro is on the rise. Renewable energy sources which include solar, wind, thermal, hydro, biofuel, and tidal power presently meet roughly 20% of world energy requirements. PV electricity powered by solar energy is amongst the most promising renewable energy alternatives since, it requires less money, is simple to install, and is economically feasible. Solar energy are also abundant and the most available than others. Solar energy based renewable sources particularly has garnered a lot of attention which is clean and emission-free because it doesn't generate harmful pollutants or by-products. As a result, it is a flourishing research industry today that is challenged by new and more effective modes of solar energy use. Solar power conversion into electricity has many areas of use. PV systems are progressively being incorporated into the worldwide electricity grid. The nonlinear structure of PV arrays in terms of ambient circumstances and changeable climatic elements, on contrary, makes it difficult to extract the utmost power produced by the PV modules. Therefore, the PV modules are able to extract a fake MPP and transform less solar energy into electricity. As a result, the efficacy of PV system suffers a decline. The solar cells presently available commercially can only harvest 10–27% of incoming solar radiation [1–7]. Because solar cells have a poor efficiency, it is necessary to guarantee that the maximum amount of solar light reaches the cells. Also, the Variations in sun irradiance and solar heat affect the output of solar cells [8–14]. When it comes to solar plants with a large installed capacity, the efficiency of PV system drops dramatically. As a result, marginally more efficient MPPT techniques can enhance the produced power. Hence, MPPT approaches have been widely explored and developed by researchers. Thus, to obtain a constant production of maximum power in a solar cell, MPPT approach is frequently utilized [15–17]. MPPT is a technology that uses a control system to allow PV systems to run at their highest power productivity. The technology varies in proportion to the number of sensors, it requires, their complexities, costs, converging speed, and precise monitoring under varying irradiance as well as temperature. When the ambient circumstances change and, as a result, the MPP of the module is adjusted, MPPT approaches can help accelerate the computation for a new MPP. Under typical environmental circumstances, an ineffective MPPT approach may, for instance, maintain the MPP with almost no harm to the power delivered to a system. But, if there are numerous moving clouds in short durations or a fake MPP is spotted, this approach may not be able to keep up with the MPP. Unfortunately, this may compromise the PV system's ability to generate electricity. As a result, selecting the best MPPT approach for the ambient circumstances is critical for maximizing power generation.

Solar cells are integrated with a solar power converter in order to utilize MPPT technique to maximize the yield. There are a number of MPPT methods like Parasitic Capacitance, Constant Voltage Method, P&O [18, 19],

Inc. Cond., [20, 21]. Nonetheless, everyone has own strengths and draw-backs [22, 23]. The Constant Voltage method is simple but an inefficient method since it collects only 80% of the available maximum. The Open Circuit Voltage method is not an accurate technique and it might not oper-ate at the highest point of power generation exactly. Also, the Short Circuit Current method is not accurate and has low efficiency. The data vary with various weather conditions and locations. The constant value must be chosen carefully, to accurately calibrate the solar panel. The Incremental Conductance (INC) method has higher complexity that reduces the sam-pling frequency and increases the overall computational time. However, until the MPP is reached, the slope of the PV curve effects the converter duty cycle in fixed or variable step sizes in INC. MPP tracking time is reduced by increasing the step size, however oscillation around MPP still persists [24]. In Parasitic capacitance method, the parasitic capacitance is very small. Hence, when used in larger PV systems, a large capacitor is essential to eliminate the minor ripples in the PV array, potentially lower-ing the PV array's parasitic capacitance. In P&O method, the voltage level is observed and perturbed until the maximum power point is grabbed. But since perturbations continually shift direction to maintain the MPP under rapidly changing solar irradiation, steady-state oscillation occurs in P&O, reducing system efficiency and increasing power losses [25]. Fuzzy Logic, Artificial Neural Network, and PSO are other commonly used MPPT techniques. Each of the techniques possesses characteristics with respect to complexity, speed, response and apparatus. A modified P&O technique with improved results by reducing the steady state oscillations was pre-sented by Alik and Jusoh [26]. Tey *et al.* [27] established evolution algo-rithm for tracking MPP within few seconds by improving global search space and achieved an accuracy of 99%. Priyadarshi *et al.* [28] projected an intelligent Fuzzy PSO under unstable atmospheric and load conditions. Execution of an enhanced P&O MPPT technique by Alik and Jusoh [29] offered higher efficiency. In comparison to the standard PSO method, Mao *et al.* [30] established a PSO-based MPPT algorithm that reduced the steady-state oscillation with an enhanced output. However, because of their ease of use and increased efficiency, P&O and Inc. Cond. are often employed among the many MPPT techniques. However, their implemen-tation suffer difficulty because the changes in incoming sunlight cause movement away from the MPP and the rate of tracking is relatively slower. It is relatively complex and expensive to incorporate other methodologies [31–33]. Most of the techniques suffer from power loss due to oscillation at the MPP. To address the issue, artificial intelligence (AI) methods such as PSO, Bee Colony optimization, GA, and others were created. The difficulty with the AI method is that if the length of the MPP search space is enormous, the timeframe for converging may be too long [34]. Furthermore, if the weather patterns change quickly, the PV system may run at or near the local maximum power points for an extended period of time.

This study presents the implementation of a PV panel controller with a customized MPPT algorithm relied upon P&O method. The method has been improved in that after achieving the MPP, it eliminates the oscillation surrounding the point in order to attain the steady-state. It continuously tracks and records the MPP. The recorded MPP is updated when a difference between 'power at MPP' and 'PV power' of 5 W is encountered, it is tracked as new MPP (MPP$_{old}$). When the algorithm achieves a new MPP, it compares it to the old MPP in order to create more power and update the previous MPP. The new MPP values are tested to see if the steady-state has been attained by computing the regular middle point. The new method intends to monitor the maximum power points quickly and efficiently. The slope of the P-V curve is used here to find the maximum power point. To monitor the voltage as well as current change in the PV panel, a DC-DC buck converter is employed. Furthermore, the DC–DC converter selection is crucial since it must monitor the MPP independent of the ambient circumstances. To put it another way, it can't have a non-operational zone on its I–V characteristic curve to ensure that the greatest amount of energy is transmitted to the load irrespective of the testing conditions. As the buck converter changes the duty cycle, the change in voltage and current of the panel is achieved that leads in a shift in output power (ΔP) in PV panel. The slope $\left(\dfrac{\Delta P}{\Delta V} \right)$ at a particular position of the P-V curve is calculated from ΔP and change in voltage (ΔV). The calculated slope determines the adjustments of the next duty cycle and until the slope reaches zero or near approximate values. The course of tracking shifts in respect to MPP depending on the slope's side point. The algorithm continually tracks irradiance changes and rapidly reiterates the computation. The precise nature of the algorithm helps to attain the maximum power point accurately with fewer iterations and sophisticated step size. The Arduino UNO board having ATmega328P processing unit is utilized to execute this computation within milliseconds. The 16MHz on-board clock frequency of Arduino offers this high processing speed with small power consumption that a 5V battery can provide. The following is an outline of the remainder of the paper: Section 10.2 has a concise summary of the impact of irradiance on solar PV efficiency. Section 10.3 describes the design and implementation of the proposed MPP tracker. Section 10.4 discusses the results. Finally, in Section 10.5, the study concludes with a conclusion.

10.2   Impact of Irradiance on PV Efficiency

The performance of PV module is commonly measured using a single operating point under IEC 61215 specified standard test conditions (STC), which includes an irradiance of 1000W/m², a module temperature of 25°C, and a spectrum of AM1.5. PV system builders can use these ratings to estimate yearly energy yields. Actual PV installation performance, on the other hand, may vary across a wide variety of real-world operating conditions, and a reliable yield estimate should reflect for this. As recommended in the rating methods of the newly formed IEC 61853 series of standards, this can be predicted or determined experimentally. When an ideal current source connected in parallel with an ideal diode, we consider it as an ideal solar cell. In essence, there is no such thing as an ideal solar cell. Hence, the electrical comparable to a non-ideal solar cell, in addition consists of shunt resistance and series resistance component along with a current source and a diode as depicted in Figure 10.1.

Here I_L, I_D, I_{SH}, and I can be given by,

$$I_L = I - I_D - I_{SH} \tag{10.1}$$

$$I_D = I_S \left(e^{\frac{q(V_L + I_L R_S)}{nKT}} - 1 \right) \tag{10.2}$$

$$I_{SH} = \frac{V_L + I_L R_S}{R_{SH}} \tag{10.3}$$

$$I = I_{ref} \left(\frac{G}{G_{ref}} \right) [1 + \alpha_T (T - T_{ref})] \tag{10.4}$$

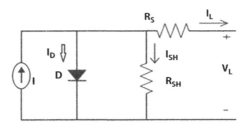

Figure 10.1 A solar cell representation diagram.

So, from the Equation (10.4), it is observed that the solar cell output current (I) is directly dependent on the irradiance (G) which changes the PCE. As a consequence, the solar cell's output power is changed accordingly which in turn varies the MPP. As a result, an efficient approach is necessary for extracting the MPP to give maximum power through a MPP tracker.

10.2.1   PV Reliability and Irradiance Optimization

10.2.1.1   PV System Level Reliability

Enhancing the efficiency of the module would be only one approach to get more energy out of it. The generated power of the PV at the system level, however, seems to be what matters in the end. So the issue is: what could be done at the system level to boost PV system yields?

Aside from the semiconductors used in PV modules, there are only two components that contribute to a PV system's efficiency: electrical and mechanical. The former section is in charge of MPP tracking, which is a step in ensuring the function of PV module at MPP on its I-V curve at a certain irradiance and temperature. At PV system's design stage, this unit cannot be optimized or changed to increase performance but, can be done through MPPT techniques. The other component is the PV system's mechanical component, which may be tuned by the developer to increase the incident radiance incident on the PV array. Physically adjusting the orientation and tilt angle of the module is the easiest technique to increase solar utility. Hence, there exists a requirement for mechanical monitoring device to follow the sun. Because the most of PV systems are permanently escalated, a single option for alignment and tilting changes based on the geographical location throughout the year.

10.2.1.2   PV Output with Varying Irradiance

The subject of how irradiance affects PV production remains unanswered. In literature, it is learnt how irradiance and temperature impact a PV cell's production. When all other factors kept invariable, the greater the irradiance, the higher the output current, and hence the higher the power generated. Because the radiation from the sun are the primary source of energy for PV systems, it's critical that the PV modules are correctly mounted to get the most radiation and minimize partial shading [35]. The unit should point normal to the incoming sun beams in order to collect the greatest irradiation intensity. There exists strong correlation between PV module voltage and current at various solar irradiation levels. One of the finest methods to capture the most solar energy is to use a solar tracking device to trace the sun's movement in the sky continually. The literature showed how the module generates more current on the vertical axis as the irradiance increases. Likewise, the voltage and power characteristics of a PV module may be observed at various levels of irradiances. As the irradiance enhances, the module is capable to produce additional power.

10.2.1.3   *PV Output with Varying Tilt*

The intensity of incoming solar rays on a PV panel determines its optimal performance. As a result, a panel must be angled so that greatest amount of sunrays hit the upper part of the panel vertically. Mounting techniques, terrain topography, and climate conditions all play a role in determining an appropriate tilt [36]. PV modules are typically oriented with the latitudes of the location. Thus, precise orientation is essential for a PV system to achieve full irradiance [37]. The tilt angle and azimuth angle are the two basic angles used to describe array alignment, with the former being the upward angle in between plane and the panel face [38]. Selecting an appropriate tilt angle for a specific installation might help capture the greatest irradiance at a given environmental scenario. Generally, a shorter tilt angle aids productivity in the summer, whereas a greater tilt angle favors low irradiance levels in the winter. Developers should consider the costs of racking and hardware mounting, which may be reduced by lowering the angle of tilt, as well as the potential of wind damage to the array. Solar designers may utilize simple tools created by NREL to discover the ideal tilt and azimuth angles without having to do complex mathematical calculations. There are available tools that lets designers calculate yearly energy output using basic factors to optimize solar utility for a given site.

10.3   Design and Implementation

When numerous units are linked in series, a PV string is generated. In this situation, the string I-V curve is identical to the individual I-V curve of each module, but it is scaled in voltage by the number of modules linked in series, while the current remains constant. PV strings can be as simple as one module or as complex as a series of modules. When strings are coupled in parallel, the current is scaled by the number of threads, but the voltage is equal to the voltage of each individual string. Depending on the size of the system, a PV system might have a single string or numerous strings. Continuing on to the shading impact on PV systems, when one module within a string is shaded, the entire string might lose power due to the limitation of current flowing through the string, similar to the modules level effect. Bypass diodes will clear the shading effect by bypassing the shaded module, as indicated by the modules solution. As a result, the overall string voltage will drop, potentially interfering with the other parallel strings in the system, because the equivalent array voltage is determined by the string with the lowest voltage. As a result, designer opt to include a blocking diode to restrict electricity from travelling back to the weak string, which also eliminates the risk of fire.

The architecture of a solar pv is based on the amount of solar irradiance available at a given location. The input power of daylight or the overall power from radiating sources hitting on a unit area is measured by irradiance. The irradiance obtained by Earth from the sun via the atmosphere is the solar constant for Earth.

$$S = E / (4\pi R^2) = 1370 \text{ W/m2} \tag{10.5}$$

Here, Solarex MSX-60 panel is used for simulation through Proteus that provides easy Arduino microcontroller compatibility as shown in Figure 10.2. The detailed specification of the panel is presented in Table 10.1. The I-V and P-V characteristic curves for Solarex MSX-60 are depicted in Figure 10.3. To model the PV panel in Proteus, a controlled current source of 3.8 ampere (A), a diode with modified Spice code, a shunt and series resistance is created. As per the MSX-60 panel specifications, the saturation current Is, ideality factor, number of cells, and band gap energy must be changed in the Spice code. A maximum of 3.8 A and 3.8128 V is generated by each cell at STC i.e. at the temperature (T) 25° C and irradiance (G) 1000 W/m². I_{sc} of 3.8 A and V_{oc} of 21.1 V is generated by the entire configuration which is encapsulated within a module like structure. The Voltage Controlled Current Source (VCCS) is controlled by DC Voltage Source (DVS) in order to model the Current Source. The diode with spice

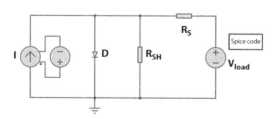

Figure 10.2 The solar panel model under proteus.

Table 10.1 Detailed description of Solarex MSX-60 panel.

Sl. no.	Features	Rating
1	Power (max)	60W
2	Cell type and efficiency	polycrystalline
3	Voltage at maximum point (V_{mp})	17.1 V
4	Current at maximum point (I_{mp})	3.5A
5	Open circuit voltage (V_{oc})	21.1 V
6	Short circuit current (I_{sc})	3.8 A
7	Ideality factor	0.9784
8	Shunt Resistance R_{sh}	153.5644 Ω
9	Series Resistance R_s	0.38572Ω
10	Test condition:	1000W/m², 25°C

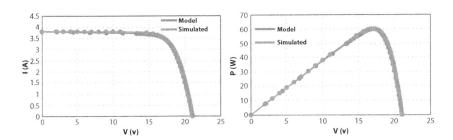

Figure 10.3 The I-V and P-V curves in Solarex MX-60 PV panel.

code is used to control the Saturation current (I_s), number of cell, ideality factor [39]. The DVS is coupled to the PV panel as variable load.

The typical P&O technique periodically monitors the change in power as the voltage is being perturbed to achieve maximum power from PV arrays. If no change of power occurs, MPP is achieved. The major drawback of the P&O system is the fact that it has a restricted tracking speed because it makes a fixed voltage change in the iterations. It thus oscillates around the MPP area for a while, which leads to poor precision when solar radiation is rapidly changing.

This study presents a novel algorithm as shown in Algorithm 1 that tracks the MPP within less than a second. Here, the P-V curve of the PV array system uses a variable step size to establish the maximum power point. Instead of a fixed duty cycle, the buck converter uses a varied duty cycle in accordance with the slope $\left(\dfrac{\Delta P}{\Delta V}\right)$ of the P-V curve. On the right side of MPP, the slope is less than zero while on the left side of MPP the slope is positive, i.e., greater than zero. The step size is therefore regulated automatically that achieves an improvement in tracking speed. Unlike the traditional P&O method, the algorithm after reaching the MPP removes the oscillation surrounding the MPP as it reaches the steady-state [40]. This is achieved in the following way: The algorithm normally tracks the MPP and recorded as 'P_{mpp}' continuously. If ($P_{mpp} - P_{pv} > \Delta P$), it is tracked as new MPP (MPP_{old}). There is a variation of 5W (ΔP=5W) in P_{pv}, if there is a variation of 30 W/m^2 in irradiance 'G', which represents that G is changed. When the algorithm attains a new MPP, it is compared with MPP_{old} to generate higher power and updates the MPP_{old}. The tracking converges at the boundary (i.e., 0.1-0.9 V_{oc}). The new MPP_{old} is checked as if the steady-state is reached, through computing the regular middle point (V_{mid}). The voltage is registered as V_{mid} if the step shifts two successive directions. If the step is V_{mid} again, the counter is incremented by 1. When the counter hits the limit, the oscillation stops and the step at V_{mid} also stops. Thus, the oscillation is stopped approximately at the MPP. As a result, the total loss of power is reduced.

Algorithm 10.1 Algorithm for MPP tracking using proposed technique.

1. Read V_n, I_n
2. Calculate P_n
   a. dP = P_n - P_{n-1}
   b. dV = V_{n-1} - V_n
   c. Slope = dP / dV
3. Calculate V_{mid}
4. If Slope = 0
   duty cycle (n) = duty cycle (n-1)
   else
   duty cycle (n) = duty cycle (n-1) + (α * Slope)
5. Goto 1.

10.3.1   The DC to DC Buck Converter

The buck converter is a simple DC-DC converter that outputs a lower voltage than the input voltage. The inductor in a buck converter typically "bucks" or works against the input voltage, thus the name. An ideal buck converter's output voltage is simply the product of the switching duty cycle and the source voltage. The DC-DC step-down (buck) converter has a controller including one or more inbuilt FETs and an additional inductor, and they provide a good blend of versatility and usability. Buck converters, both synchronous and non-synchronous, simplifies the conceptual design by decreasing the number of external components. Simultaneously, the choices external inductor allows improving the power supply for efficiency, size, or price. The DC/DC buck voltage converter and accompanying modeling tools are available to assist almost every need in order to meet the power-supply design issues. The impedance coupled to a PV panel determines its working point. The panel can, therefore, be worked on the maximum power point by adjusting the load impedance. PV panel is a DC source, so the DC-DC converter is applied as shown in the panel to adjust the load impedance. The representation diagram of the DC-DC converter is shown in Figure 10.4. Increasing the duty cycle of the converter will change the impedance. Here, a buck converter is designed for this purpose as per specifications listed in Table 10.2. Through increasing its duty cycle, the converter bucks the V_{oc} of the panel. Thus, Arduino determines the slope of the P-V curve. Arduino from one of its pulse width modulation (PWM) pins fed the successive duty cycle value to the buck converter

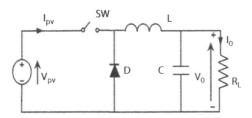

Figure 10.4 Circuit diagram of the designed buck converter.

Table 10.2 Component specifications for the BUCK converter.

1.	Inductor	0.5 mH
2.	Capacitor	150 µF
3.	Load Resistance	5 Ω
4.	MOSFET	IRFZ44N Switching Frequency: 50 kHz
5.	Diode	10BQ040

MOSFET after the required calculations. The impedance, therefore, continues to change and settles at the MPP of the P-V curve. IRFZ44N logic level MOSFET is used that can be directly driven by an Arduino PWM pin.

10.3.2   The Arduino Microcontroller

Arduino Uno is an open framework that may be used to create electrical creations. Arduino consists of a hardware configurable programmed circuitry (microcontroller) and software referred as an IDE (Integrated Development Environment), used to create and transfer programming code to the physical board. The Arduino platform has grown in popularity among those who are just getting started with circuits, and for good cause. Unlike many other prior programmable circuitry, the Arduino does not require an additional hardware device (known as a programmer) to transfer new code into the device; instead, a USB cable is all that is required. Furthermore, the Arduino IDE makes programming easier by using a simplified form of C++. Finally, Arduino offers a standard form factor that separates the microcontroller's tasks into a more manageable packaging. Simply voltage levels are sensed by the Arduino microcontroller. It can accommodate up to 5V of its analog pins. A current sensor is therefore used to capture current values. The sensor is used to sense the panel output current and converts it to a 5 V range in conjunction with a filter circuit. The value would then be transformed to the current equivalent value, which Arduino then uses for calculation. The panel's output voltage must likewise be scaled down in this range. Hence, a voltage divider circuit has been utilized with a resistance ratio of 1:7 to transform the maximum voltage of 34V within the range of 5V. Since the solar insolation level often changes quickly, the maximum power point is, therefore, to be calculated within a period of time. The schematic diagram is shown in Figure 10.5. Because of its fast processing speed, numerous built-in functionality, acoustic contents (digital operation), and versatility, the Arduino microcontroller board was chosen for this work. The following are some of the other advantages of utilizing Arduino:

1. There is no need for external PWM generating equipment.
2. It includes a supplementary 5V power supply for the current sensors and LCD operations. Additionally, ATmega328P offers features of high performance, low power consumption, fully static operation, on chip analog comparator and advance RISC architecture. Because of its sophisticated RISC design, the ATmega328P is an 8-bit AVR microcontroller

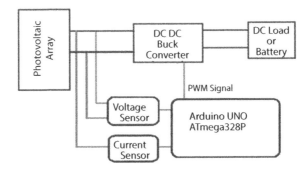

Figure 10.5 The proposed MPP tracker's schematic design.

with high efficiency and low power consumption that can execute 131 strong instructions in a single clock cycle. It's a CPU that's typically seen in Arduino boards like the Arduino Fio and Arduino Uno. Advantages of ATmega328p are the following:

1. Processors are easier to operate since they employ 8bit and 16bit instead of the more difficult 32/64bit.
2. With 32k bytes of onboard self-programmable flash program memory and 23 programmable I/O lines, it may be used without any external computational components.

Table 10.3 Various features of ATmega328P.

1.	Total number of Pins	28
2.	Processing Unit	RISC 8-Bit AVR
3.	Range of operating voltage	1.8 - 5.5 V, 5V as a standard
4.	Program Memory and Type	32KB (Flash)
5.	EEPROM	1 KB
6.	SRAM	2 KB
7.	ADC channels	8 of 10-Bit
8.	PWM Pins	6
9.	Comparator	1
10.	Oscillator	up to 20 MHz
11.	Timer/counter	3 nos, 8-Bit-2, and 16-Bit-1

3. The arithmetic logic unit (ALU) is intrinsically linked to all 31 registers, resulting in a microcontroller that is 10 times quicker than traditional CISC microcontrollers.
4. AVR improved RISC instruction set optimized. It's well-suited for power control, rectifier, and DAC applications owing to the fast PWM mode, which generates high-frequency PWM waveforms.

Other features of ATmega328P are represented in Table 10.3.

10.3.3   Dynamic Response

The response of the developed algorithm is depicted in Figure 10.6 which reveals that the proposed algorithm follows the rapid irradiation changes very quickly. For demonstration, the solar irradiance is changed from 1000 W/m^2 to 600 W/m^2 from time 2 sec and kept up to 4 sec. Again the irradiance is raised to 1000 W/m^2 at time 4 sec. The corresponding voltage and power are also shown. In both cases, the time required to track the MPP is 0.2 seconds. It is shown that, for a given change in solar irradiation, the PV power changes proportionally.

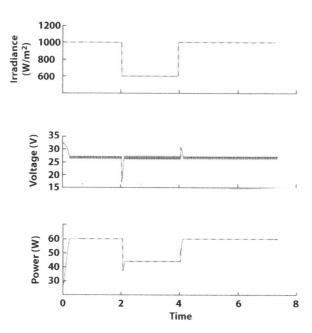

Figure 10.6 The PV power and voltage under varying solar irradiance.

10.4   Result and Discussions

In this study, Proteus is used for simulation. To simulate the PV module in Proteus, the analogous circuit is created using a controlled current source and a diode using customized Spice code, which is then used to develop a true PV panel model. The setting of the PV panel is as follows: Voc = 21.1V, Isc = 3.8A, and under STC, the maximum output power of PV is 60W. Global irradiance is varied as 1000 W/m², 811 W/m², 676 W/m², 540 W/m², 405 W/m², and 270 W/m². In PV systems, the matter of concern is the overall current and voltage that the PV module can produce, hence we create the Module I-V curve, also known as the current-voltage curve. The curve depicts the voltage and current under various operating circumstances. For instance, the maximum current refers to the short-circuit condition (when the positive and negative connectors of the PV module are attached without load, allowing extremely greater current to flow), whereas the maximum voltage arises when the positive and negative connectors of the PV module are attached to any load, allowing no power to flow. When the current and voltage beginning at the open-circuit situation is examined (where the voltage is greatest and the current is zero), and increasing the load of the circuit, the current begins to climb as the voltage declines until it approaches zero at the short-circuit condition (where the current is maximum). Other approach to see the I-V curve is to transform it to a power-voltage relationship. In this scenario, we may refer to it as the PV module's (P-V) curve. Like an I-V curve, the maximum voltage appears when the circuit is open and the current is zero, and the lowest voltage occurs when the circuit is closed and the current is largest. Because power can considered as voltage times current (P=VXI), power is exactly zero among both short-circuit and open-circuit states because either voltage or current is zero at any of these sites. If we watch the power and voltage beginning at the open-circuit state (where the voltage is greatest and the power is zero), then increasing the load of the circuit, the power begins to climb and the voltage lowers until it reaches the value at MPP (where power is maximum and voltage is zero). As the load is raised further, the voltage continues to decline. Yet, the power would decline until it hits zero in a short-circuit circumstance (where the both voltage and power are zero). It is revealed that the peak power on the P-V curve is much easier to identify than on the I-V curve since it represents a hump. The MPP has been effectively tracked and the maximum power obtained as 58.59 W. The current and voltage were measured as 3.12 A and 18.78 V respectively. The model has been checked in order to confirm if the MPP can be monitored each time. The model effectively and reliably recorded MPPs at each point which is illustrated in Figure 10.7. At lower irradiance levels the power attained was lower. For example, at 811 W/m², 676 W/m², 540 W/m², 405 W/m², and 270 W/m² the power attained is 51.97 W, 47.49 W, 36.21 W,

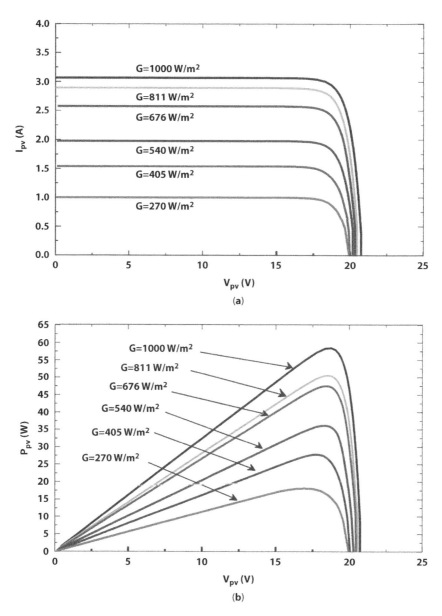

Figure 10.7 Output characteristics curve while tracking the MPP at different irradiance for Solarex MSX-60 (a) I-V (b) P-V characteristics.

Table 10.4 Comparison of simulated MPPs with measured power and efficiencies at various irradiances.

| Irradiances G (W/m²) | Simulated MPP values | | | Measured power from controller | Efficiency of power translation |
	V_{mp}(V)	I_{mp}(A)	P_{mp}(W)	P_{mp}(W)	(η %)
1000	18.78	3.12	58.5936	58.1353	99.21
811	18.43	2.82	51.9726	51.1254	98.36
676	18.41	2.58	47.4978	45.5738	95.94
540	18.29	1.98	36.2142	35.2173	97.24
405	18.13	1.54	27.9202	26.3815	94.48
270	17.71	1.01	17.8871	17.0971	95.55

Table 10.5 An assessment of the proposed method to various MPPT techniques.

Methods	Cost	Time to track MPP in seconds	Efficiency %
Constant Voltage	-	0.2-0.4	95.16
Fixed duty cycle	-	-	57.80
Incremental Conductance	Costly	0.5	98.53
Existing P&O	-	0.2-0.4	98.40
Neural network based P&O [42]	-	0.2-0.5	94-98
Improved INC [43]	Cost-effective	0.33	98.91
Proteus-Based Arduino Board Environments [44]	-	0.2-0.96	99.4
Improved INC [45]	-	0.35-0.39	94.83
Modified P&O (Proposed)	Cost-effective	0.2	99.21

27.92 W and 17.88 W, respectively. It also validates the predicted behavior of a solar-energy-converting device: output power decreases as irradiation decreases. The impact of increasing panel temperature on reduced power is not immediately apparent, but it is consistent with a large influence on open-circuit voltage V_{oc}. An external 60 W solar panel was attached to the tracker. Table 10.4 illustrates the V_{mp}, I_{mp}, P_{mp}, and efficiency of the tracker for various levels of irradiance. The efficiency of the tracker was measured within the range of 94.48% to 99.21%. The proposed method is compared to various MPPT techniques [41] as demonstrated in Table 10.5.

The proposed tracker is considered to be cost effective since it uses low cost sensors on Arduino board to track the irradiances. The time required to track the MPP is 0.2 seconds which is considerably very low. Finally, the efficiency of the tracker was measured within the range of 94.48% to 99.21%, which is quite satisfactory.

10.5   Conclusions

PV energy production has recently emerged as a potential source of energy because to its several advantages, including cheap maintenance costs, no need for relocation, and also no pollutants. Yet, the poor efficacy of panels and the expensive cost of PV system deployment may be deterrents to its adoption. Furthermore, the nonlinear behavior and strong reliance of PV modules on solar irradiance and temperature provide significant hurdles in PV system researches. To circumvent these constraints, the functioning of the PV system just at MPP is a necessity that can increase the PV reliability and capacity. As a result, the MPPT algorithm is applied. This paper showed a new approach to quickly and accurately track the MPP of solar panels. A high-speed processor clocked microcontroller board (Arduino UNO) was used to design the tracker. Proteus software is utilized to design and simulate the model. As Arduino could not accept voltages greater than 5 V, a voltage sensor is utilized to lower the Voltage level to some other value between (Vd) [0, 5] that could be recognized by Arduino. The current sensor is utilized to convey a representation of the PV panel power to the Arduino. A modified P&O algorithm is established with zero oscillation at the MPP. The new method was written in the Arduino programming language before being loaded into the microcontroller. The circuitry functioned autonomously in according to the algorithm and allowed for real-time decision making. The built MPP tracker has also been evaluated in an outside location using the experimental configuration. The circuit produces output based on the findings of the simulated model. The model was calculated as 99.21 percent as maximum efficiency. The new technique may be considered as addressing the drawbacks of traditional P&O and improving the overall efficiency.

References

1. Banakhr, F.A. and Mosaad, M.I., High performance adaptive maximum power point tracking technique for off-grid photovoltaic systems. *Sci. Rep.*, 11, 20400, 2021, doi: https://doi.org/10.1038/s41598-021-99949-8.

2. Kermadi, M., Salam, Z., Eltamaly, A.M., Ahmed, J., Mekhilef, S., Larbes, C., Berkouk, E., Recent developments of MPPT techniques for PV systems under partial shading conditions: A critical review and performance evaluation. *IET Renew. Power Gener.*, 14, 3401–3417, 2020.

3. Al-Majidi, S., Abbod, M.F., Al-Raweshidy, H.S., A novel maximum power point tracking technique based on fuzzy logic for photovoltaic systems. *Int. J. Hydrog. Energy*, 43, 14158–14171, 2018.

4. Salman, S., Xin, A.I., Zhouyang, W.U., Design of a P&-O algorithm based MPPT charge controller for a stand-alone 200W PV system. *Prot. Control Mod. Power Syst.*, 3, 25, 2018, doi: https://doi.org/10.1186/s41601-018-0099-8.

5. Sarika, P.E., Jacob, J., Mohammed, S., Paul, S., A novel hybrid maximum power point tracking technique with zero oscillation based on P&O algorithm. *Int. J. Renew. Energy Res.*, 10, 1962–1973, 2020.

6. Başoğlu, M.E. and Çakır, B., Comparisons of MPPT performances of isolated and non-isolated DC–DC converters by using a new approach. *Renew. Sust. Energ. Rev.*, 60, 1100–1113, 2016.

7. Killi, M. and Samanta, S., An adaptive voltage-sensor-based MPPT for photovoltaic systems with SEPIC converter including steady-state and drift analysis. *IEEE Trans. Ind. Electron.*, 62, 12, 2015.

8. Thongsuwan, W., Sroila, W., Kumpika, T. *et al.*, Antireflective, photocatalytic, and superhydrophilic coating prepared by facile sparking process for photovoltaic panels. *Sci. Rep.*, 12, 1675, 2022, doi: https://doi.org/10.1038/s41598-022-05733-7.

9. Dhimish, M. and Tyrrell, A.M., Power loss and hotspot analysis for photovoltaic modules affected by potential induced degradation. *NPJ Mater. Degrad.*, 6, 11, 2022, doi: https://doi.org/10.1038/s41529-022-00221-9.

10. Grubisic-Cabo, F., Nizetic, S., Marco, T.G., Photovoltaic panels: A review of the cooling technique. *Trans. Famena*, 40, SI-1, 63–74, 2016.

11. Ramaprabha, R. and Mathur, B.L., Impact of partial shading on solar PV module containing series connected cells. *Int. J. Recent Trends Eng.*, 2, 7, 56–60, 2009.

12. Moharram, K.A., Abd-Elhady, M.S., Kandil, H.A., El-Sherif, H., Enhancing the performance of photovoltaic panels by water cooling. *Ain Shams. Eng. J.*, 4, 4, 869–877, 2013.

13. Alonso-Garcia, M.C., Ruiz, J.M., Chenlo, F., Experimental study of mismatch and shading effects in the I–V characteristic of a photovoltaic module. *Sol. Energy Mater. Sol. Cells*, 90, 3, 329–340, 2006.

14. Kawamura, H., Naka, K., Yonekura, N., Yamanaka, S., Kawamura, H., Ohno, H., Naito, K., Simulation of I–V characteristics of a PV module with shaded PV cells. *Sol. Energy Mater. Sol. Cells*, 75, 3, 613–621, 2003.

15. Danandeh, M.A. and Mousavi, S.M.G., Comparative and comprehensive review of maximum power point tracking methods for PV cells. *Renew. Sustain. Energy Rev.*, 82, 2743–2767, 2018.

16. Dandoussou, A., Kamta, M., Bitjoka, L., Wira, P., Kuitché, A., Comparative study of the reliability of MPPT algorithms for the crystalline silicon photovoltaic modules in variable weather conditions. *J. Electr. Syst. Inf. Technol.*, 4, 1, 213–224, 2017.

17. Pant, S. and Saini, R.P., Comparative study of MPPT techniques for solar photovoltaic system. *International Conference on Electrical, Electronics and Computer Engineering (UPCON)*, pp. 1–6, 2019, doi: 10.1109/UPCON47278.2019.8980004.

18. Salman, S., AI, X., WU, Z., Design of a P-&-O algorithm based MPPT charge controller for a stand-alone 200W PV system. *Prot. Control Mod. Power Syst.*, 3, 25, 2018, doi: https://doi.org/10.1186/s41601-018-0099-8.

19. Elgendy, M.A., Zahawi, B., Atkinson, D.J., Assessment of perturb and observe MPPT algorithm implementation techniques for PV pumping applications. *IEEE Trans. Sustain. Energ.*, 3, 1, 21–33, 2012.

20. Shang, L., Guo, H., Zhu, W., An improved MPPT control strategy based on incremental conductance algorithm. *Prot. Control Mod. Power Syst.*, 5, 14, 2020.

21. Tey, K.S., Mekhilef, S., Seyedmahmoudian, M., Horan, B., Oo, A.M., Stojcevski, A., Improved differential evolution-based MPPT algorithm using SEPIC for PV systems under partial shading conditions and load variation. *IEEE Trans. Ind. Inform.*, 14, 10, 4322–4333, 2018, doi: https://doi.org/10.1109/TII.2018.2793210.

22. Hlaili, M. and Hfaiedh, M., Comparison of different MPPT algorithms with a proposed one using a power estimator for grid connected PV systems. *Int. J. Photoenergy*, 2016, Article ID 1728398, pages 10, 2016. 10.1155/2016/1728398.

23. Carannante, G., Fraddanno, C., Pagano, M., Piegari, L., Experimental performance of MPPT algorithm for photovoltaic sources subject to inhomogeneous insulation. *IEEE Trans. Ind. Electron.*, 56, 11, 4374–4380, 2009.

24. Kumar, N., Hussain, I., Singh, B., Panigrahi, B.K., Self-adaptive incremental conductance algorithm for swift and ripple-free maximum power harvesting from PV array. *IEEE Trans. Ind. Informat.*, 14, 5, 2031–2041, 2018.

25. Jiang, L.L., Srivatsan, R., Maskell, D.L., Computational intelligence techniques for maximum power point tracking in PV systems: A review. *Renew. Sustain. Energy Rev.*, 85, 14–45, 2018.

26. Alik, R. and Jusoh, A., Modified Perturb and Observe (P&O) with checking algorithm under various solar irradiation. *Sol. Energy*, 148, 128–139, 2017, doi: https://doi.org/10.1016/j.solener.2017.03.064.

27. Tey, K.S. and Mekhilef, S., Modified incremental conductance MPPT algorithm to mitigate inaccurate responses under fast-changing solar irradiation level. *J. Sol. Energy*, 101, 333–342, 2014.

28. Priyadarshi, N., Padmanaban, S., Kiran, M.P., Sharma, A., An extensive practical investigation of FPSO-based MPPT for grid integrated PV system under variable operating conditions with anti-islanding protection. *IEEE Syst. J.*, 13, 2, 1861–1871, 2018, doi: https://doi.org/10.1109/JSYST.2018.2817584.

29. Alik, R. and Jusoh, A., An enhanced P&O checking algorithm MPPT for high tracking efficiency of partially shaded PV module. *Sol. Energy*, 163, 570–580, 2018, doi: https://doi.org/10.1016/J.SOLENER.2017.12.050.

30. Rizzo, S.A. and Scelba, G., ANN based MPPT method for rapidly variable shading conditions. *Appl. Energy*, 145, 124–132, 2015.

31. Mao, M., Zhang, L., Duan, Q., Oghorada, O., Duan, P., Hu, B., A Two-stage particle swarm optimization algorithm for MPPT of partially shaded PV arrays. *Int. J. Green Energy*, 14, 694–702, 2017, doi: https://doi.org/10.1080/1 5435075.2017.1324792.

32. Kulaksız, A.A. and Akkaya, R., A genetic algorithm optimized ANN-based MPPT algorithm for a stand-alone PV system with induction motor drive. *Sol. Energy*, 86, 9, 2366–2375, 2012.

33. Larbes, C., Cheikh, S.A., Obeidi, T., Zerguerras, A., Genetic algorithms optimized fuzzy logic control for the maximum power point tracking in photovoltaic system. *Renew. Energy*, 34, 10, 2093–2100, 2009.

34. Hua, C.-C. and Zhan, Y.-J., A hybrid maximum power point tracking method without oscillations in steady-state for photovoltaic energy systems. *Energies*, 14, 5590, 2021, doi: https://doi.org/10.3390/ en14185590.

35. Babatunde, A., Abbasoglu, S., Senol, M., Analysis of the impact of dust, tilt angle and orientation on performance of PV Plants. *Renew. Sust. Energ. Rev.*, 90, 1017–1026, 2018.

36. Almeida, M.A.P., Recent advances in solar cells, in: *Solar Cells*, Sharma, S., Ali, K. (eds),. Springer, Cham., 2020. https://doi.org/10.1007/978-3-030-36354-3_4

37. Babatunde, A.A. and Abbasoglu, S., Evaluation of field data and simulation results of a photovoltaic system in countries with high solar radiation. *Turk. J. Elec. Eng. Comp. Sci.*, 23, 1608–1618, 2015.

38. Motahhir, S., Chalh, A., Ghzizal, A., Sebti, S., Derouich, A., Modeling of photovoltaic panel by using proteus. *J. Eng. Sci. Technol. Rev.*, 10, 2, 8– 13, 2017.

39. Hua, C.-C. and Chen, Y.-M., Modified perturb and observe MPPT with zero oscillation in steady-state for PV systems under partial shaded conditions, in: *2017 IEEE Conference on Energy Conversion (CENCON)*, pp. 5–9, 2017, DOI: 10.1109/CENCON.2017.8262448.

40. Hafez, A., Soliman, A., El-Metwally, K., Ismail, I., Tilt and azimuth angles in solar energy applications–A review. *Renew. Sust. Energ. Rev.*, 15, 713–720, 2011.

41. Tofoli, F.L., Pereira, D., Paula, W.J., Comparative study of maximum power point tracking techniques for photovoltaic systems. *Int. J. Photoenergy*, 2015, Article ID 812582, 10 pages, 2015, doi: http://dx.doi.org/10.1155/2015/812582.

42. Kacimi, N., Grouni, S., Idir, A., Boucherit, M.S., New improved hybrid MPPT based on neural network-model predictive control-kalman filter for photovoltaic system. *Indones. J. Electr. Eng. Comput. Sci.*, 20, 3, 1230, 2020.

43. Xu, L., Cheng, R., Yang, J., A new MPPT technique for fast and efficient tracking under fast varying solar irradiation and load resistance. *Int. J. Photoenegry*, Article ID 6535372, 18 pages, 2020.

44. Chellakhi, A., Beid, S.E., Abouelmahjoub, Y., Implementation of a novel MPPT tactic for PV system applications on MATLAB/Simulink and proteus-based Arduino Board Environments. *Int. J. Photoenergy*, Article ID 6657627, 19 pages, 2021, doi: https://doi.org/10.1155/2021/6657627.

45. El Hassouni, B., Armani, A.G., Haddi, A., A new MPPT technique for optimal and efficient monitoring in case of environmental or load conditions variation. *Int. J. Inf. Tec. App. Sci.*, 3, 2, 18–28, 2021, doi: https://doi.org/10.52502/ijitas.v3i2.16.

11

Axiomatic Analysis of Pre-Processing Methodologies Using Machine Learning in Text Mining: A Social Media Perspective in Internet of Things

Tajinder Singh[1], Madhu Kumari[2], Daya Sagar Gupta[3]* and Nikolai Siniak[4]

[1]Department of CSE, SLIET Longowal, India
[2]Department of CSE, Chandigarh University, India
[3]Department of CSE, RGIPT Amethi, India
[4]Private Institute of Management and Business, Belarus

Abstract

Despite of the behemoth utilization of social media platforms for various aspects, which provides opportunities to analyze and study the social behavior of users, text mining's role has been not explored fully. For this, text mining is the way to discover interesting patterns in data. The motive of text mining is to utilize discovered patterns to elucidate contemporary behavior or to predict future outcomes. Multiple disciplines participate in crawling text to discover required textual patterns such as mathematical modeling, computer science, data mining and warehousing to name a few. For this purpose, embeddings are also playing a key role and under the umbrella of machine learning, IoT (Internet of things) are coping up flawlessly at an individual level to predict the behavior in terms of security privacy, analysis, and prediction. Through this chapter, explaining the role of such strategies in social media text analysis for finding knowledgeable patterns. To illustrate and deliberate the areas of social media which are reachable on an amazing variety in the field of text mining using IoT-enabled services in terms of machine learning are also described. Outcomes can provide as a baseline for future of IoT research based on machine learning in emerging applications.

Keywords: Text mining, social media, embeddings, clustering, pre-processing, Internet of Things (IoT)

*Corresponding author: dayasagar.ism@gmail.com

Danda B. Rawat, Lalit K Awasthi, Valentina Emilia Balas, Mohit Kumar and Jitendra Kumar Samriya (eds.) Convergence of Cloud with AI for Big Data Analytics: Foundations and Innovation, (229–256) © 2023 Scrivener Publishing LLC

11.1   Introduction

In these days' social media is acting as a double edged sword to share information, at its low cost with easy usage and explosive growth. Explosion of live multimedia streams text magnetize online social clients to contribute in real time phenomenon to become an element of gigantic multitude as they want to participate by publishing information in terms of text, video, image or sharing URL. Though, the immense quantity of text available on social media beside with the redundant information demands a momentous venture of collected social text stream. Removing of unwanted information and keywords from the collected text is very common practice. Usually social users do not write a words with correct spellings due to which numerous kind of ambiguities like lexical, semantic and syntactic occurs. Various machine learning approaches are available which helps to remove unwanted information from social text and identify the key theme in extracted social patterns. Therefore online social media and text mining is expanding with a huge degree. In current era a new story of text mining has begun as vast amount of text is posted on a various kind of social media such as Twitter, Facebook, forums, and blogs etc. Numerous types of knowledgeable patterns can be analyzed as it is a knowledge intensive manner. The text is collected over a certain period of time and various analysis tools are used to seek appropriate information from various social media resources through the classification and examination of mesmerizing patterns. Unstructured formats are available as the collected text usually comes in unstructured format and the lack of knowledge to deal with such strange patterns of text forced the researchers to perform scrubbing and normalizing data.

A dynamic and attractive source can change the whole story as it can be a big resource to generate innovative pattern of information. The dynamic nature also helps the users to get updates on time whenever required which not lonely propose a baseline for the social users but also for those who are interested to participate and keep track on daily update with time. With such kind of explosion in social media provides a full freedom to participate and to be a part of current trend. Critical analysis at regular intervals is also to be maintained to keep track on social user's activities for a variety of perspectives' plausibility. Numerous methods and training ways are addressed and discussed which are communally used to share and with new users to analyze reappearance of text [1].

These all mechanism diffuses information in vast extent and helps the social media for its rapid growth. Surprising growth and evolution of World Wide Web, online users are also increasing day by day. This exponential growth is never ended and such users participate in various activities of social media and generate a huge corpus of text. Multiple schemes are available which can combine and assemble collected text for analysis such as Leipzig Corpora Collection [2] and many more. The collected text demands for pre-processing [3] from which various features can be extracted and these features can be used for further research areas such as opinion/sentiment mining [4, 5], analysis of polarity disambiguation in sentiment analysis [6], detection, classification and analysis of social media events [7–9], burst analysis and trend forecasting [10], subject/topic tracking [11], recommendation method [12], Machine leaning applications in Internet of Things (IoT) and many more. Bag of Word (BOW) is a very realistic and simple approach which is used to represent text. Semantic information is also carried forward with the text representation so that the correct analysis can be performed. Doing such analysis helps the users to understand the nature of text and also provide a freedom where the large corpus of text can be converted into numeric data. Multiple influential mining mechanisms are available which can perform this task very well to extract required information [13, 14]. Few features which can be available in social text/documents can be described as:

- *Tininess:* As we know that social media have limit of words and size to post. Therefore we can say that social media text will be usually shorter such as in Twitter there is a 280 character limit to the length of a tweet [15]. With this small length of social post, it is very difficult and challenging task to analyze and extract essential features.

- *Multitudinous Languages:* Every social media platform facilitates their users to post with different kind of languages as they want. User can use language as per their choice and can participate in multiple social media activities such as blogs, social groups, communities as in FIFA WorldCup, public can watch and participate in any language on Twitter [16]. This kind of nature of social media creates a problem for social users to extract and analyze their meaning as slangs can be out of vocabulary.

- *Belief:* Social media text contains/holds beliefs which is also known as opinion and it is a quintuple (t_{obj}, obj_f, $senti_{score}$, op_h, ꞌ), where, t_{obj} is a goal object, obj_f is a feature characteristic of the object, senti$_{score}$ is the sentiment cost, op$_h$ is opinion container, ᵗ is time [17].

- *Suitability:* As we know the dynamic nature of social media make it more flexible and users can post in precise time intervals. The summary and the specifications of the posted text changes over time and sometimes the whole scenario of the content can also be changed which is difficult to understand.

Thus, from the above features it is observed that the role of text pre-processing is quite important and it is quite challenging and interesting also to extract the actual meaning of the collected text streams. Therefore, in the next section the role of pre-processing is explained which is proving an information in various domains.

11.2   Text Pre-Processing – Role and Characteristics

Non-standard and out of vocabulary words have their own role in social media and their negative impact on decision making is quite challenging. We have seen and observed from the above discussion how the pre-processing tasks are demanding for emerging methodology. In general form, an ISBN is usually worn to symbolize "International Standard Book Number" [18] and this abbreviation can be used by someone for other purpose also. Such kind of abbreviations, which are changing their sense from one tier to another, make pre-processing task more difficult. Instead of social media, social apps such as mobile phone messaging also contains non-standard or out of vocabulary words. Such words are very common and also handy e.g. hru\how are you, ttyl/talk to you later, cu\see you [19], and many more. Therefore, in every social media, such words are increasing in rapid way and this is a very common practice in these days. Typos such as hiy/hey, bey/bye/c u soon/see you soon and repetition of words like byeeeeee/bye, helllooooo/hello, and many more are the part of social media informal abbreviations. Influence of such words in social media is very critical and needs to be addressed.

- *Power of out of vocabulary and non-standard words:* In text mining, part of speech tagging [20] and NER (Name Entity Recognition) [21, 22] are very important part to gain high precision. With these two parameters, parsing mechanisms

[18] i.e. syntax analysis parsing and machine translation are also to be considered. Because it has been observed that in many cases POS (Part of Speech) is frequently used with the combination of Penn tree bank to gain the information about particular keywords [23].

The performance and accuracy is degraded by non-standard and out of vocabulary words. To increase the performance and accuracy parsing is a best solution which helps to take care about out of vocabulary words [22]. We have seen that many researchers have used parsing on forums [24] and text diversity [25]. The authors have claimed that parsing gives best result but if errors occurs or performance degrades then the major reason behind this are unwanted population, false tokenization and out of vocabulary or non-standard words. Thus, we can say that wrong POS tagging generates error in parsing [19]. Such kind of issues is also available in machine translation in which machine interpretation can be wrong due to negative influence of our of vocabulary words. Let us consider an example of non-standard vocabulary which is pre-processed to gain the actual form of words in a sentence.

Before pre-processing: Finally he got a chance 2 wrk 2gther on a project.
After pre-processing: Finally, he got a chance to work together on a project.

Role of capital words in name entity recognition (NER) cannot be ignored which is also a part of non-standard word. Out is observed that with the increase of slangs, non-standard and out of vocabulary words on social media, segments of non-standards words are also growing. Sometimes slangs don't have global impact but they contain local impact and cannot be ignored in text mining. In text mining these all act as a part of noise and such influence of words degrades the quality and performance of the text mining task. In Twitter we know that #tag, @tag are also play a significant role which are very important to consider and in [26] authors are working on domain adoption problem which is based on tagging mechanism. So we can say that tagging and its influence on the contextual information is important to consider which leads towards a successful text mining. For this purpose in section 11.3 modern text pre-processing approaches are discussed with their application domains.

11.3   Modern Pre-Processing Methodologies and Their Scope

In text mining research, pre-processing is required and it converts non-standard and out of vocabulary words into actual word. Sometime during pre-processing contextual information lost therefore, it is also very important to understand the contextual information in a suitable form. We have seen that in social media text analytics, contextual information is not considered usually and it leads towards wrong decision. In current era, sentiment analysis, polarity disambiguation in sentiment analysis, event detection, and classification are very common areas of research and every-day new event happened on social media. It is necessary to find the contextual information to count the exact meaning of a particular keyword [19]. In human analysis, it is easy to understand and recognize the contextual information but in machine translation it becomes difficult task. Efforts are required to understand and deal with this situation. From the previous study we can say that its very complex task and such keywords demands additional information also which is usually ignored.

Previous studies related to this text mining problem are designed in which context insensitive lexical approach is commonly used. The main motive of this approach is to reduce or remove the repetitive characters to gain the exact word. It works very well for minimizing the repeated words but it is difficult to analyze the actual sense and exact meaning of the word including the contextual information. Let us consider an example to understand this scenario. *"Police will charge rupees 5 thousand fine for not tagging seat ballet in a car"* whereas in second example: *"I am absolutely fyn, What about you?"*.

Now, in these examples, fine have two aspects in which it is representing money and felling/emotions of human concerned. From this example we can say that in re-processing it is necessary to consider the contextual as well as ambiguity in social media text. Many approaches which are handling ambiguity and also taking care of contextual information are explained further. As we know that the machine translation based and spell checking based pre-processing tasks are very communal used from the last many years. Including these two we have also explained the recent approaches which are used in pre-processing and contextual polarity disambiguation.

- *Machine learning based text pre-processing approaches:* Machine learning translation for social text pre-processing is widely used to convert non-standard and out of vocabulary words into accrual words. Phrase based machine version is used commonly to convert out of vocabulary words into actual words. We have identified that in [27, 28] phrase based machine translation approach is used on SMS texts. Similarly the supervised and unsupervised machine learning approaches are also used to process out of vocabulary words into actual words. In [29] a supervised machine learning approach is used for tweets collected from Twitter. A vast approach is given by the authors who is also performing pre-processing and if any letter/character is repeating then the approach is removing that repeated words to convert into normal form. Effectiveness and accuracy of the supervised machine learning approach is evaluated and the BLEU score is also increased.

- Further, a text processing mechanism based on statistical machine translation (SMT) is explained in [30]. An automatic statistical machine translation (SMT) is explained and developed. For development of the system the authors get information from the various internet users and designed a SMT models including vast knowledge of pre-processing mechanism but lack of deep contextual information of computer knowledge. For comparing and evaluating the efficiency of the system, the proposed system is implemented BLEU score and mystification of the language model.

  Similarly, a machine learning approach based on character translation is commonly used for text pre-processing [31]. Character based machine translation can handle the sparse easily. We have observed that in social media text mining, due to sparse nature of words and non-standard words availability, it is very difficult to find a particular keyword from the collected data. Therefore, character level machine translation approach is used for informal text normalization. It is also found that when we are applying this approach database should be updated time to time when the new words are coming from various users with new abbreviations and types. For example if in the database "whr" is defined as where then it will be recognized otherwise it will be fail to understand the word due to nonexistence of information at character level translation.

- *Spell checking based Text pre-processing methodologies:* Detecting wrong spelling of various keywords and analyzing errors is a complex task in social text mining. Multiple reasons are associated with spelling mistakes such as typing errors, unintentionally typing wrong character like fair/fear and peace/piece, principle/principal and many more. Many approaches are given by various authors and in [32], it is defined that 25% and 40% of spelling errors are effective English words. But with this analysis it is also found that with this identification we have to study that either these approaches are capable to convert non-standard words into standard formats or not. If they are detecting and converting words into standard words then accuracy is to be measured for that particular approach. Dictionary based approach is quite easy to use which helps the users to find the correct word from the collected text. We have seen that many authors have used dictionary based approach to correct the spelling of words and similarly in [35], a UNIX based dictionary is used. The main motive of using dictionary based approach is to find the corrected version of the word from the huge number of wrong words.

Usually the dictionaries are designed from large list of unigrams such as Google N-gram text corpus. Likelihood approach is used and depends on the user that how to consider the prior information and then what is the probability to match the words together. Distributional patters of words are also based on probability of matching words. In this approach a query based on misspelled words is matched with the dictionary and then the various patterns of matching are designed. The probability of finding correct pattern is computed and in social media, several non-standard words totally different from their standard word forms, which is away and outside the range of a spell check due to which a standard distribution of matching pattern is to be applied. As we have discussed above the repetition of the character can be corrected and similarly several words are existing in social media text which cannot be detected by spell checkers and not available in dictionary based approach (e.g. f9, b4, str8 etc.).

Various other approaches are also based on same sequences but in [36] a supervised machine learning approach is used. They used the unsupervised approach for text pre-processing and the proposed approach applied on short text messages such as tweets and SMS to find the non-standard words. The performance was computed and analyzed with the standard data sets and in the same way in [37] a special source channel based text processing approach is designed. Four factors are included in this approach such as contextual information, orthographic factor, a phonetic aspect, a contextual aspect, and short form growth. The study proved that the sources which create error to twitter data can be minimized and improved. The authors have practically performed and convert the various abbreviations into actual words such cu/see you", which is included frequently as one of their model.

- *Modern pre-processing approaches:* In modern era numerous text mining and text pre-processing approaches have been designed. From last two years the number is increasing in a huge manner. In the above section we have given an overview about spell checking based and machine learning based approaches and without discussing the modern approaches of pre-processing it will be a discrimination. In the modern approaches, conditional random fields (CRF) based approaches are used for text pre-processing. The combination of CRF can be seen with various another modest networks such as RNN (recurrent neural networks), CNN (Convolution neural networks). Similarly in [38] CRF based approach is used for text pre-processing. A Bayesian based approach is implemented to extract the meaning of out of vocabulary words. For implementing modification in the collected text, CRF is also used which helps to update, delete and insert characters in the words. Linear chain models are also available for doing the same job and modest recurrent network can also be used.

- *On the other hand* Hidden Markov model (HMM) have also a great contribution in the area of text pre-processing. Various authors are using HMM for text mining activities and in [39], authors found its suitability for finding errors in text which are represented cognitive and typos. Cognitive errors are those errors are which are which are primarily initiated and the features of such errors are extracted on the basis of morphological or phonetic approximations. Typing errors are known as typos which occur unintentional/accidentally during typing.

Unsupervised machine learning methodology is used by authors in [40] to pre-process the text. An approach based on random walk is used on noisy unlabeled text. Contextual information and similarity is also considered from the collected sequence of text.

In this approach a graph called bipartite graph is generated which is represented as G(W, C, E), in which 'W', contains all nodes representing pre-processed keywords and noisy out of vocabulary keywords, 'C', stands for contextual information and 'E', is representing the edges. The weight is updated on the basis of the word frequency. When a same word will occur again and again the analysis stage then the weight will be updated by one every time.

Another way of text pre-processing is parsing strategy. Parsers are widely used to find the meaning of non-standard words and it is used by various researchers whose motive is to find the exact meaning of non-standard words in the collected corpus. Therefore, a parsing based approach is applied in [41] whose main motive is to analyze non-standard words and to convert them into standard words. Performance of the parser is directly associated with the normalization performance and for this purpose evaluation based approaches can be used to measure the performance of various approaches w.r.t. to existing approaches. Numerous parameters are available to compute the performance of pre-processing approaches such as F-measure, precision and recall is widely used and acceptable. A modern sequential text pre-processing approach is given in [42] in which the main focus is drawn on English lexicons. The various strategies are applied to analyze the non-standard words and in first phase these non-standard words are converted into standard words. After analysis phase, domain information of the text is analyzed in next phase which enables further processing of text.

In the modern approaches of text pre-processing an integrated, unsupervised statistical methodology is also very popular and used by various researchers to normalize the text. In [43] same approach is used which is keeping track on converting out of vocabulary words into standard regular words. Random features are selected from the collected text and log- linear method is applied to extract the exact meaning of the words. In case of real time text, usually we deals with text streams and in twitter case, a collected tweet is represented as $S=\{s_1,s_2,........s_n\}$ when we are dealing with social text streams. The main motive of generating such string is to identify the exact meaning of keywords which is represented as tweet = $\{t_1,t_2,.......t_n\}$. Similar kind of approach is used by various social media text analysis approaches to analyze the meaning of words. Finding the real time events based on various time strategy is also a part of social text stream which is dynamic in nature and changing with the change of time. Table 11.1 is showing the summarized version of various text pre-processing techniques.

Table 11.1 Summary of text pre-processing approaches.

Reference and year	Major contribution	Methodology	Scoring
[28, 47, 55]	• Hold up for various language based parameters. • Network based approach • Efficient way to translate words to exact meaning	Open-source toolkit and SMT decoder.	Machine Learning Approach (Supervised)
[29, 17]	• Supervised machine learning is implemented for tweets. • Text is pre-processed using supervised approach. • Repeated words from the various words are eliminated according to the supervised approach.	NLP (Natural Language Processing)	Machine Learning Approach (Supervised)

(Continued)

Table 11.1 Summary of text pre-processing approaches. (*Continued*)

Reference and year	Major contribution	Methodology	Scoring
[30, 41, 58]	• A comparison is drawn between various text pre-processing approaches. • A statistical method is used for language translation. • Combination of various keywords are analyzed to collect exact representation of lexicon/keywords	LI-rule, LS-rule, SMT.	Numerical Statistical based machine translation (SMT)
[10, 19, 33, 40, 49]	• A accurate pre-processing approach is designed. • The proposed approach can handle noisy data very well. • Graphical sequences of text are given. • N-gram language model is used to create sequences of text	Language model (5-gram) Pre-processing based on dictionary Generation	Machine Learning Approach (Unsupervised)
[43, 61]	• A pre-processing approach based on evaluation is given • Various performance analysis parameters such as F-measure, precision and recall are used for measuring the performance of the pre-processing method.	log-linear model and UNLOL	Machine Learning Approach (Unsupervised)

(*Continued*)

Table 11.1 Summary of text pre-processing approaches. (*Continued*)

Reference and year	Major contribution	Methodology	Scoring
[44, 52]	• Disambiguation based corpus is used for analysis. • Contextual dis-ambiguity is considered. • Experiments are compared with existing robust methods using various parameters. • Captures source and domain of noisy text in different aspects.	Language models	Machine Learning Approach (Unsupervised)

11.4   Text Stream and Role of Clustering in Social Text Stream

Temporal and continuous extraction of social text in social text stream is a power of every kind of textual features. For extracting social text from twitter, API is designed which helps to extract social text pattern based on user's query. In most of the cases, the process of extraction starts at 'T' which can be represented as closed time interval of time, [$time_1$, $time_2$] and it is defined as $T = (t_1, t_2, ...t_i, ... t_r, ..., t_n)$. A steam of social text is a sequence 'S' which is collected during various interval, $S = \{s_1, s_2, ... s_i, ..., s_r, ... s_n\}$. From these collected intervals there may be several element of S such that s_i, holding a tweets t_i. This part of tweet can be connected or linked with other entities in a social network. To analyze the actual connection and linking of tweets, various clustering mechanisms are used. Clustering is an easy way by which a stream of text can be categorized into various similar classes [44]. If in social text stream, $S = (s_1, s_2, ...s_i, ...s_r, ...s_n)$, is distributed among clusters (C') which is defined as $C' = (C_1, C_2, ... C_j)$ where, $C_1, C_2, ... C_j \in S$, such that $S = \cup (c_1, c_2, ... c_j)$. Each of the object s_i, belongs to the cluster c_j where, $c_j \subset C'$.

A similarity based function can also be used which helps to assign a cluster to every incoming text stream on the basis of similarity index.

Therefore, if the new keyword is coming then a new cluster is to be created otherwise existing cluster is to be assigned to the incoming textual data which increase its popularity and make it happening.

11.5   Social Text Stream Event Analysis

In social media event is related to anything happening surrounding. If the event will be popular then it will be very active on every kind of social media whereas other events will be ignored. If we consider a simple example as if there will be marriage function of a celebrity then it will act as a big event whereas marriage of a normal citizen will be a very common. Therefore, it is important to know the global context of an event whereas the local events does not contain any equivalent recognition in social media history as global events achieved [45]. From this discussion a social happening can be categorized into two ways:

- *Planned events:* The events which are pre planned such as IPL, president elections and many more. Various featured tagged with these events are needed to be including such as title, name, time, and place.
- *Unplanned events:* The events which can occur without any prior information such as earthquake, flood, tsunami and many more. No any information related to the event is associated about their happening but there as some signals which can helps to provide information about the occurrence of event content.

Social text stream: It can be represented as 's' which helps to extract the tweets in 'T' in a specific time interval such as, [$time_1$, $time_2$]. The extracted tweets contain chain of text which can be a combination of tweets which is represented as, $T = (t_1, t_2, ...t_i, ... t_r, ..., t_n)$. In other words we can say that social text streams are the combination of continuous and discrete time internal in which various keywords may be linked with each other directly or indirectly. Information of sender and receiver is to be recorded and this scenario may vary from network to network.

From the social text stream it is observed that when the text is extracted, it will be full of noise such as unwanted symbols, abbreviations, short forms of specific words and may be some additional information in terms of tagging and emoticons. Due to this reason a pre-processing approach is required for cleaning the social text stream. We have studied various machine learning based methods which can clean the text in an efficient way. Various methods and techniques are present which classify and detect events from and those methods can be applied to perform pre-processing.

After pre-processing the processed form of text is stored on the basis of their similarity. For this purpose, clustering is used to organize similar text in a single cluster and accordingly others will be managed. Usually in the existing study we have seen that a dynamic clustering is used [46]. In various applications such as topic detection, event classification, event detection, trend analysis and many more are dependent on clustering [47] [48]. In previous study, many authors are applied clustering approach on various applications of text mining and similarly in [48] and [49] clustering is applied on event detection and tracking. The single pass clustering is implemented to analyze the text and to understand the evolving nature of the social events adaptive filtering mechanism is used.

Clustering based on supervised and unsupervised type is also preferred for content analysis. In [50] the authors used the machine learning mechanism whereas in [51] clustering based on machine learning approaches to identify events and their evolving nature is studied. Basically in social media if we want to extract some patterns from the social text stream then usually three steps are performed which are as follows:

- Clustering based on text
- Temporal segments
- Graph analysis of social network

In [52] authors developed an approach for event burst detection based on clustering. A spatial approach is used which helps to analyze the numerous feature of collected text whereas, in [53] a feature based pivot approach based on clustering is studied based on a time window. The time window helps to analyze various kinds of social patterns over time which changes with the change of time window [54]. In [55] a spatial clustering mechanism is applied on flicker text and to extract event from images a k-mean clustering with the combination of DWT is used in [56]. LDA based methods are also very popular in social text analysis and after pre-processing the LDA based methods can also be used. Various author used Bayesian filters for the analysis of social text in extraction of various features such as location and time [57, 58]. It is observed that such applications help to study the unplanned events very well such as earthquake, tsunami, etc. [59, 60]. A language based model called Latent Dirichlet Allocation Category Language Model is designed for topic modeling and also helps to categorize text into different classes.

So, we can say that it is very clear from the discussion that the pre-processing a backbone for each and every application of text mining. Without performing the task of pre-processing further analysis is not possible and it is better to understand the role of pre-processing so that an efficient and superior approach can be followed. Here now we are going to give some issues which are analyzed from the discussion and existing in the current study.

- Spam messages, abbreviations, short forms, slangs, irregular use of English words, emoticons using ☺, ☹ and many more are the part of social media text. For analyzing and to extract knowledgeable patterns, it is important to pre-process the text accurately
- Due to dynamic nature of social media and multiple sources it is also necessary to study its changing behavior with the change of time.

Therefore, in this chapter, we explained a role of text pre-processing task in various application domains of text mining by considering various social text streams. For this purpose, the embeddings are also playing a key role in social media text analysis and they cannot be ignored. Effective vector representations for very short fragments of text in weighted form of word, embedding can be used. In various perspectives embeddings in social media can be used in which weighted embeddings are used widely and effectively. In case of embeddings it will very easy to apply clustering mechanism which helps to combine similar keywords in a group. Thus, we can say that embeddings are faster and efficient to use and for this reason we are explaining the usage of embedding in text mining domain in the next section.

11.6   Embedding

To generate and represent a social text stream or corpus into vector form embeddings are used. Figure 11.1 is describing the general architecture of embedding.

11.6.1   Type of Embeddings

Usually, it is found that there are three main types of classes on the basis of which embeddings can be classified based on the topic. Figure 11.2 is

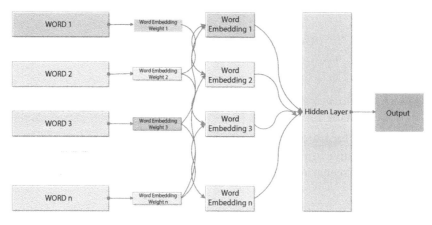

Figure 11.1 General depiction of embedding.

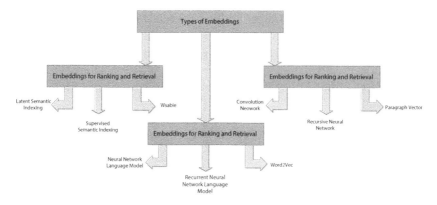

Figure 11.2 Types of embedding.

defining a way by which text can be retrieved and ranked with the help of an embeddings.

Latent semantic indexing (LDA): To identify and analyze hidden concepts and plan in the collected text LDA is widely used. In this method each keyword is represented in the form of vector. Semantic relationships between various documents and terms are analyzed to identify the hidden relationship within the social text. To produce all knowledgeable patterns, pre-processing is also required at initial stage for cleaning the text.

Figure 11.3 is a depiction of LSI (Latent Semantic Indexing). In this representation SVD (Singular Value Decomposition) is computed in in first stage. In Figure 1.3, '*D*' is a representation of '*M*' in '*r*' dimensions, where,

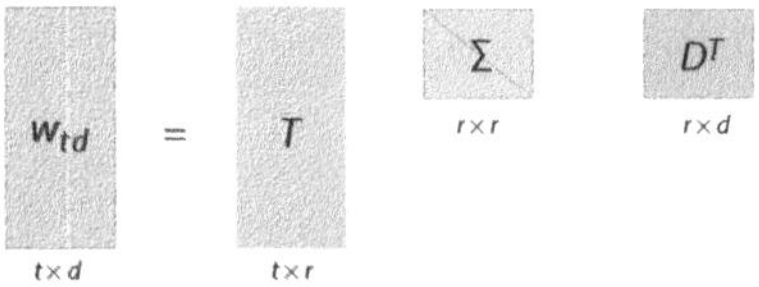

Figure 11.3 Depiction of latent semantic indexing (LSI).

'T' is a matric for transforming new documents. Σ, a diagonal matrix provides comparative importance of dimensions [61].

The overall scenario of the model is represented as:

$$f(q,d) = q^T W d = \sum_{i,j=1}^{D} q_i W_{ij} d_j$$

Here, $f(q, d)$ is standing for score between a query q and an individual text d. Weight matric which is to be learnt is $W \in \Re^{D \times D}$. For training purpose, normalized text stream/corpus $\Re$ is considered. As per the query, 'q' related 't_{r+}' and unrelated 't_{r-}' text is analyzed. We would like to choose 'S' such as and it can merge to regain information as given below:

$$q^T S t_{r+} > q^T S t_{r-}$$

$$\sum_{(q,t_{r+},t_{r-}) \in \Re} \max(0, 1 - q^T S t_{r+} + q^T S t_{r-})$$

Recurrent neural network: The popularity of acceptance of RRNs' is gaining huge interest in the field of text mining. The application of RNN in language modeling is never ended due to their neurons. These neurons can employ to access its internal its internal memory which helps to maintain information associated to preceding state. Due to this property of RNN, contextual information related to every keyword can be preserved. RNNs are recognized as recurrent as they perform the related function for each module of a cycle through the output being inclined on the preceding computations. The distributed hidden feature of RNN helps to store huge information connected or linked with past in smooth manner. On the other hand, the non-linear dynamics feature allows restoring veiled state in multifaceted means. In Figure 11.4, folded RRN is shown and Figure 11.5 describes a complete network.

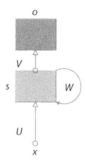

Figure 11.4 Representation of folded recurrent neural network (RNN).

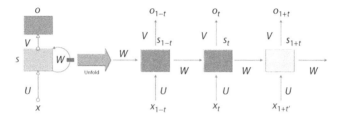

Figure 11.5 Description of unfolded recurrent neural network (RNN).

In the above Figure 1.4, 'x_t' is the input, 's_t' is describing the hidden state at time 't' and 'o_t' is the output state. In mathematical form, RNN can be described as:

$$o_t = f_w(o_{t-1}, x_t)$$

- **Word2vec:** Word2vec is also used in text mining analysis community. It helps to convert text into vector with very simple way. Many of the researchers have used this approach for various applications of text mining. Another benefit of using vector representation of text is that it gives an accurate and efficient semantic analysis. The vectors can be used for multiple tasks on social media text and we can say that the two models of word2vec such as Continuous Bag of Words (CBOW) and Skip-Gram are also doing a great work. Context information for a given context related to a particular word is easy to predict using CBOW, whereas in skip gram context is envisaged for a specified word. Figure 11.6 is describing the general view of BOW model in which various layers such as input, projection, and output are given and their link between them is also represented whereas in Figure 11.7 a depiction of skip gram is given.

- *Clustering*: It is an unsupervised process whose main motive is to search frequent features or related patterns. No any pre-defined class value is available in clustering and it collects the common features together and combines them to help the decision maker. Various applications of clustering are available in the field of text mining, machine learning, Sensor network, pattern recognition, image analysis, bioinformatics and many more. Figure 11.8 is describing the general representation of clustering.

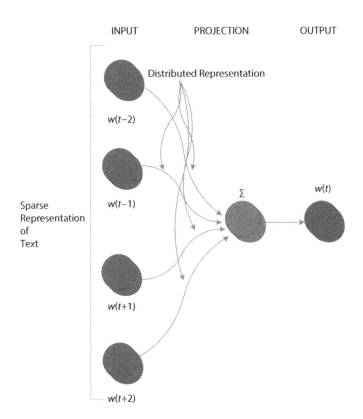

Figure 11.6 General depiction of continuous bag of words (CBOW).

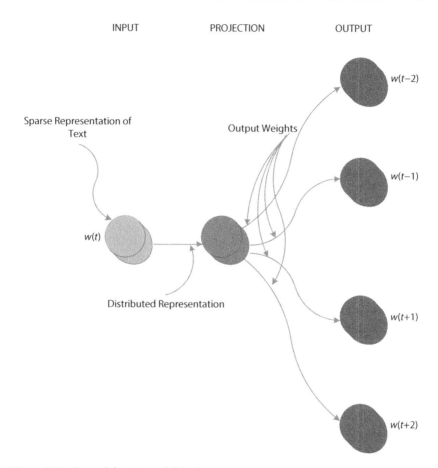

Figure 11.7 General depiction of Skip-Gram.

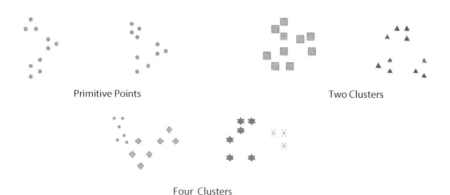

Figure 11.8 Representation of clustering.

11.7 Description of Twitter Text Stream

As we know that in text mining, for the experiment purpose, we can use existing text corpus or we can extract text from the social media called text stream. Current research is based on real time social text stream which helps to analyze social informative patterns for multiple purposes. Therefore, now in this section we present a twitter text stream. Due to its availability publically accessibility, we used this text stream for the experiment purpose also.

- *Twitter Text Stream:* For the experiment purpose, we crawled text from Twitter. The experiment is based on various features as described in Table 11.2. Total number of features extracted from the twitter text stream is 3453214 (after pre-processing) and when we perform clustering then on the basis of similarity of features we found 67540 similar features. Features. Various features were connected with each other through direct or indirect link and the connected features are 34398. These features are related with different nodes and these nodes include the information regarding sender and the receivers either in the way of direct indications from senders or their followers in the situation of transmission messages. On the other hand, on the average, each stream object contained about 84 nodes per tweet. Other features associated with this, experiments are described in Table 11.2 given below.

Table 11.2 Summary of collected statistics.

Statistics	Total values
Total feature entities	3453214
Total types of feature's categories	67540
Connected features	34398
Categories for features	5430
Average token features	564
Average predicates associated with features	432
Average total literals associated with features	289

11.8 Experiment and Result

We performed a series of experiments to answer understand the role of embeddings and its role in social text stream. For this purpose we tried our best to configure model by implementing it on various social text streams. We implemented and analyzed the result for the Skip-Gram-based and word2vec optimization step.

11.9 Applications of Machine Learning in IoT (Internet of Things)

- *To decrease the energy cost:* Machine learning approaches are widely used to minimize the energy cost in various devices such as vehicles, smart homes, smart vehicle system and many more.
- *In traffic routing:* By implementing IoT using machine learning, numerous routes can be identified and suggested by a particular node in network traffic. In this way a small route can be identified in a particular network.
- *Traffic prediction:* This is a very popular application in these days in which machine leaning can embed with IoT to improve the precision of traffic system. Real time traffic analysis and prediction can also be analyzed to identify the traffic situation. IoT based environment embedded with machine learning helps to predict the future in fraction of seconds.
- *In human living:* For the home utility IoT based services are quite useful. IoT with machine learning is very useful in healthcare and can be used for the light, measuring humidity and temperature.
- *In industry:* In various industries such as gas, energy water an interface of IoT based devices is used with machine learning to analyze the demand-supply prediction.
- *In manufacturing:* In remote monitoring, product failure analysis, prediction and production automation IoT with sensor based technology is used for improving the product quality and anomaly detection.
- *In retail and insurance:* Novel value added services related to customer's benefits is incorporated with IoT based

methodologies under the umbrella of machine learning is used in a dynamic way to increase the value of various plans among customers.

11.10   Conclusion

In this chapter, the standard insights extraction for social text stream is explained for event evaluation. We have also explained how well it applies to a grammatically complex and local slangs of languages. Various processes and embedding mechanism are studied and identified as belonging to the standard structure of social media analysis such as text preprocessing, embeddings, clustering and extraction of event related keywords from collect text. From the above discussing it is observed that embeddings are very useful in social text analysis and from the experimental studies we can say that various features associated with collected text can be distinguished from disjunctively written languages. It is also observed that if we use embeddings in Twitter social text stream they have an optimistic impact on the accuracy. In the future, we are interested in extending the embedding models to analyze the impact using large volume of data sets and social streams for pre-processing and keyword extraction.

References

1. Lifna, C.S. and Vijayalakshmi, M., Identifying concept-drift in twitter streams. *Proc. - Proc. Comput. Sci.*, 45, 86–94, 2015.
2. Goldhahn, D., Eckart, T., Quasthoff, Q., Building large monolingual dictionaries at the Leipzig Corpora Collection: From 100 to 200 Languages. In *Proceedings of the Eighth International Conference on Language Resources and Evaluation (LREC'12)*, pages 759–765, Istanbul, Turkey, European Language Resources Association (ELRA), 2012.
3. Singh, T. and Kumari, M., Role of text pre-processing in twitter sentiment analysis. *Proc. - Proc. Comput. Sci.*, 89, 549–554, 2016.
4. Bhadane, C., Dalal, H., Doshi, H., Sentiment analysis: Measuring opinions. *Proc. Comput. Sci.*, 45, C, 808–814, 2015.
5. Hamdan, H., Bellot, P., Bechet, F., Lsislif: Feature extraction and label weighting for sentiment analysis in twitter. *SemEval*, pp. 568–573, 2015.
6. Saleiro, P., Rodrigues, E.M., Soares, C., Oliveira, E., FEUP at SemEval-2017 Task 5: Predicting Sentiment Polarity and Intensity with Financial Word

Embeddings. In *Proceedings of the 11th International Workshop on Semantic Evaluation (SemEval-2017)*, pages 904–908, Vancouver, Canada, Association for Computational Linguistics, 2017.

7. Vavliakis, K.N., Symeonidis, A.L., Mitkas, P.A., Event identification in web social media through named entity recognition and topic modeling. *Data Knowl. Eng.*, 88, 1–24, 2013.

8. Zhou, X. and Chen, L., Event detection over twitter social media streams. *VLDB J.*, 23, 3, 381–400, 2014.

9. Zhao, Q., and Mitra, P., Event detection and visualization for social text streams, in: *ICWSM 2007 - International Conference on Weblogs and Social Media, International Conference on Weblogs and Social Media, ICWSM 2007*, Boulder, CO, United States, pp. 1-3, 2007.

10. Aiello, L.M. *et al.*, Sensing trending topics in twitter. *IEEE Trans. Multimedia*, 15, 6, 1268–1282, 2013.

11. Lin, J., Snow, R., Morgan, W., Smoothing techniques for adaptive online language models: Topic tracking in tweet streams. *Proc. 17th ACM SIGKDD Int. Conf. Knowledge Discovery Data Mining*, pp. 422–429, 2011.

12. Mart, L., Barranco, M.J., Luis, G.P., A knowledge based recommender system. *Int. J. Comput. Intell. Syst.*, 1, 3, 225–236, 2008.

13. Quan, C. and Ren, F., Unsupervised product feature extraction for feature-oriented opinion determination. *Inf. Sci. (NY)*, 272, 16–28, 2014.

14. Croft, W.B., Metzler, D., Strohman, T., Information retrieval in practice, pp. 1-542, Pearson Education, Inc., Boston: Addison-Wesley, 2015.

15. Ren, Z. and Meij, E., Personalized time-aware tweets summarization. *SIGIR'13*, Dublin, Ireland, July 28–August 1, 2013, pp. 513–522.

16. Ren, Z., *Monitoring social media: Summarization, classification and recommendation*, ZhaochunRen, Amsterdam, the Netherlands, 2016.

17. Pang, B. and Lee, L., Opinion mining and sentiment analysis. *Found. Trends Inf. Retr.*, 2, 1–2, 1–135, 2008.

18. Cucerzan, S., and Brill, E.,. Spelling correction as an iterative process that exploits the collective knowledge of web users, in: *Proceedings of the 2004 Conference on Empirical Methods in Natural Language Processing*, pages 293–300, Barcelona, Spain, Association for Computational Linguistics, 2004.

19. Han, B., *Improving the utility of social media with natural language processing*, The University of Melbourne, Melbourne, Australia, February 2014.

20. Gimpel, K. *et al.*, Part-of-speech tagging for twitter: Annotation, features, and experiments. *Proceedings of the Annual Meeting of the Association for Computational Linguistics, HLT '11*, vol. 2, pp. 42–47, 2011.

21. Liu, X., Zhang, S., Wei, F., Zhou, M., Recognizing named entities in tweets. *Proceedings of the 49th Annual Meeting of the Association for Computational Linguistics*, Portland, Oregon, pp. 359–367, June 19-24, 2011.

22. Owoputi, O., Connor, B.O., Dyer, C., Gimpel, K., Schneider, N., Smith, N.A., Improved part-of-speech tagging for online conversational text with word clusters, in: *Proceedings of NAACL*, pp. 380–390, June 2013.

23. Toutanova,K., Klein, D., Manning, C. D., Singer, Y.,. Feature-rich part-of-speech tagging with a cyclic dependency network, in: *Proceedings of the 2003 Human Language Technology Conference of the North American Chapter of the Association for Computational Linguistics*, pp. 252–259, 2003.

24. Foster, J., *cba to check the spelling ' Investigating Parser Performance on Discussion Forum Posts, Human Language Technologies: The 2010 Annual Conference of the North American Chapter of the ACL*, Los Angeles, California, pp. 381–384, June 2010.

25. Baldwin, T., Cook, P., Lui, M., MacKinlay, A., and Wang, L.,. How Noisy Social Media Text, How Diffrnt Social Media Sources?. In Proceedings of the Sixth International Joint Conference on Natural Language Processing, pages 356–364, Nagoya, Japan. Asian Federation of Natural Language Processing, 2013.

26. Daum, H. and Marcu, D., Domain adaptation for statistical classifiers. *J. Artif. Intell. Res.*, 26, 101–126, 2006.

27. Aw, A., Zhang, M., Xiao, J., Su, J., *A Phrase-Based Statistical Model for SMS Text Normalization Proceedings of the COLING/ACL 2006 Main Conference Poster Sessions*, Sydney, pp. 33–40, July 2006.

28. Koehn, P. *et al.*, Moses: Open source toolkit for statistical machine translation. *Proceedings of the ACL 2007 Demo and Poster Sessions*, Prague, pp. 177–180, June 2007.

29. Kaufmann, M., Syntactic normalization of twitter messages. *International Conference on Natural Language*, pp. 1–7, 2010.

30. Schlippe, Tim & Zhu, Chenfei & Gebhardt, Jan & Schultz, Tanja. (2010). Text Normalization based on Statistical Machine Translation and Internet User Support. Proceedings of the 11th Annual Conference of the International Speech Communication Association, INTERSPEECH 2010. 1816-1819.

31. Pennell, D.L., A character-level machine translation approach for normalization of SMS abbreviations, in: *Proceedings of IJCNLP*, 2007, Sasa, pp. 974–982, 2011.

32. Kukich, K., Techniques for automatically correcting words in text. *ACM Comput. Surv.*, 24, 4, 377–439, Dec. 1992. https://doi.org/10.1145/146370.146380

33. Whitelaw, C., Hutchinson, B., Chung, G.Y., Ellis, G., Using the web for language independent spellchecking and autocorrection. *Proceedings of the 2009 Conference on Empirical Methods in Natural Language Processing*, Singapore, pp. 890–899, 6-7 August 2009.

34. Hearn, L.A.W. Detection is the central problem in real-word spelling correction. Computation and Language, Cornell University Library, arXiv preprint arXiv:1408.3153, 2014.

35. Ahmad, F., Learning a spelling error model from search query logs. *Proceedings of Human Language Technology Conference and Conference on Empirical Methods in Natural Language Processing (HLT/EMNLP)*, Vancouver, pp. 955–962, October 2005.

36. Cook, P. and Stevenson, S., An unsupervised model for text message normalization. *Proceedings of the NAACL HLT Workshop on Computational Approaches to Linguistic Creativity*, Boulder, Colorado, pp. 71–78, June 2009.

37. Zhenzhen, X., Yin, D., Davison, B.D., Normalizing microtext. Workshops at the Twenty-Fifth AAAI Conference on Artificial Intelligence, 10, 74–79, 2011.

38. Chrupała, G., Normalizing tweets with edit scripts and recurrent neural embeddings. *Proceedings of the 52nd Annual Meeting of the Association for Computational Linguistics (Short Papers)*, Baltimore, Maryland, USA, pp. 680–686, June 23-25 2014.

39. Choudhury, M., Saraf, R., Jain, V., Mukherjee, A., Sarkar, S., Basu. A., Investigation and modeling of the structure of texting language. *Int. J. Document Anal. Recognit,* 10, 3-4 157–174, 2007.

40. Hassan, H., Social text normalization using contextual graph random walks. *Proceedings of the 51st Annual Meeting of the Association for Computational Linguistics*, Sofia, Bulgaria, pp. 1577–1586, August 4-9 2013.

41. Zhang, C., Baldwin, T., Kimelfeld, B., Li, Y., Adaptive parser-centric text normalization. *Proceedings of the 51st Annual Meeting of the Association for Computational Linguistics*, Sofia, Bulgaria, August 4-9 2013, pp. 1159–1168.

42. Sarker, B., and Gonzalez-Hernandez, G., An unsupervised and customizable misspelling generator for mining noisy health-related text sources, *J. Biomed. Inform.,* 88, 98–107, 2018.

43. Yang, Y., and Eisenstein, J., A log-linear model for unsupervised text normalization. in: *Proceedings of the 2013 Conference on Empirical Methods in Natural Language Processing*, pp. 61–72, Seattle, Washington, USA, Association for Computational Linguistics, 2013.

44. Aggarwal, C.C., Chapter 10 A survey of stream clustering algorithms, in: *Data Clustering. Algorithms Applications*, pp. 229–252, 2013.

45. Becker, H., *Identification and characterization of events in social media Hila Becker*, Submitted in partial fulfillment of the requirements for the degree of Doctor of Philosophy in the Graduate School of Arts and Sciences, Columbia University, New York, NY 10027, US, 1–193, 2011.

46. Allan, J. and Papka, R., Search on-line new event detection. *Proceedings of the 21st Annual International ACM SIGIR Conference on Research and Development in Information Retrieval*, pp. 37–45, 1998.

47. Lee, C.H., Unsupervised and supervised learning to evaluate event relatedness based on content mining from social-media streams. *Expert Syst. Appl.,* 39, 18, 13338–13356, 2012.

48. Aggarwal, C.C. and Wang, J., Data streams: Models and algorithms, in: *Data Streams*, vol. 31, pp. 9–38, Kluwer Academic Publishers, Boston/Dordrecht/London, 2007.

49. Allan, J., Papka, R., Lavrenko, V., On-line new event detection and tracking. *SIGIR'98*, Melbourne, Australia, ACM, pp. 37–48, 1998.

50. Aggarwal, C.C. and Subbian, K., Event detection in social streams. *Proceeding. 2012 SIAM International Conference. Data Mining*, pp. 624–635, 2012.

51. Becker, H. and Gravano, L., Learning similarity metrics for event identification in social media categories and subject descriptors. *WSDM'10*, New York City, New York, USA, February 4–6, 2010, 2010.

52. Chen, W., Chen, C., Zhang, L., Wang, C., Bu, J., Online detection of bursty events and their evolution in news streams. *Front. Inf. Technol. Electron. Eng.*, 11, 5, 340–355, 2010.

53. Fung, G.P.C., Yu, J.X., Yu, P.S., Lu, H., Parameter free bursty events detection in text streams. *VLDB '05 Proc. 31st Int. Conf. Very Large Data Bases*, vol. 1, pp. 181–192, 2005.

54. He, Q., Chang, K., Lim, E., Zhang, J., Bursty feature representation for clustering text streams. *Proceedings of the 2007 SIAM International Conference on Data Mining,(SDM)*, pp. 491–496, 2007.

55. Zeppelzauer, M., Zaharieva, M., Breiteneder, C., A generic approach for social event detection in large photo collections. *Work. Notes Proc. Mediaev. 2012 Work*, pp. 2011–2012, 2012.

56. Ghai, D., Gera, D., Jain, N., A new approach to extract text from images based on DWT and K-means clustering. *Int. J. Comput. Intell. Syst.*, 9, 5, 900–916, 2016.

57. Yin, H., Cui, B., Li, J., Yao, J., Chen, C., Challenging the long tail recommendation. *Proc. VLDB Endowment*, 5, 9, 896–907, 2012.

58. Sakaki, T., Okazaki, M., Matsuo, Y., Earthquake shakes twitter users: Real-time event detection by social sensors. *Proc. 19th Int. Conf. World Wide Web*, pp. 851–860, 2010.

59. Singh, T., Kumari, M., Pal, T.L., Chauhan, A., Current trends in text mining for social media. *Int. J. Grid Distrib. Comput.*, 10, 6, 11–28, 2017.

60. Zhou, S., Li, K., and Liu, Y., Text categorization based on topic model. *International Journal of Computational Intelligence Systems*, 2, 4, 398–409, 2009.

61. Bai, B. *et al.*, Supervised semantic indexing. *Proc. 18th ACM Conf. Inf. Knowl. Manag*, pp. 187–196, 2009.

12

APP-Based Agriculture Information System for Rural Farmers in India

**Ashwini Kumar[1], Dilip Kumar Choubey[2]*, Manish Kumar[3]
and Santosh Kumar[4]**

[1]*Cognizant Technology Solutions, Kolkata, West Bengal, India*
[2]*Department of Computer Science and Engineering, Indian Institute of Information
Technology Bhagalpur, Bihar, India*
[3]*Department of Biomedical Engineering, School of Engineering and Technology,
Mody University of Science and Technology, Lachhamangarh, Rajasthan, India*
[4]*Department of Computer Science and Information Technology, Institute of
Technical Education and Research, Siksha 'O'Anusandhan Deemed to be University,
Bhubaneswar, Odisha, India*

Abstract

Agriculture is one of the most important sectors contributing around 16% of GDP (Gross Domestic Product) in India. The majority of the land that was earlier used for the cultivation of crops is now depleting and is now replaced by an industrial cover and by urban settlements or other forms of business prospects. The lack of information and use of traditional methods, farmers had to rely upon weather condition and quality of fertilizers to expect good productivity of crops, but due to uncertainty in weather condition and other factors in which growth of crops depend the production of crops was not uniform and are not able to meet the present consumption requirement. It may lead to an increase in the poverty level and inflation to tackle this problem. The ICT and cloud computing are used as a tool to provide real-time information in the agricultural sector so that they can be made aware about the existing technology which can be used to enhance the productivity of crops along weather forecast and continuously monitor their crop growth. This can increase productivity and overcome the problem of immediate consumption requirement to a great extent in India.

*Corresponding author: dilipchoubey_1988@yahoo.in; dkchoubey.cse@iiitbh.ac.in

Danda B. Rawat, Lalit K Awasthi, Valentina Emilia Balas, Mohit Kumar and Jitendra Kumar Samriya (eds.) Convergence of Cloud with AI for Big Data Analytics: Foundations and Innovation, (257–276)
© 2023 Scrivener Publishing LLC

Keywords: ICT, cloud computing, mobile cloud computing, mobile application, farmers, agriculture

12.1   Introduction

Mobile cloud computing is the emerging technology that has recently been used in many sectors, such as transportation, education to enhance their growth and productivity. With the advent smartphones, this technology can be extended to a great extend so that its advantage could be spread to the majority of the peoples. It is well known that a majority of the people in India depend upon agriculture, and uncertainty in weather conditions affects crops' productivity to a great extent because the farmers are mainly not aware of this condition and due to lack of information. They are not able to tackle the present situation. With the advent of ICT (Information and Communication Technology) and cloud computing, it can be used to provide all the valuable information directly to the farmers and guidance from top agricultural institutes from which farmers could interact and solve their problems in real-time.

Cloud computing will enable to host of the data related to agriculture, which is processed by the app engine, which in turn will be provided in the mobile application. The execution of data in the cloud employing computation offloading and App engine presence in the cloud will process all the relevant information from different websites related to the agricultural sector. Any pertinent information will be provided to the user associated with the agricultural sector, and this will help the user save his time and utilize that time in some productive work. He has not to search for the information from a different website. The other means of the communication system will enable the user to save internet data and computational resources, which in turn reduces the power consumption of the application. It is installed on the user's smartphone. The user interface is also interactive and easy to understand. It does not require enough technical knowledge. The user has to know basic things like how to access the data and derive useful results.

This work aims to use cloud computing as a tool for ICT and provide essential information related to Agriculture in real-time to farmers and saving Energy by offloading computation through MCC (Mobile cloud computing) in the form of cloudlets from Mobile handset to the cloud server

- To provide information on the availability of new tools and technologies related to the agricultural sector which will help in assisting the farmers for better cultivating methodology and also offer training material of new tools online without wasting their time in giving to a different place for consulting the and learning how to use that specific tool efficiently in agriculture and growth of crops.
- It is providing Introduction to new farming practices and its advantage over the traditional method.
- To provide real-time information related to climate, diseases and pests, harvesting mechanisms, post-harvest strategies, and finally, proper marketing.
- Expert advice based on the uploaded image of the crops.
- Cost reduction mechanism by providing information on new government schemes.

The rest of the paper is organized as follows: Motivation is introduced in Section 12.2. Related work is present in Section 12.3. Proposed methodology and experimental results discussion in detail is discussed in Section 12.4. In the end, conclusion and future work are devoted to Section 12.5.

12.2   Motivation

The motivation for this work is noted below.

- There is no reliable information system existing that could be used by both farmers and researchers in the agricultural sector to get real-time updates and information to enhance productivity and knowledge in agriculture.
- Accessing websites on the internet is too time and energy-consuming to get different information. A person has to access a separate website that is time-consuming, and sometimes the relevant information is not present on a particular site, so the app-based information system application will fetch most of the informative website and group them in order time in which they are updated. So that the user accesses all the relevant information. It shows the tag or the heading of the information, which contains the link from which the user can read the complete information.

- This application does the computation in the cloud, so it is platform-independent and does not consume much of the Smartphone's energy and resources.
- This application can access much information from the internet, which can help in enhancing productivity. It will help the farmers to interact with experts from the agricultural sector.

12.3 Related Work

Rose *et al.* [1] have used a decision support tool, which is software for evidence-based decision making in agriculture to improve productivity and environmental outputs. By combining qualitative interviews and quantitative surveys, researchers have found that 15 factors are influential in convincing farmers and suggest using decision support tools. In the UK, this study finds a plethora of agriculture decision support tools in operation.

Lee *et al.* [2] gives an overview of four national forest fire management information system for Canada. The spatial Fire management system (sFMS) is used to implement Canada's national forest fire management information systems, the Canadian wild land fire information systems, fire monitoring, mapping, and modeling. It presents daily information on fire weather, fire behavior potential, and selected upper atmospheric conditions.

Zhang *et al.* [3] have reviewed and identified the ICT based information in china. This study analyses the development stages of china's agriculture information dissemination systems. The seven ICT-based information dissemination models are identified and discussed. It provides directions for researchers in developing futures ICT-based information dissemination systems. This research article will help other developing countries to apply emerging ICTs in agriculture information dissemination and knowledge transfer.

Ziogas [4] have developed a Farm Management Information System (FMISs) which utilizes new technologies. The developed application is focused upon the individual farmers or farmer cooperatives. The objective of this study is to perform farm financial analysis based on all farm transactions. This application was successfully tested on a winter wheat crop for one season, where all related costs were recorded.

Shahzadi *et al.* [5] have proposed an expert system based on the Internet of Things (IoT), which will use the input data collected in real-time. It will help obtain proactive and preventive actions to minimize the losses due to diseases and insects/pests.

Prasad *et al.* [6] have proposed various ways in which farmers can use Mobile Cloud Computing (MCL) on their handsets using an application called Agro Mobile, which helps them for relatively better cultivation and marketing. The main focus is on crop image analysis. Here, the framework uses MCC, by which authors believe that the cloud will be into a farmer's pocket. The framework has been tested on Android-based mobile devices.

Dahikar & Rode [7] have used Artificial Neural Network (ANN) for modeling and prediction of the crop. It is used to predict a suitable crop by sensing various soil parameters and related to the atmosphere.

Karetsos *et al.* [8] have reviewed the use of smartphones and capabilities in agriculture. They have proposed a transactional m-government app for agriculture as an add-on to an existing government portal. The app is easy to access and promising solutions for farmers.

Pal *et al.* [9] have proposed a voice-based mobile application for agricultural commodity price dissemination in the Bengali language. The automatic speech recognition incorporated app provides an excellent value-addition to the existing websites of the agriculture marketing department of the West Bengal government and Indian government.

Pongnumkul *et al.* [10] have reviewed many articles applications that use built-in Smartphone sensors to provide solutions to agriculture. They have focused on how smartphone sensors have been used in agriculture, without the need for external sensors.

Agrawal & Sattiraju [11] have designed two smartphone applications for farmers of Indian agriculture.

Zen *et al.* [12] have used geographical Information System (GIS) techniques to analyze various types of geospatial data and deal with complex situations.

Roy *et al.* [13] have used a Cordova framework based geo package mobile/application to support field applications in agriculture. After the implementation of geo package SDK on a mobile application, users can easily access, manage, and visualize.

Roy [13] have presented an innovative hybrid Agro Tick system for smart agriculture. Agro Tick is an IoT based system designed to improve the efficiency of agriculture.

Nugroho *et al.* [14] have used web-based monitor systems to monitor the oil palm plantation developed using the Progressive Web App (PWA) approaches. The PWA approach provides easy access for both field employees and plantation supervisors.

Marimuthu *et al.* [15] have developed the persuasive Technology Method (PTM) to change the farmers' mindset towards technology supported farming. The PTM with ICT models assessing their success with the farmers.

Rajeshwari *et al.* [16] have used IoT device to sense the agricultural data and is stored into the cloud database. Here, the data mining techniques have been used for the prediction by information reaches the farmer via mobile application. The objective of this study is to increase crop production and control of agricultural cost.

Kuang *et al.* [17] have presented a cloud platform for farmland environment monitoring systems by which remote control and real-time alarming is realized through the mobile terminal. The cloud platform has provided strong technical support for the realization of smart agriculture.

Vijay *et al.* [18] have proposed an aggro-app based improved monitoring system for better production of crops. The objective of this study is to enhance the productivity of crop production. Choubey *et al.* [19] have used the cloud for image processing.

Rabello *et al.* [20] have developed a mobile application to optimize the drone flight in a precision agriculture scenario.

Rupanagudi *et al.* [21] have discussed a novel approach, notably video processing, cloud computing, and robotics, to solve the problem by continually monitoring crops. It has implemented to detect pests in one of the most popular fruits in the world-the tomato.

Rachana & Guruprasad [22] have reviewed the emerging challenges, threats, and concerns in cloud computing security. The study of this article is focused on cloud computing security framework, problems, possible strategies, and technical support.

Patel & Patel [23] have demonstrated how android apps of agricultural services have impacted the farmers in their farming activities.

12.4   Proposed Methodology and Experimental Results Discussion

The methodology of computation of flooding and information sharing are noted in steps which are as follows:

1. The Google cloud platform is used as Platform as a Service for proving resources for computation and data migration in the form of cloudlets from mobile app to gcloud servers with

the help of the project creation tool. It provides project id on the cloud platform.

2. All the websites have the Html and XML data contents in which information is stored. The app accesses these websites and does computation offloading in which the computation is sent in the form of cloudlets to the cloud server from the smartphone. The data sent is received by the app engine, which does XML parsing and extracts useful data from the websites which have the latest information in the field of agriculture.

3. RI (Recent Information) algorithm is used to extract the latest and relevant data by allocating priority to each data and making a stack. It contains essential data at the top, which has the highest priority and groups according to the data's preference. The information this data is then stored in the virtual repository created in the Google cloud server and extraction is based on the latest available information.

4. The data is saved in the form of a JSON parse tree with the main node containing the main data and its sub-nodes containing subsequent data. The RI algorithm collects the latest and essential data and feeds it into the app engine. The app engine does Xml parsing and fetches the data stored in the virtual database (Figure 12.1).

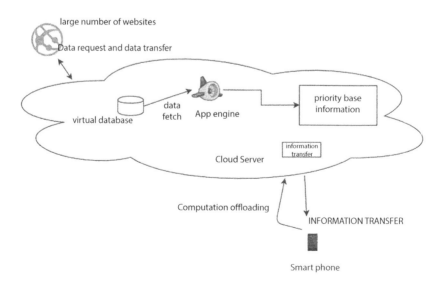

Figure 12.1 Cloud-based agriculture system.

5. The important information extracted by the app engine has fended to the mobile app.

6. This app also contains a sub module which allows users to click the picture of the crop's soil and send it to the expectations for review to check whether the crop has any diseases or to find which fertilizer to add so that to improve its growth and quality ad also provide a chat module in which the farmers could directly chat with the experts to resolve their issues and improve productivity and growth of their crops and improve the quality of agriculture.

7. This app runs in the cloud helps in saving battery and data of the users, and the users do not need to upgrade the version as it is done directly in the cloud by the person who is managing this mobile app.

The application workings are summarized below:

- When the users start the mobile app, it comes online, gets connected to the internet, and searches for the information from various websites

- The application starts loading the information from the website, and the computation offloading takes place and the app engine in the cloud process and finds important information from the websites

- As there are a large number of information from each website RI algorithm starts

- RI fetches all the data from the site. It compares the time in which it was uploaded along with the priority. It sends that data in the form of an information line to the mobile app, and the user gets the information in the form of notification.

The summa public class feedcompaer extends RecyclerView.ViewHolder {

```
        protected TextView Tileofwebsite;
//fetches the title of the page
        Protected TextView publicationDATE;
//compares the publication date of the news;

        protected RSSFeed WebsiteData;
// getting the feeds from website
//list of website for information
```

```
    public FeedListRowHolder(View view) {
      super(view);

      this.title = (TextView) view.findViewById(R.idWebsitetitle);
      this.pubDate = (TextView) view.findViewById(R.id.website
      publicationdate);

      view.setOnClickListener(new View.OnClickListener() {
        @Override
        public void on Click(View info) {
```

//info on clicking the information to read the details

```
          Intent WebsiteIntent = new Intent(info.getContext(), Web
          ViewActivity.class);

          websiteIntent.putExtra("title", rssFeed.getTitle().toString());
          websiteIntent.putExtra("url", rssFeed.getLink().toString());
          // String url=mRssFeedList.get(position).getLink().toString();
          // Log.i("onlcik Recycler",url);
          websit.getContext().startActivity(websiteIntent);
        }
      });
    }
```

}rized coding for the above statements is mentioned below:

After the data is processed, it is saved in the real-time database until the user remains online in the app. This way, all the relevant and important information is sent to the user without using much of the user's Smartphone resources. This consumer's fewer data and power, so it is

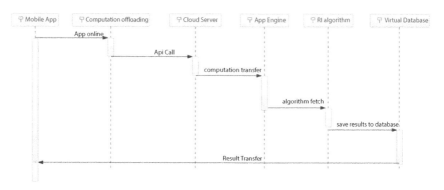

Figure 12.2 Sequence diagram of Mobile App computation.

always advantageous to use mobile cloud computing for cloud computing and computation is offloading. The computation takes place in the cloud server in real-time, and the user gets the data as soon as he comes online in the application. He has installed on his phone to get information related to agriculture for using it (Figure 12.2).

12.4.1 Mobile Cloud Computing

Mobile cloud computing comprises cloud computing and mobile computing, which takes place with wireless networks. As is known those applications which provide enormous quality contents to users such as mobile browsers and other application which was previously used in high performing computers are now used in mobile devices. It is used to access the huge processing power of computers and consumes a lot of power from the battery are now can be used in mobile devices. Still this mobile device has some limitations, such as processing speed and power supply. They run on battery power, which ranges from 2000 mAH to 4000 mAH but the smartphones with less cost, computational speed, and battery power. So to provide them also rich content, mobile cloud computing is the only solution. The main thing it does is that it offloads the computation in the form of cloudlets from Smartphone's to the cloud server with the help of a wireless network. The cloud servers have a large amount of computational resource from which it processes and does the computational task and transmits the results back to the user.

12.4.2 XML Parsing and Computation Offloading

Parsing XML means reading the XML document and changing the data contents in it. It can be used for accessing the data contents in the document. XML has a specific layout and is organized in a specific structure, which helps in identifying and changing specific data contained in the XML file. This could be done through java, which provides many ways to parse the contents. It may be present on a particular webpage.

- JDOM Parser – Its parsing is based similar to Dom parsing, but it does more efficiently.
- StAX Parser – It is more efficient than the SAX parser, which does it in, and it is similar to it.
- Due to the increased processing capability of smartphones in recent years, computationally intensive mobile applications such as image recognition, gaming, and speech

recognition are becoming increasingly popular. However, these applications also quickly drain mobile device batteries. One viable solution to address this problem utilizes computation offloading. Offloading computationally intensive tasks to remote resource-rich servers can save a mobile device's energy. The previous researchers have investigated how to make offloading decisions, i.e., determining which tasks should be offloaded to minimize mobile devices' energy consumption. Some of this work considers the trade-off between the energy saved by moving computations to the server and the energy consumed to offload it.

12.4.3   Energy Analysis for Computation Offloading

The energy analysis has been summarized in Table 12.1 when the application used in a Smartphone.

The following used notations indicate:

M: Speed of instruction per second of the mobile phone
C: Speed in instruction per second of the cloud server
D: Bytes exchanged between the mobile and the cloud
N: Number of resources for computation
G: Resources involved in offloading process
p_{tr}: Power consumed for sending and receiving data
α: Constant energy consumption when the idle state
E: Total energy consumed by the process or consumed when the smartphone is idle+ energy consumed when the process is executing

Table 12.1 Energy analysis when the application is used in smartphone.

No of websites accessed	CPU used in percentage	Battery consumption 2400 mAh in hours	Data used in MB
2	42	8.4	0.8
4	48	8.2	1
6	54	7.8	1.6
8	58	7.6	2

$$E = \alpha * N \frac{C}{M} \quad \text{(When a Smartphone is in idle state)}$$

$$E = \alpha * N \frac{C}{M} + p_{tr} * \frac{D*G}{C*M} \quad \text{(when offloading and Application is}$$

executing in the smartphone)

Energy is saved when the value of C*M is large, and when the process is offloaded to the app engine in a cloud, the processing capacity increased. So the value of C*M is always large; hence the total energy consumption will be low as compared to the normal execution of the application in the smartphone. During normal execution, the value of N will be large and it will increase as the resources are required during the application execution in a smartphone. It will also increase so this will help in conserving and making the process fast and efficient (Figure 12.3).

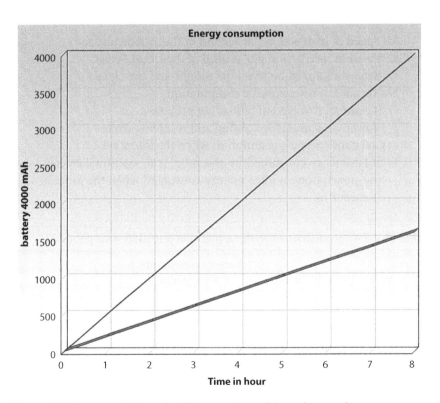

Figure 12.3 Energy analysis graph with app engine and through smartphone.

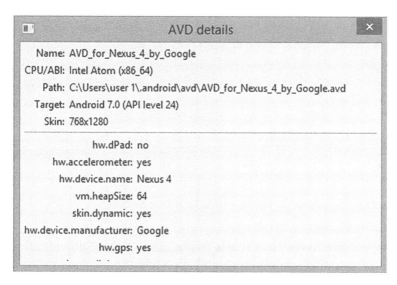

Name: AVD_for_Nexus_4_by_Google
CPU/ABI: Intel Atom (x86_64)
Path: C:\Users\user 1\.android\avd\AVD_for_Nexus_4_by_Google.avd
Target: Android 7.0 (API level 24)
Skin: 768x1280

hw.dPad: no
hw.accelerometer: yes
hw.device.name: Nexus 4
vm.heapSize: 64
skin.dynamic: yes
hw.device.manufacturer: Google
hw.gps: yes

Figure 12.4 Virtual machine specification used for testing application.

- Energy consumption through app engine
- Energy consumption through mobile computation

The battery power consumed is 1500 mah in 8 hours for running the same application, whereas in standard mobile computing, the battery drained is 4000 mah in 8 hours (Figure 12.4).

12.4.4 Virtual Database

A virtual database is a cloud-based database that is hosted in the cloud server. The virtual database is capable of storing a large amount of data. It is stored in JSON format and synchronized in real-time in which the user can read, write, and update the data. It is accessible from any platform, whether it is an android or iOS operation system. The multiple users can access the same database and read, but the administrator only provides the update. The virtual database allows secure access to the data so that only the registered uses can access the database. The virtual database provides advantages over the local database as it can be accessed from any machine from anywhere. The user does not have to maintain it. The administrator of the database can maintain it. The data is stored in several servers, so accessing the data according to requirements can also be done in less time.

Real-time database updates itself whenever any update is done locally. If the update is made when the database is offline, it synchronizes with

Figure 12.5 Virtual database formats in cloud real-time database.

the virtual databases when it gets online. The database provides flexible rules for updating, maintaining, and accessing the database to the user. The real-time database provides several authentication mechanisms for accessing the database to the user. It is mainly a NoSQL type of database and has different optimization and function compared to the relational database. It contains API, which provides quick access to the database according to user requirements related to the information stored in the database (Figure 12.5).

12.4.5   App Engine

The app engine is the platform as a service module cloud computing platform for hosting and developing. The Google managed application which can run on the cloud platform. The application runs on multiple servers and is capable of doing large computation as the scale of the resources with the existing demand for medium files. It is free but for large computation. Google charges some amount for proving resources for execution in the app engine. The App engine could be used in many languages, such as java, python, PHP. It supports many languages that are required to run several virtual machines. It is also capable of running a web app. It is used as a platform as a service. Its usability is extended to many applications (Figures 12.6, 12.7 and 12.8).

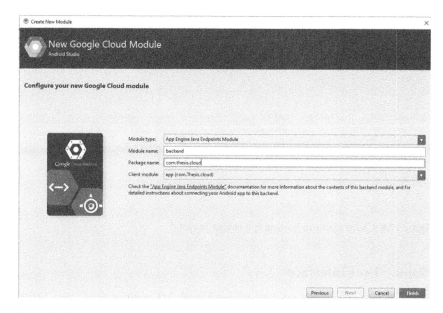

Figure 12.6 Backend module for app engine.

Figure 12.7 Cloud platform hosting app engine in cloud.

Figure 12.8 Cloud platform hosting app engine in cloud.

12.4.6   User Interface

The user interface uses a tabbed layout with a scrolling view. The information is presented in the mobile APP, it could be scrolled, viewed, and a piece of particular information could be selected to view it in more detail. The link embedded in the information is processed by the app engine to redirect it to the particular website and open in a format that could be easily read. The important information ends in the form of notification using a firebase notification service. The import information could reach the concerned information as soon as possible by which the user can make use of the information and take advantage from it (Figure 12.9).

Scrolling Activity

Figure 12.9 User interface layout app.

12.4.7   Securing Data

The security feature of the Google cloud is useful. It provides an SHA-1 key while creating the project. The project could be linked with the app in the cloud, and no modification can be done from others who are not the authorized person to make changes in the application. It also provides several login methods to the user by using their email address or logging in through social networking websites.

Securing user access is done by allowing only registers users to have access to this application. The security is implemented by allowing a user to use either email password or social sites account to login and use the application to get all the important information (Figure 12.10).

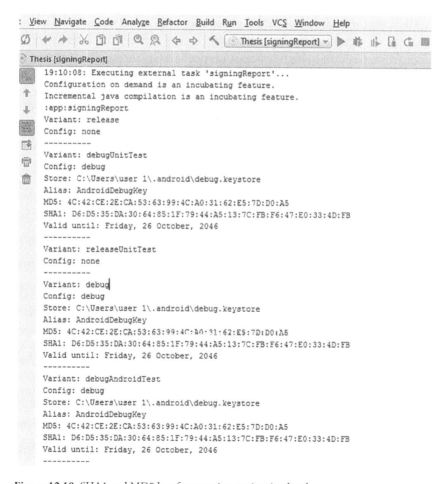

Figure 12.10 SHA1 and MD5 key for securing project in cloud.

12.5   Conclusion and Future Work

Cloud computing has always been a field of research, and its application is extending in every field. It provides software in-demand platform as a service infrastructure, as a service virtual datable, virtual processing capacity. It enables users to migrate to cloud computation for managing and processing their data. It has also emerged in the field of agriculture. It serves the purpose of information and communication technology along with managing the agriculture data in the cloud and proving them to the users. It has increased in improving and extending the processing capability of the smartphone by extending its processing capacity and saving power consumption. It also assists farmers in enhancing productivity and hence contributing to the development of the country.

MCC is composed of mobile computation and cloud computing in the presence of a computer network as processing power. The Smartphones range from medium to high processing speed in Gigahertz. The processing of large applications could be a challenge, so to take this challenge; Mobile cloud computation comes into play. It extends the processing capacity of smartphones compared to computers. The architecture of MCC enables the users to use large applications by offloading the computation to the cloud servers. It processes the user data by resources in the cloud. It is used in the agricultural sector and will be useful in increasing productivity and helping farmers to expect better growth and profit.

References

1. Rose, D.C. *et al.*, Decision support tools for agriculture: Towards effective design and delivery. *AGSY*, 149, 165–174, 2016.
2. Lee, B.S., Alexander, M.E., Hawkes, B.C., Lynham, T.J., Stocks, B.J., Englefield, P., Information systems in support of wildland fire management decision making in Canada. *Comput. Electron. Agric.*, 37, 185–198, 2002.
3. Zhang, Y., Wang, L., Duan, Y., Agricultural information dissemination using ICTs: A review and analysis of information dissemination models in China. *Inf. Process. Agric.*, 3, 1, 17–29, 2016.
4. Ziogas, V., Dietrich, A., Griepentrog, H.W., Paraforos, D.S., Griepentrog, H.W., Paraforos, D.S., Information system farm management management information system using using future internet technologies a farm management information system using future internet technologies a farm management information system using future internet technologies. *IFAC-PapersOnLine*, 49, 16, 324–329, 2016.

5. Shahzadi, R., Tausif, M., Suryani, M.A., Internet of Things based expert system for smart agriculture. *Int. J. Adv. Comput. Sci. Appl.,* 7, 9, 341–350, 2020.

6. Prasad, S., Peddoju, S.K., Ghosh, D., AgroMobile: A cloud-based framework for agriculturists on mobile platform. *Int. J. Adv. Sci. Technol.,* 59, 41–52, 2013.

7. Dahikar, S.S. and Rode, S.V., Agricultural crop yield prediction using artificial neural network approach. *International Journal of Innovative Research in Electrical, Electronics, Instrumentation and Control Engineering (IJIREEICE),* 2, 1, 683–686, 2014.

8. Karetsos, S., Costopoulou, C., Sideridis, A., Developing a smartphone app for m-government in agriculture. *J. Agric. Inform.,* 5, 1, 1–8, 2014.

9. Pal, M., Roy, R., Khan, S., Bepari, M.S., Basu, J., PannoMulloKathan: Voice enabled mobile app for agricultural commodity price dissemination in Bengali language, in: *Interspeech 2018, 19th Annual Conference of the International Speech Communication Association,* pp. 1491–1492, Hyderabad, India, 2018.

10. Pongnumkul, S., Chaovalit, P., Surasvadi, N., Applications of smartphone-based sensors in agriculture: A systematic review of research. *J. Sens,* 2015, 2015.

11. Agrawal, R. and Sattiraju, K.S., Exploring suitable interfaces for agriculture based smartphone apps in India. *Proceedings of the 11th Asia Pacific Conference on Computer Human Interaction,* pp. 280–285, 2013.

12. Ren, Z., Hou, Y., Lu, X., A case of GIS application in agricultural project management. in: *2013 Second International Conference on Agro-Geoinformatics (Agro-Geoinformatics),* pp. 2–5, 2008.

13. Roy, S. *et al.*, IoT, big data science & analytics, cloud computing and mobile app based hybrid system for smart agriculture, in: *2017 8th Annual Industrial Automation and Electromechanical Engineering Conference (IEMECON),* pp. 303–304, 2017.

14. Nugroho, L.E., Gandhi, A., Pratama, H., Mustika, I.W., Ferdiana, R., No, J.G., Development of monitoring system for smart farming using Progressive Web App, in: *2017 9th International Conference on Information Technology and Electrical Engineering (ICITEE),* pp. 1–5, 2017.

15. Marimuthu, R., Design and development of a persuasive technology method to encourage smart farming, in: *2017 IEEE region 10 humanitarian technology conference (R10-HTC),* pp. 21–23, 2017.

16. Rajeswari, S., Suthendran, K., Rajakumar, K., A smart agricultural model by integrating IoT, mobile and cloud-based big data analytics, in: *2017 international conference on intelligent computing and control (I2C2),* pp. 1–5, 2017.

17. Kuang, Y., Shen, Y., Lu, L., Li, G., Farmland monitoring system based on cloud platform. *Itaic,* pp. 335–339, 2019.

18. Vijay, K.M.A., Kumar, K.N.C., Kumar, N., Harshitha, K., Khan, M.K.K., An improved agriculture monitoring system using agri-app for better crop production, in: *2018 3rd IEEE International Conference on Recent Trends in*

Electronics, Information & Communication Technology (RTEICT), pp. 2413–2417, 2018.

19. Choubey, D.K., Kumar, A., Solutions, C.T., Srivastava, K., Pahari, S., Notification and image analysis in cloud, in: *2020 International Conference on Emerging Trends in Information Technology and Engineering (ic-ETITE)*, pp. 1–5, 2020.

20. Rabello, A., Brito, R.C., Favarim, F., Weitzenfeld, A., Todt, E., Mobile system for optimized planning to drone flight applied to the precision agriculture, in: *2020 3rd International Conference on Information and Computer Technologies (ICICT)*, pp. 12–16, 2020.

21. Rupanagudi, S.R., Ranjani, B.S., Bhat, V.G., A novel cloud computing based smart farming system for early detection of borer insects in tomatoes, in: *2015 international conference on communication, information & computing technology (ICCICT)*, pp. 1–6, 2015.

22. Rachana, S.C. and Guruprasad, H.S., Emerging security issues and challenges in cloud computing. *Int. J. Eng. Sci. Innov. Technol.*, 3, 2, 485–490, 2014.

23. Patel, II. and Patel, D., Urvey of. *International Journal of Information Sciences and Techniques (IJIST)*, 6, 1, 61–67, 2016.

13

SSAMH – A Systematic Survey on AI-Enabled Cyber Physical Systems in Healthcare

Kamalpreet Kaur[1]*, Renu Dhir[1] and Mariya Ouaissa[2]

¹Department of CSE, Dr BR Ambedkar NIT Jalandhar, India
²Moulay Ismail University Meknès, Meknès, Morocco

Abstract

In the former period, technology connects the devices for resourceful interaction, still in an atmosphere of various concerns like trust, privacy, and security. Nowadays in the real world, various protruding systems are trying their level best for creating a secure communication environment with a set of protocols. Artificial intelligence-driven healthcare systems are integrated with automatic decision-making systems that take appropriate decisions regarding the patient's health. It follows the physiological closed-loop interoperable system to control the input and output parameters of health. So, the health security of the patient should be sustained with proper security measures.

The electronic healthcare systems transmit data and perform monitoring over the numerous communication media using low-cost sensors and intelligent devices such as smart meters and watches that are constructed on the basic platform of the cyber-physical systems. The new technology like wireless sensors networks placing a milestone for these medical cyber-physical systems (MCPS). The chapter will enlighten the role of artificial intelligence in medical cyber-physical systems that are followed by certification and regulation. Also, throw light on the threats and challenges in the medical cyber-physical systems.

Keywords: Healthcare system, wireless sensor network, medical cyber-physical systems, smart devices, artificial intelligence, smart meters

Corresponding author: kamalpreetk.cs.19@nitj.ac.in

Danda B. Rawat, Lalit K Awasthi, Valentina Emilia Balas, Mohit Kumar and Jitendra Kumar Samriya (eds.) Convergence of Cloud with AI for Big Data Analytics: Foundations and Innovation, (277–298)

13.1 Introduction

Artificial Intelligence is the vertebral support for the healthcare system that manages the situations of the patient in remote areas. The medical devices are projecting towards the changes from the past that upgraded with the latest technology for communication. Initially, the patient's health is carried out with the intervention of a human. The physical presence of the experts like doctors is required in evaluating the various health parameters of the patient.

At the dawn of artificial intelligence, the health expert's team can diagnose the patients remotely and use their prerequisite knowledge to train automatic decision-making systems for excluding the human intervention and achieve the benchmark in parameter accuracy. The wide range of the network for shares the records of the patient fast and accurately to the doctors.

Ultimately, these systems are critically integrating the health of a patient, by knowing the conditional parameters that are used in the hospitals to accomplish the various high-quality results. Under the clinical scenario, the treatment procedures can be modified using the opinion of the caregiver. The latest research reveals that the medical cyber-physical systems (MCPS) help reduce the size and complexity issues in the traditional systems. The chapter will address the plentiful challenges in building a good quality medical cyber-physical system. In addition, an operational working of the systems is possible with high-quality embedded systems. The model-based technique will be taking a forward-facing in modifying the designs of the MCPS timely. The model techniques are considering the prominent properties of building a hardware system. This chapter will be thrown light on the role of artificial intelligence in medical cyber-physical systems. And the layout is as follows. Section 13.2 provides the architecture of a medical cyber-physical system. Sections 13.3-13.10 work accomplished in addressing the artificial intelligence-driven medical devices, the emergence of a new trend, challenges, and threats. Section 13.11 will sum up the chapter.

13.2 The Architecture of Medical Cyber-Physical Systems

Artificial intelligence creates integrated embedded computer systems for computing the medical processes and managing these systems through a closed feedback loop that are changing the results of computations timely.

These real-time supporting systems are secure, dependent, inter-operative, and cooperative for e-healthcare systems [2]. With the consequences, there is a usual inclination towards aspect the rising of the embedded systems that have operating variations in the process that regulates an architecture for finding an adjustable as a result for medical cyber-physical systems. The procedure regulates the architecture in various domains for designing the large and complex sensors for these systems. For an illustration, the Code Blue software framework founded at Harvard University that uses comfortable in medical applications uses a routing framework for wireless nodes Code Blue utilizes in discovery protocol so that both medical devices and handheld end-user devices could determine which sensors were currently deployed in the environment. An interface based on the query will work to request data from precise devices and to set a filter that would only transmit to a person back if the data exceeded any threshold [2]. Layered architectures of numerous styles have been proposed. Like Mobi Health utilized sensor devices that attach patients to connect through Bluetooth, which manages portable devices referred to as the Mobile Base Unit (MBU). E-health applications work with the substitute host to enquiry about the evidence that is required for the communication through the MBU of every patient [8, 9]. A comparable style was applied in Alarm Net [9]. The researcher [13] proposed a layered framework of the component layers, process layer, and application layer that captures sensor data in healthcare using the Big data framework. The component layer performs the functioning for providing the message and routing the data using the distribution services at the system level. The process layer has helped remove the unwanted information, group data that filter sensor data streams with the set of rules along with semantic knowledge. The application layer is stimulating with analytics services. The author proposed a similar architecture [6] that used an ambient intelligent compliant object along with the set of sensors in the base layer.

Generally, decision support systems are permitting proper processing of the stored data values and an accountable decision is performed according to a running situation. Earlier data analyst is doing proper analysis of the patient record and making an appropriate decision. The decision support systems are bridging the gap between the data analytics and the decision that is working efficiently in making the decisions in the system. The clinical decision systems are motivated with artificial intelligence using smart alarm systems that smartly manage the health parameters related information such as diagnosis the illness, preventive care and many more. The physiological loop system takes the input data through the directly controlled imputed device. Also, an automatic controller performs immediate action while promptly using the majority of systems where safety is at an initial priority. In the medical domain, continuous monitoring of health parameters like blood pressure, body temperature etc., are simply handled by knowledge of a physiological closed-loop system and automatically reconfiguring delivery devices, and abruptly sending a revert to a caregiver through a message if the patient's current parameters varied from the provided normal range by the practitioners. After receiving the desired changes, the caregivers can then concentrate on it and make an important clinical decision, so the caregiver is having a lesser probability of lost critical events, thereby effectively enlightening the patient safety. The major medical applications that are controlling the in-built systems by closed-loop control are cardioverter-defibrillators. The secret designing of the modeled physiological closed-loop system is the virtually existing machines that are built cost-effectively through networking with the existing medical devices, like infusion pumps and vital sign monitors. Meanwhile, new hazards are faced and need to be mitigated. As per the current challenges corresponding to the patient's modeling, an appropriate model-driven development approach is to be used to acquire an efficient result from it. There is the majority of the researcher who is well explored the patient modeling using an efficient model-driven development, to be illustrated as an extensively analyzed and modeled is glucose-insulin kinetics. Numerous control strategies on the biochemical models, like model predictive control [7], have been developed. Moreover, the researchers worked effectively on the physiological control to avoid failure or delay. The interconnection between the medical devices is proficiently defined by the physiological closed-loop system and revealed in the numerous cases studied in the real world. The patient controller analgesia (PCA) in a closed-loop [1] followed the proper safety concern in using the PCA pump for checking the dose of an analgesic and to avoid respiratory failure proper checking of an analgesic is to be checked. The most popular device for monitoring the health parameters like heart rate and blood oxygen saturation (SpO2) is known to be a pulse oximeter and circulates the reading to the desired controller for analysis. While for the diabetic and ICU patient depends upon the outer insulin and glucose for effectively maintaining the reference range. For safety purposes, it is necessary to verify and validate the system properly. According to the pre-decided clinical scenario, an appropriate model is designed with proper validation such that all the hazards are to be mitigated. The difficulty of hazard investigation is very closely related to the control objectives provided by the caregiver. Indeed, experimental results distributed by a closed-loop corresponding to the parameters fixed by the caregiver are comparable and a major challenge. The researcher [9] gave a realistic and

Table 13.1 Classification of MCPS architecture.

S. no	Architecture	Layers involved
1	CMIOT [5]	• Sensing (for execution) • Communication assistant • Network transport • Data fusion • Application service
2	ECSH [1]	• Hybrid sensor source • Data aggregator • Mobile edge node • Edge cloud • Monitoring and service provider
3	SHMM [2]	• Collection (energy) and generation (data) • Preprocessing of data • Application
4	ODAI [12]	• Acquisition • Preprocessing • Cloud behavior
5	OPHR [4]	• Client • Server
6	DEH [3]	• WSN • Side chain • Smart contract • Blockchain
7	FHE [10]	• Community member • Internet of things gateway • Cloud database • Detection (Anomaly)
8	MH [9]	• Storage at cloud • Data mining (medical) • Cloud engine-session cache • Service presentation • Service interaction
9	HT [17]	• Devices (mobile) • Storage at cloud • Centers (medical)

controlled approach under the caregiver environment providing a patient simulator for analyzing it. A proper notion is provided for a virtual clinical trial for the drug development in mass. In nutshell, the different layers used in the different architecture of MCPS are depicted in the upcoming Table 13.1. In the CMIOT architecture, medical sensors are present to analyze the health data of the community residing at various health centers that need to be uploaded at the health server timely and successfully through the IPv6 network [5]. The stored data is to be transmitted for the integration, processing, and storage according to the data collected. This author segregates the patient's health records into the blocks which are a logical division of the patient health datasets and focuses on the interoperability and distribution of the data [3]. The architecture is designed for the mobile and healthcare provider to contact patients with the web applications [12]. In summary, systems indulge all users for maintaining trust with the client (patient) for providing authentic medical records. The numerous architectures give the creation of the e-health systems that manage healthcare in a better way.

13.3   Artificial Intelligence-Driven Medical Devices

In the specified architecture of the medical cyber-physical system which sends and analyzes the medical reports that are according to decision generated by the decision support systems that use the wired and wireless interfaces for this communication. Therefore, the different parameters like body temperature, blood pressure, and many more are accessible through the monitoring devices and the report is analyzed through these devices [2]. The devices used in the medical physical systems are categorized broadly into two groups on the primary functionality in performance are as follows.

13.3.1   Monitoring Devices

The devices that analyze minutely the heart rate and oxygen level of the sick patient and provide alertness through the sensors for the relevant information about them. The monitoring devices like electrocardiograph ("ECG") machines that analyze the heart rate through electronic representation and uses, the capnography machine for checking carbon dioxide levels, a pulse oximeter for effectively calculating the oxygen level in the blood, and a sphygmomanometer to measure blood pressure. According to the clinical settings, to check the patient remote area there is the majority of applications that care for or before cases like surgery, diabetic care and many more. Although, each monitoring device is unique likely an ECG device cannot be constructed within the same piece as a glucose monitor. The monitoring devices are categorized into the following subparts:

a. **Checking devices** are efficiently utilized to monitor the patient's numerous parameters that contact or may be implanted into an individual body. To cite an example, the oximeter is checking the pulse rate of an individual by putting the piece of clip on the finger and regularly sensing the pulse using the capital equipment.

b. **The capital equipment:** The capital equipment is analyzing the records of the patients. The patient monitoring device collects the important data parameters of the patient's health and this data is sent for monitoring especially wirelessly or wired for processing, placing, and displaying. A plethora of these equipment uses the interconnection system through connectors, PCB and wire harness for monitoring the patient's health. To illustrate, the ECG P-Wave of the patient is monitored using the computer screen.

c. **The software:** Once the patient parameters are recorded, they will immediately transfer to capital equipment. The proper analysis of the records is performed by the expert team such as nurses or doctors and extracts useful information from it and useful information is to be used for further usage. The efficient software converts the analyzed data into a binary format that is machine-dependent.

13.3.2   Delivery Devices

The delivery devices are those that are proficient enough to provide therapy in changing the physiological state of the patient. In the structure of MCPS, data received from monitoring is to be analyzed using a smart controller that gives an approximation to the state of the patient's health and performs an automatic initiation to the treatment (such as medicine infusion or ventilators) by giving a command to delivery devices.

13.3.3   Network Medical Device Systems

For the patient record monitoring, the wide array of medical devices takes a bulging step to swap analogous electro-medical devices with the new microprocessor's improvements and digital networks so that the healthier diagnosis and impulsive treatment of the patient in remote areas. However, the connectivity of numerous medical devices has been scaled from minute to ultra-huge geographical distribution of electronic records. To illustrate, the networking sector remotely allows monitoring the patient's progress that gave relaxation to the majority of clinician's space at the hospital along with the period saving and reduces travel expenditures. At the worst condition of an individual the prompt action to be taken is to make an immediate ping to the doctor's office that the condition of getting re-admitted at the hospital has arrived. The different parameters like blood sugar levels, heart rates, or other metrics can be monitored at a particular residential area and then conveyed to clinics either day to day or after some interval through a wired or wireless network connection. This procedure is moderately convenient and economical for the patient to share the record. A popular concept of Remote patient monitoring (RPM) is also known as home monitoring uses the subset application for working under numerous requirements along with delivery rate. For example, an analysis of prolonged running is known as chronic diseases such as diabetes, congestive heart failure, and hypertension are completed by unremitting record checking [4].

13.3.4   IT-Based Medical Device Systems

Numerous self-driven devices are using the computational intelligence that controls the passive devices. The active usage of actuators and embedded sensors are controlling the [1]sick individual's physiology function and processes, as the systems help to reach an extremely functionally flexible and efficient cyber-physical system. To cite with an illustration, the smart alarm for the medical devices that are used in health organizations. The hospitals are developing an alarm system for dealing with multiple patients simultaneously and providing immediate medical assistance through the caregiver. In these systems, practitioners are setting the threshold alarm on the dynamic sign 24-hour care and the current alarm per the existing algorithms for examining the vital signs individually. There are abundant consequences that may commence such as low-level alarm due to over-abundance. The alarm systems are built with varied protocols under the situation that is going to be handled. To be illustrated, for the bypass graft surgery, the algorithm is designed in such a way that it should consider multiple vital signs of simultaneous monitoring like heart rate, respiration rate, oxygen saturation rate, and heart rate so that the appropriate solutions can be provided by the practitioners [5]. Three-level alarm priority systems are preferable to declining the clinical false alarm and efficiently communicating the clinical severity based on the problem and demand of the healthcare. The algorithm flows in such a manner that it takes an input flow of four vital signs from the three monitors and employees a Fuzzy Expert system to imitator the decision-related process of nursing. The decision-related tools are employed using the Bayesian theory for showing the existing complication undergone by the patient at any time and prominent risk factors.

13.3.5 Wireless Sensor Network-Based Medical Driven Systems

In the current scenario, there are a plethora of wearable devices that promptly share the data with numerous societies through the wireless body area network (WBAN); in the case of health monitoring, for various types of implantations, miniature or any wearable sensors that communicate through the wireless network. The biosensors are analyzing the various human health parameters like the temperature of the body, heart rate, breathing rate, blood sugar, and electro-cardiogram. For all the quantities that are interconnected using either a wireless or wired connection to be linked to the central node like any personal digital assistants that are providing evidence to the user's interface or communicating the gathered vital signs to the numerous health centers for assisting the patients. To meet the requirement of active arising problems, the wireless sensor networks (WSN) and mobile ad hoc network (MANET) will explore the possibilities for it [14]. The vivid usage of these cyber physical systems (CPS) in the different spheres and then exchanging the heterogeneous information flow, intelligent decision corresponds to different issues and inter-domain sensor cooperation. An illustration of common architecture used in wireless sensor networks reveals its proper utilization [11]. The medical devices and human beings are interacting with each other are possible through the medical cyber-physical systems in two ways like a human as subject or individual as operators. Patient-specific and adaptive therapy is required for patient stimulating models.

13.4   Certification and Regulation Issues

Medical physical systems are safe and critical systems that have to undergo the regulatory process of certification approval such that the systems work efficiently in the remotely accessible devices. Initially, the US Food and Drug Administration (FDA) authorized the medicinal policies for accessing the records of the patient but was unable to meet the complexity level of medical device systems. A new approach based on the regulatory regime, to work with the infusion pump improvement [14], the Food and Drug requires assurance case for documentation submission for approval. Broadly, medical devices use a plethora of software for monitoring and delivering the essential parameters. In the major cases, the software's hazards are not well understood and not excelling in evaluating the performance. In the last of designing, the verification and certification are made such that it overfills the device requirements. The design and verification approach helps in scaling the model-based techniques to implement the code generation. The new regulatory approach is that certificates have to advocate for reviewing that the system had achieved its goal. However, the model-based technique is a new process-based approach and proper evidence is required for certification. Stand-alone devices are built from scratch, so they are in-built certified, whereas virtual medical devices need to be verified and certified, to support the framework supported by the security and authentication layer with the interoperability platform established in it. The separate certification of virtual medical devices (VMD) keeps the physical realization in mind. The majority of medical applications that are using the mobile platform for executing the gain are to be at the doorstep of the majority of the persons. These applications are based on the recent software that are utilizing the sensors according to the functioning of the medical devices on a mobile platform to perform functions that, until now, were performed only by medical devices. For example, in case of emergency non-availability of the stethoscope can be overcome by the remotely available device like a cell phone that is having a software application for behaving as a stethoscope and using the microphones for listening to the heartbeat. Now updated guidance is issued by the FDA for identifying the numerous applications based on medical devices and providing a regulatory approach for such virtual devices.

13.5 Big Data Platform for Medical Cyber-Physical Systems

The word is emerging in the technological world of big data that are high-volume, velocity, and variety of informatics data for new processing forms to allow better-quality understanding of the finding, method optimization, and decision-making. The medical physical systems are generating structured or unstructured data from biological sensors, mobile sensing devices, software logs, radiofrequency identification readers and remote sensing that encompassed data related to the socially assembled open source available on the internet. The basic 4 V features of the big data support the cyber-physical system and extract the information that is like qualitative and quantifiable conversion of data in an assorted framework. The researcher explored that management of records through big data is very cost-effective and progressive information processing forms are required for analysis of the findings and decision making corresponding to it [15]. For a better health monitoring system, the adaptation capabilities are for accessing the new devices with a new set of protocols. The various small embedded systems are inserted into the human body to remotely access the numerous health parameters of the patient. The usage of commonly

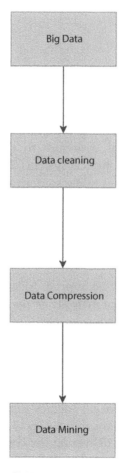

Figure 13.1 Big data processing of MCPS.

wireless sensor networks for health monitoring systems. In the real-time scenario person's health are accessible and records are privately authorized, so that proper diagnosis of the health is to be done. The processing of the facts and statistics collected for the analysis in the medical cyber-physical systems includes data collection (big data), data processing, data storage, data analysis and data applications. In the following Figure 13.1 data processing, like data cleaning, includes error detection, error recovery, consistency, and redundancy detection. The data compression is used to minimize the size of the dataset, for the proper storage. Compression of the data may be as time correlation compression, spatial correlation compression and data block compression. For the visualizing of the information, data mining and analysis need to be performed. In the case of data mining, data characterization, frequency pattern analysis, classification, aggregation, correlation, and mining.

13.6   The Emergence of New Trends in Medical Cyber-Physical Systems

There is a grouping of medical devices and useful networks that transform the complex physical dynamics to the contemporary medical devices that analyze cyber-physical systems, broadly called medical CPS [13]. The web-based facilities allow smooth access to the broader communication between the individuals such as patients, doctors, and health organization staff at a quick note, but allow sharing the patient's record frequently. The rising scenario in the medical cyber-physical systems are as follows:

a. *Heightened network abilities*: In today's era, with advancements in technology majority of the medical devices used in the MCPS are highly capable of monitoring the patient's health through local connections and storing electronic records on cloud databases.

b. *Innovative software is authorized embedded systems*: Novel possibilities are created to enhance the functionalities of the embedded systems of any medical device.

c. *Perfection in automatic monitoring of patient*: Those devices that are capable of delivering the continuous observations of the patient's state so that the prominent action could be taken, that devices are known to be automatic controllers.

d. *Expansion of computer technology for wireless communication*: The rapid progress in the field of information technology, networking and mobile broadband network is flexible in the usage of portable devices. Although, mobile healthcare systems are more prevalent and settled by the cyber-physical systems.

Furthermore, health-related applications use intelligent decision-making for predicting the results from the given parameters. Research perspective in the cloud computing technologies permit the real-time analysis of the data effortlessly and increase its scalability for future use. The cyber-physical systems use effective decision making collect the data such as active data including digital records and smart feedback whereas passive data from smart devices or biosensors in this popular healthcare system support the acquisition process. The prearrangement of data gaining and decision-making are successfully explored in a wide variety of healthcare applications.

13.7   Eminence Attributes and Challenges

The medical devices using the cyber-physical systems came across the real-world challenges that ensure the eminence attributes as follows:

A. Independency: The medical physical systems are using the computational intelligence that practices the actuation therapies with the current health state of the patient, which allows the systems to work independently. All the work is followed securely and effectually in a closed loop.
B. High Assurance Computer Software: The running of the hardware in the medical devices is based on the software. The various hardware interlocks are traditionally implemented for protection but now the transition is made into the software. So, the high assurance is grave to declare the protection and usefulness of MCPS.
C. Interoperability: For the sharing of the patient's record with healthcare timely, the communication among them must be harmless, operative, certified, and protected.
D. Context Awareness: In the case of interoperability, the general health parameters of the patient are early predictable providing emergency alertness to the care through an alarm.

Over the patient's population, the composite level in humanoid with a variation of physiological factor that evolving a high level of computational intellect is a non-trivial task.

E. Security and Privacy: The medical devices collecting the patient's record is a key issue in terms of privacy and safety. The privacy loss, discrimination, abuse and physical harm can be done by unauthorized access or tampering with the provided record. So, a shield of record in MCPS is life-threatening.

F. Authorization: The multifaceted protection in medical devices requires a value for an operative mode in software reliability and achieving altitudes in shielding them.

The new trends that support the existing cyber-physical systems have to be cost-effective to support the medical technology. As all systems are dependable on the foundation of technology that is configuring the embedded systems through networking. The advent of new technologies provides a good opportunity for dynamically sensing the systems. However, the existence of new cloud computing development opens a new perspective of exploring the new technology-based applications. For the integration of the new systems larger integration skills are required for dealing efficiently with the machine-to-machine applications. The researchers are still working to analyze the complex mesh network along with its complexity. The communication consistency is still overleaf for the medical devices. To illustrate, ZigBee, Bluetooth and WIFI are at a similar frequency band. Along with this, cyber-physical systems are facing the design challenges like energy management, real-time distributed control, system resource management and many more, though the cyber-physical systems are human cognitive driven processes.

13.8 High-Confidence Expansion of a Medical Cyber-Physical Expansion

Modern devices are dependent totally on the software for the safety of the stored records of the patient in the real world. The emerging trend in Model-based development is a mode of improving the quality of the existing software. This method allows the programmer to accomplish model verification for security and functional requirements and the proper methodical programming will preserve them for further use. The researcher presented a semiformal technique such as UML and Simulink. The model-based development process is well predictable with demonstrated case studies of an implantable pacemaker and infusion pump [17]. The numerous formal modeling and tools based for analysis were proposed by different authors for growth and validation of the model of a scheme along with code.

The case study of an infusion pump begins with system requirements using an informal state machine notation, the requirements which are overcome by timing constraints are satisfied during the execution. According to the existing requirements a structured model is developed. For testing the system, under the specification the requirements are for inspecting the behaviors of the system. The proper validity of results is not much exposable through non-trivial computation time. In the recent case, identification of the violation has been made and alteration according to measurement on the implementation found during the validation experimentations. Within a cycle of the process, for the selected platform the software implementation of the system is made executed and validation was done according.

13.9   Role of the Software Platform in the Interoperability of Medical Devices

MCPS with the help of a variety of medical devices that are framed in a specified structure and using a connection-oriented or connectionless network that checks remotely needy person. Abstractly, the devices are networked according to the clinical scenario known as *Virtual Medical Device* (VMD) [17], which follows the suitable clinical algorithm for executing a mainframe. For using the mandatory devices, the development of the VMD application is portable and easy to use for everyone. So, the interoperability manager provides a proper execution platform for detecting network faults.

13.10   Clinical Acceptable Decision Support Systems

To accomplish medical device interoperability all the medical information needs to be centralized from many to one concept. The latest technologically equipped hospitals use medical devices for continuously monitoring the patient's vital signs. However, these vital signs provide a vivid clinical window in the deterioration of health state by providing an alert signal. Recently, are configured with threshold alarms which will be activated when a dynamic value crosses a predefined threshold. Such that these threshold alarms are helpful in the detection of the emergency state, but some scenarios are not considered viable, raising false alarm, high rate of alarms which cause tiring of caretaker and will lead to ignorance and turn-off many alarms. The context-awareness in MCPS will provide flexibility in pre-processing and storing the patient data from the patient streaming. The multiple pre-processing of the available techniques helps in choosing the best technique in the context of medicine. In the case study of Generic smart alarm, that is built according to the generic architecture that is flexible for reconfigurable and provable systems. The architecture depicts the vital signs of the patient through the different pre-processing systems and under the given protocols resulting in the desired output. Sometimes, in case of surgery the false alarm generation for overcoming the high risk is made during the artery bypass graft. The accuracy of alarm in this domain will be improved through the specified architecture with a simple pre-processing and inference modulus to create a straightforward instantiation [18].

13.11   Prevalent Attacks in the Medical Cyber-Physical Systems

The valuable information used by the cyber-physical systems is met with malicious attacks and exploits the resources of these systems intentionally b/y the intruder. These attacks may be in the form of individuals or groups to destroy the content of the systems. Numerous attacks can be followed as:

a. External Threats: The threats that are suspicious and gaining access from the outer surrounding are known to be external threats. There are numerous external threats as follows:

   i. *Cyber Criminals:* The treat is possible in the group of individuals that are using the technology for performing the criminal act to fetch the information of the multi-national/international companies for their profit.
   ii. *Hacktivists:* The collection of individuals who in combination taking the action for a precious gain of information on the topic of political or religious matters by performing malicious activities on their tasks. Though they can feel they are fighting injustice.
   iii. *State-Sponsored Attackers:* The malicious activities are performed under the political, commercial, or military interest of the country. There are plentiful skilled

hackers by an administration of the country that exploits the information badly.

b. Insider Threats: A security risk known as an insider threat comes from within the target organization. It usually involves a current or former employee or business acquaintance who gain unauthorized accounts on an organization network.

The most popular attacks in the *medical physical systems:*

- *Data Breaches:* The data breaches are considered to be popular malware-based attackers fetching an important set of instructions from healthcare industries and gaining personal profits by selling them in the market.
- *Ransomware Attacks:* The computer system attackers are critically disabling the server systems till the period it is not getting the payoff for that type of attack. In the current era, there are a plethora of e-healthcare applications that will face difficulties with the attacker's middle attacks and hinder the functioning of the majority of the medical devices.
- *Social Engineers:* The social engineers are exploiting the network security of the systems that are bulls' eye on the health organizations employees by circulating the emails and creating a tricky illusion of some kind of links, such that these highly malicious for fetching internal data/records of the organization like records of any employee etc.

Among all the above-mentioned attacks on the systems that are corrupting the hidden information of any organization. Though some other attacks are popular in these cyber-physical systems are Stuxnet, DDoS, Phishing, Man in Middle attack and many more are existing in this real world and majority of the consequences related to it. To secure the data various requirements like data integrity, data availability, data audit and information privacy are shown in Figure 13.2.

Data availability certifies that the data or the data systems need to be used by an authorized user. The data availability is highly affected by unreliability or inaccurate data or through unauthorized access to existing

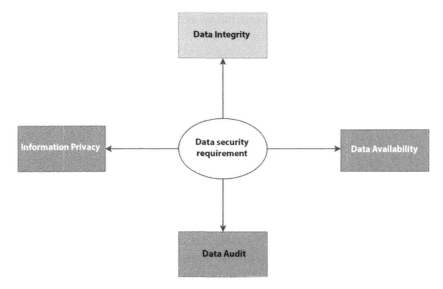

Figure 13.2 Various data security requirements for protecting data in MCPS.

information. The observation of the perfect grained audit of the database operations, alerting the risk behavior of the database and obstructive outbreak behavior, is known as data audit. The privacy of the data is required, in terms of the records that are publically accessed or the personal identification of the patient [16].

13.12   A Suggested Framework for Medical Cyber-Physical System

The medical business is abruptly in progress with the alteration that giving a big challenge to the software and network connectivity. The MCPS provides a different set of challenges that are separate from the existing CPS. The following framework will provide an idea for the designing of the medical cyber-physical systems. In this, there was a direct interaction of the patient with the medical devices (like input devices) for the analysis of the data parameters. The medical devices are supported with the administrated support and decision support system for accurate analysis of the results. The caregiver (like doctors or nurses) will work on the health parameters that are provided to them. The Figure 13.3 beneath is the framework for the medical cyber-physical system.

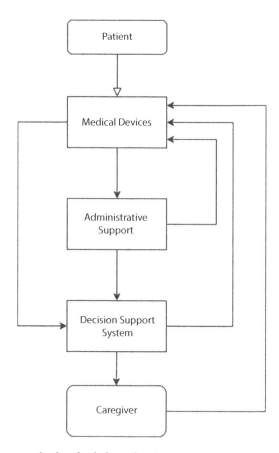

Figure 13.3 Framework of medical physical systems.

13.13   Conclusion

In nutshell, according to the rising pressure from society with a combination of technology, MCPS takes a lift in the substantial transformation developing a massive expandable and strengthening safety for caregivers and patients. The challenges facing MCPS are arduous, presenting a vast opportunity for the researcher and a plethora of ways to develop to overcome these challenges. The worldwide web and computing revolutions opened multiple potentials in controlling the life of individuals and increasing their interaction remotely. Considerable research has been made to control the different medical health-related operations and their maintenance. These human health parameters are analyzed and modeled and made convenient for the patients as well as for the practitioners to provide their services in the remote area also. Though, medical cyber-physical systems are creating an independent, self-driven system for protecting the health of the client before the caregiver reaches. Now, time to see off the dependable systems designed for providing health services after analyzing the health parameters of the patient. These versatile systems need to be protected from malicious attacks by an intruder. An appropriate set of privacy policies is to be established so that the records of an organization need to be preserved broadly.

References

1. Din, S. *et al.*, Edge computing for smart health: Context-aware approaches, opportunities, and challenges. *IEEE Access*, 7, 3, 196–203, 2019.
2. Din, S. and Paul, A., Smart health monitoring and management system: Toward autonomous wearable sensing for Internet of Things using big data analytics. *Future Gener. Comput. Syst.*, 91, 611–619, 2019.
3. Casado-Vara, R. and Corchado, J., Distributed e-health wide-world accounting ledger via blockchain. *J. Intell. Fuzzy Syst.*, 36, 3, 2381–2386, 2019.
4. Roehrs, A., da Costa, C.A., da Rosa Righi, R., OmniPHR: A distributed architecture model to integrate personal health records. *J. Biomed. Inf.*, 71, 70–81, 2017.
5. Liu, C., Chen, F., Zhao, C., Wang, T., Zhang, C., Zhang, Z., IPv6-based architecture of community medical Internet of Things. *IEEE Access*, 6, April, 7897–7910, 2018.
6. Choudhary, G., Astillo, P.V., You, I., Yim, K., Chen, I.R., Cho, J.H., Lightweight misbehavior detection management of embedded IoT devices in medical cyber physical systems. *IEEE Trans. Netw. Serv. Manage.*, 17, 4, 2496–2510, 2020.
7. O, S., Kwon, S., Son, Y.H., Park, Y., Ahn, J.H., CIDR: A cache inspired area-efficient DRAM resilience architecture against permanent faults. *IEEE Comput. Archit. Lett.*, 14, 1, 17–20, 2015.
8. Xu, Z., Xu, C., Liang, W., Xu, J., Chen, H., A lightweight mutual authentication and key agreement scheme for medical Internet of Things. *IEEE Access*, 7, 1, 2019.
9. He, C., Fan, X., Li, Y., Toward ubiquitous healthcare services with a novel efficient cloud platform. *IEEE Trans. Biomed. Eng.*, 60, 1, 230–234, 2013.
10. Alabdulatif, A., Khalil, I., Yi, X., Guizani, M., Secure edge of things for smart healthcare surveillance framework. *IEEE Access*, 7, 31010–31021, 2019.
11. Ogunduyile, O.O., Olugbara, O.O., Lall, M., Development of wearable systems for ubiquitous healthcare service provisioning. *APCBEE Proc.*, 7, 163–168, 2013.

12. Mowla, N.I., Doh, I., Chae, K., On-device AI-based cognitive detection of bio-modality spoofing in medical cyber physical system. *IEEE Access*, 7, 2126–2137, 2019.

13. Grispos, G., Glisson, W.B., Choo, K.K.R., Medical cyber-physical systems development: A forensics-driven approach. *Proceedings - 2017 IEEE 2nd International Conference on Connected Health: Applications, Systems and Engineering Technologies, CHASE 2017*, pp. 108–114, 2017.

14. Porres, I., Domínguez, E., Pérez, B., Rodríguez, Á., Zapata, M.A., A model driven approach to automate the implementation of clinical guidelines in decision support systems. *Proceedings - Fifteenth IEEE International Conference and Workshops on the Engineering of Computer-Based Systems, ECBS 2008*, pp. 210–218, 2008.

15. Humayed, A., Lin, J., Li, F., Luo, B., Cyber-physical systems security - A survey. *IEEE Internet Things J.*, 4, 6, 1802–1831, 2017.

16. Kocabas, O., Soyata, T., Aktas, M.K., Emerging security mechanisms for medical cyber physical systems. *IEEE/ACM Trans. Comput. Biol. Bioinf.*, 13, 3, 401–416, 2016.

17. Lee, I. and Sokolsky, O., Medical cyber physical systems. *Proceedings - Design Automation Conference*, pp. 743–748, 2010.

18. Verma, R., Smart city healthcare cyber physical system: Characteristics, technologies and challenges. *Wireless Personal Communications*, 122, 2, 1413–1433, 2022.

ANN-Aware Methanol Detection Approach with CuO-Doped SnO$_2$ in Gas Sensor

Jitendra K. Srivastava[1], Deepak Kumar Verma[1]*, Bholey Nath Prasad[2] and Chayan Kumar Mishra[1]

[1]Dr. Rammanohar Lohia Avadh University, Ayodhya, India
[2]Department of Physics, Integral University, Lucknow, India

Abstract

The sensors capable to detect the toxic gases such as Methanol which is known to affect the vital organs severely are needed to be developed. Methanol is a very hazardous gas and its acute exposure can produce immediate bronchial constriction, narrowing of the airways, increased pulmonary resistance, and increased airway reactivity in experimental animals. It is also reported that with the gas exposure, in sensors with microsized particles, only the surface properties of the grain change whereas in sensors with nanosized particles, whole of the grain properties change, typically, when crystal dimension is comparable to the thickness of the charge depletion layer. A suitable gas sensor structure was fabricated on 1″x1″ alumina substrate using thick film technology. The necessary paste for screen printing was also developed. The sensitivity of the sensor has been investigated at different temperatures (150°C–350°C) upon exposure to Methanol yielding a maximum value at 350°C. We have also carried out the validation of developed methanol thick film gas sensor through Artificial Neural network.

Keywords: ANN, sensor, artificial neural network, gas sensor

*Corresponding author: deepak.discrete@gmail.com
Jitendra K. Srivastava ORCID: 0000-0003-2957-5919
Deepak Kumar Verma ORCID: 0000-0001-7177-7632

Danda B. Rawat, Lalit K Awasthi, Valentina Emilia Balas, Mohit Kumar and Jitendra Kumar Samriya (eds.) *Convergence of Cloud with AI for Big Data Analytics: Foundations and Innovation,* (299–330)
© 2023 Scrivener Publishing LLC

14.1   Introduction

ANNs are the tools used to produce a map between experimental data as input and some essential output. ANN is free from model estimators in which they do-not have the foundation form for underlying data. In fact ANNs are based on observed data [1]. They opposed the traditional model and they use a non-linear data. They are considered as a powerful technique for modeling, when the underlying data relationship is unavailable. ANNs are also used to distinguished correlated patterns and the input data set and also target outputs. Undoubtedly ANNs are used to exhibit the outcome of new, unseen, and independent input. ANNs are true copy of some aspects of the brain construction and learning process the human brain. Not only this, it proceeds problems having nonlinear complex data even if data are clumsy and noisy. One of the extra ordinary properties of ANN is "learning by example" is replaced by "programming" [2–5].

This outstanding property makes such computational work very simple in application while one has incomplete and versatile brain ability, but where training data is readily available. ANN technology does not have intelligence, but it has good ability to recognize patterns and to make simple rules to handle complex problems. In practice, we can look at the computation in an ANN from the estimating perspective of unknown function based on some observations. Nevertheless, this does not mean that the ANN is a heuristic technique. ANNs are technique based on mathematical principles and mathematical computation. The ANN technique has been to be very popular in research field. The only drawback of this technique is off-the-shelf black boxes.

14.1.1   Basic ANN Model

In fact the neural network is dependent upon human brain functioning. Its evolution and existence is based upon human brain function. It tries to follow the attempts to fault-tolerance and to learn biological neural systems learn of biological neural systems by modeling of human brain [6].

Biologically human brain consists of several interconnected neurons. The neuron has several branched structure (the dendrites). It has a cell body (the soma), and a branching output structure (the axon) as shown in Figure 14.1. The axon of one cell connects to the dendrites of another through a synapse. The neuron fires and an electrochemical signal along the axon that electrochemical signal crosses the synapses to the other neurons. This process of firing goes on continuously and successively. A neuron fires

Structure of a Typical Neuron

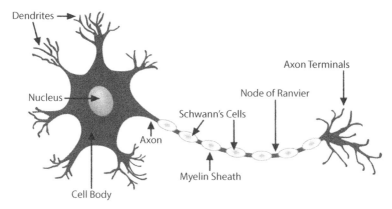

Figure 14.1 Structure of a typical neuron.

only if the total signal received at the cell body from the dendrites exceeds a certain level (the firing threshold).

The basic components of biological neurons are mention below.

Synapses – The modeling synapses is done as weights in neuron network. The strength of the connection having input and neuron is represented by the value of the weight. Signals are passed from one neuron to another through a chemical process. The neurons sending the signals is called presynaptic cell and received neurons is post synaptic cell. The presynaptic neurons and act on a postsynaptic cell. process liberate a transmitter substance that diffuses across the synaptic junction between The synapses weight of the artificial neuron lies within the range of positive and negative values. Positive weight values symbolized as excitatory connections while negative values symbolized inhibitory connections.

Cell Body – The cell body is the heart of the cell, containing the nucleus and maintaining protein synthesis. It generates the output neuron signals, a spike, which is transferred along the axon to the synaptic terminals of the other neurons.

Dendrites – The dendrites has irregular surface and is treelike structure. Dendrites receive signals from other neurons. A neuron can have many dendrites.

Axon – The axon of a neuron is very long and thin transmission lines, which grows out of cell body. When a particular amount of an input is received, then the cell fires. It transmits through axon to other cell. The axon has a smoother surface, fewer branches, and length.

The next two components model the actual activity within the neuron cell:

I. Linear Combination or adder junction-An adder is used to sum up the input signal modified by their respective weights. In these cases, the sign of the output is considered to be equivalent to the 1 or 0 of the step function systems, which enables the two methods, be to equivalent if

$$\Theta = -b \qquad\qquad (14.1)$$

II. Activation function or squashing function-The operation of an artificial neural network is to sum up the product of the associated weight and the input signal and produce an output or activation function. For the input unit this activation function is the identity function. The neuron of a particular layer gets the same type of activation function. In almost all cases non- linear activation functions are used It controls and commands the amplitude of the output of the neuron. The output the neurons are laying between 0 and 1, or -1 and 1. The various types of activation functions used in a neural network are identity function, binary step function, binary sigmoid functions and bipolar sigmoid functions.

The model illustrated in Figure 14.2 also includes an externally applied bias, b_k, which has the effect of increasing or lowering the net input of the

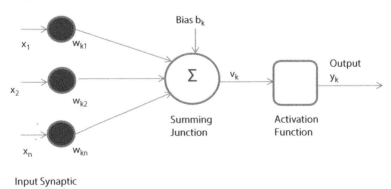

Figure 14.2 Artificial neural network model.

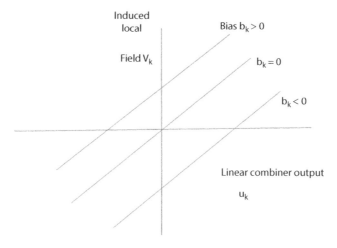

Figure 14.3 Affine transformation produced by the presence of a bias.

activation function, depending on whether it is positive or negative, respectively. Mathematically, using Figure 14.3, a neuron k can be written as:

$$y_K = \phi(v_k + b_k) \tag{14.2}$$

Where $x_1, x_2, ..., x_m$ are the input signals
w_k synaptic weights of neuron k
v_k is the linear combination output due to the input signal b_k is the bias
ϕ is the activation function
y_k is the output signal of the neuron

A bias is defined as a function to a threshold and it acts as a weight connected to a node point which is always on. The weights decide where hyperplane lies in the input space or not. The hyperplane is objected to pass through the origin without a bias term. In many problems the hyperplane produced increased performance away from the origin [7–12].

14.1.2   ANN Data Pre- and Post-Processing

Preprocessing process which is normally known as normalization or standardization, can accelerated the training process of the ANN and decrease the chances that the ANN obtain sucking in a local minima [13]. With the help of normalizing the data, the impact of outliers in the data are decrease and with this, the density of the local minima is also diminished. The application of normalization is solely to change the input features into the same range of values in order to reduce the possibility of bias within the ANN towards one specialty over another. The training time will be decrease because each feature has the same range of data values as each other and the gradient descent process will treat each feature the same. The normalization process is generally useful when the inputs of an application vary over wide range of difference in scales. There are number of ways to normalize the data, and a specific one is the statistical or Z-score normalization tool which applies the average and standard deviation for each feature across a set of training data to normalize each input feature vector [14].

14.1.2.1   Activation Function

The activation function is also called transfer function, which works as a "squashing" function so that the output of a neuron in the neural network falls between certain values. Generally, there are two types of activation function:

Threshold Function-This function limits the output of the neuron to either 0 or 1 is shown in Figure 14.4.

Sigmoid Function-Sigmoid function is usually S-shaped curve function. This is most common form of activation function used in the construction of ANNs [15]. It is refers to as a steeply increasing function that shows as a graceful balance between linear and non-linear features. Logistic and hyperbolic tangent functions are commonly used sigmoid functions. This function will limit the output of a neuron to a range between 0 and 1. As the slope parameter approaches infinity, the sigmoid function becomes simply threshold functions, which assume value of 0 or 1. The hyperbolic tangent function, limits the outputs to fall between -1 and +1 is shown Figure 14.5.

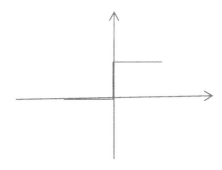

Figure 14.4 Threshold function.

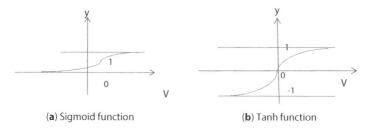

(**a**) Sigmoid function   (**b**) Tanh function

Figure 14.5 Common non-linear function.

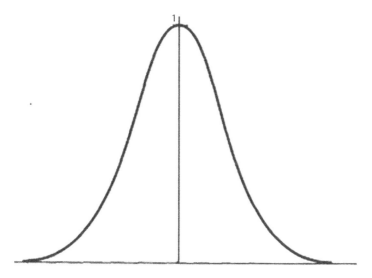

Figure 14.6 Gaussian activity function.

Gaussian Function-Gaussian functions are bell-shaped curves that are continuous as shown in Figure 14.6. The node output (high or low) is interpreted in terms of class membership (1/0), depending on how close the net input is to a chosen value of average.

14.2   Network Architectures

There are two fundamentally different classes of network architecture.

14.2.1   Feed Forward ANNs

In such type of topology, the connections between the neurons in an ANN flow from input to output only. These ANNs can be further divided into either single-layer feed forward ANNs or multi-layer feed forward

ANNs. ANNs allow signals to travel one way only: from input to output. There is no feedback (loops) i.e., the output of any layer does not affect that same layer. Feed forward ANNs tend to be straightforward networks that associate inputs with outputs. They are extensively used in pattern recognition. This type of organization is also referred to as bottom-up or top-down. The single-layer network is the easiest form of a layered network which has only one input layer that links directly to the output layer as shown in Figure 14.7(a). The perceptron is the simplest form of neural network used for classification of pattern which is linearly separable. Linearly separable pattern lie on opposite sides of a hyperplane. The model consists of single neuron with balanced synaptic weight and bias. Single neuron perceptron is limited to perform pattern classification with only two classes. To from the classification with than two classes; the output layer of the perceptron can include more than one neuron. With multi-layer feedforward ANNs, one or more hidden layers are available between the input and output layers, as shown in Figure 14.7(b). The input is propagated in a forward direction, layer by layer. These networks are called multilayer perceptron's, which is a generalization of single layer perceptron. The network is fully connected i.e. neuron in any layer of the network is connected to all the neurons in the previous layer. Signal flow in a forward direction, from left to right. The input signal propagated forward through the network and produces output as an output signal. At each neuron, through which it passes, the signal computes the function of the input and associated weights. An error signal propagates backward from right to left in the network. The error originated at the output layer is propagated backward for error correction. By combining one or more hidden layers, the network can extract higher-order statistics from its input and model more complex

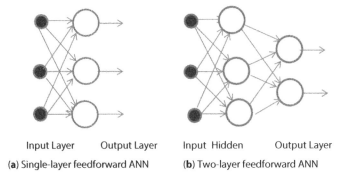

Input Layer   Output Layer   Input Hidden   Output Layer

(a) Single-layer feedforward ANN   (b) Two-layer feedforward ANN

Figure 14.7 Feedforward ANN topology.

non-linear and linear models. Feedforward neural networks are ideally suitable for modeling relationships between a set of predictor or input variables and one or more response or output variables. In other words, they are appropriate for any functional mapping problem where we want to know how a number of input variables affect the output variable. Some parameters of ANNs cannot be determined from an analytical analysis of the process under investigation. This is the case of the number of hidden layers and the number of neurons belonging to them. Consequently, they have to be determined experimentally according to the precision which is desired for the estimation. The number of inputs and outputs depends from the considered process.

14.2.2   Recurrent ANNs Topologies

In feedback or recurrent ANNs, there are linkages from later layers back to earlier layers of neurons. In this type of neural network, there is one feedback loop. Either the networks hidden neuron unit activation to the output data are feedback into the network as input as shown in Figure 14.8. The internal states of the network allow this type of network to exhibit dynamic behavior when modeling the data dependence on time or space. With one or more than one feedback links whose state fluctuates with time, the network has balanceable weights. This causes the state of its neuron being based not only on the current input signal, but also on the earlier states of the neuron. In other ways, the network feature is based on the current input and the results of processing previous inputs.

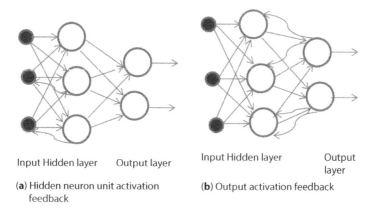

Input Hidden layer   Output layer

(a) Hidden neuron unit activation feedback

Input Hidden layer   Output layer

(b) Output activation feedback

Figure 14.8 Recurrent ANN topologies.

14.2.3 Learning Processes

The learning processes through which ANNs function can be categorized as supervised learning and unsupervised learning.

14.2.3.1 Supervised Learning

This type of learning can be considered as similar to learning with a teacher, whereby the teacher has the knowledge of the environment. The knowledge is represented as input- output summation. This environment is unfamiliar to the neural network system. The network parameters are adjusted one by one under the combined impact of the training vector until and unless the network emulates the teacher, generating the desired outputs for the respective inputs. In this way, the knowledge of the environment having with the teacher is transferred to the neural network through training and stored data in the form of fixed synaptic weights, representing long-term memory. When this condition is achieved, the network is released from the teacher to describe with the environment by itself. With a sufficient set of input-output examples, and sufficient time in which to do the training, a supervised learning system is generally able to approximate an unknown input-output mapping.

The mean square errors over the training example are good performance measure for the system, which can be visualized as error surface with coordinates as free parameter. The true error surface is averaged over all possible input-output examples. The supervised learning is useful for pattern classification and function approximation tasks [16–20].

14.2.3.2 Unsupervised Learning

In this type of learning, the networks study on their own as a kind of self-study. When a set of data is conveyed to the network, it learns to recognize patterns of the data. To perform unsupervised learning, a competitive-learning methods may be used a neural network with two layers – an input layer and a competitive layer. Each of the output layer neuron is connected to the input nodes. This is called feedforward synaptic connection or excitatory connection. The input layer can receive the available data. The competitive layer contains the neurons that compare with others for the chance to respond to behavior contained in the input data. The output of the network is not compared with acceptable output. Instead of the input vector, to be compared with the weight vectors leading to the competitive layer. The neuron with the weight vectors most closely matching the input vector is the winning neuron. Only single output neuron is active at any time. Due to this feature, competitive learning is suitable for discovering statistically salient features that are used to classify a set of input patterns [21].

14.2.4   ANN Methodology

Training, Validation, and Testing Datasets
As soon as the network architecture is finalized and the data required are collected, the next stage of the ANN methodology is the training of the ANN model. The training aim is to search the training parameters that result in the best performance, as decided by the ANN''s performance. To explore the optimum ANN configuration, an ideal approach is to bifurcate the data into three independent sets: training, validation and testing.

Training set – A set of samples uses to adjust or train the weights in the ANN to produce the desire outcome.
Validation set – The validation error is used to check the training. The validation error is verified to find the optimum point to check training. Usually, the validation error decrease during the initial stage of training. Nevertheless, when the ANN begins to over fit the data, the output error generated by the validation set, begin to rise. When the validation error increases for a considerable number of iterations, thus exhibiting the trend is rising, the training is halted, and the weights that were produced at the minimum validation error are used in the ANN for the operation.
Testing set – To evaluated the performance of the ANN. As the real prediction accuracy will be generally worse than that for the holdout sample, there is a need to evaluate the developed model with some real problem [22].

14.2.5   1%CuO–Doped SnO$_2$ Sensor for Methanol

Response of 1% CuO-Doped SnO$_2$ based thick film gas Sensor for Methanol at 150°C
Response of 1% Pd-doped SnO$_2$ thick film gas sensor on exposure to methanol is shown in Figure 14.9 and Table 14.1. To measure the sensitivity of the 1% CuO-doped SnO$_2$- based thick film gas sensor, first of all, the value of resistance of thick film gas sensor in air (R$_a$) is measured with the digital multi-meter (DMM). Secondly, the value of resistance in sample gas is calculated by digital multi-meter (DMM). The sensitivity is define as

$$S = \frac{R_a - R_g}{R_a} \times 100$$

where
  R_a = Resistance of a thick film sensor in air
  R_g = Resistance in a sample gas
  S = Sensitivity

When the concentration of methanol was 100 (ppm) the sensitivity was found to be 3.03%. When the concentration of methanol was increased

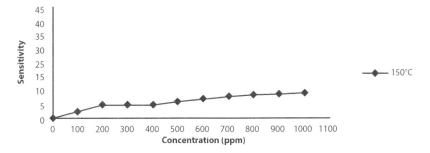

Figure 14.9 Response of 1% CuO-doped SnO$_2$ based think film gas sensor on exposure to methanol.

Table 14.1 Variation of sensitivity with concentration for SnO-$_2$based 1% CuO-doped thick film gas sensor for methanol at 150°C.

Concentration (ppm)	R_a	R_g	R_a-R_g	%S (Sensitivity)
0.00	0.00	0.00	0.00	0.00
100	2.31	2.24	0.07	3.03
200	2.31	2.17	0.14	6.06
300	2.31	2.17	0.14	6.06
400	2.31	2.17	0.14	6.06
500	2.31	2.14	0.17	7.36
600	2.31	2.11	0.2	8.66
700	2.31	2.08	0.23	9.96
800	2.31	2.07	0.24	10.39
900	2.31	2.06	0.25	10.82
1000	2.31	2.05	0.26	11.26

to 200 (ppm) the sensitivity also increased considerably to 6.06%. This increase in sensitivity remains almost constant till 400 (ppm) of methanol concentrations. From 500 (ppm) methanol concentration the sensitivity gradually increased with the increase in concentration of methanol. However, the rate of increase of the sensitivity at higher level of methanol was relatively slower. This could be due to the fact that has the resistivity of tin oxide increases with the increase in the temperature and after some time the resistance becomes almost constant.

14.2.6   Experimental Result

At constant temperature of 150°C, the experimental data exhibit that with the increase in concentration of methanol (toxic liquid) the sensitivity of SnO_2 based thick film gas sensor increased provided R_a (Resistance of a thick film sensor in air) should be constant. It is also observed that with increased the concentration R_g (Resistance in a sample gas) decreases.

Artificial Neural Network (ANN) model may be used as alternative method for technological analysis and Matlab based calculation. Artificial Neural Networks have two main components- the processing element called neurons and the connection between them, each connection have their own weights. The neurons are the information processors and the connection functions are the information storage. Each processing element first calculates a weighted sum of the input signals and then applies the transfer functions. The term 'Feed Propagation' comes due to the training method used during the training process-back propagation of error. The error between the desired and true output is computed. A Gradient Descent Backpropagation with adaptive learning rate algorithm is used to adjust the weights in the hidden and output layer nodes. The result is a network that produces the mapping between the input values and output values with help of the neurons. In this model perception, Feed Forward Propagation is one of suitable method of artificial neural network, designed for the testing and training of data. Three training methodologies based upon forward propagation was used. Purelin, logsin, and tansin network transfer function for all the neurons, which reflects the relationship between concentration as input and sensitivity for different concentration as output of SnO_2 based 1% CuO-doped thick film gas sensor. Sensitivity is tested by artificial neural network. In neural network architecture one layer acts as input layer, ten neurons acts as the hidden layer and other layer output layer. In this model input is concentration of methanol and output is the sensitivity of sensor. Though in present work single sensor is exposed to single gas or vapor at a time and ANN is utilized to confirm it with experiments so that the data collected can be used to train the network when sensor is replaced by sensor array and single gas is replaced by group of gases or vapors to achieve high selectivity. This model was trained to generate a mapping between the input concentration of the methanol and output as the sensitivity of the methanol. Neural network structure is shown in Figure 14.10. Sensitivity is dimension less quantity which is obvious from its expression.

$$\text{i.e.,} \quad S = \Delta R/R_a$$

The experimental data was first extrapolated by the Matlab tool and 10 extrapolated data were obtained for the different concentration of methanol at 150°C. Out of these first six data were used for the training purpose

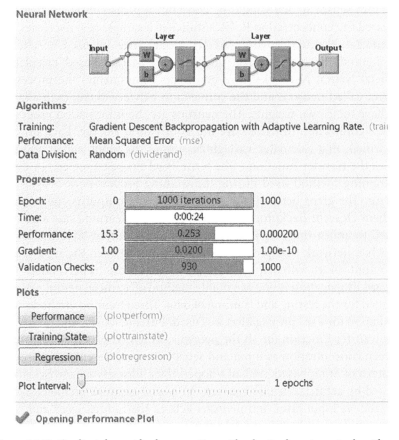

Figure 14.10 Gradient descent backpropagation with adaptive learning rate algorithm training function.

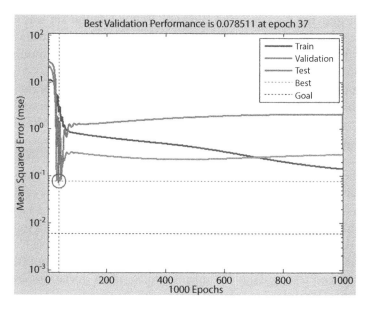

Figure 14.11 Results of validation performance in logsin network transfer function.

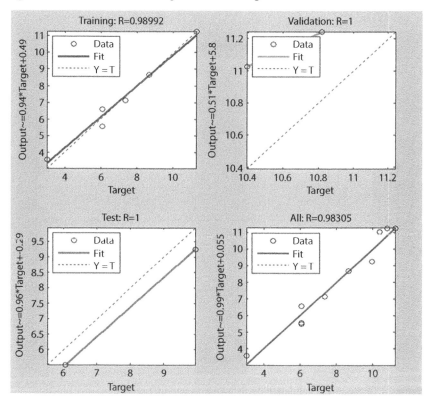

Figure 14.12 Results of regression logsin transfer function.

and rest four for the validation purpose. The validation set was used to stop the training of the neural network, when the neural network begins to over fit the data. The test data set was not used during the training and validation of neural network model.

The multilayer perceptron feed forward ANN was design for the testing and training purpose using Gradient Descent Backpropagation with adaptive learning rate algorithm of feed forward propagation. LEARNGDM is used as its adaptation learning function and mean square error is used as performance function. To evaluate the effectiveness of the training network, the mean square error is introduced as the training goal. The smaller the mean square error is the better performance and accuracy of the network in the real life achieve tansin, logsin and purelin were used as transfer function for all the neurons respectively one by one each set of input and output data. The usual way of data preprocessing for ANNs is to obtain the standard deviation and mean from the training data, but not from the validation and testing data. The means and standard deviations are computed for each feature over the set of training data, and used to scale each

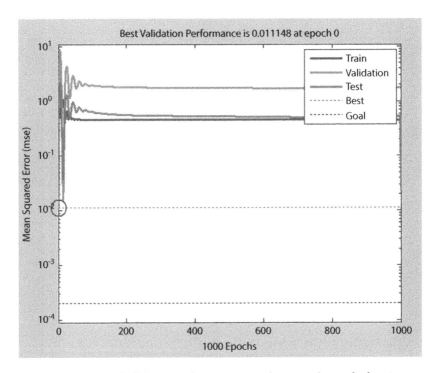

Figure 14.13 Results of validation performance in purelin network transfer function.

sample of the validation and testing data. The performance of the ANN will vary significantly as the data was trained on a different data representation. After building the neural network by the Matlab setting the right network type and parameters and training for 1000 iterations and ten hidden neuron.

Logsin network transfer function retrieval capability of the 1% CuO-doped SnO_2 based thick film gas sensor for methanol at 150°C. At thirty seven epochs the validation performance goal was (0.078) achieved by using the logsin network transfer function in Figure 14.11. The Gradient Descent Backpropagation with adaptive learning rate algorithm was used regression parameter of train data (0.9899) and output target train data (0.98305) in Figure 14.12.

Purelin transfer function retrieval capability of the 1% CuO-doped SnO_2 based thick film gas sensor for methanol at 150°C. The validation performance goal was (0.011) achieved at zero epochs for purelin network transfer function network in Figure 14.13. The Gradient Descent Backpropagation

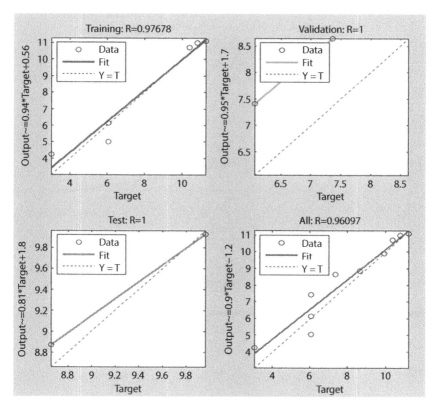

Figure 14.14 Results of regression Purelin network transfer function.

with adaptive learning rate algorithm was used regression parameter of train data (0.97678) and output target train data (0.96097) as shown in Figure 14.14.

Tansin network transfer function retrieval capability of the 1% CuO-doped SnO_2 based thick film gas sensor for methanol at 150°C. The tansin transfer function network is providing the validation performance goal (0.011) achieved at twenty-five epochs as shown in Figure 14.15. The Gradient Descent Backpropagation with adaptive learning rate algorithm was used regression parameter of train data was (0.9996) and output target data (0.9723) are shown in Figure 14.16. Amongst the three-transfer function network, Purelin is most suitable function as at zero epoch maximum validation performance was achieved.

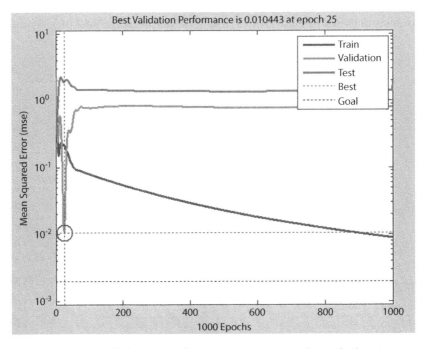

Figure 14.15 Results of validation performance in tansin network transfer function.

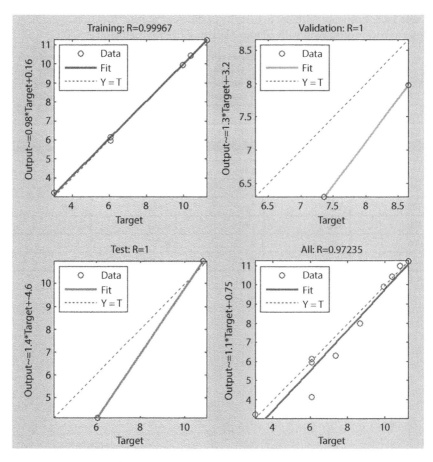

Figure 14.16 Results of regression tansin transfer function.

The maximum sensitivity recorded for 1% CuO-doped SnO_2 based thick film gas sensor was 11.25% at 150°C (Table 14.2). When the sensitivity was tested by Matlab software neural network tool through Gradient Descent Backpropagation with adaptive learning rate network function, the maximum sensitivity for purelin network transfer function was found to be 11.24% at 150°C compare to other transfer network function as shown in Figure 14.17 (Table 14.2).

Table 14.2 Compare different Sensitivity of different transfer function in gradient descent backpropagation with adaptive learning rate for methanol at 150°C.

Concentration (ppm)	Practical sensitivity for methanol	Logsin network transfer function sensitivity	Purelin network transfer function sensitivity	Tansin network transfer function sensitivity
0.00	0.00	0.00	0.00	0.00
100	3.03	5.673	3.477	3.347
200	6.06	5.516	3.922	4.116
300	6.06	5.381	4.714	5.609
400	6.06	5.379	5.932	6.559
500	7.36	5.649	7.438	7.228
600	8.66	6.809	8.868	8.601
700	9.96	9.250	9.925	10.495
800	10.39	10.410	10.570	11.037
900	10.82	11.215	11.237	10.980
1000	11.26	11.228	11.250	11.026

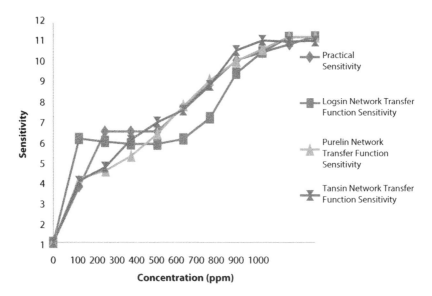

Figure 14.17 Response of 1% CuO-doped SnO$_2$ based thick film gas sensor on exposure to methanol in different network transfer function.

The Gradient Descent Backpropagation with adaptive learning rate network function was found to having minimum error in Purelin transfer function network. The multilayer perceptron feed forward ANN was design for the testing and training purpose using Levenberg–Marquardt feed forward propagation. Tansin, logsin, and purelin were used as transfer function for all the neurons respectively one by one each set of input and output data. The error graph is shown in Figure 14.18.

Logsin network transfer function retrieval capability of the 1% CuO-doped SnO_2 based thick gas film sensor for methanol at 150°C. At one thousand epochs the validation performance goal (0.18048) was achieved by using the logsin network transfer function as shown in Figure 14.19. The Levenberg–Marquardt feed forward propagation algorithm was used regression parameter of train data (0.99922) and output target data (0.98369) as shown in Figure 14.20.

Purelin transfer function retrieval capability of the 1% CuO-doped SnO_2 based thick film gas sensor for methanol at 150°C is shown in Figure 14.21. By using the Purelin network transfer function at one epoch the validation performance goal (0.735) was obtained as illustrated in Figure 14.22. The Levenberg–Marquardt feed forward propagation algorithm regression parameter of train data was (0.95788) and output target data (0.96477) are shown in Figure 14.23.

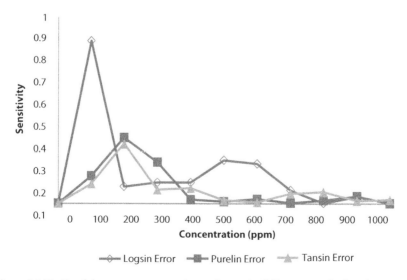

Figure 14.18 Graph between concentration and error in different transfer function.

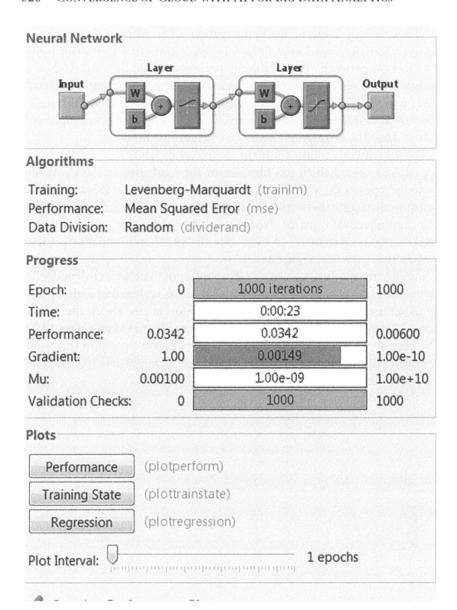

Figure 14.19 Levenberg–Marquardt feed forward propagation neural network at 150°C.

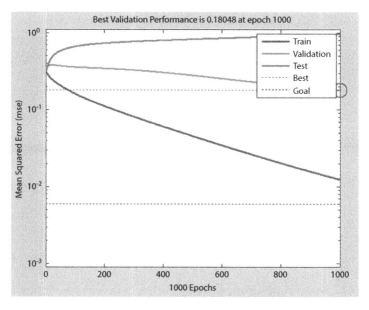

Figure 14.20 Results of validation performance in logsin network transfer function.

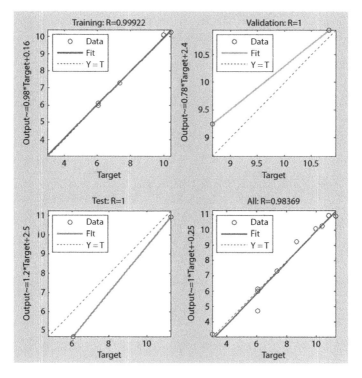

Figure 14.21 Results of regression logsin transfer function.

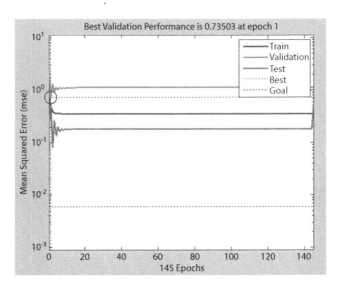

Figure 14.22 Results of validation performance in Purelin network transfer function.

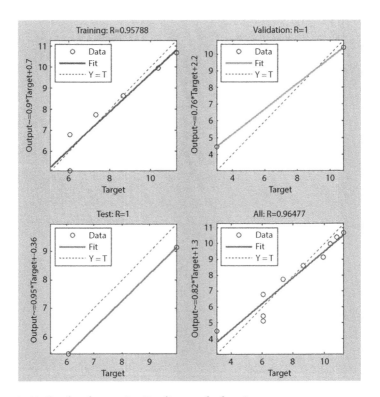

Figure 14.23 Results of regression Purelin transfer function.

Tansin transfer function retrieval capability of the 1% CuO-doped SnO$_2$ based thick film gas sensor for methanol at 150°C. At two hundred eight epochs the performance goal (0.735) was achieved by using the tansin transfer function in Figure 14.24. The Levenberg–Marquardt feed Forward Propagation algorithm regression of train data was (0.99974) and output target data (0.99739) are shown in Figure 14.25. Amongst the three transfer function network, Tansin network transfer function is most suitable function as at two hundred eight epochs maximum validation performance was achieved. The Levenberg–Marquardt feed forward propagation algorithm tansin network transfer function training data regression function given better performance compared to the other training network transfer data function.

The performance of 1% CuO-doped SnO$_2$ based thick film gas sensor was best predicted by artificial neural network as shown in Table 14.4. The maximum sensitivity recorded for 1% CuO doping sensor was calculated as 11.25% at 150°C (Table 14.4). When the sensitivity was tested by Matlab software neural network tool through Levenberg–Marquardt feed forward propagation algorithm, the maximum sensitivity in tansin network transfer function was found to be 11.187% at 150°C (Table 14.4) compare to various network transfer function.

Tansin network transfer function predicts less error as compared to the other neural network transfer function.

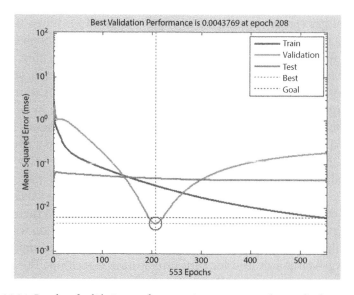

Figure 14.24 Results of validation performance in tansin network transfer function.

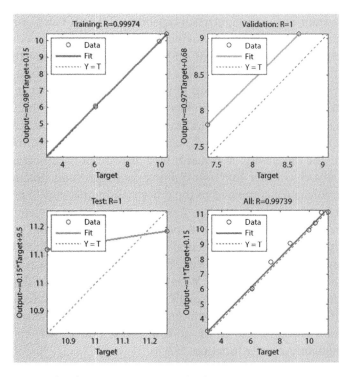

Figure 14.25 Results of regression tansin transfer function.

The maximum sensitivity recorded for 1% CuO-doped SnO_2 based thick film gas sensor was 11.26% at 150°C (Table 14.3). When the sensitivity was tested by Matlab software neural network tool through Gradient Descent Backpropagation with adaptive learning rate algorithm network function in purelin network transfer function, the maximum sensitivity for network was found to be 11.25% at 150°C (Table 14.3) as compared to Levenberg–Marquardt feed forward propagation algorithm in tansin network transfer function, the maximum sensitivity for network was found as 11.18 % at 150°C (Table 14.4). We have deliberately selected a neural network technology just compare the values of sensitivity one from practically calculated value and another from theoretically calculated value (neural network). There is some small discrimination between two values due to physical condition not remaining the same at all time. Even then the two values are almost the same. Gradient Descent Backpropagation with adaptive learning rate algorithm is the best suitable technique in comparison to Levenberg–Marquardt feed forward propagation algorithm. The different performance function of ANN has been shown for 1% CuO based thick film gas sensor is shown in Figures 14.26 and 14.27 respectively.

Table 14.3 Different types of error in different transfer network function in gradient descent backpropagation with adaptive learning rate at different concentration for methanol at 150°C.

Concentration (ppm)	Logsin network transfer function error	Purelin network transfer function error	Tansin network transfer function error
0.00	0.00	0.00	0.00
100	0.872	0.148	0.105
200	0.090	0.353	0.321
300	0.112	0.222	0.074
400	0.112	0.021	0.082
500	0.232	0.011	0.018
600	0.214	0.024	0.007
700	0.071	0.003	0.054
800	0.002	0.017	0.062
900	0.037	0.039	0.015
1000	0.003	0.001	0.021

Table 14.4 Compare different sensitivity of different network transfer function for Levenberg–Marquardt feed forward propagation algorithm for methanol at 150°C.

Concentration (ppm)	Practical sensitivity for methanol	Logsin network transfer function sensitivity	Purelin network transfer function sensitivity	Tansin network transfer function sensitivity
0.00	0.00	0.00	0.00	0.00
100	3.03	3.205	4.128	3.369
200	6.06	4.715	4.680	5.900
300	6.06	5.996	5.416	6.234
400	6.06	6.132	6.317	5.990
500	7.36	7.310	7.310	7.309
600	8.66	9.248	8.283	8.739
700	9.96	10.100	9.135	9.911
800	10.39	10.277	9.811	10.518
900	10.82	10.944	10.306	11.120
1000	11.26	10.992	10.647	11.187

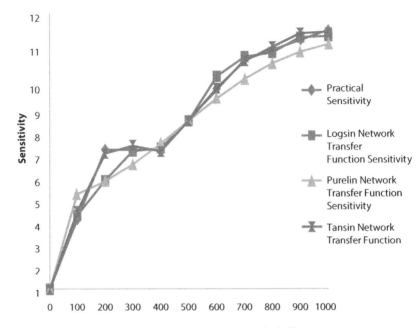

Figure 14.26 Response of 1% CuO-doped SnO$_2$ based thick film gas sensor on exposure to methanol in different transfer function.

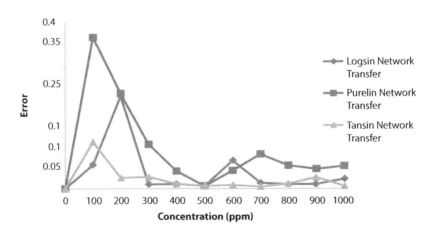

Figure 14.27 Graph between concentration and error in different transfer function.

Table 14.5 Different types of error in different transfer function for Levenberg–Marquardt feed forward propagation algorithm at different concentration for methanol at 150°C.

Concentration (ppm)	Logsin network transfer function error	Purelin network transfer function error	Tansin network transfer function error
0	0	0	0
100	0.058	0.362	0.112
200	0.222	0.228	0.026
300	0.011	0.106	0.029
400	0.012	0.042	0.012
500	0.007	0.007	0.007
600	0.068	0.044	0.009
700	0.014	0.083	0.005
800	0.011	0.056	0.012
900	0.011	0.048	0.028
1000	0.024	0.054	0.006

References

1. Albert, S., Viricelle, J.P., Tournierb, G., Breuil, P., Pijolat, C., Detection of oxygen traces in nitrogen- and hydrogen-rich atmosphere. *Sens. Actuators B*, **139**, 1, 298–303, 2009.
2. Baranov, A., Spirjakin, D., Akbari, S., Somov, A., Optimization of power consumption for gas sensor nodes: A survey. *Sens. Actuators B*, **233**, 1, 279–289, 2015.
3. Bagal, L.K., Patil, J.Y., Bagal, K.N., Mulla, I.S., Suryavanshi, S.S., Acetone vapour sensing characteristics of undoped and Zn, Ce doped SnO_2 thick film gas sensor. *Mater. Res. Innovations*, **17**, 2, 98–105, 2013.
4. Blatter, G. and Grenter, F., Carrier transport through grain boundaries in semiconductors. *Phys. Rev.*, **33**, 6, 3952–3962, 1986.
5. Botter, R., Aste, T., Beruto, D., Influence of microstructures on the functional properties of tin oxide-based gas sensors. *Sens. Actuators B*, **22**, 1, 27–36, 1994.

6. Brattain, W.H. and Garrett, C.G., Surface properties of germanium and silicon. *Ann. N. Y. Acad. Sci.*, **58**, 1, 951–958, 1954.

7. Butta, N., Cinquegrani, L., Mugno, E., Taglieuete, A., Pizzini, S., A family of tin oxide based sensors with improved selectivity to methane. *Sens. Actuators B: Chem.*, **6**, 1, 110–113, 1992.

8. Carotta, M.C., Dallara, C., Martinelli, G., Passari, L., Camanzi, A., CH_4 thick film gas sensors: Characterization method and theoretical explanation. *Sens. Actuators B: Chem.*, **3**, 3, 191–196, 1991.

9. Chang, D.H. and Islam, S., Estimation of soil physical properties using remote sensing and artificial neural network. *Remote Sens. Environ.*, **74**, 3, 534–544, 2000.

10. Choe, Y.S., New gas sensing mechanism for SnO_2 thin-film gas sensors fabricated by using dual ion beam sputtering. *Sens. Actuators B: Chem.*, **77**, 1, 200–208, 2001.

11. Chowdhari, A., Gupta, V., Sreenivas, K., Enhanced catalytic activity of ultra-thin CuO islands on SnO_2 films for fast response H_2S gas sensors. *IEEE Sens. J.*, **3**, 6, 231–235, 2003.

12. Chowdhari, A., Gupta, V., Sreenivas, K., Kumar, R., Mozumdar, S., Patanjali, P.K., Response speed of SnO_2 based H_2S gas sensors with CuO nano particles. *Appl. Phys. Lett.*, **84**, 7, 1180–1182, 2004.

13. Choudhary, M., Mishra, V.N., Dwivedi, R., Effect of temperature on palladium-doped tin oxide thick film gas sensor. *Adv. Sci. Eng. Med.*, **5**, 1, 932–936, 2013.

14. Cominia, E., Ferronib, M., Guidib, V., Fagliaa, G., Martinellib, G., Sberveglieria, G., Nanostructured mixed oxides compound for gas sensing applications. *Sens. Actuators B: Chem.*, **84**, 1, 26–32, 2002.

15. Comini, C., Faglia, G., Sberveglieri, G., Calestani, D., Zanotti, L., Zha, M., Tin oxide nano belts electrical and sensing properties. *Sens. Actuators B: Chem.*, **112**, 1, 2–6, 2006.

16. Dawson, C.W. and Wilby, R., An artificial neural network approach to rainfall-runoff modelling. *Hydrol. Sci. J.*, **43**, 1, 47–66, 1998.

17. Demuth, H., Beale, M., Hagan, M., *Neural network toolbox 6, user's guide*, Mathworks Inc., Nattick, MA, 2007.

18. Fam, D., Tok, A., II, Palaniappan, A., Nopphawan, P., Anup, L., Mhaisalkar, S.G., Selective sensing of hydrogen sulphide using silver nanoparticle decorated carbon nanotubes. *Sens. Actuators B: Chem.*, **138**, 1, 189–192, 2009.

19. Friestch, M., Zudock, F., Goschnick, J., Bruns, M., CuO catalytic membrane as selectivity trimmer for metal oxide gas sensors. *Sens. Actuators B: Chem.*, **65**, 1, 379–381, 2000.

20. Gadlikas, A., Mironas, A., Setkus, A., Copper doping level effect on sensitivity and selectivity of tin oxide thin film gas sensor. *Sens. Actuators B: Chem.*, **26**, 1, 29–32, 1995.

21. Garje, A.D. and Sadakale, S.N., LPG sensing properties of platinum doped nano crystalline SnO_2 based thick films with effect of dipping time and sintering temperature. *Adv. Mater. Lett.*, **4**, 1, 58–63, 2013.

22. Haykin, S., *Neural network: A comprehensive foundation*, Macmillan, New York, 1994.

15

Detecting Heart Arrhythmias Using Deep Learning Algorithms

Dilip Kumar Choubey[1]*, Chandan Kumar Jha[2], Niraj Kumar[2], Neha Kumari[2] and Vaibhav Soni[3]

[1]*Department of Computer Science and Engineering, Indian Institute of Information Technology Bhagalpur, Bihar, India*
[2]*Department of Electronics and Communication Engineering, Indian Institute of Information Technology Bhagalpur, Bihar, India*
[3]*Department of Computer Science and Engineering, Maulana Azad National Institute of Technology, Bhopal, M.P., India*

Abstract

An electrocardiogram measures the electrical activity of the heart and has been widely used for detecting heart diseases due to its simplicity and non-invasive nature. It is possible to detect some of the heart's abnormalities by analyzing the electrical signal of each heartbeat, which is the combination of action impulse waveforms produced by different specialized cardiac tissues found in the heart, as it is challenging to visually detect heart disease from the ECG signals. Implementing an automated ECG signal detection system can aid in the identification of arrhythmia and increase diagnostic accuracy. In this chapter, we proposed ECG signal (continuous electrical measurement of the heart), implemented, and compared multiple types of deep learning models to predict heart arrhythmias for classifying normal signals and abnormal signals. The MIT-BIH arrhythmia dataset has been used. Finally, authors have discussed the limitations and drawbacks of the methods in the literature presenting concluding remarks and future challenges.

Keywords: Heart, deep learning algorithms, Jupyter, Python, DNN, CNN, LSTM, accuracy

*Corresponding author: dilipchoubey_1988@yahoo.in; dkchoubey.cse@iiitbh.ac.in
ORCID: 0000-0002-1233-7159

Danda B. Rawat, Lalit K Awasthi, Valentina Emilia Balas, Mohit Kumar and Jitendra Kumar Samriya (eds.) *Convergence of Cloud with AI for Big Data Analytics: Foundations and Innovation*, (331–386)
© 2023 Scrivener Publishing LLC

15.1 Introduction

The necessity for effective monitoring of sub health issues is steadily increasing. Cardiac disease or heart disease, is now the largest cause of death. Heart disease identification is important because it affects not only adults but also youngsters all around the world. It can happen to anyone who has an improper diet, has high cholesterol, smokes, has an alcohol or drug addiction, or is diabetic. An electrocardiograph (ECG) is a quick and straightforward tool to identify, diagnose, and treat cardiac arrhythmia. It's also not difficult for expert cardiologists to distinguish between dozens of various types of heartbeats. Researchers, on the other hand, have yet to be able to successfully apply state-of-the-art supervised machine learning approaches to attain the same degree of diagnosis.

Cardiac Arrhythmia is a medical term that describes cardiac rhythms that do not follow a regular pattern. A total of 12 different forms of aberrant arrhythmia rhythms exist. The process of finding and classifying arrhythmias can be extremely difficult for a human person since it is often essential to assess each heartbeat of ECG readings obtained by a Holter monitor over hours or even days. Furthermore, due to weariness, there is a risk of human mistake during the processing of ECG records. So, Computational approaches for automatic classification would be a better option.

The objective of this article may be summarized:

- To study and examine the arrhythmia classification techniques as practically implementable.
- To overview the existing research studies based on arrhythmia classification benefits and further direction.
- Identify the latest research trends and publications interests based on arrhythmia classification.
- Detection of heart disease in an early stage by using various Deep Learning algorithms on MIT-BIH Arrhythmia dataset from Physionet to train the model.
- To build three different prediction algorithms on collected dataset.
- Also, the validation part of prediction labels will be processed in the testing phase and compared to existing models. After training among our dataset, we would predict normal and abnormal signals.

- To compare the performance of different prediction algorithms.

We are detecting heart arrhythmias using deep learning algorithms so deep learning is stated below.

15.1.1   Deep Learning

Deep learning (also known as deep structured learning) is part of a broader family of machine learning methods based on artificial neural networks with representation learning. Learning can be supervised, semi-supervised, or unsupervised. The term Deep Learning was introduced to the machine learning community by Rina Dechter in 1986, and to artificial neural networks by Igor Aizenberg and colleagues in 2000, in the context of Boolean threshold neurons.

Over the years many Deep learning and neural network approaches are adopted to identify the disease. Various Deep Learning models like Convolutional neural network, Dense neural network, Recurrent neural network, Long short-term memory are introduced to determine the threat level these disease possess but the data from the last few decades define that many person are having these disease at an early stage and even some new born children are suffering or died from a heart disease. Machine Learning aspects can play a major role in prediction of these diseases and the threat level it possesses. The major applications of deep learning are: Virtual Assistants, Chatbots, Healthcare, and entertainment. Deep learning algorithms like Convolutional neural network, Long short-term memory and Data Mining methods have been used to predict these disease [1, 2, 7, 8] by calculating the accuracy on a dataset. We proposed various approaches like Convolutional neural network, Dense neural network, and Long short-term memory on MIT-BIH Arrhythmia dataset from physionet to train the model. These trained models are then used for predicting normal and abnormal signals. Also, the validation part of prediction labels will be processed in the testing phase and compared to existing models. Furthermore, we have compared the performance of Dense NN, CNN, and LSTM by comparing the AUC values of the above-mentioned algorithms.

The rest of the chapter may be organized as: Motivation have been stated in section 15.2, Literature Review has been discussed in section 15.3, Proposed Approach are elaborated in section 15.4, Experimental Results and Discussion are presented in section 15.5, Conclusion and Future Scope are committed to section 15.6.

15.2   Motivation

It is challenging to visually detect heart disease from the electrocardiographic (ECG) signals. Implementing an automated ECG signal detection system can aid in the identification of arrhythmia and increase diagnostic accuracy. The main motivation of doing this project is to present a heart disease prediction model for the prediction of occurrence of heart disease. Further, this project work is aimed towards identifying the best classification algorithm for identifying the possibility of heart disease in a patient.

15.3   Literature Review

Several research articles covering the application of Machine Learning and Data Mining are evaluated in this study in order to acquire an overall understanding of how to deal with the dataset, which algorithms should be used, and how the accuracy can be increased to create an efficient system. The reviews of some of the studies are included below, along with the approach and approach employed.

Gawande and Barhatte [1] utilized a system, which consist CNN configured in 7 layers consist of input signal, convolution matrix, pooling, stack of line conversion, sigmoid function, another activation function and softmax function at the output stage. The researchers achieved an accuracy of 99.46%.

Sarvan and Özkurt [2] proposed a model, CNN algorithm has 3 basic layers: a convolutional linear layer, a pooling layer, and fully connected layer. The overall accuracy of the model achieved is 93.72%.

ŞEN and ÖZKURT [3] proposed a CNN model consist of convolutional layer, pooling layer and fully-connected layer. The researchers achieved accuracy for Time-series signal (97.10%) and spectrogram images (99.67%).

Rajkumar *et al.*, [4] proposed approach uses Machine Learning to classify ECG signals in Time Series Analyses. The data is processed through different layer consist of DENSE layer, ELU activation function and Softmax layer. Researchers achieved an accuracy of 93.60%.

Qayyum *et al.*, [7] proposed a 2D CNN model, two different CNN is used one-dimensional and the other is two-dimensional. Even the temporal vector cardiogram (TVCG) approach optimized by the particle swarm optimization (PSG) algorithm and the Support Vector Machine (SVM) with decreased features beat both of these convolutional models. Researchers achieved an accuracy of 2D CNN 94.37% and 1D CNN 92.67%.

Singh *et al.*, [8] proposed CNN model architecture uses a six-layer CNN model with input ECG signal, convolution, pooling, FC, and output layers to generate feature maps. For learning, a stochastic gradient algorithm (SGD) is applied to the CNN architecture. This is a cost function optimization method based on calculative repetition. The overall accuracy of the model is 87.50%

Rana and Kim [9] proposed LSTM networks which are an advancement over typical recurrent neural networks in that they avoid the vanishing gradient problem. Backpropagation through time (BPPT) and its derivatives can be used to train LSTM networks. Tensorflow library's single layer LSTM model was employed in the methodology. The authors achieved an accuracy of 95%.

Sangeetha *et al.*, [10] proposed CNN which is used as Exponential Linear Units with Xavier initialization for all layers. The suggested CAPE displays the detection of cardiac arrhythmias and the categorization of individuals with similar symptoms in three steps: ECG includes ECG 1D signal to 2D picture conversion, data augmentation and heartbeat classification, and patient grouping based on predictive similarity learning. The overall accuracy of the model is 93.57%.

Takalo-Mattila *et al.*, [12] proposed a system that included a preprocessing unit, ECG windowing, a trained classification model, and compression. Maximum pooling- and dropout-layers are utilized to prevent overfitting. Using extracted features from CNN layers, the MLP classifier is trained to categories ECG beats into five different beat classes, demonstrating that CNN layers may be used as a feature extractor. The authors achieved sensitivity of 92%.

Xu and Liu [13] proposed a method which is composed of two main steps: pre-processing and classification. The raw signal was divided into six levels using the Daubechies wavelet, with the wavelet coefficients from the third to sixth levels being kept and used for reconstruction. Four convolutional layers, two subsampling layers, two fully connected levels, and one Softmax layer make up the CNN classifier's nine layers. The overall accuracy of the proposed method is 99.43%

Wasimuddin *et al.*, [15] proposed method entails the dataset is collected, the R-R interval of the ECG signal is extracted and represented as a 2-D picture for pre-processing, a CNN classifier is created and trained. The CNN model has ten layers, which include two convolutional layers, the Relu activation function, and finally a pooling layer. The loss function used in this model is cross entropy. The overall accuracy of the proposed method is 97.47%.

Gupta *et al.*, [20] proposed machine intelligence framework for heart disease diagnostics is to maximize the system's capability in predicting heart disease in order to improve patient survival rates by detecting disease accurately, precisely, and early. constructs Data Imputation and Partitioning, Feature Extraction using FAMD, and Data Imputation and Partitioning are only a few of the phases in MIFH. FAMD also aids in the visualization of object graphical representations, correlation between numeric and categorical data, and feature association. The authors achieved accuracy of 93.44%

Huang *et al.*, [21] have stated that there are two important parameters in the proposed architecture of the 2D-CNN model: the learning rate and the batch size. The phase of model parameter optimization is required to attain the best classification performance of ECG heart rhythm abnormalities. The processing of features in feature-extraction-pattern techniques is substantially more complicated. The overall accuracy of the proposed architecture is 99.0%.

Sarmah [22] proposed methodology consists of 3 steps, Registration, Login and Verification. Huffman coding is a lossless compression strategy based on the frequency of the symbol's appearance in the file. The patient's data is encrypted with the Patient Id, Doctor Id, and Hospital Id-Advanced Encryption Standard (PDH-AES) Algorithm. The PDH-AES technology, which is used in secure data transfer, produces the greatest results, with the highest level of security (95.87%) and the quickest encryption and decryption times. The model achieved accuracy of 96.80%.

Kiranyaz *et al.*, [24] proposed approach are in training (offline) and real-time classification and monitoring phases. The raw ECG data from each individual patient in the database is feature extracted and classified using adaptive 1D CNNs. The neurons of the hidden CNN layers are expanded to be capable of both convolution and down-sampling in order to simplify the CNN analogies and have the freedom of any input layer dimension independent of the CNN parameters. The overall accuracy of the proposed approach is VEB – 99.00% and SVEB – 97.60%.

Zhai and Tin (2018) [25] proposed a CNN-based framework for heartbeat classification using dual-beat ECG coupling matrix consist of three convolutional layers, two sub-sampling layers (1 maximum sub-sampling layer and 1 average sub-sampling layer), one fully connected layer with dropout, and a softmax loss layer. The activation function is Rectified linear units (ReLU). To improve classification performance, an automatic selection approach for selecting the most useful training beats was presented. The authors achieved accuracy of VEB – 98.60% and SVEB – 97.50%.

Dang *et al.*, [26] proposed network structure model consists of four convolution layers, two BLSTM layers, two full connection layers, and additional computational activities (pooling layers, ReLU activate, batch normalization, dropout, and so on). Input layer, convolution layer, polling layer, activation function layer, completely connected layer or completely convolution layer, and SoftMax layer are all part of the CNN network model for feature extraction and learning. The overall accuracy of the proposed network structure model is 99.94% (train), 98.63% (validation), and 96.59% (test).

JSonawane and Patil [27] proposed technique for the classification and retrieval of image by using self-organizing map (SOM). In this methodology, the image texture is classified in two phases: the first phase extracts color features, and the second phase uses a self-organizing map to classify the image texture based on the color features. The photos in each class from the first phase are categorized again in the second phase using a self-organizing map based on texture features collected with the GLCM matrix. Multilayer perceptron and other neural networks are trained using the back-propagation algorithm. The model achieved accuracy of 93.39%.

Chauhan *et al.*, [29] proposed a system for heart disease prediction. It analyses a data mining system for properly predicting cardiac disease, which will assist both analysts and doctors. On the patient's dataset, frequent pattern growth association mining is used to develop strong association rules. Assist doctors in analyzing their data and accurately predicting cardiac problems. The overall accuracy of the proposed a system for heart disease prediction is 61.07% (training) and 53.33% (testing).

Gavhane *et al.*, ([31]) proposed Mechanism used the neural network algorithm multi-layer perceptron (MLP) to train and test the dataset. The multi-layer perceptron algorithm is a supervised neural network approach with one input layer, a second output layer, and one or more hidden layers between these two levels. To obtain the output, the activation function is applied to the weighted input. The input and output layers are connected by the hidden layer, which processes the data internally. The authors achieved precision of 0.91.

Yuwono *et al.*, [32] proposed MKNN (Modified K-Nearest Neighbor) which is a method for recognizing data based on specified ECG component data values such as PR interval, PR segment duration, QRS interval, ST segment duration, QT interval duration, and ST interval duration. There are multiple steps in the MKNN algorithm, including identifying K, computing validity, computing Euclidean distance, calculating the weights and determination of data classes evaluated based on selected k. The overall accuracy of the proposed methodology is 71.20%.

Ambekar and Phalnikar [33] proposed a system for classification which are nave Bayes and KNN. Researchers can estimate if a patient is at high or low risk using the CNN-UDRP algorithm. The Nave Bayes classifier provides input to CNN-UDRP (highest accuracy value as compared to KNN classifier). The CNN algorithm is used to extract features. The SoftMax classifier is used to classify the risk of heart disease. Researchers achieved accuracy of 82%.

Suvarna et al., [35] proposed system uses CPSO (Constricted Particle Swarm Optimization) and PSO (Particle Swarm Optimization) for prediction of heart disease. The proposed prediction algorithm in action. A particle evaluates its own experience, which is specified by the Euclidean distance between two particles positions, or as a sociometric neighborhood, while selecting where to move next. The overall accuracy of the proposed system is 53.1%.

Singh et al., [37] proposed technique generates Classification Association Rules (CARs) and determine which approach provides the highest percentage of accurately projected values for early heart disease diagnosis. The proposed method was compared to existing state-of-the-art procedures in a comparative analysis. Selection, Pre-processing and Transformation, Selection of Associative rules, Performance Evaluation, and Predict Diseases the IHDPS (Intelligent Heart Disease Prediction System) is designed to detect heart disorders based on improved performance and correctly identified cases of the applied algorithm. The model achieved accuracy of 99.19%.

Ramprakash et al., [39] used the neural network acquired a training dataset. Pattern recognition is accomplished using neural networks, which are a set of algorithms. Activation functions make up the neural network's layers. The number of guidelines used to determine the network's behavior has an impact on its performance. Low capacity occurs from a model with fewer parameters, resulting in underfitting. Overfitting occurs when a model contains more parameters than is required. The overall accuracy of the proposed methodology is 94%.

Nikhar and Karandikar [40] employed the Decision Tree Classification method and the Nave Bayes Classifier algorithm. Both category and numerical data are handled by the Decision Tree Classification method. It provides a categorical solution, such as Yes/No, based on specified conditions. The Decision tree Classification technique is commonly used to handle medical datasets. The most efficient and economical classification technique is the Nave Bayes Classifier Algorithm, which can handle vast, difficult, non-linear, dependent data. The authors achieved accuracy of 91% (DT model) and 87% (NB model).

Table 15.1 Summary of existing work for heart disease.

Ref. no.	Dataset used	Technique used	Tool used	Advantages	Issues	Accuracy
[1]	MIT-BIH cardiac arrhythmia database-based ECG signals	Convolutional Neural Network Algorithm	MATLAB R2015a	Reduced the error rate (correctness of classification is higher)	Required rapidity and computational effectiveness.	99.46%
[2]	MIT-BIH database	1-D CNN and Data mining methods	MATLAB compatible WFDB toolbox	Increase the performance of the classification of the heart signals	Required more data sets to train the algorithm and to increase the accuracy	93.72%
[3]	MIT-BIH arrhythmia database	Convolutional Neural Network, Deep learning and spectrogram method	MATLAB	The sensitivity for PVC class is increased by 20% using the spectrogram method.	Time-series signal classification approach is not more successful as compared to spectrogram images classification approach	Time-series signal (97.10%) spectrogram images (99.67%)

(Continued)

Table 15.1 Summary of existing work for heart disease. (*Continued*)

Ref. no.	Dataset used	Technique used	Tool used	Advantages	Issues	Accuracy
[4]	MIT-BIH Database from Physiobank. com	CNN a Deep Learning algorithm and Regularization technique -	…….	The system designed gives better results than the ELU activation function.	We need to increase the epoch to get higher accuracy	93.60%
[6]	MIT-BIH arrhythmia dataset	CNN and LSTM algorithms		CNN performs better than LSTM which is evident from its large AUC.	…………..	…….
[7]	PhysioNet's MIT-BIH dataset	One- and Two-Dimensional Convolutional Neural Network	Kaggle (Tensorflow)	Two-dimensional convolutional model performs better than the one-dimensional convolutional model.	Pre-processing method Time Fourier Transform (STFT) is applied on the data set.	2D CNN 94.37%, 1D CNN 92.67%

(*Continued*)

Table 15.1 Summary of existing work for heart disease. (*Continued*)

Ref. no.	Dataset used	Technique used	Tool used	Advantages	Issues	Accuracy
[8]	MIT Physionet atrial fibrillation arrhythmia database	Deep learning and CNN	....	At 0.01 learning rate the CNN network performs better as compared to other values of learning rate.	CNN does not have the tendency to directly model the dynamic characteristic of time series data.	87.50%
[9]	Physio net's MIT-BIH Arrhythmia dataset	Recurrent Neural Network and LSTM	....	It accurately classifies 5 different arrhythmias with only one layer LSTM	The mode does not converge for lower value of epochs	95%
[10]	MIT-BIH ECG database	Convolution Neural Network and Signal Processing	....	The proposed CAPE is proved to be more efficient than the cardiac arrhythmia prediction techniques	....	93.57%

(*Continued*)

Table 15.1 Summary of existing work for heart disease. (*Continued*)

Ref. no.	Dataset used	Technique used	Tool used	Advantages	Issues	Accuracy
[11]	MIT-BIH dataset	Deep learning, convolutional neural network	....	Using dropout layer and tuning learning rate can help solving over fitting problem	There is a constraint on leaning rate dropout layer and epoch number for optimum performance	94.2%
[12]	MIT-BIH Arrhythmia dataset	Deep Convolutional Neural Network	MLP network	Fully automatic ECG classifcation system that can classify heartbeats into 5-AAMI classes based on 'heartbeats and save time'	Required a pre-processing dataset before feeding it to the network.	92% (Sensitivity)

(*Continued*)

Table 15.1 Summary of existing work for heart disease. (*Continued*)

Ref. no.	Dataset used	Technique used	Tool used	Advantages	Issues	Accuracy
[13]	MIT-BIH Arrhythmia dataset	Coupled-Convolutional Neural Network	....	This model performed better in terms of VEB, SVEB and accuracy.	The dataset is always sampled to 360Hz before processing.	99.43%
[14]	MIT-BIH Arrhythmia Database (360Hz)	Convolutional Neural Network	....	Proposed automatic classification framework without pre-processing of dataset.	Misclassification between VT and VF occurs, resulted in downfall of accuracy	90%
[15]	European ST-T dataset	2-D Image Classification with convolutional Neural Network	AliveCor app	Reduces the requirement of a multiple-lead signal and can work on a single-lead ECG signal record.	Required to pre-processed data in form of 2-D image	97.47%

(*Continued*)

Table 15.1 Summary of existing work for heart disease. (*Continued*)

Ref. no.	Dataset used	Technique used	Tool used	Advantages	Issues	Accuracy
[16]	MIT-BIH arrhythmia dataset	Convolutional Neural Network and Generative Adversarial Networks	....	Reduced the computation significantly by augmenting the heartbeats using GAN	There is a need of a smoothing filter and outliers' removal before using the generated samples.	First approach 98.30% Second approach 98.00%
[17]	Statlog and Cleveland; termed datasets I and II, respectively	....	Flask V1.0.2 as a Python Web Server	The HDPM model minimizes miss-rate and optimizes prediction accuracy for both negative and positive subjects.	The data pre-processing for data transformation and feature selection are conducted, leads to complex computation	98.40%

(*Continued*)

Table 15.1 Summary of existing work for heart disease. (*Continued*)

Ref. no.	Dataset used	Technique used	Tool used	Advantages	Issues	Accuracy
[18]	UCI machine learning repository	Hybrid Machine Learning Techniques	R Studio Rattle	The highest accuracy is achieved by HRFLM classification method as compared to existing methods.	New feature selection methods can be developed to increase the performance	88.7%
[19]	MIT-BIH arrhythmia database	Generalized regression neural network (GRNN)	…………	The proposed methods have comparative advantage over speed and classification accuracy	Computational complexity of pattern layer and summation layer causes CPU to run slowly.	95.00%

(*Continued*)

Table 15.1 Summary of existing work for heart disease. (*Continued*)

Ref. no.	Dataset used	Technique used	Tool used	Advantages	Issues	Accuracy
[20]	UCI heart disease Cleveland dataset	MIFH(D), Data Imputation, Dataset Stratif ication_ HoldOut, FAMD, Dataset_ Normalization and F AMD_MLBox algorithms	Linux machine	MIFH returns the best classifier based upon the weight matrix corresponding to performance metrics.	The data pre-processing for data standardization, data stratification and one hot encoding increase complexity.	93.44%
[21]	MIT-BIH arrhythmia database	STFT-based spectrogram and convolutional neural network.	....	2D-CNN can achieve better classification accuracy without manual pre-processing of the ECG signals unlike 1D-CNN.	For analysis of a non-stationary signal (ECG), it is assumed that it is approximately stationary within the span of a temporal window.	99.00%

(*Continued*)

Table 15.1 Summary of existing work for heart disease. (*Continued*)

Ref. no.	Dataset used	Technique used	Tool used	Advantages	Issues	Accuracy
[22]	The Hungarian HD dataset	Modified Huffman Algorithm, Deep Learning Modified Neural Network and Cuttlefish Optimization Algorithm.	Implemented in JAVA	Modified Huffman algorithm utilized in DC gives the highest values of CR and takes less time for DC. And to reduce the file size, compressed PHR is saved in a CS format.	The pre-processing of HD dataset consists of removal of redundancy, normalization led to increase complexity	96.80%
[23]	2019 Tianchi Hefei High-Tech Cup ECG Human-Machine Intelligence Competition	1D-convolution Resnet, depthwise separable convolution	....	The SE module and depthwise separable convolution work together to reinforce and extract the connection between different channel data.	The dataset does not cover all types of arrhythmias and not yet been clinically verified.	86.30%

(Continued)

Table 15.1 Summary of existing work for heart disease. (*Continued*)

Ref. no.	Dataset used	Technique used	Tool used	Advantages	Issues	Accuracy
[24]	MIT/BIH arrhythmia database	1D Convolutional Neural Networks	Using C++ over MS Visual Studio 2013	There is significant low computational cost for the beat classification in proposed approach	The critical anomaly beats, such as the S beats, are characterized.	VEB- 99.00% SVEB- 97.60%
[25]	MIT-BIH arrhythmia database	Convolutional neural network (CNN)	cuDNN	Reduce the misclassification of N beat to S beat to improve the classifier's performance and stability, particularly for S beat Ppr.	As the number of different types of beats decrease, then the proposed method is more biased in assessing the classifier performance.	VEB-98.60% SVEB- 97.50%

(*Continued*)

Table 15.1 Summary of existing work for heart disease. (*Continued*)

Ref. no.	Dataset used	Technique used	Tool used	Advantages	Issues	Accuracy
[26]	MIT-BIH Atrial Fibrillation databases	Deep CNN-BLSTM network	TensorFlow o	In traditional machining learning, professional knowledge in the biomedical field or handcrafted feature extraction methods are required. But now it is not required.	Between all the RR intervals, input signals are just two points of RR peaks, which do not include the other signal values between the RR intervals.	99.94% (train) 98.63% (validation) 96.59% (Test)
[27]	Cleveland heart disease database	Multilayer perceptron, machine learning and back-propagation	MATLAB R2012	Useful and accurate technique for the classification and retrieval of image by using self-organizing map (SOM) is proposed and developed	....	93.39%

(*Continued*)

Table 15.1 Summary of existing work for heart disease. (*Continued*)

Ref. no.	Dataset used	Technique used	Tool used	Advantages	Issues	Accuracy
[29]	Cleveland Database	Weighted Association Rule	Java based tool called KEEL	Assist doctors in analyzing their data and accurately predicting heart disease.	....	61.07% (Training) 53.33% (testing)
[30]	Cleveland Clinic Foundation databases at the University of California, Irvine (UCI)	Artificial neural networks (ANNs) and Data mining	Weka 3.6.4 tool	reducing system complexity, reducing archive size, and lowering the cost of the health checklist	In the training data set, the accuracy gap between 13 and 8 features is 1.1%, while in the validation data set, it is 0.82%.	88.46% (Training) 80.17% (Testing)
[31]	Cleveland dataset from UCI library	neural network algorithm multi-layer perceptron (MLP)	PyCharm IDE.	Multi Layered Perceptron (MLP) in the proposed system because of its efficiency and accuracy	New algorithms can be proposed to achieve more accuracy and reliability.	0.91 (Precision)

(*Continued*)

Table 15.1 Summary of existing work for heart disease. (*Continued*)

Ref. no.	Dataset used	Technique used	Tool used	Advantages	Issues	Accuracy
[32]	MIT BIH	Modified K-Nearest Neighbor (MKNN)	....	Implementation of computer assistance to help diagnosis.	The result of the decision model is dependent on, chosen value of K	71.20%
[33]	UCI Repository	Naïve Byaes, KNN Algorithm and CNN-UDRP Algorithm	....	naïve Bayes algorithm accuracy is near about 82% which is more than KNN algorithm	Time required for execution of KNN algorithm is more comparatively	82%
[34]	UCI repository	support vector machine and f k-means clustering algorithm	WEKA	Execution time and accuracy of proposed algorithm is less as compared with existing algorithm.	KNN classifier give higher accuracy as compared to SVM	83%

(*Continued*)

Table 15.1 Summary of existing work for heart disease. (*Continued*)

Ref. no.	Dataset used	Technique used	Tool used	Advantages	Issues	Accuracy
[35]	Cleaveland dataset University of California, Irvine (UCI)	Particle Swarm Optimization and Constricted Particle Swarm Optimization	Data mining tool KEEL V2.0	Using the constriction factor method when limiting the velocity is the best approach to use for particle swarm optimization.	The accuracy of CPSO is more as compared as PSO	53.1%
[36]	Cleveland Data Set	Machine Learning and Internet of things	Weka tool	Reduces the barriers for patient monitoring outside hospitals and it helps to reduce the cost of spending patient monitoring.	Required a pre-processing dataset before feeding it to the model.	Naïve Bayes (82.90%), Decision Tree (81.11%), KNN-(81.85%) SVM (82.94%)

(*Continued*)

Table 15.1 Summary of existing work for heart disease. (*Continued*)

Ref. no.	Dataset used	Technique used	Tool used	Advantages	Issues	Accuracy
[37]	Cleveland Heart Disease databases	IBk with a prior Algorithm	Weka environment	IBk with Aprior associative algorithms provides better results for early detection of heart disorders with high prediction accuracy.	Mean absolute error is higher as compared to few of the classifiers.	99.19%
[39]	Cleveland coronary disorder dataset online UCI AI archive.	Deep Neural Network and x^2-statistical model	....	During the prognosis method, the proposed framework increases the level of prediction.	A model with less parameters has a lower capacity, resulting in underfitting.	94%
[40]	UCI Machine learning repository	Decision Tree (DT) Classification and Naïve Bayes (NB) Classification Algorithm	WEKA	For managing medical data, the decision tree classification algorithm is the best.	Required a pre-processing dataset before feeding it to the model.	91% (DT model), 87% (NB model)

Jangir *et al.*, [41], Choubey *et al.*, [42, 43, 50, 52, 54, 67, 68] have used similar data science and machine learning algorithms for the identifications and predictions of medical diabetes. The idea conceived through the review [49, 53, 57, 59–61, 64, 66] of many published articles, text and references like comparative analysis of classification methods, performance evaluation of classification methods [44], rule based diagnosis system [45] and classification techniques diagnosis [46–48, 58] for diabetes, classification techniques diagnosis [51] for leukemia, classification techniques diagnosis [55, 56] for heart disease, classification techniques diagnosis [62] for dengue, image detection [63] using computer vision are found to be of great help in accomplishment of the present work.

Table 15.1 consists of the summary of existing work for heart disease.

Table 15.2 consists of the used techniques with their advantages and issues.

Table 15.3 consists of the summary of future works over exiting works.

Table 15.2 Technique used with their advantages and issues.

Ref. no.	Technique used	Advantages	Issues
[1, 3, 7, 11–16, 21, 24, 25]	Convolutional Neural Network	The main advantage of CNN compared to its predecessors is that it automatically detects the important features without any human supervision. For example, given many pictures of cats and dogs it learns distinctive features for each class by itself. CNN is also computationally efficient.	CNNs don't develop the mental models that humans have about different objects and their ability to imagine those objects in previously unseen contexts. Another problem with convolutional neural networks is their inability to understand the relations between different objects.

(Continued)

Table 15.2 Technique used with their advantages and issues. (*Continued*)

Ref. no.	Technique used	Advantages	Issues
[3, 4, 8, 11, 22]	Deep learning	Feature engineering can be automatically executed inside the Deep Learning model. Can solve complex problems, flexible to be adapted to new challenge in the future (or transfer learning can be easily applied) high automation. Deep learning library (Tensorflow, keras, or MATLAB) can help users build a deep learning model in seconds (without the need of deep understanding)	Need huge amount of data, Expensive and intensive training, Overfitting if applied into uncomplicated problems, No standard for training and tuning model. It's a black box, not straightforward to understand inside each layer
[6, 9, 26]	LSTM	LSTM is well-suited to classify, process and predict time series given time lags of unknown duration. Relative insensitivity to gap length gives an advantage to LSTM over alternative RNNs, hidden Markov models and other sequence learning methods. The structure of RNN is very similar to the hidden Markov model.	LSTM requires 4 linear layers (MLP layer) per cell to run at and for each sequence time-step. Linear layers require large amounts of memory bandwidth to be computed, in fact they cannot use many compute units often because the system has not enough memory bandwidth to feed the computational units.

(Continued)

Table 15.2 Technique used with their advantages and issues. (*Continued*)

Ref. no.	Technique used	Advantages	Issues
[16]	Generative Adversarial Networks	GANs generate data that looks similar to original data. If you give GAN an image then it will generate a new version of the image which looks similar to the original image. Similarly, it can generate different versions of the text, video, audio. GANs go into details of data and can easily interpret into different versions so it is helpful in doing machine learning work. By using GANs and machine learning we can easily recognize trees, street, bicyclist, person, and parked cars and also can calculate the distance between different objects.	Harder to train: You need to provide different types of data continuously to check if it works accurately or not. Generating results from text or speech is very complex
[19]	Generalized regression neural network (GRNN)	It can be used for regression, prediction, and classification, Single-pass learning so no backpropagation is required. High accuracy in the estimation since it uses Gaussian functions, It can handle noises in the inputs, It requires only a smaller number of datasets.	The main disadvantages of GRNN are: Its size can be huge, which would make it computationally expensive. There is no optimal method to improve it.

Table 15.2 Technique used with their advantages and issues. (*Continued*)

Ref. no.	Technique used	Advantages	Issues
[22]	Modified Huffman	Adaptive Huffman coding has the advantage of requiring no preprocessing and the low overhead of using the uncompressed version of the symbols only at their first occurrence. The algorithms can be applied to other types of files in addition to text files.	It is not optimal unless all probabilities are negative powers of 2. This means that there is a gap between the average number of bits and the entropy in most cases. Despite the availability of some clever methods for counting the frequency of each symbol reasonably quickly, it can be very *slow* when rebuilding the entire tree for each symbol. This is normally the case when the alphabet is big and the probability distributions change rapidly with each symbol.

(*Continued*)

Table 15.2 Technique used with their advantages and issues. (*Continued*)

Ref. no.	Technique used	Advantages	Issues
[2, 30, 35]	Data mining	It is helpful to predict future trends, It signifies customer habits, Helps in decision making, Increase company revenue, It depends upon market-based analysis, Quick fraud detection.	Data mining in healthcare include reliability of medical data, data sharing between healthcare organizations, inappropriate modelling leading to inaccurate predictions. Taking financial or political decisions based on data mining can lead to catastrophic results in some cases. As mentioned before, discriminating people based on a few baseless information can lead to unpredictable decisions, which can cost money and brand value for many companies. Data mining also has its own disadvantages e.g., privacy, security, and misuse of information.

(*Continued*)

Table 15.2 Technique used with their advantages and issues. (*Continued*)

Ref. no.	Technique used	Advantages	Issues
[36, 40]	Decision tree	Easy to read and interpret. One of the advantages of decision trees is that their outputs are easy to read and interpret, without even requiring statistical knowledge, Easy to prepare, Less data cleaning required.	They are unstable, meaning that a small change in the data can lead to a large change in the structure of the optimal decision tree. They are often relatively inaccurate. Many other predictors perform better with similar data.
[32–34, 36]	K-Nearest Neighbor Algorithm	Quick calculation time, Simple algorithm – to interpret, Versatile – useful for regression and classification, High accuracy – you do not need to compare with better-supervised learning models.	Accuracy depends on the quality of the data, With large data the prediction stage might be slow, Sensitive to the scale of the data and irrelevant features, Require high memory – need to store all of the training data, Given that it stores all of the training, it can be computationally expensive.

(*Continued*)

Table 15.2 Technique used with their advantages and issues. (*Continued*)

Ref. no.	Technique used	Advantages	Issues
[33, 36]	Naïve Bayes Algorithm	It is simple and easy to implement, It doesn't require as much training data, It handles both continuous and discrete data, It is highly scalable with the number of predictors and data points. It is fast and can be used to make real-time predictions.	If we test data set has a categorical variable of a category that wasn't present in the training data set, the Naive Bayes model will assign it zero probability and won't be able to make any predictions in this regard. This algorithm is also notorious as a lousy estimator.
[34, 36]	support vector machine	SVM works relatively well when there is a clear margin of separation between classes. SVM is more effective in high dimensional spaces. SVM is effective in cases where the number of dimensions is greater than the number of samples. SVM is relatively memory efficient.	SVM algorithm is not suitable for large data sets. SVM does not perform very well when the data set has more noise i.e., target classes are overlapping. In cases where the number of features for each data point exceeds the number of training data samples, the SVM will underperform.

(*Continued*)

Table 15.2 Technique used with their advantages and issues. (*Continued*)

Ref. no.	Technique used	Advantages	Issues
[35]	Particle Swarm Optimization	The main advantages of the PSO algorithm are summarized as: simple concept, easy implementation, robustness to control parameters, and computational efficiency when compared with mathematical algorithms and other heuristic optimization techniques. maximum iteration number, current iteration number.	The disadvantages of particle swarm optimization (PSO) algorithm are that it is easy to fall into local optimum in high-dimensional space and has a low convergence rate in the iterative process.

Table 15.3 Summary of future work over existing work.

Ref. no.	Existing work	Future work
[3]	Two methods were used to classify CNN heartbeat arrhythmias: ECG spectrogram image classification and ECG time series signal classification. For both methods, CNN is an effective classifier and feature extractor.	In future research, the various forms of arrhythmias will be studied, and CNN parameters will be improved.
[5]	Propose a reference network (network A) and a multi-scale fusion CNN architecture (network B) based on network A to automatically recognize various forms of ECG heartbeats, which is vital for ECG heartbeat diagnosis.	Other arrhythmia signals, such as atrial fibrillation and ventricular fibrillation, will be classified in the future. We can also extend to other public databases in order to assess the accuracy and generalizability of models.

(*Continued*)

Table 15.3 Summary of future work over existing work. (*Continued*)

Ref. no.	Existing work	Future work
[6]	The performance of CNN and LSTM algorithms is compared in terms of AUC and ROC curve for a publicly accessible MIT-BIH dataset in this paper. CNN is said to perform better than LSTM, as evidenced by its large size.	The features of CNN and LSTM algorithms will be combined to create a hybrid deep learning model with the aim of improving results.
[8]	For the input of an ECG image, an effective CNN classifier is proposed. Regularization, learning parameter, momentum coefficient, and cross-validation are all important parameters to consider when optimizing the CNN.	It is left for future work to apply RNN and LSTM to remove problems. Since CNN has a proclivity for not explicitly modelling the dynamic characteristics of time series results.
[12]	Proposes a fully automated ECG classification system that can categories heartbeats into five AAMI-recommended groups based on morphological characteristics.	Intend to look at both active and unsupervised learning approaches.
[13]	Using a coupled convolution layer structure and the dropout function, they created a Holter data CNN heartbeat classifier based on the MLII lead.	They want to investigate a stable and high-accuracy R-peak detection algorithm in the future.
[15]	Deep learning CNN was used as a computer vision technique to identify abnormalities in the ECG signal, specifically the ST episode for myocardial infarction, in the proposed study.	Their long-term development goal is to create an ECG system application that uses Apple Watch data as input.

(*Continued*)

Table 15.3 Summary of future work over existing work. (*Continued*)

Ref. no.	Existing work	Future work
[16]	To solve the imbalance problem, a novel data augmentation technique using GAN was proposed for ECG data.	Different GAN variants will be developed in the future, as well as different classification architectures, sampling rates, and deployment of the proposed models in real-time monitoring and classification systems.
[17]	To improve prediction accuracy, researchers proposed an efficient heart disease prediction model (HDPM) that integrates DBSCAN, SMOTE-ENN, and XGBoost-based MLA.	They will compare other data sampling with the model hyper-parameters and a larger medical dataset in the future.
[18]	The proposed hybrid HRFLM solution combines the advantages of Random Forest (RF) and Linear Method (LM) (LM). HRFLM has been shown to be very effective in predicting heart disease.	To improve the efficiency, various combinations of machine learning techniques and new feature selection methods can be created.
[20]	The proposed method MIFH can be used to predict cases in both healthy people and heart patients.	Multi-class classification of heart disease datasets may be proposed in the future.
[23]	On the basis of the ECG 12-lead data collection, investigate the form of arrhythmia multi-label classification.	Replacing the backbone network with a cutting-edge network model like Efficient Net is likely to produce better performance, and that is exactly what we will do in the future.

(*Continued*)

Table 15.3 Summary of future work over existing work. (*Continued*)

Ref. no.	Existing work	Future work
[24]	Proposed a patient-specific ECG heartbeat classifier based on an adaptive implementation of 1D Convolutional Neural Networks (CNNs) capable of integrating the two main blocks of conventional ECG classification into a single learning body: feature extraction and classification.	Researchers plan to design the hardware implementation of the proposed solution as a future project.
[25]	Using a dual-beat ECG coupling matrix, proposed a CNN-based method for heartbeat classification. This ECG dual-beat coupling matrix, encoded in two dimensions, is an accurate representation of both heartbeat morphology and rhythm.	The classification system's robustness in long-term usage will be investigated in future research.
[26]	To detect the AF signal from ECG records, a new deep CNN-BLSTM network was created. The model combines CNN and BLSTM function extraction methods.	Multiple arrhythmia signals are classified, and the approach is extended to other public databases to determine the method's accuracy and model's generalization capacity.
[31]	The Heart Disease Prediction Method, which employs the MLP machine learning algorithm, provides users with a prediction result that shows a user's likelihood of developing CAD.	With the aid of recent technologies like machine learning, fuzzy logics, and image processing, similar prediction systems can be designed for a number of other chronic or fatal diseases like Cancer, Diabetes, and others to achieve greater accuracy and reliability.

(*Continued*)

Table 15.3 Summary of future work over existing work. (*Continued*)

Ref. no.	Existing work	Future work
[33]	Researchers use structured data to test the CNN-UDRP algorithm for disease risk prediction.	Researchers will add more diseases in the future and estimate the probability that a patient will develop a particular disease.
[34]	Data mining is used to retrieve valuable information from a raw dataset. The knowledge that is identical and dissimilar is grouped together.	The proposed method would be improved in order to create hybrid classifiers for heart disease prediction.
[35]	With the aid of data mining and optimization techniques, this project focuses on creating a prediction algorithm.	To pre-process data and minimize uncertainty, researchers may use techniques like Principal Component Analysis. Reinforcement Learning may also be used to ensure that the system continues to improve.
[36]	To detect the absence or presence of heart diseases, an iOS mobile application with IoT architecture and a machine learning model was developed.	In the future, this research hopes to use Deep Learning to increase the precision of detecting heart diseases.
[37]	To predict heart diseases, various association and classification methods are applied to heart datasets.	Future research will focus on reducing the number of characteristics and evaluating the most important ones that contribute to the diagnosis of heart disease.
[39]	Using a deep neural network, researchers created a self-operating diagnostic model for cardiac disorder disease detection.	In the future, genetic algorithms may be used to improve accuracy.

(Continued)

Table 15.3 Summary of future work over existing work. (*Continued*)

Ref. no.	Existing work	Future work
[40]	Two supervised data mining algorithms were used to predict the likelihood of a patient having heart disease, and the results were analyses using a classification model.	The developed framework, which employs a machine learning classification algorithm, could be used to predict or diagnose other diseases in the future, or it could be improved for heart disease analysis automation.

In this chapter various studies were reviewed on the basis of the technique used, tool used, algorithm used and thereby ending with the conclusion. These studies helped the authors to get prepared for the upcoming situation.

15.4   Proposed Approach

We started by making a list of all the patients in the data path. We used a pypi package wfdb for loading the ECG and annotations and made a list of the non-beat and abnormal beats. Then we made a dataset that is centered on beats with +- 3 seconds before and after. We then split our data by patients into a train and validation set because technically the same patient can show up in both the training and validation sets. This means that we may accidentally leak information across the datasets. Therefore, we split on patients instead of samples.

The following software and hardware are required for the designed algorithms which is mentioned below: (a) Software: Ubuntu 16 or above/ Windows 7 or above, Python, Packages (Numpy, Sklearn, Matplotlib, Pandas, Numpy, Wfdb), Jupyter Notebook, Sublime Text, Google Chrome (b) Hardware: 4 GB RAM or above, 1 TB ROM or above, Processor Speed 1.4 GHz or above.

The dataflow diagram for the proposed approach is shown below in Figure 15.1.

To prevent the model from overfitting and tracing the training process, 70% of the training data is actually used to train the model, while 30% of the training data is used to validate the performance of the network at the end of each epoch. The model is trained for 5 epochs using the Dense NN,

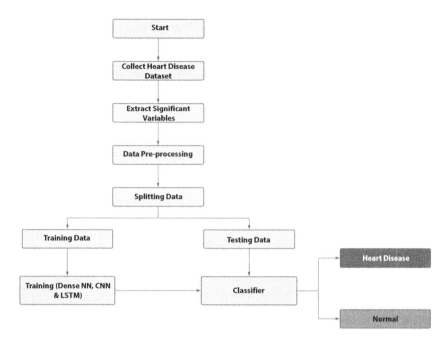

Figure 15.1 Dataflow diagram.

CNN and LSTM algorithm with a batch size of 32. The learning rate is set to 0.001 and is also applied to Adam optimizer so as to accelerate the learning process. The total training and validation process was processed under the GPU acceleration environment.

The work descriptions deal into two stages: (a) Dataset (b) Algorithms

15.4.1   Dataset Descriptions

An arrhythmia describes an irregular heartbeat. With this condition, a person's heart may beat too quickly, too slowly, too early, or with an irregular rhythm. Arrhythmias occur when the electrical signals that coordinate heartbeats are not working correctly. An irregular heartbeat may feel like a racing heart or fluttering. Many heart arrhythmias are harmless. However, if they are highly irregular or result from a weak or damaged heart, arrhythmias can cause severe and potentially fatal symptoms and complications.

The MIT-BIH Arrhythmia Database contains 48 half-hour excerpts of two-channel ambulatory ECG recordings, obtained from 47 subjects studied by the BIH Arrhythmia Laboratory between 1975 and 1979. Twenty-three recordings were chosen at random from a set of 4000 24-hour ambulatory ECG recordings collected from a mixed population of inpatients (about 60%) and outpatients (about 40%) at Boston's Beth Israel Hospital; the remaining 25 recordings were selected from the same set to include less common but clinically significant arrhythmias that would not be well-represented in a small random sample.

Table 15.4 Beat annotations

Code	Description
N	Normal beat (displayed as "·" by the PhysioBank ATM, LightWAVE, pschart, and psfd)
L	Left bundle branch block beat
R	Right bundle branch block beat
B	Bundle branch block beat (unspecified)
A	Atrial premature beat
a	Aberrated atrial premature beat
J	Nodal (junctional) premature beat
S	Supraventricular premature or ectopic beat (atrial or nodal)
V	Premature ventricular contraction
r	R-on-T premature ventricular contraction
F	Fusion of ventricular and normal beat
e	Atrial escape beat
j	Nodal (junctional) escape beat
n	Supraventricular escape beat (atrial or nodal)
E	Ventricular escape beat
/	Paced beat
f	Fusion of paced and normal beat
Q	Unclassifiable beat
?	Beat not classified during learning

The recordings were digitized at 360 samples per second per channel with 11-bit resolution over a 10-mV range. Two or more cardiologists independently annotated each record; disagreements were resolved to obtain the computer-readable reference annotations for each beat (approximately 110,000 annotations in all) included with the database. Annotations are labels that point to specific locations within a recording and describe events at those locations. For example, many of the recordings that contain ECG signals have annotations that indicate the times of occurrence and types of each individual heart beat ("beat-by-beat annotations"). The dataset we used is from the MIT-BIH arrhythmia dataset from https://physionet.org/content/mitdb/1.0.0/.

Table 15.4 depicts the beat annotations of code.

15.4.2   Algorithms Description

In this study, we used Jupyter Notebook to determine the prediction of arrhythmia using Python. It has inbuild libraries to do the statistical computation in few seconds.

Figure 15.2 presents the proposed architecture.

The detailed description of the algorithms used in the model are given below.

15.4.2.1   Dense Neural Network

A deep neural network (DNN) is an artificial neural network (ANN) with multiple layers between the input and output layers There are different types of neural networks but they always consist of the same components: neurons, synapses, weights, biases, and functions. These components functioning similar to the human brains and can be trained like any other ML algorithm.

DNNs are typically feedforward networks in which data flows from the input layer to the output layer without looping back. At first, the DNN creates a map of virtual neurons and assigns random numerical values, or "weights", to connections between them. The weights and inputs are multiplied and return an output between 0 and 1. If the network did not accurately recognize a particular pattern, an algorithm would adjust the weights. That way the algorithm can make certain parameters more influential, until it determines the correct mathematical manipulation to fully process the data.

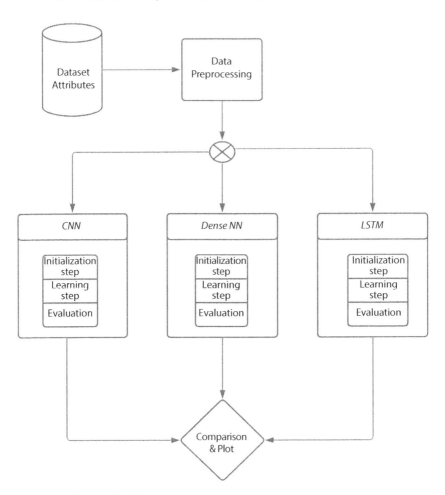

Figure 15.2 Proposed architecture.

Dense NN-pseudo-code involves training of the required dataset and after that, evaluation of the model is performed on the test dataset. Finally, accuracy, recall, precision, specificity, and prevalence will be the output of the model.

The Algorithm 15.1 of DNN is as noted below.

Figure 15.3 depicts the DNN architecture.

15.4.2.2   Convolutional Neural Network

A Convolution Neural Network (CNN) is a special type of deep learning algorithm which uses a set of filters and the convolution operator to

---

Algorithm 15.1 Dense Neural Network.

Input: *X_train, y_train, sym_train, X_valid, y_valid, sym_valid.*
1. Procedure Dense NN MODEL
2. BatchSize=32, epoch=5, verbose=1
3. Input_length=80614, rate = 0.25
4. model = Sequential()
   # Dense Layer
5. model.add (Dense(32, activation = 'relu', input_dim = X_train. shape[1]))
   # Dropout Layer
6. model.add (Dropout(rate = 0.25))
   # activation Layer
7. model.add (Dense(1, activation = 'sigmoid'))
   # Compile Function
8. model.compile (loss = 'binary_crossentropy', optimizer = 'adam', metrics = ['accuracy'])
   # Summary of the model
9. print (model.summary())
10. **For** all epochs in (1: NEpoch) **do**
    # Fitting a Model
11. model.fit (X_train, y_train, batch_size = 32, epochs= 5, verbose = 1)
    # Model Prediction
12. model.predict (X_train, verbose = 1)
13. model.predict (X_valid, verbose = 1)
14. **End for**
    # Model Evaluation
15. Evaluate thresh = (sum(y_train)/len(y_train))[0]
16. To print (y_train, y_train_preds_dense, thresh)
17. To print (y_valid, y_valid_preds_dense, thresh);
18. **End Procedure**
Output: *AUC, Accuracy, Recall, Precision, Specificity, Prevalence.*

---

reduce the number of parameters. This algorithm sparked the state-of-the-art techniques for image classification. Essentially, the way this works for 1D CNN is to take a filter (kernel) of size kernel_size starting with the first-time stamp. The convolution operator takes the filter and multiplies each element against the first kernel_size time steps. These products are then summed for the first cell in the next layer of the neural network.

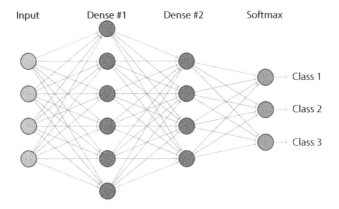

Figure 15.3 DNN architecture.

The filter then moves over by stride time steps and repeats. The default stride in keras is 1, which we will use. In image classification, most people use padding which allows you to pick up some features on the edges of the image by adding 'extra' cells, we will use the default padding which is 0. The output of the convolution is then multiplied by a set of weights W and added to a bias b and then passed through a non-linear activation function as in a dense neural network. We can then repeat this with addition CNN layers if desired. Here we will use Dropout which is a technique for reducing overfitting by randomly removing some nodes.

CNN-pseudo-code involves training of the required dataset and after that, evaluation of the model is performed on the test dataset. Finally, accuracy, recall, precision, specificity, and prevalence will be the output of the model.

The Algorithm 15.2 of CNN is as noted below.

Figure 15.4 presents the CNN architecture.

15.4.2.3   Long Short-Term Memory

Long short-term memory (LSTM) is an artificial recurrent neural network (RNN) architecture used in the field of deep learning. Unlike standard feedforward neural networks, LSTM has feedback connections. It can not only process single data points (such as images), but also entire sequences of data (such as speech or video). For example, LSTM is applicable to tasks such as unsegmented, connected handwriting recognition, speech recognition and anomaly detection in network traffic or IDSs (intrusion detection systems).

Since this data signal is time-series, it is natural to test a recurrent neural network (RNN). Here we will test a bidirectional long short-term memory (LSTM). Unlike in dense NN and CNN, RNN have loops in the network

Algorithm 15.2 Convolutional Neural Network.

Input: *X_train & X_valid*
1. Procedure CNN MODEL
2. BatchSie=32, epoch=2, filters=128, verbose=1
3. input_length=2160, kernel_size = 5, rate = 0.25
4. model=Sequential()
Dropout Layer
5. model.add (Dropout(rate = 0.25))
Convolutional Layer
6. model.add (Conv1D(filters = 128, kernel_size = 5, activation = 'relu', input_shape = (2160,1)))
Flatten Layer
7. model.add (Flatten())
Dense Layer
8. model.add (Dense(1, activation = 'sigmoid'))
Compile Function
9. model.compile (loss = 'binary_crossentropy',optimizer = 'adam',metrics = 'accuracy'])
Summary of the model
10. print(model.summary())
11. For all epochs in (1:NEpoch) **do**
Fitting a Model
12. model.fit (X_train_cnn, y_train, batch_size = 32, epochs= 2, verbose = 1)
Model Prediction
13. model.predict (X_train_cnn,verbose=1)
14. model.predict (X_valid_cnn,verbose=1)
15. **End for**
Model Evaluation
16. Evaluate thresh=sum (y_train)/length of y_train
17. To print (y_train, y_train_preds_cnn, thresh)
18. To print (y_valid, y_valid_preds_cnn, thresh)
19. **End Procedure**
Output: *AUC, Accuracy, Recall, Precision, Specificity, Prevalence*

to keep a memory of what has happened in the past. This allows the network to pass information from early time steps to later time steps that usually would be lost in other types of networks. Essentially there is an extra term for this memory state in the calculation before passing through a

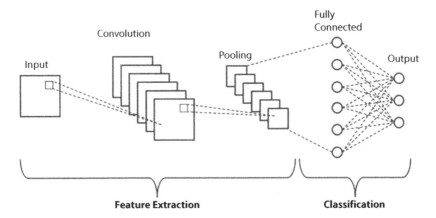

Figure 15.4 CNN architecture.

Algorithm 15.3 Long Short-Term Memory.

Input: *X_train & X_valid*

1. Procedure LSTM MODEL
2. BatchSie=32, epoch=1, verbose=1
3. input_length=10000, rate = 0.25
4. model = Sequential()
   # **Bidirectional layer**
5. model.add(Bidirectional(LSTM(64, input_shape= (X_train_cnn.
   shape[1], X_train_cnn.shape[2]))))
   # **Dropout layer**
6. model.add (Dropout (rate = 0.25))
   # **Dense layer**
7. model.add (Dense(1, activation = 'sigmoid'))
   # **Compile Function**
8. model.compile (loss = 'binary_crossentropy', optimizer = 'adam',
   metrics = ['accuracy'])
   # **Summary of the model**
9. Print (model.summary())
10. For all epochs in (1:NEpoch) **do**
    # **Fitting a Model**
11. model.fit (X_train_cnn, y_train, batch_size = 32, epochs= 1,
    verbose = 1)
    # **Model prediction**
12. model.predict (X_train_cnn,verbose = 1)
13. model.predict (X_valid_cnn,verbose = 1)

(Continued)

Algorithm 15.3 Long Short-Term Memory. (*Continued*)

14. **End for**
  # Model Evaluation
15. Evaluate thresh=sum (y_train)/length of y_train
16. To print (y_train, y_train_preds_lstm, thresh)
18.To print (y_valid, y_valid_preds_lstm, thresh)
19. End Procedure

Output: *AUC, Accuracy, Recall, Precision, Specificity, Prevalence*

---

non-linear activation function. Here we use the bidirectional information so information can be passed in both direction (left to right and right to left). This will help us pick up information about the normal heart beats to the left and right of the center heartbeat.

Figure 15.5 shows the LSTM network.

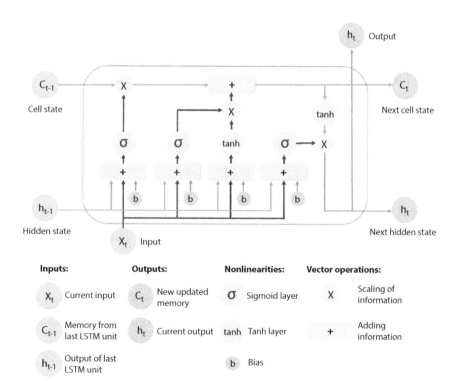

Figure 15.5 Structure of LSTM network.

15.5 Experimental Results of Proposed Approach

We have used DNN, CNN and LSTM on MIT-BIH Arrhythmia Database. The performance has been evaluated in tabular forms.

Table 15.5 presents the training performance of DNN, CNN and LSTM.

The above table represents the training parameter values such as AUC, Accuracy, Recall, Precision, Specificity and Prevalence of DNN, CNN, and LSTM.

Table 15.6 presents the testing performance of DNN, CNN and LSTM.

The above table represents the testing parameter values such as AUC, Accuracy, Recall, Precision, Specificity and Prevalence of DNN, CNN, and LSTM.

Table 15.7 presents the comparison of proposed algorithms with existing in context of accuracy.

Table 15.5 Training performance of DNN, CNN and LSTM.

Parameters	DNN	CNN	LSTM
AUC	0.992	0.993	0.772
Accuracy	0.969	0.960	0.677
Recall	0.959	0.973	0.518
Precision	0.944	0.901	0.744
Specificity	0.974	0.954	0.829
Prevalence	0.315	0.299	0.489

Table 15.6 Testing performance of DNN, CNN and LSTM.

Parameters	Dense-network	CNN-network	LSTM-network
AUC	0.988	0.905	0.560
Accuracy	0.964	0.812	0.565
Recall	0.952	0.832	0.642
Precision	0.934	0.699	0.428
Specificity	0.969	0.801	0.522
Prevalence	0.314	0.358	0.358

Table 15.7 Comparison of proposed algorithms with existing in context of accuracy.

Source	Algorithm	Accuracy
Khemphila and Boonjing (2011)	Artificial neural networks (ANN)	80.17%
Suvarna *et al.*, (2017)	Constricted Particle Swarm Optimization	53.1%
Chauhan *et al.*, (2018)	Weighted Association Rule	53.33%
Yuwono *et al.*, (2018)	Modified K-Nearest Neighbor (MKNN)	71.20%
Mohan *et al.*, (2019)	Hybrid Machine Learning Techniques	88.7%
Cai *et al.*, (2020)	1D- convolution Resnet, depth wise separable convolution	86.30%
Our Study	DNN	96.4%
	CNN	81.2%
	LSTM	56.5%

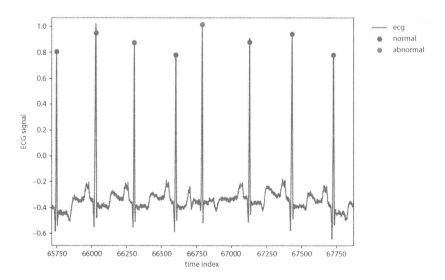

Figure 15.6 ECG signal vs. time index of abnormal beats.

In above table, it may be observed that proposed algorithm i.e., DNN achieved the best performance than existing.

Figure 15.6 shows the ECG Signal vs. Time Index of Abnormal Beats.

Figure 15.7 shows AUC vs. Number Training Points.

Figure 15.8 shows the ROC curve of DNN, CNN and LSTM.

Figure 15.9 shows the ROC curve of LSTM.

Figure 15.10 shows validation of CNN, DNN, and LSTM.

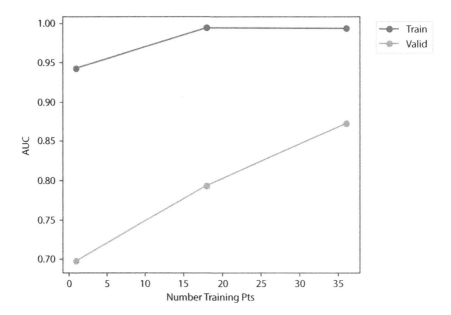

Figure 15.7 AUC vs. number training Pts.

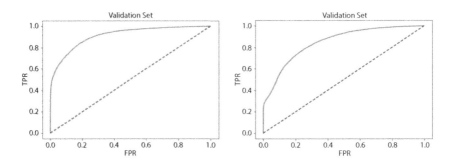

Figure 15.8 ROC curve of DNN and CNN.

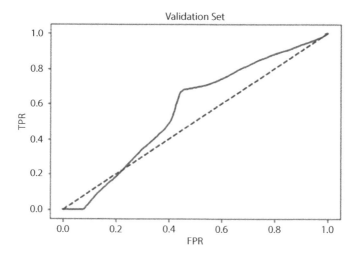

Figure 15.9 ROC curve of LSTM.

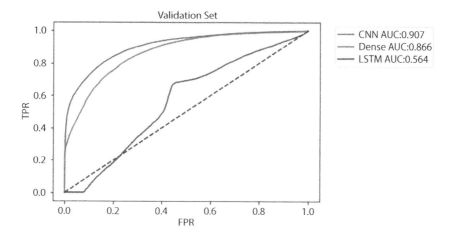

Figure 15.10 ROC curve of DNN, CNN, and LSTM.

15.6 Conclusion and Future Scope

More data set can be taken in consideration with optimized hyperparameters in order to achieve even higher values for CNN, Dense CNN and LSTM network.

Determining any heart disease on some raw data is really difficult for even a doctor which is why many healthcare sectors are opting for machine learning techniques to determine it. In our project we took the MIT-BIH

Arrhythmia dataset from https://physionet.org/content/mitdb/1.0.0/ and applied pre-processing to drop the data with missing values and applied some deep learning models like Dense neural network, CNN, LSTM of which Dense NN gives an accuracy of 96.4%, CNN gives an accuracy of 81.2%, and LSTM gives an accuracy of 56.5%. However, the accuracy can be improved by using some data mining techniques for feature extraction from the samples. The ROC curve for Dense NN gives an AUC of 0.866, CNN gives an AUC of 0.907, and LSTM gives an AUC of 0.564.

For further implementation, we can try to take in consideration of huge data set for model training and validation, further more optimize the hyperparameters or number of layers. More data set can be taken in consideration as suggested by learning curve. Instead of taking in consideration of 6 second window centered on the peak of the heartbeat, it can be increased (keeping in mind the degree of complexity of handling the huge information).

References

1. Gawande, N. and Barhatte, A., Heart diseases classification using convolutional neural network, in: *2017 2nd International Conference on Communication and Electronics Systems (ICCES)*, 2017, October, IEEE, pp. 17–20.
2. Sarvan, Ç. and Özkurt, N., ECG beat arrhythmia classification by using 1-D CNN in case of class imbalance, in: *2019 Medical Technologies Congress (TIPTEKNO)*, 2019, October, IEEE, pp. 1–4.
3. ŞEN, S.Y. and Özkurt, N., ECG arrhythmia classification by using convolutional neural network and spectrogram, in: *2019 Innovations in Intelligent Systems and Applications Conference (ASYU)*, 2019, October, IEEE, pp. 1–6.
4. Rajkumar, A., Ganesan, M., Lavanya, R., Arrhythmia classification on ECG using deep learning, in: *2019 5th International Conference on Advanced Computing & Communication Systems (ICACCS)*, 2019, March, IEEE, pp. 365–369.
5. Dang, H., Sun, M., Zhang, G., Zhou, X., Chang, Q., Xu, X., A novel deep convolutional neural network for arrhythmia classification, in: *2019 International Conference on Advanced Mechatronic Systems (ICAMechS)*, 2019, August, IEEE, pp. 7–11.
6. Hassan, S.U., Zahid, M.S.M., Husain, K., Performance comparison of CNN and LSTM algorithms for arrhythmia classification, in: *2020 International Conference on Computational Intelligence (ICCI)*, 2020, October, IEEE, pp. 223–228.

7. Qayyum, A.B.A., Islam, T., Haque, M.A., ECG heartbeat classification: A comparative performance analysis between one and two dimensional convolutional neural network, in: *2019 IEEE International Conference on Biomedical Engineering, Computer and Information Technology for Health (BECITHCON)*, 2019, November, IEEE, pp. 93–96.

8. Singh, S., Sunkaria, R.K., Saini, B.S., Kumar, K., Atrial fibrillation and premature contraction classification using convolutional neural network, in: *2019 International Conference on Intelligent Computing and Control Systems (ICCS)*, 2019, May, IEEE, pp. 797–800.

9. Rana, A. and Kim, K.K., ECG heartbeat classification using a single layer LSTM model, in: *2019 International SoC Design Conference (ISOCC)*, 2019, October, IEEE, pp. 267–268.

10. Sangeetha, D., Selvi, S., Ram, M.S.A., A CNN based similarity learning for cardiac arrhythmia prediction, in: *2019 11th International Conference on Advanced Computing (ICoAC)*, 2019, December, IEEE, pp. 244–248.

11. Prawira, R.H., Wibowo, A., Yusuf, A.Y.P., Best parameters selection of arrhythmia classification using convolutional neural networks, in: *2019 3rd International Conference on Informatics and Computational Sciences (ICICoS)*, 2019, October, IEEE, pp. 1–6.

12. Takalo-Mattila, J., Kiljander, J., Soininen, J.P., Inter-patient ECG classification using deep convolutional neural networks, in: *2018 21st Euromicro Conference on Digital System Design (DSD)*, 2018, August, IEEE, pp. 421–425.

13. Xu, X. and Liu, H., ECG heartbeat classification using convolutional neural networks. *IEEE Access*, 8, 8614–8619, 2020.

14. Kido, K., Ono, N., Altaf-Ul-Amin, M.D., Kanaya, S., Huang, M., The feasibility of arrhythmias detection from a capacitive ECG measurement using convolutional neural network, in: *2019 41st Annual International Conference of the IEEE Engineering in Medicine and Biology Society (EMBC)*, 2019, July, IEEE, pp. 3494–3497.

15. Wasimuddin, M., Elleithy, K., Abuzneid, A., Faezipour, M., Abuzaghleh, O., ECG signal analysis using 2-D image classification with convolutional neural network, in: *2019 International Conference on Computational Science and Computational Intelligence (CSCI)*, 2019, December, IEEE, pp. 949–954.

16. Shaker, A.M., Tantawi, M., Shedeed, H.A., Tolba, M.F., Generalization of convolutional neural networks for ECG classification using generative adversarial networks. *IEEE Access*, 8, 35592–35605, 2020.

17. Fitriyani, N.L., Syafrudin, M., Alfian, G., Rhee, J., HDPM: An effective heart disease prediction model for a clinical decision support system. *IEEE Access*, 8, 133034–133050, 2020.

18. Mohan, S., Thirumalai, C., Srivastava, G., Effective heart disease prediction using hybrid machine learning techniques. *IEEE Access*, 7, 81542–81554, 2019.

19. Li, P., Wang, Y., He, J., Wang, L., Tian, Y., Zhou, T.S., Li, J.S., High-performance personalized heartbeat classification model for long-term ECG signal. *IEEE Trans. Biomed. Eng.*, 64, 1, 78–86, 2016.

20. Gupta, A., Kumar, R., Arora, H.S., Raman, B., MIFH: A machine intelligence framework for heart disease diagnosis. *IEEE Access*, 8, 14659–14674, 2019.

21. Huang, J., Chen, B., Yao, B., He, W., ECG arrhythmia classification using STFT-based spectrogram and convolutional neural network. *IEEE Access*, 7, 92871–92880, 2019.

22. Sarmah, S.S., An efficient IoT-based patient monitoring and heart disease prediction system using deep learning modified neural network. *IEEE Access*, 8, 135784–135797, 2020.

23. Cai, J., Sun, W., Guan, J., You, I., Multi-ECGNet for ECG arrythmia multi-label classification. *IEEE Access*, 8, 110848–110858, 2020.

24. Kiranyaz, S., Ince, T., Gabbouj, M., Real-time patient-specific ECG classification by 1-D convolutional neural networks. *IEEE Trans. Biomed. Eng.*, 63, 3, 664–675, 2015.

25. Zhai, X. and Tin, C., Automated ECG classification using dual heartbeat coupling based on convolutional neural network. *IEEE Access*, 6, 27465–27472, 2018.

26. Dang, H., Sun, M., Zhang, G., Qi, X., Zhou, X., Chang, Q., A novel deep arrhythmia-diagnosis network for atrial fibrillation classification using electrocardiogram signals. *IEEE Access*, 7, 75577–75590, 2019.

27. Sonawane, J.S. and Patil, D.R., Prediction of heart disease using multilayer perceptron neural network, in: *International Conference on Information Communication and Embedded Systems (ICICES2014)*, 2014, February, IEEE, pp. 1–6.

28. Babu, S., Vivek, E.M., Famina, K.P., Fida, K., Aswathi, P., Shanid, M., Hena, M., Heart disease diagnosis using data mining technique, in: *2017 International Conference of Electronics, Communication and Aerospace Technology (ICECA)*, 2017, April, vol. 1, IEEE, pp. 750–753.

29. Chauhan, A., Jain, A., Sharma, P., Deep, V., Heart disease prediction using evolutionary rule learning, in: *2018 4th International Conference on Computational Intelligence & Communication Technology (CICT)*, 2018, February, IEEE, pp. 1–4.

30. Khemphila, A. and Boonjing, V., Heart disease classification using neural network and feature selection, in: *2011 21st International Conference on Systems Engineering*, 2011, August, IEEE, pp. 406–409.

31. Gavhane, A., Kokkula, G., Pandya, I., Devadkar, K., Prediction of heart disease using machine learning, in: *2018 Second International Conference on Electronics, Communication and Aerospace Technology (ICECA)*, 2018, March, IEEE, pp. 1275–1278.

32. Yuwono, T., Franz, A., Muhimmah, I., Design of smart electrocardiography (ECG) using Modified K-Nearest Neighbor (MKNN), in: *2018 1st*

International Conference on Computer Applications & Information Security (ICCAIS), 2018, April, IEEE, pp. 1–5.

33. Ambekar, S. and Phalnikar, R., Disease risk prediction by using convolutional neural network, in: *2018 Fourth International Conference on Computing Communication Control and Automation (ICCUBEA)*, 2018, August, IEEE, pp. 1–5.

34. Chakarverti, M., Yadav, S., Rajan, R., Classification technique for heart disease prediction in data mining, in: *2019 2nd International Conference on Intelligent Computing, Instrumentation and Control Technologies (ICICICT)*, 2019, July, vol. 1, IEEE, pp. 1578–1582.

35. Suvarna, C., Sali, A., Salmani, S., Efficient heart disease prediction system using optimization technique, in: *2017 International Conference on Computing Methodologies and Communication (ICCMC)*, 2017, July, IEEE, pp. 374–379.

36. Dharmasiri, N.D.K.G. and Vasanthapriyan, S., Approach to heart diseases diagnosis and monitoring through machine learning and iOS mobile application, in: *2018 18th International Conference on Advances in ICT for Emerging Regions (ICTer)*, 2018, September, IEEE, pp. 407–412.

37. Singh, J., Kamra, A., Singh, H., Prediction of heart diseases using associative classification, in: *2016 5th International Conference on Wireless Networks and Embedded Systems (WECON)*, 2016, October, IEEE, pp. 1–7.

38. Shouman, M., Turner, T., Stocker, R., Using data mining techniques in heart disease diagnosis and treatment, in: *2012 Japan-Egypt Conference on Electronics, Communications and Computers*, 2012, March, IEEE, pp. 173–177.

39. Ramprakash, P., Sarumathi, R., Mowriya, R., Nithyavishnupriya, S., Heart disease prediction using deep neural network, in: *2020 International Conference on Inventive Computation Technologies (ICICT)*, 2020, February, IEEE, pp. 666–670.

40. Nikhar, S. and Karandikar, A.M., Prediction of heart disease using machine learning algorithms. *Int. J. Adv. Eng. Manage. Sci.*, 2, 6, 239484, 2016.

41. Jangir, S.K., Joshi, N., Kumar, M., Choubey, D.K., Singh, S., Verma, M., Functional link convolutional neural network for the classification of diabetes mellitus. *Int. J. Numer. Methods Biomed. Eng.*, e3496, 37, 8, 1–12, 2021.

42. Choubey, D.K., Tripathi, S., Kumar, P., Shukla, V., Dhandhania, V.K., Classification of diabetes by Kernel based SVM with PSO. *Recent Adv. Comput. Sci. Commun. (Formerly: Recent Patents Comput. Science)*, 14, 4, 1242–1255, 2021.

43. Choubey, D.K., Kumar, M., Shukla, V., Tripathi, S., Dhandhania, V.K., Comparative analysis of classification methods with PCA and LDA for diabetes. *Curr. Diabetes Rev.*, 16, 8, 833–850, 2020.

44. Choubey, D.K., Kumar, P., Tripathi, S., Kumar, S., Performance evaluation of classification methods with PCA and PSO for diabetes. *Netw. Model. Anal. Health Inform. Bioinform.*, 9, 1, 1–30, 2020.

45. Choubey, D.K., Paul, S., Dhandhenia, V.K., Rule based diagnosis system for diabetes. *Int. J. Med. Sci.*, 28, 12, 5196–5208, 2017.
46. Choubey, D.K. and Paul, S., GA_RBF NN: A classification system for diabetes. *Int. J. Biomed. Eng. Technol.*, 23, 1, 71–93, 2017.
47. Choubey, D.K. and Paul, S., Classification techniques for diagnosis of diabetes: A review. *Int. J. Biomed. Eng. Technol.*, 21, 1, 15–39, 2016.
48. Choubey, D.K. and Paul, S., GA_SVM: A classification system for diagnosis of diabetes, in: *Handbook of Research on Soft Computing and Nature-Inspired Algorithms*, pp. 359–397, IGI Global, USA, 2017.
49. Bala, K., Choubey, D.K., Paul, S., Lala, M.G.N., Classification techniques for thunderstorms and lightning prediction: A survey, in: *Soft-Computing-Based Nonlinear Control Systems Design*, pp. 1–17, IGI Global, USA, 2018.
50. Choubey, D.K., Paul, S., Bala, K., Kumar, M., Singh, U.P., Implementation of a hybrid classification method for diabetes, in: *Intelligent Innovations in Multimedia Data Engineering and Management*, pp. 201–240, IGI Global, USA, 2019.
51. Rawal, K., Parthvi, A., Choubey, D.K., Shukla, V., Prediction of leukemia by classification and clustering techniques, in: *Machine Learning, Big Data, and IoT for Medical Informatics*, pp. 275–295, Academic Press, UK, 2021.
52. Choubey, D.K., Paul, S., Kumar, S., Kumar, S., Classification of Pima Indian diabetes dataset using naive Bayes with genetic algorithm as an attribute selection, in: *Communication and Computing Systems: Proceedings of the International Conference on Communication and Computing System (ICCCS 2016)*, 2017, February, pp. 451–455.
53. Bala, K., Choubey, D.K., Paul, S., Soft computing and data mining techniques for thunderstorms and lightning prediction: A survey, in: *2017 International Conference of Electronics, Communication and Aerospace Technology (ICECA)*, 2017, April, vol. 1, IEEE, pp. 42–46.
54. Choubey, D.K., Paul, S., Dhandhania, V.K., GA_NN: An intelligent classification system for diabetes, in: *Soft Computing for Problem Solving*, pp. 11–23, Springer, Singapore, 2019.
55. Kumar, S., Mohapatra, U.M., Singh, D., Choubey, D.K., IoT-based cardiac arrest prediction through heart variability analysis. *Advanced Computing and Intelligent Engineering: Proceedings of ICACIE*, 2018, vol. 2, p. 353, 2020.
56. Kumar, S., Mohapatra, U.M., Singh, D., Choubey, D.K., EAC: Efficient associative classifier for classification, in: *2019 International Conference on Applied Machine Learning (ICAML)*, 2019, May, IEEE, pp. 15–20.
57. Pahari, S. and Choubey, D.K., Analysis of liver disorder using classification techniques: A survey, in: *2020 International Conference on Emerging Trends in Information Technology and Engineering (ic-ETITE)*, 2020, February, IEEE, pp. 1–4.
58. Kumar, S., Bhusan, B., Singh, D., Kumar Choubey, D., Classification of diabetes using deep learning, in: *2020 International Conference on Communication and Signal Processing (ICCSP)*, 2020, July, IEEE, pp. 0651–0655.

59. Parthvi, A., Rawal, K., Choubey, D.K., A comparative study using machine learning and data mining approach for leukemia, in: *2020 International Conference on Communication and Signal Processing (ICCSP)*, 2020, July, IEEE, pp. 0672–0677.

60. Sharma, D., Jain, P., Choubey, D.K., A comparative study of computational intelligence for identification of breast cancer, in: *International Conference on Machine Learning, Image Processing, Network Security and Data Sciences*, 2020, July, Springer, Singapore, pp. 209–216.

61. Srivastava, K. and Choubey, D.K., Soft computing, data mining, and machine learning approaches in detection of heart disease: A review, in: *International Conference on Hybrid Intelligent Systems*, 1179, pp. 165–175, Springer, Cham, 2021.

62. Choubey, D.K., Mishra, A., Pradhan, S.K., Anand, N., Soft computing techniques for dengue prediction, in: *2021 10th IEEE International Conference on Communication Systems and Network Technologies (CSNT)*, 2021, June, IEEE, pp. 648–653.

63. Bhatia, U., Kumar, J., Choubey, D.K., Drowsiness image detection using computer vision, in: *Soft Computing: Theories and Applications*, pp. 667–683, Springer, Singapore, 2022.

64. Pahari, S. and Choubey, D.K., Analysis of liver disorder by machine learning techniques, in: *Soft Computing: Theories and Applications*, pp. 587–601, Springer, Singapore, 2022.

65. Choubey, D.K., Mishra, A., Pradhan, S.K., Anand, N., Soft computing techniques for dengue prediction, in: *2021 10th IEEE International Conference on Communication Systems and Network Technologies (CSNT)*, 2021, June, IEEE, pp. 648–653.

66. Choubey, D.K., Paul, S., Bhattacharjee, J., Soft computing approaches for diabetes disease diagnosis: A survey. *Int. J. Appl. Eng. Res.*, 9, 21, 11715–11726, 2014.

67. Choubey, D.K. and Paul, S., GA_J48graft DT: A hybrid intelligent system for diabetes disease diagnosis. *Int. J. Bio-Sci. Bio-Technol.*, 7, 5, 135–150, 2015.

68. Choubey, D.K. and Paul, S., GA_MLP NN: A hybrid intelligent system for diabetes disease diagnosis. *Int. J. Intelligent Syst. Appl.*, 8, 1, 49, 2016.

16

Artificial Intelligence Approach for Signature Detection

Amar Shukla, Rajeev Tiwari*, Saurav Raghuvanshi, Shivam Sharma and Shridhar Avinash

University of Petroleum and Energy Studies, Dehradun, Uttarakhand, India

Abstract

The globe today relies on multiple security systems to protect its data and monetary transactions. Handwritten signature recognition uses a variety of methods and algorithms. In this paper we leverage the OpenCV library and Qt for GUI to implement Support Vector Machine (SVM) and Histogram of Oriented Gradients (HOG). By using the SVM algorithm, one can find an N-dimensional plane that provides a distinctly classifiable classification of data points on a plane. Meanwhile, HOG is a feature descriptor of an image that simplifies the image by extracting the helpful information while discarding the extraneous information. We will convert the image into a feature vector of length according to the precision set by the end-user or developer, using HOG feature descriptors.

Keywords: HOG, SVM, machine learning, Open CV, signature recognition

16.1 Introduction

The Security Systems are designed for the authentication of the user who is trying to access any kind of confidential data with the verification techniques like Iris Scanner, Fingerprint detection, Handwritten signature Recognition, Vocal sound recognition system, any alphanumeric pass code, and many more techniques for the same.

---

*Corresponding author: rajeev.tiwari@ddn.upes.ac.in; errajeev.tiwari@gmail.com

Danda B. Rawat, Lalit K Awasthi, Valentina Emilia Balas, Mohit Kumar and Jitendra Kumar Samriya (eds.) *Convergence of Cloud with AI for Big Data Analytics: Foundations and Innovation*, (387–400) © 2023 Scrivener Publishing LLC

With the advancement of technologies in today's era, the number of intruders is also increasing all over the globe and fraudsters are multiplying day by day. Keeping this main aspect in mind, our project has derived which will initiate a basic security system in regard to Actual Signature and Frauds being caused due to Signature Forgery. There are ample cases intercepted daily in banks or places where a signature is still a must as an authentication factor that there are forged signatures that are so similar that normal people can neglect it and it won't be cached.

This Handwritten Signature Security System will work on precision and if it detected any forgery, the output will be shown as wrong or Fraud! In the future this handwritten security system along with face detection algorithms can be used in ATM to withdraw cash to enhance security the OTP will send to the registered customer. Handwritten signatures are used regularly for a variety of purposes. Every individual will utilize a personal signature to sign a contract, approve a check payment, or review a job paper.

Haar Cascade Classifier (HCC) [1] is a machine learning technique for quick object detection based on a boosted cascade of hairlike features. The HCC technique had not previously been employed for handwritten signature identification and verification. The Persian writer database contains 8,280 pictures, while the GPDS synthetic Signature database contains information on 4,000 people. Every classifier was trained and tested using hundreds of thousands of signatures created by digitally modifying a signature image. This method outperformed other machine learning models in terms of results.

The text that follows provides a proposed practical [2] offline signature recognition system that uses the ORB feature extraction technique, which was created for a similar reason. The new technique they have proposed is simple to use and requires only a few signatures per user to achieve a high level of accuracy. The solution achieves a 91 percent recognition rate with a median matching time of only 7 ms.

The Support Vector Machine was used as the classification approach that we used. This approach enables student's [3] signatures to identify and classify documents from the University of Mostar, such as essays and exams.

The most prevalent method of identifying a [4] person is through signature verification. This verification system was created to distinguish between false and genuine signatures. CNN's have been used to learn attributes from preprocessed authentic and fraudulent signatures. The Inception V1 project served as the foundation for the CNN architecture (GoogleNet).

The study describes a method for [5] recognizing signatures and manuscripts on mobile devices that uses the Gray Level Co-occurrence Matrix (GLCM) for texture-based feature extraction and bootstrap for a single classification model. The strategy is successfully implemented for both offline and online use. During a user-based assessment, the experiment has an accuracy level of between 34% and 44%. Data from the same person produces 84.62% and 88.46% accuracy when it comes to online signature recognition. It has a success rate of 70% to 90% for online handwriting recognition.

- With the advancement of technologies in today's era, the number of intruders is also increasing all over the globe and fraudsters are multiplying day by day.
- Keeping this main aspect in mind, our project has derived which will initiate a basic security system in regard to Actual Signature and Frauds being caused due to Signature Forgery.
- There are ample cases intercepted daily in banks or places where a signature is still a must as an authentication factor that there are forged signatures that are so similar that normal people can neglect it and it won't be cached.
- This Handwritten Signature Security System will work on precision and if it detected any forgery, the output will be shown as wrong or Fraud!
- In the future this handwritten security system along with face detection algorithms can be used in ATM to withdraw cash to enhance security the OTP will send to the registered customer.

With the advancement of technologies in today's era, the number of intruders is also increasing all over the globe and fraudsters are multiplying day by day. Keeping this main aspect in mind, our project has derived which will initiate a basic security system in regard to Actual Signature and Frauds being caused due to Signature Forgery.

There are sample cases intercepted daily in banks or places where a signature is still a must as an authentication factor that there are forged signatures that are so similar that normal people can neglect it and it won't be cached. This Handwritten Signature Security System will work on precision and if it detected any forgery, the output will be shown as wrong or Fraud. In the future this handwritten security system along with face detection algorithms can be used in ATM to withdraw cash to enhance security the OTP will send to the registered customer.

16.2   Literature Review

The below study describe the detailed literature analysis in the field of signature recognition and the open CV techniques.

It is the method of verifying [6] authorship by comparing the signature to previously investigated and stored samples. This method is available both on-premises and off-premises and focuses on offline techniques. The work uses SIFT and SURF to improve offline signature recognition. To train and evaluate the SVM classifier, we used bag-of-words and radial basis functions (RBF). Vector quantization, each training picture was converted into a uniform dimensional histogram. Images were processed with OpenCV C++. This article compares SIFT and SURF on SVM-based RBF kernels. SIFT has 98.75 percent accuracy with the SVM-RBF kernel system, whereas SURF has 96.25 percent accuracy.

Facial Recognition Through Camera (FRTC) is a [7] case study that seeks to demonstrate the current state of the art in biological signature recognition in the wild with minimal data and maximum accuracy. Modern recognition technologies (OpenCV and Face API) were added to the FRTC system to improve the field recognition of biological signals. FRTC was supposed to outperform OpenCV and Face API. However, when these systems were tested in the field, their accuracy dropped substantially. The FRTC is 7.02 percent more accurate than OpenCV and -1 percent more accurate than Face API. The FRTC case study will be scrutinized based on students' unknowing attendance.

A handwritten signature [8] is used in several applications regularly. One's signature will be used to sign a contract, job papers, petitions, or authorize check payments. We can recognize and classify the work of University of Mostar students and other test materials using this daily-based biometric characteristic. This work accomplished feature extraction using an image processing tool known as the OpenCV library. We used a Support Vector Machine (SVM) to categorize our data.

Bank checks [9] are widely used for financial transactions in a variety of industries. Cheques are always hand examined. The traditional verification technique will always include the date, signature, legal information, and payment printed on the cheques. Preprocessing the image, extracting the relevant information, and finally recognizing and confirming the handwritten fields are steps in extracting legal information from a recorded cheque image. Image processing techniques such as thinning, median filtering, and dilation are also used in this procedure.

This article [10] processes photos using convolution neural networks for deep learning. Binary classification can be used to determine the origin of a signature. The most successful method is to insert the signature region of a scanned document into the trained model. It is the same sort of paper with the exact signature location. Tensor-slicing on Numpy arrays is used to choose a document element. Text and signatures are extracted using OpenCV. On a short data set, the researchers evaluated premade neural network models. The general audience is familiar with well-known writers' signatures. Convolution networks can beused for real-world problems. The findings might be an excellent resource for students learning deep learning and applying it to computer vision problems.

Signatures are [11] vital to human existence as they represent identity. Innovative home solutions that leverage the Internet of Things are becoming more popular (IoT). Signature verification and recognition may also benefit finance, banking, home security, and insurance. This project aims to build a signature recognition system utilizing a Raspberry Pi 3 with an LCD touchscreen. Cropping and resizing the acquired signature picture Then, a binary image was used to train the artificial neural network (ANN). The trained ANN categorized the input signature to distinguish authenticity or counterfeit. A 99.77 percent identification rate was achieved during testing using an 85% confidence level.

Handwritten Signature Verification [12] has much room for improvement. It is challenging building feature extractors that can distinguish between valid signatures and sophisticated forgeries without dynamic information about the signing process. Writer-independent circumstances make this verification effort more difficult. This paper proposes an offline writer independent Deep Learning Ensemble model. So we RGBT categorized our final prediction vector using two CNNs. To ensure the data set is diversified, we tested it on various data sets. Many data sets showed the best results.

Document identification, authentication, and indexing are all typical uses of signatures. Open document analysis has lately gotten more complex due to the prevalence of free-form items such as signatures. It has two main problems. Multiscale signature detection and segmentation from document pictures are proposed in this work. A new method computes 2D contour segments' dynamic curvature rather than focusing on local changes. An LDA-based supervised learning approach for merging complementary shape information is presented herein. We investigate modern form representations, shape matching, dissimilarity measures, and multiple-instance querying of documents for document picture retrieval. Offline, our matching methods are put to action. For this, we analyzed enormous datasets of printed and handwritten English and Arabic writings.

Denoising and extraction [13] are crucial in defect prognostics because noise obscures weak features. The wavelet transform has been widely used to minimize noise because it can encode frequency and time. SVD determines the optimal wavelet scale for periodicity detection. Both simulated and real-world data validate the proposed signal denoising technique. There are many ML based techniques which offers denoising and improve the scalability of images using various augmentation techniques [14–17].

It is difficult to detect and separate [18] free-form items in cluttered backgrounds. However, no suitable methods for document signature detection exist yet. This work presents a revolutionary multi-scale approach for recognizing and segmenting signatures on various materials. Our approach captures a signature's structural saliency rather than its local aspects. This strategy is easy and customizable. A saliency metric measures the dynamic curvature of 2D contour pieces. These results were validated on vast datasets of handwritten and machine-printed texts.

16.3 Problem Definition

Recognizing signatures ignoring the variations such as: Variations due to different pens; variations arising out of the fact that "No two signatures of the same person are exactly the same"; any marks on the paper or any such element; overcoming the above variations and establishing the authenticity of a Signature; handwritten signature verification has been extensively studied and implemented. Its many applications include banking, credit card validation, security systems, etc. In general, handwritten signature verification can be categorized into two kinds of online verification and offline verification. On–line verification requires a stylus and an electronic tablet connected to a computer to grab dynamic signature information. Offline verification, on the other hand, deals with signature information that is in a static format.

16.4 Methodology

The basic workflow of the project which constitute the training and the testing phase of the process involved in the recognition system.

A signature recognition and verification system (SRVS) is a system capable of efficiently addressing two individual but strongly related tasks:

- Identification of the signature owner as described in the Figure 16.4.1.
- The decision whether the signature is genuine or forger as described in the Figure 16.4.2.

The procedure for classification of the signature image is as follows:

- Acquire the Signature images.
- Enhance image to remove noise and blurring.
- Extract the various features.
- Use these features to train the system using Feed Forward neural network.
- Employ unknown Signature image to extract its features.
- Perform the pattern matching with the data set.
- Do the classification.
- Decide between originals or forgeries.

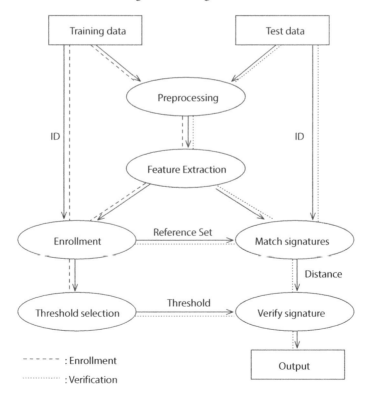

Figure 16.4.1 Flow chart for the entire process.

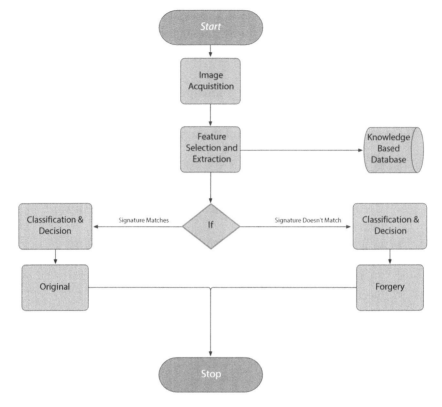

Figure 16.4.2 Overall architecture of the signature recognition system contains signature acquisition, preprocessing, feature extraction, and classification.

Signatures are scanned in gray. The purpose of this phase is to make signatures standard and ready for feature extraction. The preprocessing stage includes the following steps:

- Image binarization
- Background elimination
- Noise reduction
- Width normalization
- Thinning.

16.4.1 Data Flow Process

The below process contains the data flow, which state the exact precision of the data in the right direction where the signature detection and the creation of the model is proposed in Figures 16.4.1.1 and 16.4.1.2.

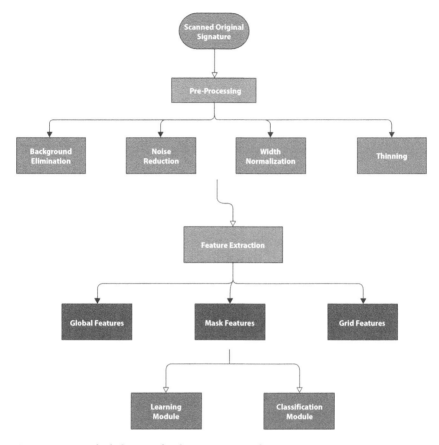

Figure 16.4.1.1 Block diagram for the signature verification.

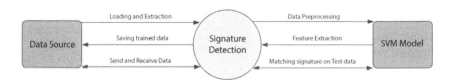

Figure 16.4.1.2 Data flow process.

16.4.2   Algorithm

The below algorithm contains the preprocessing of the images where it contains the specific feature set of the signature to normalize the images and the removal of unnecessary noise this process becomes essential as achieved through the algorithm represented in the Table 16.4.2.1.

Table 16.4.2.1 Algorithm for the preprocessing of the images.

1. Algorithm for the preprocessing of the Image
Input: Image Data
Output: Image Data

> *Mat deskew(Mat& img)*
>
> *{*
>
> *Moments m = moments(img); if(abs(m.mu02) < 1e-2)*
>
> *{*
>
> *return img.clone();*
>
> *}*
>
> *// Calculate skew based on central moments. double skew = m.mu11/m.mu02;*
>
> *// Calculate affine transform to correct skewness. Mat warpMat = (Mat_<double>(2,3) << 1, skew,*
>
> *-0.5*SZ*skew, 0, 1 , 0);*
>
> *Mat imgOut = Mat::zeros(img.rows, img.cols, img.type()); warpAffine(img, imgOut, warpMat, imgOut.size(),affineFlags);*
>
> *return imgOut;*
>
> *}*

The below algorithm in Table 16.4.2.2 describes about the histogram of gradient approach for the detection of the hand written recognition which is essential for the demonstration of the intensity level in the images for detecting out the correct signature proportion.

Table 16.4.2.2 Algorithm for the histogram of gradients.

Algorithm for the preprocessing of the images
Input: Image Data
Output: Image Data

> *HOGDescriptor hog(*
> *Size(20,20), //winSize*
> *Size(10,10), //blocksize*
> *Size(5,5), //blockStride,*
> *Size(10,10), //cellSize,*
> *;//Use signed gradients*

// im is of type Mat vector<float> descriptors; hog.compute(im,descriptor);
// Set up SVM for OpenCV 3 Ptr<SVM> svm = SVM::create();
// Set SVM type

svm->setType(SVM::C_SVC);
// Set SVM Kernel to Radial Basis Function (RBF) svm->setKernel(SVM::RBF);
// Set parameter C svm->setC(12.5);
// Set parameter Gamma
svm->setGamma(0.50625);
> *// Train SVM on training data*
> *Ptr<TrainData>td=TrainData::create(trainData,*
> *ROW_SAMPLE, trainLabels);*

svm->train(td);
// Save trained model
> *svm->save("digits_svm_model.yml");*

// Test on a held out test set
> *svm->predict(testMat, testResponse);*
>> *return img*

16.5 Result Analysis

There has been certain observation in the process of the algorithm where it contains the significant approach for the detection of the signature and

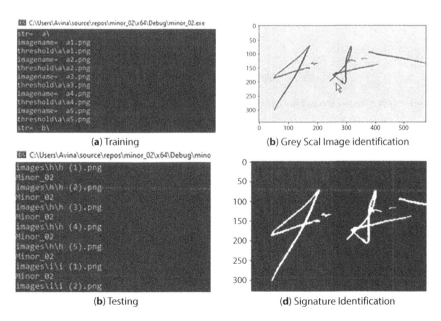

(a) Training

(b) Grey Scal Image identification

(b) Testing

(d) Signature Identification

Figure 16.5.1 Training, testing phase of the data set and the grey scale and signature identification of the image set.

```
Saving features for person id- 001
Saving features for person id- 002
Saving features for person id- 003
Saving features for person id- 004
Saving features for person id- 005
Saving features for person id- 006
Saving features for person id- 007
Saving features for person id- 008
Saving features for person id- 009
Saving features for person id- 010
Saving features for person id- 011
Saving features for person id- 012
```

Figure 16.5.2 Features of the desired object are saved.

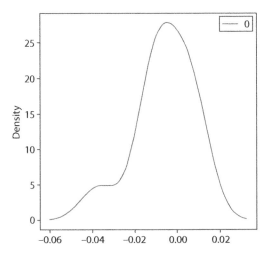

Figure 16.5.3 Intensity and the density observation on the basis of the image.

also the descriptive analysis on the basis of the result achieved is shown in Figures 16.5.1, 16.5.2 and 16.5.3.

There has been the certain observation which continues the better observation of the Signature and demonstrates the effective prediction rate of the Signature. Since other graph base analysis is also performed in the study which demonstrates the intensity level of the identified Signature. Calculating the feature of the person which has to be identified from the image data set.

The average rate of the thresholding of the predicted signature from the data set.

16.6 Conclusion

We suggested a unique signature detection and segmentation technique based on the idea that object recognition may be seen as a process. A Substantial approach has determined the motivation that can enrich the application's use in all the e verification and documentation. It is also one of the effective signature identification techniques that have to be achieved to detect and recognize the signature in document verification. This novel approach provides better accuracy in detecting the signature, a natural handwriting approach.

References

1. Blajer, J.A.G.W. and Krawczyk, M., The inverse simulation study of aircraft flight path reconstruction. *Transport*, **XVII**, 3, 103–107, 2002.
2. Al-Tamimi, A.K., Qasaimeh, A., Qaddoum, K., Offline signature recognition system using oriented FAST and rotated BRIEF. *Int. J. Electr. Comput. Eng. (2088-8708)*, **11**, 5, (2021).
3. Marušić, T., Marušić, Šeremet, Identification of authors of documents based on offline signature recognition, in: *2015 38th International Convention on Information and Communication Technology, Electronics and Microelectronics (MIPRO)*, pp. 1144–1149, 2015.
4. Mohapatra, R.K., Shaswat, K., Kedia, S., Offline handwritten signature verification using cnn inspired by inception v1 architecture, in: *2019 Fifth International Conference on Image Information Processing (ICIIP)*, pp. 263–267, 2019.
5. Hiryanto, L., Yohannis, A.R., Handhayani, T., Hand signature and handwriting recognition as identification of the writer using gray level co-occurrence matrix and bootstrap, in: *2017 Intelligent Systems Conference (IntelliSys)*, pp. 1103–1110, 2017.
6. Nasser, A.T. and Dogru, N., Signature recognition by using SIFT and SURF with SVM basic on RBF for voting online, in: *2017 International Conference on Engineering and Technology (ICET)*, pp. 1–5, 2017.
7. Gandhi, V. and Singh, J., Intensified biological signature recognition in the wild: A case study, in: *2021 12th International Conference on Computing Communication and Networking Technologies (ICCCNT)*, pp. 1–6, 2021.
8. Marušić, T., Marušić, Šeremet, Identification of authors of documents based on offline signature recognition, in: *2015 38th International Convention on Information and Communication Technology, Electronics and Microelectronics (MIPRO)*, pp. 1144–1149, 2015.
9. Dhanawade, A., Drode, A., Johnson, G., Rao, A., Upadhya, S., Open CV based information extraction from cheques, in: *2020 Fourth International*

Conference on Computing Methodologies and Communication (ICCMC), pp. 93–97, 2020.

10. Afanasyeva, Z.S. and Afanasyev, A.D., Signature detection and identification algorithm with CNN, Numpy and OpenCV, in: *Proceedings of the Computational Methods in Systems and Software*, pp. 467–479, 2020.

11. Gunawan, T.S., Hamzah, N.A., Kartiwi, M., Effendi, M.R., Ismail, N., Anwar, R., Security enhancement of smart home system using signature recognition on raspberry Pi, in: *2020 6th International Conference on Wireless and Telematics (ICWT)*, pp. 1–6, 2020.

12. Das, S.D., Ladia, H., Kumar, V., Mishra, S., Writer independent offline signature recognition using ensemble learning. *arXiv preprint arXiv:1901.06494*, 2019. https://doi.org/10.48550/arxiv.1901.06494.

13. Qiu, H., Lee, J., Lin, J., Yu, G., Wavelet filter-based weak signature detection method and its application on rolling element bearing prognostics. *J. Sound Vib.*, **289**, 4-5, 1066–1090, 2006.

14. Kaur, P., Harnal, S., Tiwari, R., Upadhyay, S., Bhatia, S., Mashat, A., Alabdali, A.M., Recognition of leaf disease using hybrid convolutional neural network by applying feature reduction. *Sensors*, 22, 2, 575, 2022.

15. Kaur, P., Harnal, S., Tiwari, R., Upadhyay, S., Bhatia, S., Mashat, A., Alabdali, A.M., Recognition of leaf disease using hybrid convolutional neural network by applying feature reduction. *Sensors*, 22, 2, 575, 2022.

16. Kaur, P., Harnal, S., Tiwari, R., Alharithi, F.S., Almulihi, A.H., Noya, I.D., Goyal, N., A hybrid convolutional neural network model for diagnosis of COVID-19 using chest X-ray images. *Int. J. Environ. Res. Public Health*, 18, 22, 12191, 2021.

17. Nagaraju, M., Chawla, P., Upadhyay, S., Tiwari, R., Convolution network model based leaf disease detection using augmentation techniques. *Expert Syst.*, 39, e12885, 2022.

18. Zhu, G., Zheng, Y., Doermann, D., Jaeger, S., Multi-scale structural saliency for signature detection, in: *2007 IEEE Conference on Computer Vision and Pattern Recognition*, 39, pp. 1–8, 2007.

17

Comparison of Various Classification Models Using Machine Learning to Predict Mobile Phones Price Range

Chinu Singla[1]* and Chirag Jindal[2]

[1]*Department of Computer Science and Engineering, Punjabi University Patiala, Punjab, India*
[2]*Department of Computer Science and Engineering, Thapar Institute of Engineering and Technology, Patiala, Punjab, India*

Abstract

Classification is the Machine Learning technique used for classifying categorical data. In this chapter, different classification models are used to predict the price range of the different mobile phones based upon their features. The use and demand of Mobile phones seem to be at their peak today, and this trend does not seem to go down in the near future. Therefore, an efficient system needs to predict the mobile prices' range based on its features. We have taken the mobile phone dataset containing information about their various features and functions for our research. After that, pre-processing is being performed to remove the ambiguities before applying the classification models. The Price range can be of any category between 0 and 3, where 0 represents cheapest and 3 costliest. We aim to find the classification model with the best results. Accuracy and R2 score are used to select the best model.

Keywords: Classification, mobile phones, decision tree, logistic regression, Naive Bayes, support vector machine KNN, accuracy, prediction

Corresponding author: cheenusingla10@gmail.com

Danda B. Rawat, Lalit K Awasthi, Valentina Emilia Balas, Mohit Kumar and Jitendra Kumar Samriya (eds.) Convergence of Cloud with AI for Big Data Analytics: Foundations and Innovation, (401–420)
© 2023 Scrivener Publishing LLC

17.1   Introduction

Machine Learning (ML) is all about creating a machine that can be as close to the human mind as possible. The ML algorithms are created to copy the human approach of learning, which can sometimes be from previous knowledge like supervised learning or sometimes from new experiences like unsupervised learning [1]. Since price is the most essential and foremost factor that comes into a person's mind when anyone thinks about buying or exploring something, one has to keep it as an output variable. Budget is the main thing that decides what a person is looking for. Our model will help the customer in finding the features and phones available in his budget.

The application of Artificial Intelligence is possible through Machine Learning Techniques, which are mainly regression and classification. Classification is used to analyses discrete data types, while regression is used for continuous data types [2]. Here output variable is in the form of discrete data, so we apply various classification models. Also, this is an example of supervised learning since the previous values of the data are already known [3]. For our application, code is written in Python and the four main libraries used are numpy, pandas, matplotlib, and scikit learn [4]. Different classification models mentioned here are Logistic Regression, KNN, SVM, Decision tree, and Gaussian Naive Bayes. We apply a few optimization techniques to our dataset, such as feature scaling [5].

Mobile phones are the most in-demand and must device in today's world. Everyone has one and is planning to update it. There is a somewhat race going on between different companies who come up with a better mobile phone. In this case, people require a system that can help them choose the phones in their budget and the features they require [6]. Keeping this rising trend of mobile phones in our mind, we take the dataset of the mobile phones and the features they possess. Like mobile phones, our research can be applied to laptops, cars, and other gadgets, just with a few minor changes. The dataset contains many mobile phone features like battery, camera, RAM, memory, etc., and based upon these features, we can predict price ranges.

Here, we predict the price of these mobile phones based upon the features which they have. We have implemented five classification models in total and tried to draw a comparison between these models based upon their accuracy and R2 score.

The organization of the research papers as follows. Under section 17.2, explanation of dataset and classification techniques, followed by data pre-processing in section 17.3 and the application of these classification models in a further section. In the end, metrics and finding the most suitable model are applied and elaborated under Section 17.6. Lastly, the conclusion and future scope are elaborated in Section 17.7.

17.2   Materials and Methods

17.2.1   Dataset

In this chapter, the data we consider is the *"Mobile Price Classification"* training and testing dataset from *Kaggle* [7]. The dataset contains the features of Mobile Phones along with their Prices [7].

There are 21 features in the dataset, with the 21st representing the price, as shown in Table 17.1. Some of the features are discrete data, while some are continuous data(Mobile Weight). The ones in the form of discrete are further of two types, i.e., binary (Bluetooth and Wi-Fi) and Multi-valued (Camera Pixels).

17.2.2   Decision Tree

A decision tree is one of the influential and most suitable classification algorithms used in Machine Learning. The concept behind it is that it causes the best possible split of the tree based on our features. It can be made in two ways: Entropy and Gini Index. Here, we have used Gini Index. The results remain the same in both cases [8].

It is a powerful method not just for classification and prediction of data but also for interpretation and data manipulation. Decision tree is also robust to outliers and provides an easy way of handling missing values.

Table 17.1 Some of the dataset values.

Battery	BT	Clock speed	Dual SIM	Int memory	Depth	Width	N_cores	pc	RAM
842	0	2.2	0	7	0.6	188	2	2	2549
1021	1	0.5	1	53	0.7	136	3	6	2631
563	1	0.5	1	41	0.9	145	5	6	2603
615	1	2.5	0	10	0.8	131	6	9	2769
1821	1	1.2	0	44	0.6	141	2	14	1411
1859	0	0.5	1	22	0.7	164	1	7	1067
1821	0	1.7	0	10	0.8	139	8	10	3220

Decision Tree has a disadvantage as well that it can subject to under-fitting and over fitting especially when the dataset is small. Strong correlation between input variables of the decision tree can be another problem for us as those variables are selected sometimes which just improve model statistics and the outcome of interest is actually not related to them. Skewed data can be handled by decision tree without the need of transformation.

Gini Index computes how often a randomly selected value would be wrongly recognized. This means the attribute with less Gini Index should be preferred. Gini Impurity can be calculated with the help of the formula shown in Eq. (17.1):

$$\text{Gini Index} = 1 - \sum_{i=1}^{n}(h)^2 \qquad (17.1)$$

$$\text{Gini Index} = 1 - [(h(+))^2 + (h(-))^2]$$

Where h is the probability of belonging to the current attribute and n is the no. of attributes.

17.2.2.1   Basic Algorithm

We import the DecisionTreeClassifier from sklearn.tree library. The code for decision tree is as follows:

1. From sklearn.tree import DecisionTreeClassifier
2. classifier= DecisionTreeClassifier(criterion='entropy', random_state=0)
3. classifier.fit(x_train, y_train)

Here, two main parameters are considered;

"criterion='entropy'": It measures quality of split.
random_state=0": To generate same random numbers.

17.2.3   Gaussian Naive Bayes (GNB)

GNB is an algorithm works on the basis of Bayes theorem. In Gaussian Naïve Bayes, sequential values linked with each characteristic are supposed to be distributed in accordance to the Gaussian distribution. It has a principle that every pair of classified features is independent of each other [9].

In this, continuous values of each feature follow Gaussian distribution. It produces a bell-shaped curve that is symmetric about the mean of the feature values.

Naive Bayes is very fast and works quite well in real life based problems. Naive Bayes can be of further types as well:

Multinomial Naive Bayes: The frequency with which specific events were created by a multinomial distribution is expressed by feature vectors. This is the most common event model for document categorization.

Bernoulli Naive Bayes: Features are independent Booleans that describe inputs in the multivariate Bernoulli event model. This model, like the multinomial model, is useful for document classification tasks when binary term occurrence characteristics instead of term frequencies are used.

Bayes theorem finds the probability of an event occurring given another event that has already occurred. Bayes theorem formula is given by (Eq. 17.2):

$$H(A|B) = \frac{H(B|A)H(A)}{H(B)} \tag{17.2}$$

Where H (A) is the probability of A, H (B) is the probability of B, and H (B|A) is the probability of event B given that event A has already occurred [10].

This formula gives the probability of happening of event A given that event B has already happened.

17.2.3.1 Basic Algorithm

We used the Naive Bayes classifier to the Training dataset. The code for the same is as follows:

1. from sklearn.naive_bayes import GaussianNaiveBayes
2. classifier = GaussianNaiveBayes()
3. classifier.fit(a_train, b_train)

17.2.4 Support Vector Machine

SVM works for both classifications and regression issues. The objective of SVM is to build the boundary of decision which can separate

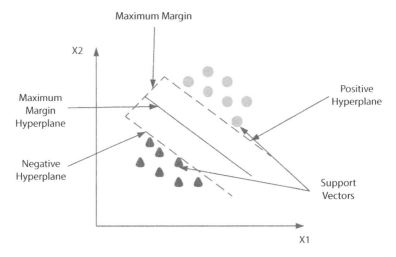

Figure 17.1 Two different classes using SVM.

multidimensional coordinates to classes so that one can quickly use the latest data set to the category it belongs to. SVM chooses the extreme point that helps create the hyper-plane [11], as shown in Figure 17.1. These extreme endpoints are called support vectors and give the algorithm its names [12]. SVM can also be made nonlinear using different types of kernel. Among many kernels, one of the most common is anisotropic radial basis. Therefore it can produce accurate results even when the data is non-linear and cannot be separated by a single line of plane.

The figure above shows how SVM draws a fine line which is equidistant from both the categories with the help of Positive, Negative Hyperplanes, and Maximum Margin.

17.2.4.1   Basic Algorithm

SVM is implemented using the following code: We extract support vector class from **Sklearn.svm** library. The code is as follows:

1. from sklearn.svm import SVC
2. classifier = supportvector(kernel='linear', randomstate=0)
3. classifier.fit(a_train, b_train)

Since data is linearly separable, we'll use the linear kernel. Afterwards we used the classifier to the training dataset(a_train, b_train).

17.2.5   Logistic Regression (LR)

LR is mainly used for binary outcomes but can also be used for non-binary outcomes. It is named after the function it is based on, i.e., Logistic function, also known as Sigmoid Function. It is an S-shaped Curve that can take any real-valued number and map it into a value between 0 and 1 but never strictly at the boundaries as depicted in Figure 17.2.

It becomes a classification technique only when a decision threshold is applied based upon the classification problem [13]. This technique is of further three types.

- Binary Logistic Regression: This is used when output is binary or has only two possible outcomes. For example 0 or 1.
- Multinomial Logistic Regression: This is the one we used here. This is used when output variable has three or more possible values without ordering as in our case.
- Ordinal Logistic Regression: This is used when output variable has three or more possible values with ordering.

17.2.5.1   *Basic Algorithm*

We create a classifier for implementing Logistic Regression as given below:

1. from sklearn.linear_model import LogisticRegression
2. classifier= LogisticRegression(random_state=0)
3. classifier.fit(x_train, y_train)

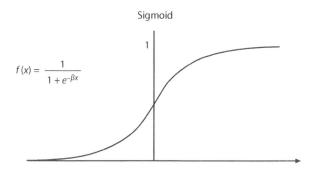

Figure 17.2 Logistic regression curve and its equation.

17.2.6   K-Nearest Neighbor

KNN is a classification algorithm in which the data point is assigned the category most of its neighbors belong to. KNN assumes that things which are closer to each have similar behavior. Apart from Classification, KNN can also be used for search and regression. No need to create a model, tweak a few parameters, or make any more assumptions in KNN. The fundamental downside of KNN is that it becomes substantially slower as the volume of data grows, making it an unsuitable solution in situations when

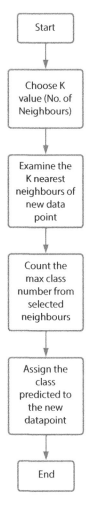

Figure 17.3 KNN implementation steps.

predictions must be made quickly. In the case of classification and regression, we observed that the best way to choose the proper K for our data is to try a few different Ks and see which one performs best.

First, we select the number k, usually the square root of n, i.e., the total number of data points. Then we sort all data points based upon their Euclidean distance from the given data point as shown in Figure 17.3. Euclidean distance is calculated by using Eq. 17.3:

$$d = \sqrt{[(r_2 - r_1)^2 + (s_2 - s_1)^2]}$$

(17.3)

Where r_1 and s_1 are the coordinates of the given data point in focus and r_2 and s_2 are the coordinates of the data point from which we calculate distance. Then we select the first K data points and check their class. Our data-point is assigned the class to which the majority of those K data-points belong [14].

17.2.6.1   Basic Algorithm

We fit the K-NN classifier to the training data. We first import the KNeighborsClassifier class of Sklearn Neighbors library. After that, we create the Classifier object of the class. The Parameter of this class will be n_neighbors: The number of neighbors to be considered.

> metric='minkowski': Parameter for deciding distance between two objects.
> p=2: It is equivalent to the standard Euclidean metric.

The code is as follows:

1. from sklearn.neighbors import KNeighborsClassifier
2. classifier= KNeighborsClassifier(n_neighbors=5, metric=' minkowski', p=2)
3. classifier.fit(x_train, y_train)

17.2.7   Evaluation Metrics

The Accuracy, R-score, and confusion matrix are being used to evaluate the models described previously.

A confusion matrix is an $N \times N$ matrix that summarizes the Accuracy of the Classification Model's predictions. N is the number of classes. Here

N = 4. In binary problem, N = 2. Confusion Matrix is a correlation between the actual labels and the models' predicted values. One axis represents actual values while the other represents predicted values [15].

Accuracy is the total number of values accurately analyzed upon the total number of values predicted by the model. The formula for Accuracy is given by Equation (17.4):

$$\text{Accuracy} = \frac{\text{True Positives} + \text{True Negatives}}{\text{All Samples}} \tag{17.4}$$

True Positives means the accurate values predicted by the model, and True Negative means, the negative values analyzed by the model. All Samples are the total number of values predicted.

17.3   Application of the Model

In the study, five models are used independently to predict the class of the mobile phone price, as shown in Figure 17.4. First, we read the dataset and assign the input and output variables to x and y, respectively.

Firstly we split the dataset into training and testing with a ratio of 3:1, and our model will be trained on 75% dataset while the rest of the 25% dataset will be used to test the model. After that, we performed feature scaling on the dataset to narrow the range of the values. A technique we use here is standardization [16]. The whole procedure to predict the prices of mobile phones is illustrated in Figure 17.4.

The feature scaling was followed by the actual implementation of the classification models whose detailed implementation is explained below. Once the models were implemented, we evaluated the results of the same using metrics library. At the end, these results were compared and we found out the best and the worst in this chapter.

Figure 17.5 roughly divides our chapter into four rough categories of data collection, data preprocessing and model creation, model optimization and

Figure 17.4 Implementation steps.

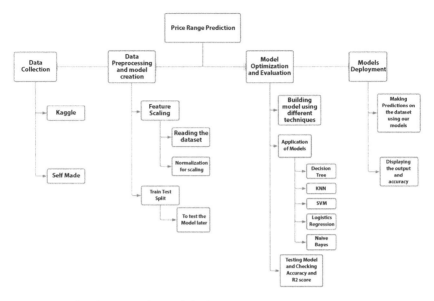

Figure 17.5 Flowchart to predict mobile phone price range.

evaluation and finally model deployment. It shows further the sub steps of each step.

17.3.1 Decision Tree (DT)

Here we implement a decision tree here using the criterion entropy and keeping the random state = 0 so that every time we run the code [17], the same values are chosen. After implementing the decision tree, we get the confusion matrix (Figure 17.6) where rows shows the predicted values while column shows the actual values.

	0	1	2	3
0	114	10	0	0
1	9	98	3	0
2	0	17	104	4
3	0	0	30	111

Figure 17.6 Decision tree confusion matrix.

17.3.2   Gaussian Naive Bayes

We use sklearn to import and implement Gaussian naive Bayes. There is no need for parameters while implementing the Naive Bayes.

The confusion matrix (Figure 17.7) where rows shows the predicted values while column shows the actual values we get is.

17.3.3   Support Vector Machine

Firstly we import SVC from sklearn. While implementing SVM, we require an input parameter called Kernel. In this case, we take Kernel as linear.

The resultant confusion matrix (Figure 17.8) where rows shows the predicted values while column shows the actual values is.

17.3.4   Logistic Regression

We import Logistic Regression from sklearn.linear_model and give the random state as the only input parameter as similar to decision tree. The confusion matrix (Figure 17.9) where rows shows the predicted values while column shows the actual values is as follow.

	0	1	2	3
0	121	3	0	0
1	8	84	18	0
2	0	31	86	8
3	0	0	20	121

Figure 17.7 Gaussian Naive Bayes confusion matrix.

	0	1	2	3
0	121	3	0	0
1	10	99	1	0
2	0	15	109	1
3	0	0	14	127

Figure 17.8 Support vector machine confusion matrix.

	0	1	2	3
0	124	0	0	0
1	18	71	21	0
2	0	34	85	6
3	0	0	5	136

Figure 17.9 Logistic regression confusion matrix.

	0	1	2	3
0	83	37	4	0
1	40	51	15	4
2	18	45	51	11
3	1	14	61	65

Figure 17.10 KNN confusion matrix.

17.3.5   K Nearest Neighbor

K neighbors classifier is imported from sklearn. Neighbors to implement KNN. The parameters required are n_neighbors, metric, and p-value. The n_neighbors is the k value we use in our model building. The distance Metric we use is Minkowski, whose formula is.

$$\left(\sum_{i=1}^{n} |u_i - v_i|^p\right)^{\frac{1}{p}} \tag{17.5}$$

Where u and v are the coordinates of the data point in focus.

The third parameter is the p-value in the above formula, which is 2 in the case of Euclidean Distance which we use for our model [18]. The confusion matrix (Figure 17.10) where rows shows the predicted values while column shows the actual values.

17.4   Results and Comparison

We calculate R2 as well as the Accuracy score for all the five models we applied. The Accuracy for all the models turned out to be pretty good except for the KNN. The Accuracy score for Decision Tree, Naive Bayes, SVM, and Logistic Regression turns out to be in a pretty close range that is 85.4%, 82.4%, 91.2% and 83.2%, respectively.

The accuracy of K Nearest Neighbor turned out to be just 50% since we took the number of neighbors k as a fixed number instead of using the generic rule of root n where n is the total number of data points. The Bar plot (Figure 17.11) given below compares the accuracy scores of the different models. Here the model of Decision Tree, Naive Bayes, Support Vector Machine, Logistic Regression, and K Nearest Neighbor are written in the form of DT, NB, SVM, LR, and KNN respectively. The Bar plot shows how the accuracy of SVM is the highest while that of KNN is the lowest thereby giving us a clear idea of the chapter.

We also calculate the R2 score or coefficient of determination for all the models. It came out to be 0.888, 0.865, 0.933, 0.871, and 0.421 for Decision Tree, Naive Bayes, SVM, Logistic Regression, and KNN. The same trend is observed in the case of R2 score as well since the score of KNN is way less than that of others which are in a pretty close range to each other. The Bar Plot (Figure 17.12) showing the R2 scores of different classification Models. Here the model of Decision Tree, Naive Bayes, Support Vector Machine, Logistic Regression, and K Nearest Neighbor are written in the form of DT, NB, SVM, LR, and KNN respectively. The Bar plot shows how the R2 score of SVM is the highest while that of KNN is the lowest thereby giving us a clear idea of the chapter.

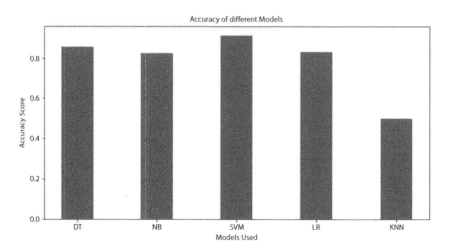

Figure 17.11 Accuracy of different models.

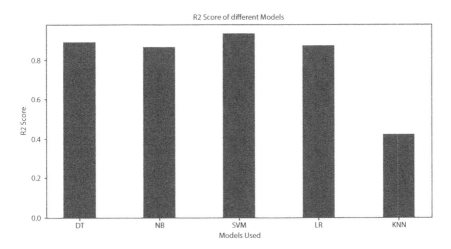

Figure 17.12 R2 score of different model.

The similar nature of the above two plots also shows us that the accuracy and R2 score vary according to each other and are somehow codependent thereby confirming a directly proportional relationship between them. As we can see that the model which have the highest accuracy also displays highest R2 score i.e. SVM in this case while the model giving the lowest accuracy also gives the lowest R2 score i.e. KNN in this case. The relationship between the Accuracy and R2 score can be displayed by the following formula:

$$Accuracy = K * R2\ Score \qquad (17.6)$$

Where K is a constant.

Table 17.2 describes comparison of different machine learning models in terms of accuracy and R2 score.

The above table summarizes the entire comparison between the five models for us. It compares the five models in six different contexts. Basic Concept tells us the algorithm or the basic principle the model is based on. Then number of parameters tells the number of parameters that are required in the implementation of each model which is maximum in the case of K Nearest Neighbor, i.e., 3 while 0 in Support Vector Machine which is then followed by the name of those parameters. The next two contexts are the Accuracy and R2 score calculated by us as shown above. The last context tells us their limitations or what these models lack in.

Table 17.2 Comparison of various machine learning models.

Features	Decision tree	Naive bayes	Support vector machine	Logistic regression	K-nearest neighbors
Basic concept	Based on Entropy or information gain	Based on Bayes Theorem	Based on extreme point boundary Based differentiation	Based on application of Sigmoid function on Linear Regression	Based upon K Closest neighbors
Number of parameters	2	0	1	1	3
Parameter names	Criterion and random state	-	Kernel	Random State	Number of neighbors, metric and p value

(Continued)

Table 17.2 Comparison of various machine learning models. (*Continued*)

Features	Decision tree	Naive bayes	Support vector machine	Logistic regression	K-nearest neighbors
Accuracy	85.4%	82.4%	91.2%	83.2%	50%
R2 score	0.888	0.865	0.933	0.871	0.421
Limitations	Unstable as a little change in the dataset can cause massive change in the tree structure.	If it encounters a case or category which was not present in the training dataset, it will assign it 0 automatically	It does not perform very efficiently if the dataset has noise.	It always assume linear relationship between dependent and independent variables.	Gets effected by the amount of data and irrelevant features.

17.5   Conclusion and Future Scope

In the study, we compared the five different classification models on the dataset of mobile phones, taking the price class as the output variable. We split our data into training and testing datasets and performed feature scaling as well. Then we applied the classification models. We find their Accuracy Score and R2 score, and based upon the values of these scores, we discovered that the Support Vector Machine proves to be the suitable model in this case with the Accuracy of 91.2% R2 score of 0.933. We also found that all the models except for KNN showed decent results and concluded that the low value of K taken compared to the size of the dataset is the reason behind the poor performance of KNN. The results of Decision Tree, Logistic Regression, and Naive Bayes are pretty close.

Further improvement can be made by applying a combination of multiple classification models or changing some parameters of the already applied models. Random Forest can also be applied to the dataset. Few more steps can be included in the pre-processing part to make the dataset consistent and even better.

References

1. Talwar, A., and Kumar; Y. Machine Learning: An artificial intelligence methodology. *Int. J.of Eng. & Comput. Sci.*, 2, 12, 3400–3404, 2013.
2. Singh, A., Thakur, N., S., A., A review of supervised machine learning algorithms. *D. (INDIACom)*, 2016, ieeexplore.ieee.org.
3. Singh, A., Thakur, N., and Sharma, A. A review of supervised machine learning algorithms. In *2016 3rd International Conference on Computing for Sustainable Global Development (INDIACom)*, 1310-1315, IEEE, 2016, March.
4. Albanese, D., Merlere, S., Jurman, G., Visintainer, R., MLPy: High-performance python package for predictive modeling. *NIPS, MLOSS Work*, 2008.
5. Akritidis, L. and B., P., A supervised machine learning classification algorithm for research articles. *P. of the 28th A. A. Symposium*, 2013, pp. 115–120, 2019, doi: 10.1145/2480362.2480388, dl.acm.org.
6. Arroyo-Cañada, F.-J., Lafuente, G., J., *Influence Factors in Adopting the m-Commerce Resources, and Users*, pp. 46–50, 2011.
7. Mobile price classification | Kaggle, 2018. https://www.kaggle.com/iabhishek official/mobile-price-classification.
8. Song, Y. Y., and Ying, L. U. Decision tree methods: Applications for classification and prediction. *Shanghai archives of psychiatry*, 27, 2, 130, 2015.

9. R.-I., I., An empirical study of the Naive Bayes classifier. *2001 Workshop on Empirical Methods in Artificial and Undefined*, 2001, cc.gatech.edu.

10. Friedman, N., Geiger, D., Goldszmidt, M., Bayesian network classifiers. *Mach. Learn.*, 29, 2–3, 131–163, 1997.

11. Cortes, C. and V., V., Support-vector networks. *Mach. Learn.*, Springer, 20, 273–297, 1995.

12. Evgeniou, T. and Pontil, M., Support vector machines: Theory and applications. *Lect. Notes Comput. Sci.*, 2049 LNAI, 249–257, 2001.

13. Peng, C., Lee, K., I., G., An introduction to logistic regression analysis and reporting. *J. Educ. Taylor Fr.*, 96, 1, 3–14, 2002, doi: 10.1080/00220670209598786.

14. Wang, L. Research and implementation of machine learning classifier based on KNN. In *IOP Conference Series: Materials Science and Engineering*, 677, 5, 052038. IOP Publishing, 2019 December.

15. Moksony, F., and Heged, R. Small is beautiful. The use and interpretation of R2 in social research. *Szociológiai Szemle*, Special issue, 130–138, 1990

16. Nasser, I., Al-Shawwa, M., Abu-Naser, S., Developing artificial neural network for predicting mobile phone price range. *Int. J. Acad. Inf. Syst. Res.*, 3, 1–6, 2019.

17. Han, L.W., Manipulating machine learning results with random state, Towards Data Science, 2019, https://towardsdatascience.com/manipulating-machine-learning-results-with-random-state-2a6f49b31081.

18. Güvenç, E., Cetin, G., K., H., Comparison of KNN and DNN classifiers performance in predicting mobile phone price ranges. *Adv. Artif. Intell.*, 1, 1, 19–28, 2021, dergipark.org.tr.

Index

Also of Interest

**Check out these published and forthcoming titles
in the "Advances in Learning Analytics for Intelligent
Cloud-IoT Systems" series from Scrivener Publishing**

Convergence of Cloud with AI for Big Data Analytics
Foundations and Innovation
Edited by Danda B. Rawat, Lalit K Awasthi, Valentina Emilia Balas, Mohit Kumar and Jitendra Kumar Samriya
Published 2022. ISBN 978-1-119-90488-5

Artificial Intelligence for Cyber Security
An IoT Perspective
Edited by Noor Zaman, Mamoona Humayun, Vasaki Ponnusamy and G. Suseendran
Published 2022. ISBN 978-1-119-76226-3

Industrial Internet of Things (IIoT)
Intelligent Analytics for Predictive Maintenance
Edited by R. Anandan G. Suseendran, Souvik Pal and Noor Zaman
Published 2022. ISBN 978-1-119-76877-7

The Internet of Medical Things (IoMT)
Healthcare Transformation
Edited by R. J. Hemalatha, D. Akila, D. Balaganesh and Anand Paul
Published 2022. ISBN 978-1-119-76883-8

Integration of Cloud Computing with Internet of Things
Foundations, Analytics, and Applications
Edited by Monika Mangla, Suneeta Satpathy, Bhagirathi Nayak and Sachi Nandan Mohanty
Published 2021. ISBN 978-1-119-76887-6

Digital Cities Roadmap
IoT-Based Architecture and Sustainable Buildings
Edited by Arun Solanki, Adarsh Kumar and Anand Nayyar
Published 2021. ISBN 978-1-119-79159-1

Agricultural Informatics
Automation Using IoT and Machine Learning
Edited by Amitava Choudhury, Arindam Biswas, Manish Prateek
and Amlan Chakraborty
Published 2021. ISBN 978-1-119-76884-5

Smart Healthcare System Design
Security and Privacy Aspects
Edited by SK Hafizul Islam and Debabrata Samanta
Published 2021. ISBN 978-1-119-79168-3

Machine Learning Techniques and Analytics for Cloud Security
Edited by Rajdeep Chakraborty, Anupam Ghosh and Jyotsna Kumar
Mandal
Published 2021. ISBN 978-1-119-76225-6

www.scrivenerpublishing.com

Printed and bound by CPI Group (UK) Ltd, Croydon, CR0 4YY

27/10/2024

14580133-0003